Population History and the Family

The *Journal of Interdisciplinary History* Readers

Health and Disease in Human History
Edited by Robert I. Rotberg

Social Mobility and Modernization
Edited by Robert I. Rotberg

Politics and Political Change
Edited by Robert I. Rotberg

Population History and the Family
Edited by Robert I. Rotberg

Population History and the Family: A *Journal of Interdisciplinary History* Reader

Edited by Robert I. Rotberg

The MIT Press
Cambridge, Massachusetts
London, England

9615554

Maris Vinovkis, "Socioeconomic Determinants of Interstate Fertility Differentials in the United States in 1850 and 1860" *JIH* VI, 3 (Winter, 1976); W. R. Lee, "Bastardy and the Socioeconomic Structure of South Germany" *JIH* VII, 3 (Winter, 1977); Robert Y. Eng and Thomas C. Smith, "Peasant Families and Population Control in Eighteenth Century Japan" *JIH* VI, X (1976); Barbara A. Hanawalt, "Childrearing among the Lower Classes of Late Medieval England" *JIH* VIII, 1 (Summer, 1997); Michael R. Haines, "Fertility, Nuptiality, and Occupation: A Study of Coal Mining Populations and Regions in England and Wales in the Mid-Nineteenth Century" *JIH* VIII, 2 (Fall, 1977); Michael Craton, "Changing Patterns of Slave Families in the British West Indies" *JIH* XI, 1 (Summer, 1979); Rudolph A. Zambardino, "Mexico's Population in the Sixteenth Century: Demographic Anomaly or Mathematical Illusion" *JIH* XI, 1 (Summer, 1980); Darrett B. Rutman, Charles Wetherell, and Anita H. Rutman, "Black and White Seasonality in the Early Chesapeake" *JIH* XI, 1 (Summer, 1980); Edward Byers, "Fertility Transition in a New England Commercial Center: Nantucket, Massachusetts, 1680–1840" *JIH* XIII, 1 (Summer, 1985); David Cressy, "The Seasonality of Marriage in Old and New England" *JIH* XVI, 1 (Summer, 1985); Francis J. Brooks, "Revising the Conquest of Mexico: Smallpox, Sources, and Populations" *JIH* XXIV, 1 (Summer, 1993); Daniel C. Quinlan and Jean A. Shackelford, "Economy and English Families, 1500–1850" *JIH* XXIV, 3 (Winter, 1994); Daniel H. Kaiser, "Urban Household Composition in Early Modern Russia" *JIH* XXIII, 1 (Summer, 1992)

Selection and Introduction © 2001 by the Massachusetts Institute of Technology and The Journal of Interdisciplinary History, Inc.

Library of Congress Cataloging-in-Publication Data

Population history and the family : a Journal of interdisciplinary history reader / edited by Robert I. Rotberg.
   p. cm.—(Journal of interdisciplinary history readers)
   Includes bibliographical references.
   ISBN 0-262-18212-2 (hc.: alk. paper)—ISBN 0-262-68130-7 (pbk.: alk. paper)
   1. Family—History. 2. Family demography—History. 3. Fertility, Human—History.
4. Population—History. I. Rotberg, Robert I. II. Journal of interdisciplinary history.
III. Series.

HQ503 .F314   2001
306.85'09—dc21   00-068384

Contents

Contributors

Robert I. Rotberg is Co-Editor of the *Journal of Interdisciplinary History,* President of the World Peace Foundation, Director of Harvard University's Program on Intrastate Conflict, Adjunct Professor at the Kennedy School of Government, and former professor of history and political science at MIT. He is the author or editor of three dozen books on Africa, Asia, and the Caribbean. His most recent books are *Creating Peace in Sri Lanka: Civil War and Reconciliation* (1999) and *Peacekeeping and Peace Enforcement in Africa* (2000).

Francis J. Brooks is Senior Lecturer in History, Flinders University of South Australia. He wrote "Disease and Population in the Conquest of Mexico: Twenty-Five Years of Scholarship," in Brooks and Martin J. Scurrah (eds.), *Iberia and Latin America: The Last Twenty-Five Years, 1966–1991* (1992).

Edward Byers was Senior Analyst at Cambridge Reports, Inc. He is the author of *The Nation of Nantucket: Society and Politics in an Early American Commercial Center, 1660–1820* (1987).

Michael Craton is Professor of History, University of Waterloo. He is the author of *Empire, Enslavement, and Freedom in the Caribbean* (1997).

David Cressy is Professor of History, Ohio State University. He is the author of *Birth, Marriage, and Death: Ritual, Religion, and the Life-Cycle in Tudor and Stuart England* (1997).

Robert Y. Eng is Professor of History at the University of Redlands. He is the author of *Economic Imperialism in China: Silk Production and Exports, 1861–1932* (1986).

Michael R. Haines is the Banfi Vintners Professor of Economics, Colgate University. He is the author of *Fertility and Occupation: Population Patterns in Industrialization* (1979), and co-author of *Fatal Years: Child Mortality in Late Nineteenth-Century America* (1991).

Barbara A. Hanawalt is Professor of History, University of Minnesota. She is the author of *Of Good and Ill Repute: Gender and Social Control in Medieval England* (1998).

Daniel H. Kaiser is Professor of History and Rosenfield Professor of Social Studies, Grinnell College. He is the author of *The Growth of Law in Medieval Russia* (1980).

W. R. Lee is Chaddock Professor of Economic and Social History, University of Liverpool. He co-edited *State, Social Policy and Social Change in Germany, 1880–1994* (1997).

Daniel C. Quinlan is Professor of Sociology, Emory & Henry College.

Anita H. Rutman co-authored several books with Darrett Rutman, including *Small Worlds, Large Questions: Explorations in Early American Social History, 1600–1850* (1994), until her death in 1997.

Darrett B. Rutman was Professor of History, University of Florida, at his death in 1997. He was the author of *American Puritanism, Faith and Practice* (1970), and co-author of *Small Worlds, Large Questions: Explorations in Early American Social History, 1600–1850* (1994).

Jean A. Schackelford is Professor of Economics at Bucknell University. She is the author of *Urban and Regional Economics: A Guide to Information Sources* (1980).

Thomas C. Smith is Professor of History, Emeritus, University of California, Berkeley. He is the author of *The Agrarian Origins of Modern Japan* (1959) and *Political Change and Industrial Development in Japan: Government Enterprise, 1868–1880* (1955).

Maris A. Vinovskis is Professor of History, University of Michigan. He is the author of *History and Educational Policymaking* (1999).

Charles Wetherell is Associate Professor of History at the University of California, Riverside. He is the editor of *Historical Methods*.

Rudolf A. Zambardino is in the Department of Computing, North Staffordshire Polytechnic.

Robert I. Rotberg

Recovering Lost Worlds:
The Demographic Dimension in History
From its very first number, in 1970, the *JIH* appreciated the significance of the revolution then underway in recovering and expressing social history. The people who constituted history—those who participated in social movements, rebelled and rioted, lived and worked in nuclear households, or changed the ways in which they were fertile or expressed their procreative instincts—were no longer lost. A vein of imaginative and pioneering research had developed a method of reconstituting populations and thus permitting a new kind of historical richness.

The *JIH* opened its pages to scholars who were pushing back the frontiers of family and demographic history. It embraced some of the then most innovative work about the age of menarche, family organization, the sexual revolution, medieval marriage, early modern childrearing, and dozens of other fresh subjects. To date, the *JIH* has remained one of the premier outlets for imaginative and pathbreaking scholarship on a broad array of topics within the parameters of population history, broadly construed.

This volume, like the three others in the *JIH* series of interdisciplinary history readers, contains articles culled from a cornucopia of family and demographic riches. Selecting the best of thirty years of publication in these fields with attention to chronology, geography, and decades of publication diversity—in order to offer readers an intriguing and representative cross-section of articles in the *JIH*—was hardly easy, especially given limitations of space. The *JIH* has published so much on these subjects that several of the new volumes could have been filled with nothing but excellent and innovative family and demographical articles. Indeed, two special issues on family history were published in the *JIH* as long ago as 1971, and reprinted in a single volume, together with two additional *JIH* articles on the same subject from 1970 and 1972, as Theodore K. Rabb and Robert I. Rotberg (eds.), *The Family in History: Interdisciplinary Essays* (New York, 1973). Articles from that special issue are excluded from this collection. A second volume, drawn from the pages of the *JIH,* was published at the beginning of the next decade: Robert I. Rotberg and Theodore K. Rabb (eds.) *Marriage and Fertility: Studies in Interdisciplinary History* (Princeton, 1980). Of its fourteen articles, only Barbara Hanawalt's article on medieval England and W. R. Lee's article on Germany are reprinted in the current volume.

This new reader arrays articles from the succeeding twenty-seven years of the *JIH* first chronologically and then geographically. It begins with Hanawalt's formative article on childrearing in medieval England, and continues with Daniel C. Quinlan and Jean A. Shackelford on English families and economic changes since 1500. Rudolph Zambardino's controversial and important discussion of the population of Mexico in the sixteenth century spawned several responses and revisions; this reader includes Zambardino's article as well as Francis Brooks on the population of Mexico during the conquest period. The next article is Michael Craton's analysis of slave families in the West Indies, one of many contributions on that subject that have been published in the *JIH*.

This volume contains articles on Japan and Russia: Robert Y. Eng and Thomas C. Smith on population control in eighteenth century Japan and Daniel Kaiser on household composition in early modern Russia. Lee's article on bastardy in Germany is one of several on either bastardy or German family structures that were published in the *JIH* and were suitable for inclusion in this reader. A chapter on modern Britain rounds out the non-American section of this volume: Michael Haines analyzes the relationships among fertility, nuptiality, and occupation in the nineteenth century, especially among the families of coal miners.

The United States section of the reader includes two complementary articles that explore the nature of seasonality in the colonial period: David Cressy on marriage in old and New England and Darrett Rutman, Charles Wetherell, and Anita Rutman on black and white birth, death, and marriage in the Chesapeake region. Edward Byers's chapter on Nantucket indicates that the residents of the island were practicing family limitation by the middle of the eighteenth century, much earlier than their peers on the mainland. Maris Vinovskis concludes this volume by explaining why U. S. fertility rates declined east of the Mississippi River in the nineteenth century.

Concentrating on then lower classes in late medieval England, Hanawalt tested prevailing theories concerning the size and function of the pre-industrial family: the ages at which children were sent out of the family to work, and the manner in which children were reared, using coroner's rolls as sources of information. She was thus able to go beyond previously employed unrepresentative class-biased data: church chronicles, other ecclesiastical writings, and artistic representations. The reports of coroner's inquests better reflect the daily life of peasants, villagers, and townspeople of the middle- and lower-classes. Their accidents, their abodes, and much about their lives is contained in the inquest materials, each account being a fresh vignette usually recorded soon after death. Hanawalt's specific evidence came from London, Oxford, Bedfordshire, and Northhamptonshire.

The typical late Bedfordshire rural household—rolls from that part of thirteenth-century England show—was a nuclear one (half of the small sample), with one or two children per household. But rolls from elsewhere suggest fewer nuclear households, with fewer children (usually one child) per household, and they are frank about the existence of households with concubines and other non-nuclear components. In other words, children grew up in a variety of circumstances, not all nuclear, in late medieval England. There was monogamy, but also bigamy, and many illegitimate children.

The families of the thirteenth century lived in houses of wattle and daub, usually insubstantial, but the physical quality of the dwellings improved throughout the century, in some cases becoming reasonably grand by the beginning of the fourteenth century. Some were multi-roomed, even with courtyards. The floors were covered with straw, and straw pallets were used for beds. A main room contained a raised hearth and a fire pit. Children and animals wandered freely across the small houses, or were bedded down within.

Hanawalt discovered that occupational segregation was not rigid in England during this period. Both men and women were engaged in outdoor tasks, although men seemed to die more often than women while involved in agriculturally related pursuits. Unlike women, men dealt with livestock and performed the hard physical chores of milling, carpentry, masonry, and carting, the most dangerous medieval activity. Men also worked the quarries. Women performed most of the purely domestic chores, like laundering and weaving. They brewed beer, at least outside London.

The children in Hanawalt's sample succumbed to accidents in the cradle, where some suffered burns. Later, they wandered into ditches, fell into wells and ponds, and pulled pots of scalding water onto themselves. There were many examples of children ambling off, being cared for only absent-mindedly by neighbors or older children, and so on. Hanawalt found that the percentage of children under four who were victims of accidents in medieval England was eight times larger than that of similarly aged children in modern times.

Accident numbers in medieval times decreased after that age, presumably because children were spending more time working with their parents, or at least learning household and field tasks. It was from much later, however, from about twelve or thirteen, that children began to move into a life of work. Before then they lived at home and were more underfoot than economically productive. Some of the urban young men went to school, but many others sold eels, gathered wood, minded younger children, and harvested in the fields.

Hanawalt was surprised to find the medieval English family congenial. At least, family members did not seem to maim or kill each other with the expected frequency. There were remarkably few intrafamilial murders. Parents were much more sentimental and involved with their children than historians and chroniclers had hitherto assumed.

Quinlan and Shackelford continued this examination of the social structure and behavior of families, this time for the sixteenth, seventeenth, and eighteenth centuries, and the first half of the nineteenth century. They argued that the nature of middle- and upper-class families altered substantially as England's agrarian and industrial economy matured. The gradual withdrawal of the landed nuclear family away from "the larger universe of kinship and clientage," and the shift of yeoman families away from the communalism of peasant villages, were rational economic responses to the coming of the agrarian revolution (46). Enclosure, capital improvements, and the efficient management of landed property became more important than kin alliances. Likewise, traditional village relations fell before the commercialization of tenancies and an increasingly competitive market. Furthermore, as the social relations of production and the upward mobility of new social classes affected domestic patriarchy, so wage labor linked to new techniques and new levels of competition encouraged new forms of discipline, thrift, and industry. These responses to changing levels of competition were carried over into homes and intensified domestic patriarchy.

The authors suggested that falling rates of fertility and nuptiality and a rising age at first marriage among the landed classes before 1750 resulted from difficulties of making suitable provision for lesser heirs. Before 1750, rents and land values stagnated, interest rates slowly declined, and landed families delayed the marriages of their children and reduced family sizes.

The authors' analysis began with the disintegration of the collectively organized English village in the sixteenth century. Landowners became more patriarchal. Lingering feudal traditions lapsed. Childrearing came to focus on "breaking the child's will," often by floggings (49). A sharp division between the roles of men and women became apparent. Among villagers, relations became more hierarchical, more competitive, more contractually based, more unequal, and more tense.

Fertility fell among the landed classes even though levels of child mortality rose. This fall in fertility resulted from rising ages at first marriage, falling rates of nuptiality (as low as 84 percent in the eighteenth century) and remarriage, and slowing rates of childbearing. Men of the landed classes married later, and so did women. Remarriages were both delayed and more rare after the seventeenth century.

Agrarian production changed during the sixteenth- and seventeenth-centuries, and brought about a restructuring of family patterns. Enclosures gradually forced the abandonment of traditional medieval village life; more and more people across the class spectrum became dependent on the market. Peasants became agricultural workers or employees of domestic industry. Landlords may have grown more prosperous, but they, too, were subject to market mechanisms. Excess children became a drain on capital. So did jobs for relatives, dowries for daughters, and finding employment for younger sons. The costs of children, in other words, rose faster than income. Quinlan and Shackelford showed the many ways in which the realities of competition and modernization squeezed the wealth of the landed classes, and eroded the solidarity of villagers. Indeed, peasants could become freeholders and yeo-

man, and thus disown or abandon customary agricultural practices.

The debt burdens of the seventeenth- and eighteenth-centu-
ries compelled landed families to limit family sizes, negotiate dowries and marriages with greater deliberateness, and reduce the pace
and number of marriages. Quinlan and Shackelford linked these
rational shifts to the "restocking" of the peerage in the seventeenth century by newly prosperous merchants and agro-business-
men. Indeed, gentleman farmers became entrepreneurial in
response to the changing competition of the times; frugality, ac-
countability, and a shift from passive rent collection to active enterprise led to a hardening of patriarchy, among yeomen as well as
gentry.

The authors associated the rise of Puritanism and other evangelical activities with the new entrepreneurialism, and patriarchy,
of English villages and towns. Small-property holders provided a
strong backbone for Puritanism. In turn, their needs and approaches to life influenced the teachings and writings of the ministers and moralists who were the evangelists of the new religious
and social movement. When Anglicanism subsequently trumped
Puritanism, the established church became dependent on the patronage of landed wealth. The gentry preferred a religion that
preached the inevitability and reasonableness of the new status quo
rather than a creed which questioned it.

The role and status of women also changed after the Restoration. According to the authors, the triumph of agrarian capitalism
led to or was accompanied by a revival of libido. Given the new
mobility, marriages began to be based more on romance than ar-
rangement. Women came to be regarded more as partners than as
chattel. The domestic status of women improved. They gained
new rights to transfer property and wealth to heirs. Parents began
taking responsibility for the care and nurturing of their offspring
away from servants.

These several societal shifts coincided with reversals in the
long-term decline in the fertility of the upper classes. Infant and
child mortality fell, and adult mortality rates stayed steady. Median
ages of marriage rose slightly, but more children were born to
these groups, especially to peer families. The likely explanations
are that aristocratic children were marrying in greater number, and

then having children at unprecedented rates thanks to rising wealth. Profiting from new capitalistic opportunities, like enclosure and investments in urban property, plus the new canals, turnpikes, and coal mines, an enriched and growing class of persons arose beyond the traditional aristocratic family nexus.

The expanded role of women lasted only until the growth of industrial capitalism and the second rise of patriarchy at the end of the eighteenth century brought a new emphasis on virtue, innocence, and purity, and thus a narrowing of the opportunities and spheres of women until about 1850. Children were raised more punitively, with curbs on young wills. These attitudes also reached beyond the gentry to the newly mobile and prosperous middle class. They joined a revival of discipline, thrift, and responsibility in vocational as well as family pursuits. Methodism, Quakerism, Unitarianism, and like-minded creeds became popular—"a collective theological parapet" from which the middle class could attack the indolence, frivolity, and extravagance of their nominal societal betters (74).

According to Quinlan and Shackelford, the English family's patterns of childrearing and fecundity, as well as its ideological underpinnings, shifted in response to larger market forces, capitalistic opportunity, and a fluctuating set of economically-driven priorities. Change, not steady amelioration or lineal progress, was the dominating feature of family life.

Just as Hanawalt and Quinlan and Shackelford revised received wisdom about English families from medieval times to the industrial revolution, so the contributions by Zambardino and Brooks fundamentally reshaped the subsequent understanding of pre-conquest and early colonial Mexico. Zambardino rejected all previous, standard estimates of the population of central Mexico on the eve of the Spanish occupation as much too high, and too dependent on a series of false assumptions. If the indigenous population were, in fact, considerably less than the 25 million estimated by the then leading historians of the conquest, then many fewer Mexicans would have succumbed to the brutalities and imported illnesses associated with the arrival of Spaniards in this part of the new world.[1] Zambardino's re-analysis of the statistical basis of the

1 Beginning in the 1950s, and culminating with a comprehensive revisionist publication in 1963, Woodrow Wilson Borah and Sherbourne F. Cook proposed the new standard numbers in their final re-working of the impact and result of the conquest on the indigenous populations of central Mexico. See Borah and Cook, *The Indian Population of Central Mexico*,

earlier assumptions and estimates called for a fundamental rethinking of the entire nature of sixteenth century Central American cultural contact and cultural survival.

At the 25 million level, central Mexico's population would have been the most densely populated sizable area in the world, and among the globe's largest political entities in the sixteenth century. Moreover, not until the modern 1960s did central Mexico begin to approximate the supposed figure for 1518.

Zambardino's skepticism about the earlier population estimates was important because potentially it shed new light on the extent to which (and on the way in which) a handful of foreign soldiers were able to overcome the opposition of a numerically preponderant receiving population. The Aztecs were defenseless against several of the diseases that accompanied the Spaniards, notably smallpox. One-third of the local population may have died from smallpox during the first century of the occupation.

As Brooks wrote, if the pre-conquest population were 25 million—five times larger than had been assumed before Borah and Cook—then the collapse of the population to the widely accepted figure of 1 million in 1600 would have been truly catastrophic as well as wildly unprecedented. But, as Zambardino explained, Borah and Cook's suppositions were riddled with error. They used a multipliers method and thus produced results so inaccurate "as to be meaningless." (86) Zambardino showed in some detail how Borah and Cook developed their population estimates for various decades in the sixteenth century, and how their methods were flawed. He demonstrated the inconsistencies in their arguments and in their employment of the available data. Particularly suspect were the ways in which Borah and Cook calculated the population numbers for 1532 and 1568, the two years around which nearly all of their other assumptions pivot. Even more problematic, Zambardino concluded, was Borah and Cook's determination of the 1518 population from pictographic tribute records coupled with extrapolating backward from the estimates for later years. This particular reworking by Zambardino of the Borah and Cook figures is a triumph of rigorous statistical thinking over methodologically less compelling estimates.

1531–1610 (Berkeley, 1960), idem, *The Aboriginal Population of Central Mexico on the Eve of the Spanish Conquest* (Berkeley, 1963).

Using Borah and Cook's own data, Zambardino suggested that the pre-conquest population of central Mexico in 1518 was between 5 and 10 million, and probably much closer to 5 million. Brooks built his argument directly on Zambardino's, and also on independent complementary research supporting the new estimates for Mexico's population before and during the first phase of the conquest. But what about the cause of the catastrophical numerical collapse throughout the century? Was smallpox the sole culprit, as had long been assumed? Was Mexico truly a case of a virgin soil epidemic, with smallpox spreading "like wildfire?"

Brooks suggested that smallpox need move neither fast nor far. Modern evidence indicates that the disease was not highly contagious. Its virulence has varied considerably. Moreover, Brooks wondered whether contemporary sixteenth century accounts of smallpox in Mexico were reliable, and not just a mixture of conjecture and conflation. (A later article in the *JIH*—Robert McCaa, "Spanish and Nahuatl Views on Smallpox and Demographic Catastrophe in Mexico," XXV (1995), reprinted in Robert I. Rotberg (ed.), *Health and Disease in Human History* (2000), 167–200—strongly questioned Brooks' skepticism about particular redactions of the time.)

The catastrophe described in several sets of accounts, Brooks decided, was war. "Smallpox was incidental." (133) Indeed, Brooks' re-analysis of the texts of the time indicated that the smallpox that accompanied the Spaniards was mild, and of little effect. The melodramatic histories were overdone. The Aztec population was not killed off in enormous numbers by smallpox. Certainly, the death count was less than one-third of the preconquest population. "No such catastrophe actually occurred."(135)

Although Brooks' account was subsequently challenged by McCaa and the original texts that he questioned deemed authentic, thus diluting the lasting impact of his pronouncement on the extent or not of "catastrophe," the importance of his article, and Zambardino's (in company with the other chapters in this volume) lies more in the manner in which received wisdom was challenged and new conclusions advanced. In Brooks' case, this was done by examining epidemiological evidence for smallpox, and then attempting to link those data to the available sources from the sixteenth century. Zambardino brought the power of statistical logic to bear on evidence already presented by his predecessors in a putatively convincing quantitative form. But more advanced re-examination of what Borah and Cook had done persuaded Zambardino (and subsequent authors like Brooks) that Borah and Cook had not fully understood the conceptual weaknesses of their own methods.

With regard to the nearby islands, before the 1970s many authorities on Caribbean families asserted that the life of slaves throughout the islands was characterized by polygyny, matrifocality, and instability. The nuclear family, it was confidently declared, had rarely existed during the centuries of slavery in the West Indies. Craton's chapter builds and elaborates upon the work of Higman, who first elsewhere and then in the *JIH* showed that the nuclear family was the norm (or at least extremely common) in the sugar colonies, and that single-headed maternal households were the minority.[2]

Examining the situation in the non-sugar colony of the Bahamas, Craton found a similar configuration of families during the nineteenth century. He reconstituted slave households and families by using the returns under the colony's slave registration act, a sample for the early 1820s that comprised more than 3000 slave groups from eleven different islands. The incidence of family was high—85 percent, with more than 54 percent living in "simple" nuclear families. More than 63 percent of the adults were listed as couples. The Outer Islands—the more isolated and rural ones—had more family life while the surrounds of the long-established white settlements displayed more disrupted conjugal patterns. There were more female-headed families, and more families with absent males. Miscegenation was more common on the inner islands, too.

Some of these patterns could have resulted from serial relationships, or from polygyny. But Craton's analyses of the Bahamian censuses from 1822 to 1834 detected little serial monogamy and less polygyny. The evidence, reported Craton, "proves the vigorous existence of [modern] families among Bahamian slaves." (149) But, he asked, was this pattern the result of the slaves' own decisions or of decisions by their Eurocentric masters?

There were well-known paternalist, prescriptive masters. Christian influences were of growing significance. Yet, Craton

---

2 Barry W. Higman, "Household Structure and Fertility on Jamaican Slave Plantations: A Nineteenth-Century Example," *Population Studies*, XXVII (1973), 527–550.

concluded, "the widespread incidence and consistent form of slave families suggest customary choice" by slaves (151). There was a strong retention of African cultural preferences, including the nuclear family. Indeed, Africans were much more likely than Creoles to live in families in the Bahamas. The establishment of elementary nuclear families was the response of African-born first-generation slaves. "The impress of Africa was indelible." (168) Yet, size of plantation, urbanization, differences between the various colonies, and the temporal period of research all influenced the extent to which the Bahamian and Jamaican patterns were typical. Even so, the nuclear family pattern remained common everywhere until, paradoxically, emancipation weakened family institutions and led to new kinds of instability.

The nuclear family was strong in Japan, too. Yet the fact that the population of Japan grew very slowly in the eighteenth century had long been ascribed to high mortality as a result of food shortages and the ills of urbanization. But Eng and Smith, in line with a few similarly revisionist studies, discovered no mortality crises. Instead, their examination of the population registers in a single fishing village demonstrated both low mortality and low fertility between the censuses of 1721 and 1846. Eng and Smith traced the family members and employed the methods of modern demography to explain the unexpected conclusion of low mortality.

Fertility in the village was average for Japan, and low compared to a sample of European villages during roughly the same time period. This resulted not from the practice of birth control but from infanticide and, less probably, abortion. Infanticide was not practiced, however, to maximize the number of males nurtured by villagers. Eng and Smith found, instead, that infanticide was practiced against both sexes so as to create families containing both girls and boys. But the families of the fishing village sought a distribution rather more complicated than equality. Nor did they seek a perfect balance. Eng and Smith inferred this conclusion by carefully analyzing alternative hypotheses in the light of demographic theory.

The Japanese wanted mixed and comparatively large families. Eng and Smith show that "early stopping" occurred deliberately when an ideal family size or an appropriately mixed family had been achieved; "late stoppers"—the median age of mothers in the fishing village at the birth of their last children was 37.5—bore children well past their prime years in order to achieve the preferred family size and/or the preferred mixture of offspring.

The size of the family farm strongly influenced the size of the family preferred and achieved in the fishing village. Additionally, the larger the family, the more evenly balanced was the sex of the children. The smaller the family, the more boys, since a minimum number of boys was required for farms to be run effectively. But since too many boys created unhealthy competition for family succession, girls were preferred as a way to round out families, and to create future links with other households.

Eng and Smith suggested that whereas infanticide elsewhere in the world may have reflected social demoralization, in Japan, and especially in the fishing village that they studied, infanticide was practiced by the most respectable and stable members of the village, by the wealthiest and largest land-holders, and in good years and bad.

Petrine Russia, like early modern Japan, began thoroughly counting its people, and therefore providing better sources for the study of family composition, early in the eighteenth century. Before Kaiser, most analysis of the demographic composition of Russia for this period was confined to aggregated data, despite significant sources of error. Kaiser's conclusions instead derived from a close inspection of twelve population inventories compiled in ten somewhat dissimilar towns of European Russia between 1710 and 1720.

These were towns with between about 1000 and 4000 common people (the households of gentry were excluded from tax liability, and therefore from being counted), with more females than males because of war and labor conscription. The overwhelming majority were "townsmen," although very small percentages were men and women of the clergy, scribes and chancery officials, and soldiers. The reported mean household sizes (MHS) in these samples were smaller than those for peasants, and the mean of the MHS was closer to English sizes of the same period, but the town totals varied considerably. (Kaiser used town inventories, which omitted 80 to 90 percent of Russia's eighteenth-century population—peasants and serfs living in rural areas.)

Poverty influenced the MHS in the towns, with tax-exempt households being small and very poor, and often headed by widows. Only the well-to-do, Kaiser concluded, could sustain sub-stantially-sized households. Among them, social estate influenced the MHS, with those in the higher strata having larger households and, presumably, being able to afford them. Priests and other clergy lived in smaller households than did townsmen, scribes in larger ones.

Kaiser found that simple family households predominated, but complex households were not exceptional. Multiple-family units seem to have been more common higher up the social scale, simple ones lower down. Social station was decisive in household formation, in size, and in composition. Although households headed by able-bodied males might have had every reason to extend families or aggregate them, thereby multiplying the able hands and decreasing the taxation per capita, in fact more powerful factors determined tax liability. Indeed, "aggregation brought no tax relief," Kaiser decided (232). Aggregation had no effect on taxation, with larger households paying higher average per capita taxes.

Kaiser demonstrated that in the towns of eighteenth-century Russia, simple family households of modest size were common, as in Western Europe. Indeed, much about the size and composition of the early eighteenth-century Russian family in the city (but not in the countryside) was reminiscent of the prevailing pattern in Western Europe, "further undermining the hypothesis of a distinct Western European experience." (234)

Nineteenth-century Germany, unlike Russia, experienced a great sexual revolution. Or did it? Illegitimacy rates rose dramatically, especially in Bavaria, early in the century. Many contemporaries decried the period's growing moral decay as Germany industrialized, urbanized, and became more "enlightened." Yet Bavaria and the rest of southern Germany were and are staunchly Roman Catholic in belief and practice; Lee cited attendance rates that testified to the hold of the Church over Bavarians, and to a lack of social decay—if churchgoing is any indication.

The striking growth in illegitimacy in Bavaria and the rest of southern Germany—the highest rate in all of Germany—seems unlikely in a largely pre-industrial, church-triumphant region. Yet, the growth of rural industry in Bavaria, together with the increasing strength of the nuclear family, may unwittingly have weakened the social fabric of this region during the early years of the last century. The growth of rural industry could have stimulated new social behavioral norms. So could the nuclear family have been dysfunctional and unable to cope with societal shifts during the century. Lee argued, however, that neither the rise of rural industry nor the spread of the nuclear family contributed significantly to rising rates of illegitimacy.

Restrictive marriage legislation could have played a part in encouraging illegitimacy, but Lee reported that it was not decisive. Nor was the legal secularization of Germany at the beginning of the century, the rapid rise of an advanced educational system, and reductions in literacy. All present plausible but insufficient reasons for the dramatic increases in illegitimate births. Indeed, most of the available explanations point to the strengthening, not the loosening, of family ties in Bavaria and elsewhere. These factors would all have reinforced cohesion, not loosened it. So, absent any effective straw men, what explains such high illegitimacy rates?

Illegitimacy was never a reason for exclusion from society in southern Germany, as it was elsewhere in Europe. Nor were illegitimate children killed, as they were in parts of France. In fact, illegitimacy was a social norm in southern Germany, not a threat to existing family structures. (In a subsequent issue of the *JIH*, Edward Shorter, "Bastardy in South Germany: A Comment," VIII (1978), 459–469, called this conclusion "simply wrong." He asserted that the rise in bastardy in south Germany in fact had involved a sexual revolution.) Nineteenth-century Bavarian legislation even reflected that indifferent, if not positive, attitude toward bastardy. "Rural society was . . . indifferent as to whether children listed in the parish register were legitimate or not," reported Lee (252).

This conclusion flew in the face of experience elsewhere, especially in northern Europe. Yet, Lee advanced a number of practical reasons why Bavaria should have been so tolerant. Infant mortality was high, and higher still for illegitimate children. There were rural labor shortages, sometimes acute, during the first half of the nineteenth century. Whether the now more valuable worker was illegitimate or not became less and less relevant. These shortages naturally bid up wage levels, and made farmers, rural entrepreneurs, and laborers wealthier, and much more secure.

Staunch parishioners could and did tolerate high levels of rural illegitimacy, but not because Bavaria experienced a social revolution. If Lee is right, bastardy had no stigma attached to it, and it was no obstacle to employment. Rural prosperity and accompanying shortages of workers played a significant role in creating a zone of tolerance around illegitimacy.

In Britain during the same era, fertility and nuptiality rates reflected occupational choices, economic factors, and social norms. To test this assumption, Haines focused on coal miners in England and Wales. In part, he did so because coal mining was geographically concentrated, and an analysis of small areas (registration districts) could substitute for occupational data not otherwise available for the nineteenth century.

Coal miners in Britain, unlike high income business and professional persons, but like agricultural laborers and unskilled manual laborers, had large families and experienced high levels of fertility. These differentials persisted over time, but also widened from at least the 1850s. Relative to the national average, the fertility of higher socioeconomic groups declined as that of mining and laboring families rose appreciably. For wives of miners over forty-five in 1911, for example, the number of children ever born per one hundred couples was 630, or 129 percent of the national average. Miners' wives ranked first in fertility of all occupational groups, followed by wives of blast furnace workers. Miners' wives with incomplete fertility (under forty-five) also ranked high, second to the blast furnace wives. High total fertility, in both cases, compensated for very high levels of infant mortality in coal mining families.

Mining families in England and Wales exhibited very low ages of first marriage for both males and females. In 1884–1885, they had the lowest mean age in the country. More miners were married (according to registration district figures) than other occupational groups (derived from a random sample of non-mining-specific British registration districts). In the 1951 British census, as a century before, the highest proportion married by age twenty-five were spouses of miners or quarrymen. Wives of professionals were least married by twenty-five.

Haines sought explanations for these results for mining families. What was it about coal mining and mining more generally that caused or became associated with such consistently high levels of marriage and fertility? Haines argued that, for mining families, the answers lay at the intersection of a mining life style and expectations of income. Although miners worked in rural areas, and were socialized by rural mores, they experienced the opportunities for wage growth of more urbanized industrial workers. Moreover, mining districts showed far more men than women as compared to non-mining British registration districts. These high sex ratios and imbalances were associated with high rates of marriage and fertility.

Women in these rural or semi-rural mining areas had reduced access to employment outside their homes; wives of textile workers, for example, had many more opportunities for outside employment than wives in mining districts. The absence of employment opportunities also influenced the ages of marriage. Textile wives exhibited later marriages and much lower levels of fertility than the wives of miners.

Miners in nineteenth century Britain were relatively wealthy. In addition to garden plots, they received free cottages and free coal for heating and cooking. Their life styles were better ordered than those of factory workers. Significantly, miners earned more earlier (relative to their counterparts in other manual occupations); men of twenty-five brought home bigger pay packets than those in the same cohort who worked in industry, on farms, or at sea.

Children of miners could work above ground even after child labor underground was prohibited in 1842. Schooling became compulsory only in 1876, and even then only until age twelve. There was a perceived family income advantage, and a bias toward more children, in mining areas. Even more influential may have been the social security motive: Because miners expected short, brutish working lives, they married earlier and developed their own social safety nets by having more children than the British average for laboring families.

Haines employed a range of appropriate statistical and demographic tests to verify and support his conclusions. His article suggested that the model used could and should be applied to other occupational groups. Marriage was more important than marital fertility in explaining differences among regions, a conclusion that fitted the general, and elsewhere discussed, predominant nineteenth century Western European marriage pattern: marriage controlled overall fertility.

Across the Atlantic, especially in seventeenth- and eighteenth-century New England, the timing of marriage was largely freed from the ecclesiastical constraints of the old world. New Englanders could marry at any time of the year, even during Advent and Lent. Nevertheless, Cressy discovered a distinct seasonality of marriage in New England.

In England during the same centuries, weddings were rarely scheduled during the harvest, for obvious reasons. Autumn, with a bounty of produce at the end of the agricultural season, was the most popular period for the marital knot to be tied. Late spring and early summer—May and June—were the rival times. Looking more carefully at regional variations within England, arable southeastern England distinctly favored autumn whereas pastoral northern and western England exhibited more frequent marriages in early summer, after the birth of lambs and calves. Urbanization and proto-industrialization muted these variations, but even in the towns marriages avoided Lent and peaked in the autumn.

Cressy asked whether the immigrants from East Anglia (and elsewhere) to Massachusetts carried seasonal notions of marriage with them when they settled in the new colony. Was there an underlying continuity in old-world and new-world rhythms of fertility and mortality even though there were no ecclesiastical constraints? The Pilgrims called the ancient holidays pagan, papish, and profane, so there may well have been positive peer encouragement to celebrate marriages at random times throughout the year. But the new colonists were farmers, and the solemnizing of their unions might have reflected the demands of a harsh new frontier enterprise.

Cressy's examination of the marriage registers of Boston and five other Massachusetts towns revealed a striking seasonal pattern unlike anything discerned in the French and English records. During the seventeenth century, most weddings outside of Boston took place in winter, especially during Advent; some occurred in the spring; and summer was an unusual time to be married. June and August marriages were rare. In Boston, marriages were distributed throughout the year, and showed a mild preference for November and a distaste for March.

During the eighteenth century, possibly connected to a strengthening of religious Anglicanism, there was a mild shift in seasonality in Massachusetts back toward the older English pattern. In both centuries, however, aside from Boston there was the expected agricultural rhythm: farmers were busiest in the fields in the summer, and then harvested in the early autumn, when marriages were few. October was a popular month for marriages in England, but not in Massachusetts because servant contracts were not renewed in the same way or at the same time and, predominantly, because New Englanders sowed winter wheat in October.

When the days turned dark and the nights cold, and when winter provisions had been laid away, it was appropriate to marry and to feast. Having abandoned their English calendar, the New England colonists and their successors followed a new calendar for marriage.

Farther south, in the Chesapeake Bay region at approximately the same time, a Virginia county inhabited by blacks and whites showed two variations of seasonality. Rutman, Wetherell, and Rutman showed that births of whites followed a pronounced seasonal pattern, peaking in March and falling in June, that was not dissimilar from pre-industrial birth timings in the other colonies, in Canada, in Sweden, and in France. The births of blacks were more numerous in June, however, and their general seasonal pattern was the reverse of the white experience. Black and white death rates were similar in their peaks and troughs during the first half of the year, but diverged in the second.

For marriage, since black unions were not recorded, only the white rhythm could be determined. The months of frequent marriage in the Virginia county were February and April (not March and June). Marriages occurred randomly throughout the remainder of the year.

Comparisons with other counties in the Bay area suggested to the authors that their data were representative. But did the recorded events accurately reflect the seasonality of the actual events. How were the records transcribed and collected? And by whom for what purposes? Perhaps there was a heaping of events, reported as they were by heads of households, whenever agricultural or other demands lessened. But the authors found no sequencing or patterning, and so dismissed the need for possible correctives. There was no systematic bias with regard to the recording of white or black events.

Rutman, Wetherell, and Rutman concluded that the early Virginians avoided the Lenten period for marriage, the frequency of marriages in the weeks immediately before or after Lent strengthening the differences between these colonists and their New England cousins.

For deaths, the killer months in an area like the Chesapeake clustered in the winter for both white and black. Whites also died in early autumn, presumably from malaria (against which blacks may have been immunized).

What about births? The authors found that their data from whites appeared to reflect the pattern of agricultural, pre-modern societies and the opposite of modern American rhythms. But the pattern of births to blacks, which might have responded to environmental or latitudinal determinants, was entirely different. The timing of births to blacks may have reflected nutritional peaks and troughs in a tobacco-growing society where all of the hard labor was supplied by slaves.

Why did fertility levels decline in the colonies and, from the end of the eighteenth century, in the United States? Did American rural and urban families consciously devise a number of strategies like later marriage and family limitation to fit the availability of land and other economic resources? Byers tested the prevailing hypotheses with regard to those questions not in the customary agrarian settings of his predecessors but with data from the commercial center and port city of Nantucket from the seventeenth century through the middle of the nineteenth century. In the late eighteenth century, until the Revolution, Quaker-dominated Nantucket, with its pacifist instincts and Tory sympathies, was the most important whaling center in the world.

Byers reconstituted the families of Nantucket, based on the city's vital records. He noticed a substantial decline in the number of children ever born throughout the period of his study, with two distinct sharp downturns in the 1740s and 1780s. Families became smaller over the same period. There was a pronounced early shift downward in the fertility behavior of the island's permanent families.

Ages at marriage rose for women, and also (but less substantially and less evenly) for men. Later marriages reduced fertility and family sizes. So did age-specific fertility after 1740, possibly as a result of conscious decision. Byers demonstrated that the mean ages of Nantucket mothers at last birth fell, especially during the 1740s. The distribution of the ages of mothers at last birth continued to shift downward as the century passed and the new one began. That finding, and other tests run by Byers, supported the conclusion that Nantucketeers practiced family limitation beginning in the 1730s, decades earlier than other New Englanders.

Nantucket's permanent families consciously, albeit gradually, limited the size of their families. This was a transition that continued until the 1790s, by which time (if not before) there was community-wide acceptance of voluntary fertility control. They did so not because of population density—Nantucket was crowded from the beginning—nor because of the scarcity of arable land. Rather, as the island prospered, childrearing became more expensive than on the mainland. The opportunities for paid child labor were minimal. Since men were at sea for long periods, wives established themselves in business, especially the dry goods trade, many becoming comparatively independent financially. Indeed, Quaker Nantucket was an early stronghold of feminism. All of these factors contributed to a secular fertility decline on the island.

The final essay in this volume also addresses fertility patterns in the United States during the first half of the nineteenth century. Vinovskis asked whether land availability and urbanization, rather than land scarcity alone, could explain the long-term fertility decline that Byers's chapter also attempted to understand. Vinovskis employed methods more sophisticated than those of his predecessors who had postulated land scarcity as the key reason for fertility decline. He scrutinized returns for 1850 and 1860 for all American census divisions east of the Mississippi River.

Vinovskis created an index of agricultural opportunity based on average values for farms, and defined urbanization as the percentage of the population living in towns over 2,500. Educational levels were measured by the percentages of the populations older than twenty who could read and write. Multiple regression and linear least-squares procedures allowed him to develop appropriate relationships between the independent and dependent variables, and then to test the relative ability of each variable to explain the white-refined fertility ratio.

There were positive correlations, especially in 1850, between the white-refined fertility ratio and the white sex ratio and the percentage of functionally illiterate white adults. In that year, farm values and urban populations were strongly correlated, too. Vinovskis also found the white-refined fertility ratio and the percentage of the free population who were foreign born positively related.

Fertility differentials over time were therefore accounted for by the percentage of the population that lived in towns (an index of commercialization was even more robust) and the percentage that was illiterate. Indeed, the "single best predictor" of fertility differentials among the states was the educational level of its white population (387). The value of the family farm was weakly relevant in 1850, but not in 1860, whereas the white sex ratio was more important in 1860 than in 1850. (Growing land scarcity proved a poor explanation lowered fertility.) The percentage of the population that was foreign born was weak and positive.

Despite these carefully elaborated conclusions, Vinovskis also suspected that fertility declines in nineteenth-century America reflected broad attitudinal shifts in both urban and rural settings that preceded the eras of industrialization and urbanization. Lower fertility ratios in the nineteenth century might have anticipated and helped to prepare for the growth of towns and industry.

Whether focusing chronologically on the medieval, early modern, or modern periods, or on Europe, Asia, or the Americas, the contents of this volume demonstrates the critical contribution to understanding the dimensions of past time that has come in recent decades from the practitioners of family and population history. Without careful attention to fertility transitions and their causes, shifting ages of marriage, seasonality of vital events, mean household size differentials, childrearing methods across cultures, infanticide, and population dynamics generally, history would be less thick and complex and our appreciation of it much the poorer. The essays in this volume are representative of the contributions that demographically-informed historians, using increasingly sophisticated and mathematically refined methods, have made over the past three decades to the interdisciplinary rewriting, reconceptualizing, and revitalizing of history and the process of historiography.

Barbara A. Hanawalt

Childrearing among the Lower Classes
of Late Medieval England

Anxiety about the breakdown of the modern family, the application of Freudian and Eriksonian models of child development to historical subjects, and the study of households by demographers combined to make Ariès' *Centuries of Childhood* the center of debate and the object of attack among social historians. Ariès suggested that the sentimental concept of the family existing for the sake of rearing children was a modern idea which developed in early modern Europe in response to the loss of other familial functions to the centralized state and the exigencies of industrialization. In the Middle Ages, he argued, the family had extensive kinship and community ties which shared and could outweigh the emotional bonds of the family to children.[1]

Although Ariès drew his data primarily from the upper class, his theory has raised issues which should be investigated for all ranks of society. First, he assumed that the medieval household was a large one in which both extended family and outsiders lived together, a view of the preindustrial family which Laslett has denied.[2] Second, he argued that children became valuable to society only when they reached the age of seven and could be sent out to another house to work, in other words, only when they became economically productive.[3] Third, he ignored the actual process of childrearing before the age of seven, leaving this issue unexplored. In this essay I have studied these three problems and have used coroners' rolls, a source often ignored by historians of the family,

Barbara A. Hanawalt is Assistant Professor of History at Indiana University and the author of *Crime in East Anglia in the Fourteenth Century: Norfolk Gaol Delivery Rolls* (Norwich, England, 1976).

The author would like to thank the Southeastern Summer Institute for Medieval and Renaissance Studies for the opportunity to join a seminar on the medieval household with David Herlihy in 1974. His direction and help during the seminar were very much appreciated.

1 Philippe Ariès (trans. Robert Baldick), *Centuries of Childhood; a Social History of Family Life* (New York, 1962), 368.
2 Peter Laslett, "The Comparative History of Household and Family," *The Journal of Social History*, IV (1970), 75–87.
3 Ariès, *Centuries of Childhood*, 128.

in order to move the investigation of childrearing away from the elite minority to the practices of the majority.

One of the central issues in the criticisms of Ariès and in the general discussion about childrearing in the Middle Ages and later has been that, although the literate upper classes left some records of childrearing, the lower classes, who comprised the bulk of society, did not.[4] The approaches of peasants and the lower urban class to raising children were usually not represented in artistic and literary remains. For the Middle Ages the problem is particularly difficult because many of these sources were the works of ecclesiastical writers who had little direct experience with normal family life. Even the usual sources of information on childrearing in the Middle Ages are inconclusive. For instance, medievalists have countered early modernists' contentions that the Middle Ages lacked a concept of childhood by indicating the instances in artistic representations, chronicles, saints' lives, and ecclesiastical pronouncements where children were treated as children. However, the mere representation of a child *qua* child rather than as a little man does not indicate a sentimental attachment to children. Injunctions of church synods and penitentials about infanticide may only indicate an extension of the commandment, "Thou shalt not kill," rather than a particular love for the children who might be killed.[5] In the hands of a skilled historian, such as McLaughlin, these literary sources become the basis for a serious discussion of trends in childrearing and attitudes toward childhood in the Middle Ages. She has shown that the attitudes of writers move from a threatening view of children in the ninth century to a greater interest and concern for children by the end of the thirteenth century. Understandably, however, works such as hers and Hunt's return repeatedly to the qualification that the literary remains of the upper classes of medieval and early modern Europe may or may

4 Lutz Berkner, "Recent Research on the History of the Family in Western Europe," *Journal of Marriage and the Family*, XXXV (1973), 395–405. Berkner provides an excellent survey of current literature on the history of the family. He emphasizes the lack of studies of peasant families.

5 Richard H. Helmholtz, "Infanticide in the Province of Canterbury during the Fifteenth Century," *History of Childhood Quarterly*, II (1975), 384. Helmholtz has shown that there was a legal punishment for infanticide which was no more or no less severe than, for example, sex offenses. The Church does not seem to have had any particular sentiment for childhood in pursuing the ecclesiastical court trials of those who killed their children.

not reflect what practices were used by the bulk of the population.[6]

The coroners' inquests are a unique source of information on the daily life of the peasants, villagers, and middle to lower classes in towns. The nobility and wealthier urban families seldom appeared because they were less likely to meet with ordinary accidents or homicides and because they would usually be exempt from most judicial procedures, including the coroners' inquests. The inquests record cases where conflicts among members of a community or family led to homicide and where work, play, or neglect led to accidental deaths. Evidence on the rolls which specifically relates to the family permits a study of the activities of children and other members of the household, an estimate of the types of family structures and number of people in the household, and, to a certain extent, the emotional relations of family members. For instance, if a child died in a cradle fire, the inquests indicated not only the cause of death but who first discovered the accident, how the fire got started, the people who were present or should have been, and the date on which it happened. The victims in a household struck by fire or attacked by robbers would all be listed along with their relationships to each other, their activities before death (if known), and the layout of the house. The most obvious bias in the source is that it is a sample of those people in society who were careless, accident prone, unfortunate, or violent. Nevertheless, an analysis of any accident or homicide statistics is a study of the practices and mores of the society. The people who appear in them are representative of their society; they are simply more unlucky or aggressive than their neighbors.

Each inquest reads like a vignette of medieval life, having freshness and immediacy because it was recorded so soon after death, in the language of the jurors and witnesses. When a person died violently or suddenly, i.e. by homicide, misadventure (accidental death), or suicide, the neighbors were required by law to summon one of the county coroners to come and view the body. The coroner empanelled a jury of the neighborhood in which the body was found and held an inquest to determine the cause of

6   Mary Martin McLaughlin, "Survivors and Surrogates: Children and Parents from the Ninth to the Thirteenth Centuries," in Lloyd de Mause (ed.), *The History of Childhood* (New York, 1974), 101–181; David Hunt, *Parents and Children in History* (New York, 1970).

death. Like the modern coroner, he inspected the wounds and inquired into the date and hour of death, the place and circumstances surrounding it, witnesses, the death instrument, suspects, the age of the victim if he were a minor, and perhaps even motivations in the cases of homicide. The information was recorded on pieces of parchment at the time of the inquest and later copied onto rolls which were presented to the king's justices upon demand.[7]

The coroners' rolls used in this paper give a sampling of different social and economic conditions in late medieval England. Urban life is represented by two series of published rolls: the London rolls, containing 205 cases, and the Oxford rolls, containing 110 cases from the fourteenth century. The data for rural society come from published Bedfordshire inquests, containing 189 cases, and from a run of over 100 years of Northamptonshire coroners' rolls in manuscript, yielding 1307 cases from the fourteenth and early fifteenth century.[8] Many of these cases deal with families. Children are specifically involved as victims in 17 percent of the Northamptonshire cases (214), 18 percent of the Bedfordshire cases (33), 6 percent in London, and .9 percent in Oxford. The ages of the children were recorded up to their twelfth birthday when they legally assumed adult responsibilities.

Since children are not reared without interaction with their environment, we will want to know the size of the household, its physical description, and the relationship of the occupants. Esti-

---

7 After the justices from the central court tried the homicide suspects who had been arrested and collected the money due from the *deodands* (i.e. the value of the death instrument in accidents), they deposited the rolls with the Exchequer, where they were preserved. The *deodand* was a revenue source for the king. Initially, the death instrument was to be sold and the money contributed to prayers for the soul of the victim. It later became a contribution to the royal treasury. The collection and preservation of the rolls was sporadic. Those counties which were visited most frequently by the justices of the king's bench have very good series, while those that had few visitations have poor ones. The amount of detail on the record depends very much on the interest an individual coroner took in recording information and how busy he was. For a complete description of the coroners see R. F. Hunnisett, *The Medieval Coroner* (Cambridge, 1961).

8 R. R. Sharpe, *Calendar of Coroners' Rolls of the City of London, A.D. 1300–1378* (London, 1913); H. E. Salter, *The Records of Medieval Oxford* (Oxford, 1912); Hunnisett, *Bedfordshire Coroners' Rolls* (Bedfordshire, 1960), XLI. I have also used a few examples from his *Calendar of Nottinghamshire Coroners' Inquests 1485–1558* (Nottingham, 1969), XXV; the Northamptonshire coroners' rolls are preserved in the Public Record Office in London under the classification of Just. 2. In addition to the coroners' rolls, I have used the jail delivery rolls of 1300–1348 for Northamptonshire, Yorkshire, and Norfolk, which are the records of trials for felonious offenses. The rolls examined contained about 10,500 criminal cases. They are preserved in the Public Record Office under the classification of Just. 3.

mates of the number of people living under one roof have varied somewhat depending on the nature of the source. Russell estimated 3.5 persons per household, but Hallam, working with more complete census data, placed the size at 4 people in the rather densely populated fenland area of Lincolnshire.[9] Both Russell and Hallam found that the nuclear family predominated, although in the fens of thirteenth-century Lincolnshire there were instances of single-person households and extended families. The coroners' rolls give some information, particularly in burglary cases, of the number of people living in a household. Yet the evidence is not entirely reliable because some members of the household, particularly young children, might have escaped attack from the burglary and therefore not be listed. Nevertheless, the Bedfordshire coroners' rolls, which are among the most detailed, show that the late thirteenth-century rural household was far from being a static unit. The sample is a small one, twenty-five cases, but of these just over half were nuclear families. The rest of the families were either extended families with the husband's mother living with her son's family, or two brothers or two sisters living together, or a single woman or man either living alone or with young children. The families had from one to four children. The number of children per household was probably greater after the Black Death because, prior to 1349, 24 percent of the accident victims were children. After the plague the percentage increased to 31 percent. The presence of more children per household is consistent with demographic studies which show that marriages and births tended to increase after a plague. In addition to immediate members of the family, some households also contained servants who lived with their master or guests who had been staying for extended periods of time.

Aside from a preference for living with family, convenience seemed to determine living arrangements in rural Bedfordshire.[10] The twenty-five cases indicate that there were upwards of 3.5 per-

---

9   Josiah Cox Russell, *British Medieval Population* (Albuquerque, 1948), 24–26; H. E. Hallam, "Some Thirteenth-Century Censuses," *Economic History Review*, X (1958), 352; Edwin D. DeWindt, *Land and People in Holywell-cum-Needingworth* (Toronto, 1972), 171, placed the size at 3.8; John Kraus, "The Medieval Household: Large or Small?" *Economic History Review*, IX (1956–57), 420, puts the household size at 4.5.
10   Hunnisett, *Bedfordshire Coroners' Rolls*, cases 20, 52, 71, 73, 102, 111, 179, 203, 224, 249. "Swetalys" had been staying at the house of Thomas Saly of Riseley throughout the autumn, before she was found dead.

sons per household, most of them related and part of the nuclear family. In London and Oxford the household picture was altogether different for the lower classes. The rolls speak more frankly about transitional relationships with concubines, and the nuclear families which do appear were limited to a husband, wife, and one child. The smaller number and size of nuclear families accounts for the very low percentage of children appearing in the urban coroners' rolls.[11]

The evidence of coroners' rolls on the composition of the households must remain more suggestive than conclusive, but lacking other reliable evidence, the tentative conclusions it suggests deserve comment. For instance, although the rural families seem to have lived in predominantly nuclear units at one hearth, other arrangements were common to the society. Because the coroners' rolls record deaths, they particularly draw attention to the transitory aspects of the family: if the grandmother died, it would become a simple nuclear family; if a wife died, the house would become that of a widower; and so on. Stepparents must have been common because of the tendency of widows and widowers to remarry in order to increase land holdings and insure labor on the land.[12] The evidence indicates that both Laslett's em-

---

An interesting sidelight which the Bedfordshire data suggest is that the theory of constant households does not hold for late thirteenth-century England. According to this theory, the number of households remains constant so that in periods of economic contraction a control will be maintained over the distribution of resources. If the number of hearths remains fixed, then around each hearth one might expect to find extended families with the married and single children living with their parents. Although the late thirteenth century was a time of scarcity and over-population in Bedfordshire, households there do not show any evidence of being impacted. On the contrary, the wattle and daub houses seem to have been easy to acquire. There are even cases of accidents occurring in vacant houses. The real shortage seems to have been food rather than housing, for a number of inquests mention poor people dying from exposure while returning to their homes from begging, or dying in their homes from accidents due to their weakened condition. One of the fallacies of the constant household theory is the assumption that because fields and food are in limited supply, housing is also limited and existing hearths will be called upon to accept more members. Housing was obviously available in thirteenth-century Bedfordshire, but not food.

11   The difference between the urban and rural household picture is similar to that which Herlihy is finding for rural and urban Florence. Cities have more single people and smaller nuclear families among the poorer classes, while the peasantry have larger families and fewer single people. David Herlihy, "Mapping Households in Medieval Italy," *Catholic Historical Review*, LVIII (1972), 1–22; Diane Hughes, "Urban Growth and Family Structure in Medieval Genoa," *Past & Present*, 66 (1975), 2–4.

12   J. Z. Titow, "Some Differences between Manors and the Effects on the Condition of the Peasant in the Thirteenth Century," *Agricultural History Review*, X (1962), 1–13, notes the demand for widows in marriage. The extensive remarriage may account for some of the medieval folk and fairy tales about wicked stepmothers and stepfathers.

phasis on the nuclear family and Ariès' assumption of an extended family were correct. Although the small nuclear family was the most common type of family, it was certainly not the only one with which a growing child would be acquainted. Furthermore, to list the number and relationships of the people living under one roof does not completely define "family." One also wants to know the extent to which relatives and communities assumed some of the social functions now normally associated with a family.[13] The size of the household in which the child grew up and the amount of community interaction in its rearing might depend on the wealth and status of its family. Wealthier families or those of greater status might have had more living family members due to better diet.

A physical description of the household in which the child was reared emerges from the evidence jurors gave to the coroner on the circumstances surrounding deaths. In the thirteenth century many peasant houses were made of wattle and daub so insubstantial that burglars pushed the walls down rather than enter through the doors. For the poorer members of the peasant community this type of housing must have continued well into the fourteenth century, but by the end of the century houses were more substantial. They had courtyards with walls or ditches surrounding them and wells and ovens within. There would probably be two rooms and often two floors. The floors, covered with straw, were highly flammable, as were the straw pallets used for beds. The main room contained a raised hearth in the center of the floor. The child spent the first years of life in a cradle near the fire. Also around the fire were pots, pans, and trivets. Tables, chairs, and beds were the only other furniture mentioned. During the day the open door provided light and children and animals wandered through freely. At night candles were used, which seem to have been left to burn all night, sometimes catching the houses on fire. In the city the child was raised in a shop or a tenement, the construction of which was better than wattle and daub, but they burned easily nonetheless.

A brief description of the roles of parents in the household is also essential, for they were the models of behavior for their offspring. In describing the different tasks of men and women in the

13 Familial compounds of peasant families linked by an overall family patriarch are not indicated in coroners' roll data. Italian peasant and patrician families had this structure. See Hughes, "Urban Growth and Family Structure," 4.

rural social order, historians have tended to follow John Ball's classification that Adam delved, Eve span, and all men and women since then have been locked into the first parental model.[14] The evidence from the coroners' rolls shows that the sexes were assigned distinct tasks, but these tasks cannot be divided between field and home with easy facility. Reaping and stacking of hay and straw were done by both men and women. Taking grain to the mill was also a task for either. By and large, the heavy work was done by men in both urban and rural society. In rural society men worked more outside than women and more of them died in work-related accidents.[15] An analysis of the instruments of their death shows that men's work was more dangerous. They did all of the digging in marl pits and quarries, and in both urban and rural society they did all of the masonry and carpentry. They also did the milling, carting (this was the most dangerous activity, accounting for a quarter of the accidents of rural men), barn work, herding of animals, and training of horses. In urban society the heavy work, with the exception of the shipping and building industries, was mostly carried on indoors in a variety of crafts or shops. The women in the rolls are pictured as working in kitchens or the courtyard or doing errands about the town or village. They also gathered herbs and wood, did the laundry, weaving, and, one of the most important tasks, the brewing (in London, this was done by men). Beyond those mentioned, there were many activities of both sexes which did not appear in the inquests because they were not dangerous. Nevertheless, certain patterns of fairly well-defined role structure emerge from the coroners' rolls. The children would be expected to imitate and eventually perform the tasks of their model parent. Because of the sex differentiation in division of labor in the household, we may expect that males were raised differently than female children.

The matrimonial pattern in the households seems to have been as traditional as the division of labor. The majority of references in the coroners' rolls are to husbands and wives. But as Sheehan has shown, the bond of marriage might be very loose and the possibility of bigamous unions common.[16] In addition to the

---

14 George C. Homans, *English Villages of the Thirteenth Century* (Cambridge, Mass., 1940), 353–381.
15 65 percent of the men compared to 48 percent of the women.
16 Michael M. Sheehan, "The Formation and Stability of Marriage in Fourteenth Century England, Evidence of an Ely Register," *Medieval Studies*, XXXIII (1971), 228–263.

children of legitimate marriages, manorial records indicate illegitimate children. The actual extent of illegitimacy is impossible to measure. Women are mentioned in the coroners' inquests of London and Oxford as concubines and more quaintly in the country as "entertaining" men. For instance Lucy Pofot, widow of Thomas of Houghton, came from a local tavern accompanied by a "ribald stranger" who asked for entertainment and Lucy complied. The ungrateful guest murdered her in the night. The concubine of a clerk in fifteenth-century Nottinghamshire sought a solution to her unwanted pregnancy by swallowing poison to cause an abortion, but it killed her instead.[17]

What happened to unwanted babies at birth? Given the nature of the coroners' rolls, one would assume that they would be an ideal source for studying the incidence of infanticide. However, out of a sample of about 4,000 homicide cases taken from coroners' rolls and jail delivery rolls, there were only two cases of newborn infants being murdered. In one case Alice Grut and Alice Grym were indicted for drowning a three-day-old baby in a river at the request of Isabell of Bradenham, her son, and her daughter. They were all acquitted. In the other case, the jurors of Oxford said that a baby girl, one-half-day old, was carried downstream, and they knew nothing about the father or the mother. They assumed that she had not been baptized since the navel was not tied.[18] The murder of toddlers and older children was also extremely rare in the circuit court records (2 percent of all homicides). Some of these children were killed in accidental slayings and some in the course of burglaries, but only three were killed out of malice. Out of a sample of 2,969 homicide cases taken from the jail delivery rolls, only nine involved the killing of young children by an insane mother.[19] Even Helmholtz, looking through ecclesiastical records for cases of infanticide, could find only a few examples.[20]

The extraordinarily low incidence of recorded infanticide and child murder does not necessarily mean that it was rare. A plausi-

17 Hunnisett, *Bedfordshire Coroners' Rolls*, cases 35 and 94.
18 Just. 3/48 m. 4d; Salter, *Oxford Coroners' Rolls*, 27.
19 This amounts to .03 percent of all the cases, hardly enough evidence to bear the weight of the psychoanalytical superstructure which Barbara Kellum in "Infanticide in England in the Later Middle Ages," *History of Childhood Quarterly*, I (1974), 371–75 tried to build on evidence in my "The Female Felon in Fourteenth Century England," *Viator*, V (1974), 259–261.
20 Helmholtz, "Infanticide in Canterbury," 384.

ble argument can be made that infanticide was not consistently illegal in the Middle Ages. A statute law against mothers killing their illegitimate children was not passed until 1623,[21] and Hurnard correctly observed that "women who killed in childbirth were sometimes regarded as responsible and sometimes not."[22] In any case, the crime was easily concealed, making criminal prosecution difficult. The Church was well aware of the methods of concealment. In penitentials, and particularly in the English synodal legislation of the thirteenth century, parents were told not to sleep with children because they might smother them, not to leave them alone, and not to leave them unattended near fires. Helmholtz found that the Church heard cases involving accusations and confessions of these practices, but the extent of the practices remains a mystery.[23] One might argue that they were concealed through reporting them as accidental deaths. Among the accidental deaths of infants in our sample, there were no reported cases of overlaying, but 50 percent of the cases involving children one year and under were caused by fire and 21 percent by drowning (see Tables 1 and 2). Was this neglect or premeditated murder? A fairly consistent pattern associated with infanticide is that female children were killed more frequently than male.[24] The coroners' rolls, however, show that in Northamptonshire the percentage of accidental deaths of boys of all ages was much higher than that of girls—63 percent of all accidental deaths among children were male and 37 percent were female (see Table 3).[25] In the age group of one year and under, twenty-eight boys died compared to twenty girls. The low discrepancy of death from accidents between male and female children in this age group is consistent with modern accident figures, which show male children having higher accident rates than females in general, but the degree of excess of male deaths over female deaths is lowest in infancy and increases with

21 William S. Holdsworth, *A History of English Law* (Boston, 1924), IV, 501.
22 Naomi D. Hurnard, *The King's Pardon for Homicide before 1307* (Oxford, 1969), 169.
23 McLaughlin, "Survivors and Surrogates," 120–121; Helmholtz, "Infanticide in Canterbury," 380–382.
24 Emily R. Coleman, "L'infanticide dans le Haut Moyen Age," *Annales Economic, Société, Civilisations*, XXIX (1974), 315–335. Richard C. Trexler, "Infanticide in Florence: New Sources and First Results," *History of Childhood Quarterly*, I (1973), 98–116.
25 This is very close to modern figures, where 63.5 percent of all accidental death victims fourteen and under are males: *Accident Facts, 1968 Edition* (Chicago, 1968), 14.

Table 1 Distribution of Causes of Accidents for Male Children by Age

	1	2	3	4	5	6	7	8	9	10	11	12	UNSPECIFIED
Animals		3						2		1			
Water													
wells	3	13	11	4	1								
ditches	3	8	7	1	2					2		3	1
ponds	1	5	3		1					1			
streams		2	1		2	2	2	2	1			3	
Equipment													
cart			2			1							2
mill												1	
knife	1					1							1
pot	6	5	4					1					2
arrow												1	1
hatchet													1
Fire	13	4	3	1	1						1		2
Heavy object	1	1			1		1					1	
Victim falls	1	1						1				1	1

Table 2 Distribution of Causes of Accidents for Female Children by Age

	AGE												
	1	2	3	4	5	6	7	8	9	10	11	12	UNSPECIFIED
Animals	1	2	2										2
Water													
wells	2	5	1										
ditches		6	3	1	1								4
ponds	1	1	1										2
streams	1	1			2	2		1					
Equipment													
cart		1	1										
mill	1	1											
knife	1												1
pot	3	6	5						1				3
arrow		1	1										
hatchet													
Fire	11	4											5
Heavy object				2	2					1			
Victim falls	3					1							

Table 3 Distribution of Children's Accidents by Age and Sex

							AGE						
	1	2	3	4	5	6	7	8	9	10	11	12	UNSPECIFIED
male	28	47	31	2	7	4	3	7	1	5	2	10	9
female	22	26	15	5	5	1	0	1	1	0	1	0	16
Total	50	73	46	7	12	5	3	8	2	5	3	10	25
Total n =	249												

age.[26] Concrete evidence for infanticide is still lacking. There are four possibilities: 1) infanticide was a widespread phenomenon but was accepted by society and, therefore, ignored in the records; 2) it was successfully concealed; 3) infant mortality being between 30 percent and 50 percent, willful murder was unnecessary; 4) all children were valued because of the need for laborers in peasant society of the fourteenth century.[27]

Those children who survived the dangers of birth, disease, and homicide had to be fed, sheltered, and attended to during the first years of their lives. When one looks at the accident pattern, the stages of the developing child fall into four clearly defined groups: birth to one year old, two to three years old, four to seven years old, and eight to twelve years old (see Tables 1 and 2). These four stages are remarkably close to those which Hunt has adapted from Erik Erikson's work on child development, and reference will be made to Hunt's *Parents and Children* throughout.

The first stage of the child's life was occupied with problems of feeding, warmth, and attention. We may assume, along with McLaughlin, that both peasant and urban lower-class mothers nursed their own children.[28] Probably the child was not given milk on demand because, as we shall see, the children seemed to be left alone for long periods. Peasant women occasionally nursed other children. In one inquest a husband lost his temper and killed his wife because he claimed that she spent too much time at his neighbor's house giving milk to Robert Asplon's son.[29]

When not being nursed, the baby was kept in a cradle by the fire. The most common accident for both male and female infants was to be burnt in the cradle (50 percent of female infants and 46 percent of male). There is no proof that children were swaddled, but they might have been.[30] As described in the coroners' rolls, a typical case showed a child lying in its cradle next to the hearth when a chicken or pig came in and knocked burning straw or an ember into the cradle. Since the infants were wrapped in linen,

26 Albert P. Iskrant and Paul V. Joliet, *Accident and Homicide* (Cambridge, Mass., 1968), 23. Indeed, the ratio is extremely close to the modern one they give on 138.
27 The percentages are from E. A. Wrigley, *Population and History* (New York, 1969), 116-131.
28 McLaughlin, "Survivors and Surrogates," 115-116. Nursing continued from one to three years.
29 Hunnisett, *Bedfordshire Coroners' Rolls,* case 255.
30 McLaughlin, "Survivors and Surrogates," 113-114.

linsey-woolsy, or wool, the smell of buring cloth, if not the cry of the child, would call attention to the accident if an adult were in the house. In one case a child's entire legs were burned. The extent of the burns seems to indicate that infants were often left alone in the house, and a few cases tells us this directly. In one inquest the jurors said that the father was in the fields and the mother had gone out to the well when the child was burned. In a London case of neglect Johanna, daughter of Bernard de Irlaunde, a child of one month, was killed in her cradle by a sow bite. Her mother had left her alone in their shop with the door open and a sow wandered in and bit her head. The jurors go on to say that "at length" her mother returned to the shop and found her.

By the third year of the child's life cradle deaths were no longer common and the children appeared to have entered into the second phase of development, reception to outside stimulus.[31] By the end of the first year swaddling cloths, if used at all, were not kept on children all the time, for they were mobile enough to get into trouble.[32] They wandered around courtyards and fell into wells, ponds, and ditches on their parent's property. They also got into accidents in the house, the most common of which was pulling pots off trivets and scalding themselves. Falls and playing with knives also brought death (see Tables 1 and 2).

The second stage of childhood in Hunt's Eriksonian model and the second readily definable accident grouping is from two to three, when children obviously have considerable motor skills and a lively interest in their environment.[33] Although cradle fires continued to be a hazard in the early stages of this period, the accident pattern indicates that the process of exploring, reaching out to the world around, and imitating adults became more intensified. Wells were the most dangerous object of the children's new lives as wanderers (25 percent of the deaths), but ditches (20 percent), ponds (8 percent), and streams and rivers (3 percent) also figured in their perambulations. For instance William, son of William

31 Just. 2/111 m. 17; 2/112, m. 38; 2/113 m. 27, 31; 2/255 m. 5; Sharpe, Coroners' Rolls of London, 56–7; Just. 2/113 m. 31 (a boy of three dies in a cradle fire).
32 Hunt found that young Louis XIII was sometimes free of swaddling cloths, and completely free by eight months: Parents and Children, 128.
33 Ibid., 135–136. This is the period which Erikson describes: "The development of the muscle system gives the child a much greater power over the environment in the ability to reach out and hold on, to throw and to push away, to appropriate things and to keep them at a distance." It is also the stage at which the child learns about authority.

Faunceys (aged 3½), fell into a ditch at Robert Wreng's house while his mother was in Robert's house getting ale. In another case a father was going to the mill and did not know that his three-year-old son was following him. The child fell into the river and drowned. Children got into accidents which show an increased interest in the work of their parents. One little boy was killed watching his father cut wood.[34] Both boys and girls of this age group became interested in cooking, ale making, and laundry. In trying to stir the pots or look into them they fell into the pots or dumped the scalding liquid on themselves. Sex differentiation appeared early—27 percent of the girls and only 14 percent of the boys this age were involved in accidents playing with pots or cauldrons. In the accidents which occurred outside the home in bodies of water, only 44 percent of the girls met their death while 64 percent of the boys did. Modern studies of accidental death indicate that male children are more adventurous, take more fatal risks, and venture further from home.[35] Such developmental explanations for the greater death rate of boys and the statistics for drowning and other risk-taking adventures perhaps hold true for medieval children as well. The explanation may also have a psychological basis. According to the coroners' roll evidence, children of two and three were already identifying with the roles of their parents in the household and were imitating them—little girls copied their mothers by cooking and boys followed their fathers about their tasks.

Greater physical mobility without sufficient motor control caused many of the accidents of two- and three-year-olds. For instance, one child was playing with a duck and holding it in her arms. She wanted to put it into the river but fell in herself. Children would be attracted to feathers floating in the water and would drown trying to grasp them; or, in trying to throw an object into the water, would throw themselves in as well.

Toddlers, like infants, seemed to have been often left alone or in inadequate care. One child wandered off and drowned, having been left in the care of a blind woman while her parents were in the fields. In other cases, a child may have been left in the care of older

---

34 Hunnisett, *Bedfordshire Coroners' Rolls*, cases 18, 62, 77; Just. 2/106 m. 1d, m. 2; 2/107, 2/109 m. 8.
35 Iskrant and Joliet, *Accident and Homicide*, 23. In modern figures boys are predominant in drownings.

siblings. William Claunche's daughters, Muriel (almost six years old) and Beatrice (almost three), were left in his house in Great Barford while William and his wife were in the fields. A fire broke out and the younger girl was unable to escape. In another case two sisters, eight and four, were left home at night while their parents were in a tavern. A neighbor, committing a burglary in the house, killed the two girls. A little boy (two) was left at home apparently in the care of older children while his parents went to church. He went outside to look for the other boys and fell into a well. His sister found him.[36] Other accidents occurred when one or both parents were present but otherwise occupied.[37] Were these medieval parents negligent of their children's safety by leaving them unattended or inadequately supervised? If adults were present when children fell into water, they could be of little help because they themselves did not know how to swim—40 percent of all adult accidents were drownings, sometimes in shallow water. A comparison with modern figures would indicate, however, that medieval parents probably spent less time supervising children. In 1968 in the United States only 7.5 percent of all accident victims were children under four, although in our medieval sample 68 percent were children under four.[38] Furthermore, while the modern curve indicates infancy as the highest period for accidents, with a sharp decrease at two and three, the medieval pattern reverses this curve.[39]

In spite of their apparent negligence, the parents of these active two- and three-year-olds were obviously able to instill some sense of caution into their wandering children, for the number of

36 Hunnisett, *Bedfordshire Coroners' Rolls*, cases 14, 25, 109; Just. 2/109 m. 7.
37 One couple was trying to heat their oven in the courtyard when their son went to another part of the courtyard and drowned; *ibid.*, case 236. Another father was eating lunch when his child wandered outdoors and drowned; *ibid.*, case 33.
38 *Accident Facts*, 14. The validity of this comparison may be questioned because of the greater proportion of children in medieval society. Still, the difference in the number of children would have to be very great to account for a difference of almost 60 percent. Even if inaccurate, the comparison does provide some perspective in understanding the accidents of children in the middle ages.
39 Iskrant and Joliet, *Accident and Homicide*, 19, 22, 138. The death rate in infants is nearly three times that of children one to four. It is interesting that in folklore of this period two to three was considered to be the most dangerous age. It is in that period that children in northern mythology were most likely to be stolen by elves. Carl Haffter, "The Changeling: History and Psychodynamics of Attitudes to Handicapped Children in European Folklore," *Journal of the History of the Behavioral Sciences*, IV (1968), 55–61.

accidents dropped dramatically for both boys and girls after they reached the age of four: only 11 percent of children involved in misadventure died in the period of four to seven. What accounts for the drop in the number of accidents? According to Hunt's Eriksonian schema, this is supposed to be the age when children discover infantile sexuality, but the coroners' rolls give no evidence that children suddenly took their fingers out of the pots and put them on their genitals instead.[40] There is not a great deal of evidence on the disciplining of children or ways in which they were taught to be more responsible.

There are a few cases of children dying from extreme forms of discipline. An eleven-year-old boy was whipped to death by his enraged mother and a five-year-old London urchin who stole some wool died from a punch on the ear delivered by the woman keeping the shop.[41] But discipline alone did not bring about the reduction in the accident rate. From the age of four children began to spend more time with their parents. Ironically, in medieval society the children seemed to have had more adult supervision from the age of four to seven than they did from infancy through three years old. This greater supervision did not appear to come about because the children were suddenly more valuable to the parents, but because their greater mobility made it possible for them to be with adults more. Contrary to Ariès' assumption that the children suddenly became productive, their accident pattern indicates that they were doing little work. Their misadventures were still almost entirely related to playing children's games. The work which they did perform must have been rather minimal: some herding, babysitting, and perhaps some work in family gardens.[42]

The most striking change in the child's life in its progress to adulthood seems to have come at ages eight through twelve. The children during this period were independent from adults and were given tasks of their own to perform. They still lived at home for the most part, contrary to Ariès' belief that all children older

40 Hunt, *Parents and Children,* 159–179.
41 Just. 2/107 m. 5; Sharp, *Coroners' Rolls of London,* 83. It is interesting to note that the shopkeeper was not even indicted for the homicide. The coroners' jury returned a verdict of misadventure indicating that the discipline of killing a thief caught in the act, even if a child, was excusable.
42 Just. 2/109 m. 7.

than seven were sent to live in another person's home.[43] Boys from eight to thirteen were shepherds, mill hands, reapers, and servants.[44] Their tasks show that they were moving into adult life and were being trained for the work they would eventually perform as men. Their accident pattern both in work and play became much closer to that of men. They no longer chased feathers or played with ducks; they were learning to have mock fights with staffs, to shoot at targets with bows and arrows, and to play such games as getting an arrow to glance off the ground and rise up and hit a target.[45] In the urban setting as well, young boys were being groomed for adult life during the period of eight through twelve. In Oxford and London this meant school for some boys. The evidence is indirect, but it is there. In Oxford a school master fell from a willow tree into the river and drowned as he was cutting willow switches with which to beat his students. In London an eight-year-old boy on his way to school was crossing London Bridge and playing a game he had often enjoyed in which he caught hold of a projecting beam and swung on it. He fell into the Thames and drowned. Other boys appeared in the coroners' rolls as selling eels and other goods in the streets, as apprentices, and as beggars. The girls in both urban and rural society were approaching the adult female pattern of accidents. They took up the duties of gathering wood, minding children, and working in the fields at harvest.[46]

The coroners' rolls show that the children growing up in the medieval household went through distinct developmental stages closely compatible with those described by Erikson, but, in addition, the inquests tell us something about the emotional climate in the home. One would assume that the rolls would reflect only negative feelings within the family since they record homicides

43 Ariès, *Centuries of Childhood*, 365. Some lower-class children were sent away in fourteenth-century England. In London and other urban centers the pattern was different than that among the rural lower classes because of apprenticeship. Among the upper classes as well it was customary to send children to another family.
44 Hunnisett, *Bedfordshire Coroners' Rolls*, cases 31, 117, 119, 247, 252; Just. 2/106, 2/109 m. 1, 7.
45 Just. 2/109 m. 1; in the last case mentioned, the arrow hit a thirteen-year-old boy in the stomach: Just. 2/255 m. 6.
46 Salter, *Oxford Coroners' Rolls*, 60; Sharpe, *Coroners' Rolls of London*, 25, 61, 169; Hunnisett, *Bedfordshire Coroners' Rolls*, cases 58, 228; Just 2/109 m. 7.

and violent death. But the evidence raises the possibility that the medieval family was remarkably congenial: only 8 percent of all homicides involved intrafamilial murders. This is low compared to the 53 percent of all murders which are intrafamilial in modern Britain and 30 percent in the United States.[47] Does this low incidence of intrafamilial crime indicate remarkable domestic tranquility within the medieval home? The evidence which Raftis and his students have been accumulating from manorial court rolls indicates that the main village families were very much concerned with preserving peace within the family and thereby perpetuating their status and control in the community. The familial relationships which led most frequently to intrafamilial homicides were husbands and wives (55 percent), followed far behind by fathers and sons and brothers (about 11 percent each). The father-daughter and mother-son relationships each produced only about 8 percent of the homicides. In nonhomicidal disputes in manorial courts, the children tended to be pursuing actions against the parents, but in homicides, the parent was usually the slayer. On the whole, there is little evidence of homicidal violence within the family.[48]

But to argue a sentimental attitude toward children, there must be more than a forbearance in killing them. We would expect emotional outpourings from the parents upon finding a dead child. The rolls, unfortunately, stop short of the parents' lament. Certain indirect expressions of parental emotions are present, as in the case of the Nottinghamshire woman who tried to save her daughter from a beating. An Oxford mother gave her life in an attempted rescue of her twenty-week-old son.

> On Friday last [9 Aug. 1298] John Trivaler and Alice his wife were in a shop where they abode in the parish of St. Mary late at night, ready to go to bed, and the said Alice fixed a lighted candle on the wall by the straw which lay in the said shop, so that the flame of the

47 Barbara Hanawalt Westman, "The Peasant Family and Crime in Fourteenth-Century England," *The Journal of British Studies,* XIII (1974), 4.

48 J. Ambrose Raftis, *Tenure and Mobility* (Toronto, 1964), 32–63; *Warboys; Two Hundred Years in the Life of an English Medieval Village* (Toronto, 1974), 225–240; DeWindt, *Land and People,* 191. These works show that the family tended to be a cohesive unit, at least in the higher strata of peasant society. Indeed, only 2 percent of all assaults and bloodlettings involved a family in Wakefield manor courts. See Westman, "Peasant Family and Crime," 5–6, 17.

candle reached the straw before it was discovered and immediately the fire spread throughout the shop, so that the said John and Alice scarce escaped without, forgetting that they were leaving the child behind them. And immediately when the said Alice remembered that her son was in the fire within, she lept back into the shop to seek him, and immediately when she entered she was overcome by the greatness of the fire and choked.[49]

In another case, a father rushed to protect his young daughter from rape and was killed himself. Finally, there is the case of a boy ten years old who was shooting at a dung hill with his bow and arrow. Missing the dung hill, he shot a five-year-old girl instead. He fled from the scene because he was afraid of her father's anger.[50] These three cases indicate that the parents may have had a great love for their children, even enough to risk their own lives saving them, but they do not necessarily indicate sentimental love for children. Likewise, the fact that when a child was lost or killed the mother or father was almost always the first finder may not indicate anything more than that the community considered it the parent's responsibility to take on the burdens of being first finder.[51] None of the cases show parents playing with children when the accidents occurred. The coroners' rolls, therefore, tell us that the parents did not hate their children enough to kill them except in rare cases and that they often loved them enough to risk their own lives for them. They do not indicate one way or another a sentimental attachment to the state of childhood, which Ariès would find essential for the modern family.

The coroners' rolls provide solid information on the childrearing of the lower classes of society and additional information on the nature of the medieval household. The growing child of the lower classes lived in a household which was fairly small and may or may not have had servants and aged relatives living in it. While there is a tendency to look upon the lower class as monolithic, there were many gradations of wealth and status within rural and urban communities. It is possible that in cases where infants died of neglect, the household was a poor one which needed every

49 Salter, *Oxford Coroners' Rolls*, 7.
50 Hunnisett, *Bedfordshire Coroners' Rolls*, cases 58, 74.
51 The first finder had to find pledges and come to the court sessions. There is some evidence that the actual first finder went and told the parents about the death so that they could be the official first finders. *Ibid.*, cases 128, 197.

able-bodied hand in the field. Servants might have been out of the question or the parents may have been working for hire themselves and could only leave an infant with an older sibling or with the old and handicapped. The demand for labor may have been so great in these households that infanticide was not generally practiced. At two and three when the children were mobile they began to follow their parents about and to imitate them. The types of accidents of male and female children began to differentiate following the pattern of activities for adult men and women which the children saw in their home. Children from four through seven were less likely to have accidents but this seems to arise not from their usefulness to society but because they were more often in the company of responsible adults and their parents had, by this time, instilled some sense of caution and responsibility in them. After the age of seven the children did become a part of the productive economy of the household, but it was usually their own household rather than another.

The stages of child development indicated in the coroners' rolls are remarkably close to those blocked out by Erikson. Their motor development and, to a certain extent, their psychological development is reflected in the sorts of accidents that they encountered. But the emotional climate within the lower-class household continues to be elusive. Ariès' suggestions that children competed for their parents' affection with extended kin and neighbors may be correct. Homicide statistics certainly indicate that the emotional contacts which led to fatal attacks tended to be with fellow villagers and friends rather than family members.[52] Since homicide is seldom random and most often occurs between people who know each other well, it is possible that the strong ties were with the outside rather than with members of the immediate household.

52 Hanawalt, "Violent Death in Fourteenth and Fifteenth Century England," *Comparative Studies in Society and History*, XVIII (1976), 297–320.

Daniel C. Quinlan and Jean A. Shackelford

Economy and English Families, 1500–1850

Once only of incidental concern in economic history, the relationship between the everyday social behavior of lower-class families and fundamental economic transformations has lately been the subject of intensive research and broad theoretical consideration. We have, as a result, a much richer picture of how waves of wholesale changes in the English economy between 1500 and 1850 realigned marriage, reproduction, communal relations, and production and consumption among lower-class families, and how those realignments in turn affected the transition to a modern industrial economy. Over the last thirty years, several major studies have also appeared which shed new light on how marriage, fertility, and mortality, the upbringing of children, the structure of kinship and clientage, and the distribution of power in the family shifted between Henry VII and Victoria among the landed classes, the commercial bourgeoisie, and the industrial and professional classes. Yet, unlike similar progress in the study of lower-class families, such strides in our factual understanding of the organization of middle- and upper-class families have not produced any striking theoretical developments that bind these changes to the radical restructuring of the early modern English economy. As new productive techniques and new forms of agricultural and industrial organization were adopted, and as the composition and the economic foundation of social classes shifted, both lower-class *and* middle- and upper-class families were bound to respond in ways that would maintain either their precarious foothold or their privileged position in a rapidly changing economy.[1]

Daniel C. Quinlan is Associate Professor of Sociology, Emory and Henry College. Jean A. Shackelford is Professor of Economics, Bucknell University.

The authors thank David Levine, John Gillis, Lawrence Stone, Jack Roper, Charlie Sydnor, Frank Ryan, Adrienne Birecree, and two anonymous reviewers for comments that not only pointed out several glaring errors, but also helped us to tighten the arguments.

1   Lawrence Stone, "Family History in the 1980s: Past Achievements and Future Trends," *Journal of Interdisciplinary History*, XII (1981), 51–56. On the lower-class family, see Richard

Our argument is that changes in the structure of the English middle- and upper-class family during the early modern period were largely the products of a radical reworking of the agrarian and industrial economy. We argue first that both the gradual withdrawal of the landed nuclear family from the larger universe of kinship and clientage, and the breakaway of the yeoman family from the communalism of the peasant village, were rational and effective economic responses to the onset of the agrarian revolution early in the sixteenth century. As commercial impulses began to redefine relations between lord and peasant, the economic and social rewards that politico-military alliances with kin and other landed families had yielded declined in value relative to the gains to be made from enclosure, capital improvements, and the efficient management of landed property. Similarly, an increasingly competitive market and rising rents made the traditions governing the agricultural affairs of the village obstacles to the profitable running of the yeomanry's tenancies.[2]

We next make a case that the two upswings in domestic patriarchy, one occurring during the Tudor and Stuart ages and the other during the Romantic and Victorian ages, were propelled by the restructuring of social relations of production, first in agriculture and later in industry, and by the resulting growth and upward mobility of new social classes. Competition increased

---

M. Smith, "Fertility, Economy, and Household Formation in England over Three Centuries," *Population and Development Review*, VII (1981), 600; David Levine, "Production, Reproduction, and the Proletarian Family in England, 1500–1851," in *idem* (ed.), *Proletarianization and Family History* (Orlando, 1984), 93–94; *idem*, *Family Formation in the Age of Nascent Capitalism* (New York, 1977), 26–29, 47, 61–64, 147–149; Peter Kriedte, Hans Medick, and Jürgen Schlumbohm (eds.), *Industrialization before Industrialization* (Cambridge, 1977), 54, 80, 87–89; Louise A. Tilly and Joan W. Scott, *Women, Work, and Family* (New York, 1978), 105–114; Neil McKendrick, "Home Demand and Economic Growth: A New View of the Role of Women and Children in the Industrial Revolution," in *idem* (ed.), *Historical Perspectives: Studies in English Thought and Society* (London, 1974), 168–191.

2 In formulating these arguments, we make extensive use of Stone's important *The Family, Sex, and Marriage in England 1500–1800* (New York, 1977). Although we disagree in fundamental ways with its explanations, it is the most systematic and comprehensive account of the development of the modern bourgeois and landed family, and as such, represents a landmark in the historical study of the family. We have also learned much from Levine, whose work has improved and enriched historical understanding of the interplay between long-term economic changes and the organization and demography of the lower-class family. See his *Reproducing Families: The Political Economy of English Population History* (Cambridge, 1987).

markedly during the formative stages of both industrial and agrarian capitalism, as the coupling of wage labor to advanced techniques created new productive fields and markets and remade established ones, and opened up both old and new fields to new competitors. Those social groups that fared better under such competition were the ones that were better able to impose a new work discipline on their workers and themselves, to cut expenses and save, and to make capital improvements. They—the commercial nobility, gentry, and yeomanry during the first period and the commercial, manufacturing, and professional bourgeoisie during the second—were also, we believe, bound to carry this discipline, thrift, and industry into the home and to intensify domestic patriarchy.

Finally, we argue that the falling rates of fertility and nuptiality and the rising age at first marriage experienced by the landed class between 1600 and 1750 were mainly due to the difficulty that the landed class had in financing the provision of lesser heirs. Stagnant rents and land values, slowly declining interest rates, periodic domestic and international crises, and the rapidly increasing size of the portions bestowed upon daughters and later younger sons combined during this period to raise drastically the cost of settling lesser heirs and put pressure on landed families to reduce the size of their families and to delay the marriages of their children.

Such profound changes in the nature of production and in the character of communities and families upset the way that people of all social classes saw their and other's proper roles in the world around them. As people go about the mundane tasks of maturing, working, living in communities, and discharging domestic duties both within and across classes, they learn what is expected of them and what is expected of others, and what sort of people are likely to live up to these expectations and what sort are not. As these multilateral expectations become more and more ingrained through repeated interactions with others, they come to take on the tenor of moral evaluations; that is, they become world views. When the form and content of these relationships and the patterns of interaction on which they are based change, as they usually do in any fundamental economic upheaval, world views of how the world does and ought to run are called into question. At least in the beginning, the erosion of customary practices and their replacement by new practices are likely to generate moral outrage, and if sufficient conditions are met, active resistance. In the long run, they will either produce or borrow new or modified world views that are more closely in line with the system of relationships and patterns of interaction that emerged with the economic transformation. The development of Puritanism, Evangelicalism, and a more heavy-handed conception of patriarchy were such creations associated with the economic transformations of agrarian and industrial capitalism. In nonconformist religion, the successful groups of these two periods found the doctrine to translate an economically necessary code of conduct—diligence, frugality, and discipline—into an ethical system.[3]

AGRARIAN CAPITALISM, LANDED FAMILY, AND PEASANT VILLAGE
Late in the fifteenth century, complex webs of social relations still surrounded the families of the landowning class and the peasantry. The nuclear family of the English aristocracy and gentry was, in Stone's words, "no more than a loose core at the center of a dense network of lineage and kin relationships." Decisions regarding property, inheritance, and marriage had to be made in consultation with important kin, and everyday matters were usually settled amid the bustle and confusion of the landed household, swelled by a host of servants and retainers. Further demands arose from the system of clientage that locked the landowning family into a grid of local, regional, and, sometimes, national political connections and alliances. The wealthier and more powerful the seigneurial family was, the more heavily these outside obligations lay on it. The peasant family, too, was merely a link in a tangled chain of interlocking interests, rights, and obligations. Despite the often sizable inequality in villager's holdings, various formal and informal arrangements placed strict bounds on the independent economic action of peasant families. Under the open-field system, the village as a collectivity regulated and organized the agricultural cycle and oversaw access to the community's commons, meadows, and waste, in many cases periodically reallocating rights to these resources according to the varying size and

3 For a brilliant discussion of the social antecedents of moral outrage and its relationship to revolt, see Barrington Moore, *Injustice: The Social Bases of Obedience and Revolt* (White Plains, 1978), 49–116, 458–505.

needs of each peasant household. The various demands that church, royal, and manorial authorities imposed on communal manpower and resources further fostered cooperation, and numerous traditional observances brought the entire village together several times a year for games and feasting.[4]

Beginning in the sixteenth century, both the kin-centered family and the collectively organized village began to disintegrate. The family of the English landowning class slowly retreated into its conjugal carapace and became more patriarchal. Symptomatic of its growing insularity were the declining reliance on the "good offices" of kin and patrons to secure lucrative civil and clerical positions, loans, and other favors, the widespread use of the legal innovation of "breaking entails," and the waning feudal traditions of homage and "good lordship." Nearly concurrent with the gradual paring of external obligations, was an intensification of patriarchy within the landed family. Child-rearing practices came to focus increasingly on breaking the child's will, which parents accomplished both by compelling their children to display outward signs of submission and respect and by the liberal application of floggings. A sterner paternal absolutism also fell on wives, although the deterioration in their position probably did not go as far as it did in the nineteenth century, when a much sharper division between male and female roles emerged. Among villagers, more competitive, hierarchical, and contractually based relationships gradually pushed aside the intricate web of customary rights and obligations that had governed village relations, in the process exacerbating inequality, heightening social tensions, and widening the social gulf between the yeomanry and their considerably poorer neighbors.[5]

4 Stone, *Family*, 85–91; Ralph Houlbrooke, *The English Family, 1450–1700* (London, 1984), 52–53; Barbara A. Hanawalt, *The Ties That Bound: Peasant Families in Medieval England* (Oxford, 1986), 19–30, 124–140; Edward Britton, *The Community of the Vill* (Toronto, 1977), 77–86; Edwin Brezette Dewindt, *Land and People in Holywell-Cum-Needingworth* (Toronto, 1972), 25–161; Edward Miller and John Hatcher, *Medieval England: Rural Society and Economic Change, 1086–1348* (New York, 1978), 89–133; Frances and Joseph Gies, *Life in a Medieval Village* (New York, 1989), 131–144; Jerome Blum, "The European Village as Community: Origins and Functions," *Agricultural History*, XLV (1971), 157–178; *idem*, "The Internal Structure and Polity of the European Village Community from the Fifteenth to the Nineteenth Century," *Journal of Modern History*, XLIII (1971), 542–576; Keith Thomas, "Work and Leisure in Pre-Industrial Society," *Past & Present*, 29 (1964), 50–66.
5 Houlbrooke, *English Family*, 143–145; Stone, *Family*, 124–132, 151, 161–174; Chris-

How the English landed class went about forming families changed as well. Between 1600 and 1750, but most severely after 1640, fertility among the upper gentry and aristocracy dropped from well above 5 children to a low of about 3.8 children born per ever-married offspring (# CHILDREN BORN in Figs. 1–3), from over 1.6 to about 0.8 same-sexed children born for every member of the previous generation born (REPLACEMENT RATE in Figs. 2–3), and from a mean of 0.8 children born to an average of 0.5 children born from remarriages (CHILDREN-REMARRIAGE in Fig. 1), even though child mortality was to stay throughout this period substantially above what it had been in the late sixteenth century. This decline in fertility seems to have been the combined result of rising ages at first marriage, falling rates of nuptiality (between 1650 and 1750) and remarriage, and slowing paces at which women bore children (AGE AT FIRST MARRIAGE, RATE OF NUPTIALITY, RATE OF REMARRIAGE, AND COMPLETED FERTILITY in Figs. 1–4).[6]

Over this period, the median age at which the upper landed class first married increased among men from twenty-four to between twenty-eight and twenty-nine and, for women, from nineteen to around twenty-three years. Although movement in the rates of nuptiality among male peers was erratic, hovering near 82 percent throughout, rates for female children of peers and male members of the upper gentry declined steadily, falling for female offspring of the peerage from a high of 95.8 percent during the first quarter of the seventeenth century to near 74 percent between 1725 and 1750 and for gentlemen from 95 percent between 1600 and 1650 to 84 percent during the first half of the eighteenth century. The consistent drop in the rate at which married members of the upper landed class remarried occurred after the Restoration, when the rate of remarriage fell at a minimum

topher Hill, *Society and Puritanism in Pre-Revolutionary England* (New York, 1964), 443–480; Leonore Davidoff and Catherine Hall, *Family Fortunes* (Chicago, 1977), 403–415; Keith Wrightson, *English Society, 1580–1680* (New Brunswick, 1982), 39–65, 155–178.

6   Figures on fertility, mortality, and nuptiality of the peerage were either taken or computed from T.H. Hollingsworth, "The Demography of the Peerage," supplement to *Population Studies*, XVIII (1964), 9, 14, 20–22, 25, 30–34, 40, 63; *idem*, "Mortality in the Peerage," *Population*, XXXII, 328, 332–335. For similar data on the upper landed class (squires, knights, baronets, and peers), whose seats were in the counties of Northamptonshire, Hertfordshire, and Northumberland, see Stone and Jeanne C. Fawtier Stone, *An Open Elite? England 1540–1880* (Oxford, 1984), 458, 460. Whenever the numbers are very close, we have combined the two series to make the exposition easier to read.

by more than 35 percent for male and female children of the peerage and male children of the upper landed class. Finally, the rate at which aristocratic wives bore children after five, ten, fifteen, twenty, and twenty-five years of marriage declined fairly steadily from the cohort born during the first quarter of the seventeenth century to that born between 1700 to 1724, resulting in considerably reduced completed fertility.[7]

The reorganization of agrarian production during the sixteenth and seventeenth centuries put increasing pressure on the landed class to restructure its families. As enclosures gradually replaced the typical medieval pattern of a small demesne nestled within the open fields of the village with a more orderly system of larger, consolidated tenancies leased to and farmed by a few prosperous yeomen, more and more people of all social classes became at least partly dependent on the market. Those peasants

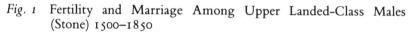

Fig. 1 Fertility and Marriage Among Upper Landed-Class Males (Stone) 1500–1850

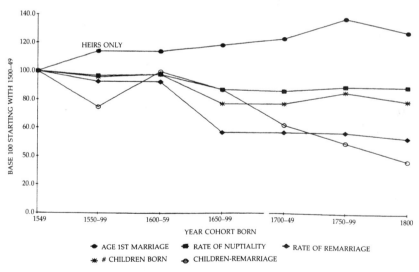

SOURCE   Data for Figure 1 were computed from Lawrence Stone and Jeanne C. Fawtier Stone, *An Open Elite? England 1640–880* (Oxford, 1984), 458, 460. All figures have been converted to a standard of 100 based on the period 1500–1549.

7 *Ibid.;* Hollingsworth, "Demography of the Peerage," 20–22, 25, 40.

Fig. 2 Marriage and Fertility Among Male Children of Peers, 1550–1850

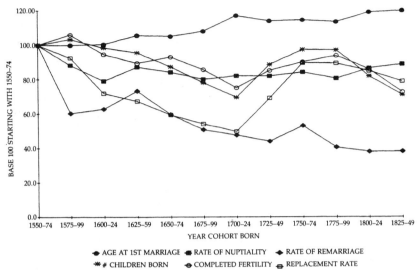

YEAR COHORT BORN

◆ AGE AT 1ST MARRIAGE ◼ RATE OF NUPTIALITY ◆ RATE OF REMARRIAGE
✳ # CHILDREN BORN ⊖ COMPLETED FERTILITY ⊟ REPLACEMENT RATE

SOURCE   Data for Figure 2 were computed from T. H. Hollingsworth, "The Demography of the Peerage," supplement to *Population Studies*, XVIII (1964), 9, 20–22, 25, 30–34, 40. All figures have been converted to a standard of 100 based on the period 1550–1574.

who either lost their land or were left with insufficient land to maintain a family were forced to seek employment as agricultural workers or in domestic industry and to obtain a growing share of their subsistence on the market. At the other end, the select few, who benefited from enclosure by becoming larger holders themselves or the large tenants of the nobility or both, were forced onto the market to pay the wages that they owed their neighbors and the rents that were due their lords. What remained after these payments could be kept for subsistence and reinvestment. In this way, both the lord's and the yeoman's prosperity became steadily more determined by the market. An incentive was created for lords and yeomen to take advantage of an expanding market through more careful management and greater use of known techniques to increase productivity and to extend production. As a result, kinship, clientage, and excess children became, for the

Fig. 3   Marriage and Fertility Among Female Children of Peers, 1550–1850

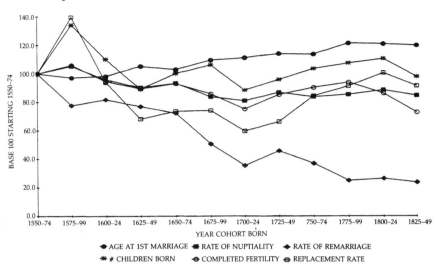

SOURCE   Data for Figure 3 were computed from T. H. Hollingsworth, "The Demography of the British Peerage," supplement to *Population Studies*, XVIII (1964), 9, 20–22, 25, 30–34, 40. All figures have been converted to a standard of 100 based on the period 1550–1574.

landed class, drains on funds that could be more prudently invested.[8]

At a time when capital investment could substantially improve the vitality of the landed estate, finding suitable positions

8   On sixteenth- and early seventeenth-century enclosures, see Richard H. Tawney, *The Agrarian Problem in the Sixteenth Century* (New York, 1967; orig. pub., 1912); Eric Kerridge, *The Agrarian Problems of the Sixteenth Century and After* (London, 1969); James A. Yelling, *Common Field and Enclosure in England 1450–1850* (Hamden, 1977); Ian Blanchard, "Population Change, Enclosure, and the Early Tudor Economy," *Economic History Review*, XXIII (1970), 427–445; J. Ross Wordie, "The Chronology of English Enclosure, 1500–1914," *Economic History Review*, XXXVI (1983), 483–505; John Chapman, "The Chronology of English Enclosure," *Economic History Review*, XXXVII (1984), 557–562; Joan Thirsk, "Enclosing and Engrossing, 1500–1640," in *idem* (ed.), *Chapters from the Agrarian History of England and Wales, 1500–1750* (Cambridge, 1990), III, 54–109. On the yeomanry, see Mildred Campbell, *The English Yeoman* (New Haven, 1942); Gordon Batho, "Landlords in England, 1500–1640: Noblemen, Gentlemen and Yeomen," in Christopher Clay (ed.), *Chapters* (Cambridge, 1990), II, 66–71; Wrightson, *English Society*, 30–33, 134–139; Patricia Croot and David Parker, "Agrarian Class Structure and Economic Development,"

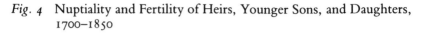

Fig. 4 Nuptiality and Fertility of Heirs, Younger Sons, and Daughters, 1700–1850

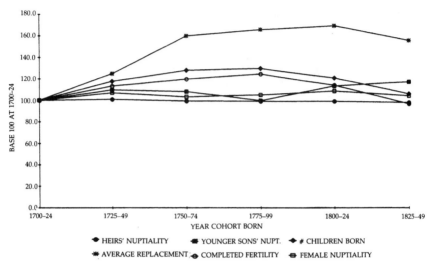

YEAR COHORT BORN

◆ HEIRS' NUPTIALITY   ◆ YOUNGER SONS' NUPT.   ◆ # CHILDREN BORN
✳ AVERAGE REPLACEMENT   ◉ COMPLETED FERTILITY   ◉ FEMALE NUPTIALITY

SOURCES   Data for Figure 4 were computed from T. H. Hollingsworth, "Demography of the British Peerage," supplement to *Population Studies*, XVIII (1964), 9, 20–2, 25, 30–34, 40; David Thomas, "The Social Origins of Marriage Partners of the British Peerage in the Eighteenth and Nineteenth Centuries," *Population Studies*, XXVI (1972), 101. All figures have been converted to a standard of 100 based on the period 1700–1724.

for near and distant relatives, attendance at court and the quest for favors from patrons, "good hospitality," raising dowries for daughters, and securing employment and setting aside portions for younger sons were serious impediments to the full exploitation of landed property. Extra-familial connections remained valuable assets for the gentry and nobility well into the nineteenth century, and children, however expensive was their transition to adulthood, still remained the overwhelmingly preferred vessel through which landowners preserved their lineage and transmitted their property. But, the rewards that kinship and clientage provided steadily diminished in value relative to those to be gained by the rational, efficient organization of the landed estate and from other financial opportunities, and the costs that children placed on the landed estate rose faster than income, despite the increases that capital improvement and better administration yielded.[9]

The mounting expense of children derived principally from the competition that the increasingly wealthy and numerous families who were tied to commerce, high governmental office, and the military brought to the marriage market. Between 1475 and 1725, the average size of aristocratic dowries increased dramatically from £625 to over £9,500, and in all likelihood, so did marriage portions conferred by untitled landowners, although a comparable series on their settlements is lacking. Younger sons, on the other hand, were comparatively shortchanged, either having to be content with a modest life-lease or annuity or having to secure an apprenticeship in business or the professions, which still offered only limited opportunities. Only after 1650 did provisions for younger sons apparently begin to grow in value. The development of a market in mortgages, the greater security and liquidity that equity of redemption offered to creditor and debtor alike, and falling interest rates enabled landowning familes to reduce substantially the yearly costs of providing for younger sons and to raise the amount settled on them by replacing leases of one to three lives, or annuities, with cash settlements financed through long-term mortgages. The net effect of mortgaging estates to provide for both daughters and younger sons, if a favorable balance were not achieved across generations between wealth gained by the heir's marriage and portions lost to lesser heirs, was to project a rising amount of debt onto succeeding generations and make them more vulnerable to rapid shifts in economic,

9 On the expenses of the Tudor and Stuart landed class, see Stone, *The Crisis of the Aristocracy, 1558–1641* (Oxford, 1965), 445–504; idem, *Family*, 85–91, 129; Clay, "Property Settlements, Financial Provision for the Family, and Sale of Land by the Greater Landowners, 1660–1790," *Journal of British Studies*, XXI (1981), 27. Stone nearly adopts our argument when he cites what the father of a potential spouse said to John Verney in 1671: his daughter "brought in no kindred with her, neither of great persons to be a charge by way of entertainment, nor of mean to be a charge by way of charity and neediness": Francis P. and Margaret M. Verney (eds.), *Memoirs of the Verney Family During the Seventeenth Century* (London, 1907), II, 271, cited in Stone, *Family*, 150. Stone concluded that "kinship was clearly now regarded more as a potential burden than a potential opportunity."

political, or fiscal conditions and more dependent on rising land values and rents.[10]

One such crisis was the reverse in aristocratic fortunes and, to a much lesser extent, in the fortunes of the squirearchy and upper gentry, which the development of agrarian capitalism, inflation, and rising standards of consumption largely produced during the sixteenth and early seventeenth centuries. Another crisis was the Civil War, during and after which much of the landed class fell deeply into debt paying stiff wartime exactions with shrunken rental incomes and financing the recovery of confiscated property. The wars with Louis XIV between 1691 and 1715, when higher land taxes, higher interest rates, and a shortage of credit seriously undermined landowners' ability to carry debt, formed still another. Beyond these times of acute financial distress, there never was a period between 1600 and 1720 when credit law, interest, food prices and rents, and land values moved in unison to improve markedly the capacity of the upper landed class to carry and discharge debts. The steep climb in agricultural prices and the opportunities that it afforded to raise rents during the period between Elizabeth and the Civil War increased rental incomes and, in turn, land values. Greater equity and higher revenues allowed landowners to negotiate larger loans, but interest rates near 10 percent and the lopsided advantage that creditors had over debtors made servicing debt both risky and relatively burdensome (Fig. 5). After the Restoration, the fall in interest rates and greater legal protections for debtors were offset by stagnant agricultural prices, rents, and land prices. The landown-

---

10   On the rapid inflation of dowries, see Stone, *Crisis of the Aristocracy*, 790; John Phillips Cooper, "Patterns of Inheritance and Settlement by Great Landowners from the Fifteenth to the Eighteenth Centuries," in Jack Goody, Joan Thirsk, and Edward P. Thompson (eds.), *Family and Inheritance: Rural Society in Western Europe 1200–1800* (Cambridge, 1976), 307. For a discussion of mortgages, credit laws, and interest rates, see Clay, *Economic Expansion and Social Change: England 1500–1700* (Cambridge, 1984), I, 125, 159; idem, "Property Settlements," 28–32; idem, "Landlords and Estate Management in England, 1640–1750," in idem (ed.), *Chapters*, II, 320–323; H. John Habakkuk, "The Rise and Fall of English Landed Families, 1600–1800," *Transactions of the Royal Historical Society*, XXIX (1979), 201. The plight of younger sons and the limited occupational outlets they had until after the Restoration is discussed in Thirsk, "Younger Sons in the Seventeenth Century," *History*, LIV (1969), 358–377; Stone and Stone, *An Open Elite?*, 228–239; Richard Bruce Grassby, "Social Mobility and Business Enterprise in Seventeenth Century England," in Donald H. Pennington and Keith Thomas (eds.), *Puritans and Revolutionaries* (Oxford, 1978), 356; R.G. Lang, "Social Origins and Social Aspirations of Jacobean London Merchants," *Economic History Review*, XXVII (1964), 31.

Fig. 5 Peer Fertility and Mean Annual Increase in Agricultural Prices

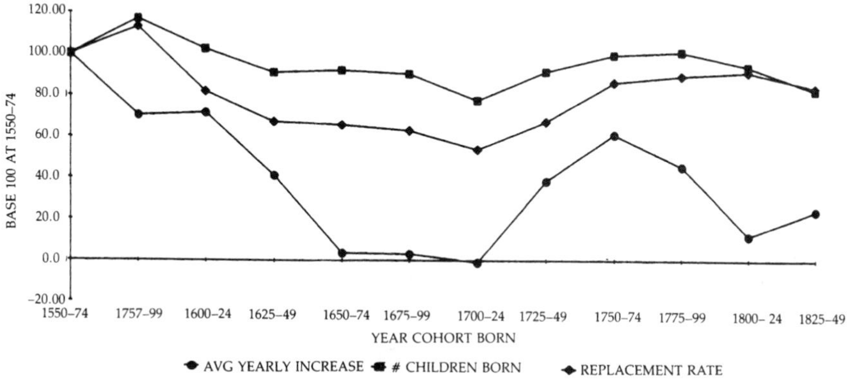

AVG YEARLY INCREASE   # CHILDREN BORN   REPLACEMENT RATE

SOURCE   Data for Figure 5 were computed from T. H. Hollingsworth, "Demography of the British Peerage," supplement to *Population Studies*, XVIII (1964), 30–33; Peter J. Bowden, "Statistical Appendix, 1500–1640" and "Statistical Appendix III: Statistics," in *idem, Chapters from the Agrarian History of England and Wales, 1500–1750* (Cambridge, 1990), 150–152, 339–341; Ernest H. Phelps Brown and Sheila V. Hopkins, "Seven Centuries of the Prices of Consumables Compared with Builders' Wage-rates," *Economica*, XXIII (1956), 312–314. The agricultural figures were obtained by computing the average yearly increase in the price of a weighted average of both arable crops and animal products for the 50 years during and after each 25-year birth cohort. Both the demographic and the agricultural figures were standardized to 100 based on the 50 years between 1550 and 1599.

ing class breathed more easily later in the eighteenth century, as interest dropped to 4 percent, the capital value of land gradually increased to thirty years' purchase, and agricultural prices and rental incomes rose steadily.[11]

11   On the financial difficulties of large landowners between 1540 and 1640, see Stone, *Crisis of the Aristocracy*, 129–198; John T. Cliffe, *The Yorkshire Gentry from the Reformation to the Civil War* (London, 1969), 93–145; Batho, "Landlords in England," 45–50; Habakkuk, "The Rise and Fall of English Landed Families, 1600–1800: III," *Transactions of the Royal Historical Society*, XXXI (1981), 204–208. On the effects of the Civil War on landowners, see Thirsk, "The Restoration Land Settlement," *Journal of Modern History*, XXVI (1954), 320–328; Habakkuk, "Landowners and the Civil War," *Economic History Review*, XVIII (1965), 139–148; *idem*, "The Rise and Fall of English Landed Families, 1600–1800: II," *Transactions of the Royal Historical Society*, XXX (1980), 202–213; Hill, *Puritanism and Revolution* (London, 1958), 153–188; Clay, *Economic Expansion and Social Change*, I, 159–160; *idem*, "Landlords and Estate Management," 246–289. On interest rates, taxes, and credit between 1692 and 1715, see Habakkuk, "English Landownership, 1680–1740," *Economic History Review*, XIX (1940), 9–14; *idem*, "Rise and Fall of English Landed Families," 197–202; Gordon Edmund Mingay, *The Gentry: The Rise and Fall of a*

Large debts forced many landed families within the bounds of contemporary contraceptive practice, to limit the number of children that they had in order to reduce both day-to-day expenses and future outlays for marriage portions. In addition, given the enormous impact that larger and larger dowries had on the finances of both parties, marital negotiations over the size of dowries and annuities probably became more and more deliberate, causing marriages to be delayed. More important, during times of acute financial difficulty, plans for an heir's marriage, if he were of age, were apt to be put off, since the funds that the dowry would bring in represented little net capital when set beside the family's standing debts *and* obligations to pay current and next generation's portions, and since a share of the family's yearly income would, in any case, have to be set aside for the heir's and his wife's maintenance.[12]

For younger sons and daughters, heavy debts often meant not only postponed marriages but also reduced or retracted portions, which damaged their marital prospects. Financial difficulties also diminished opportunities to remarry. Lesser heirs, their portions already committed, had little to bring to an increasingly competitive marriage market, unless by chance they came into a fortune. Even heirs, despite their prestige, must have lost some of their appeal alongside younger, less-encumbered scions of

---

Ruling Class (London, 1976), 67; Arthur Henry John, "Insurance Investment and the London Money Market of the Eighteenth Century," *Economica*, XX (1953), 145–146; Clay, "Property Settlements," 27–30. On the movement of rents and agricultural prices, see Eric Kerridge, "The Movement of Rent, 1540–1640," *Economic History Review*, VI (1953), 16–34; Peter J. Bowden, "Agricultural Prices, Farm Profits and Rents, 1500–1640"; "Agricultural Prices, Wages, Farm Profits and Rents, 1640–1750," in *idem* (ed.), *Chapters from the Agrarian History of England and Wales, 1500–1750* (Cambridge, 1990), I, 110–114, 250–271; Ernest Henry Phelps Brown and Sheila V. Hopkins, "Seven Centuries of the Prices of Consumables Compared with Builders' Wage-Rates," *Economica*, XXIII (1956), 296–314. On price of land and the rate of interest, see Habakkuk, "The Long-Term Rate of Interest and the Price of Land in the Seventeenth Century," *Economic History Review*, V (1952), 26–45; Clay, "The Price of Freehold Land in the Later Seventeenth and Eighteenth Centuries," *Economic History Review*, XXVII (1974), 174; *idem, Economic Expansion and Social Change* (Cambridge, 1984), II, 281.

12 A detailed discussion of economic and other incentives behind the use of contraception by the upper landed class and of the methods to stop or abort conception is found in Stone, *Family*, 415–424. On the financial perils of portions and the need to reduce expenditure, see *idem, Family and Fortune: Studies in Aristocratic Finance in the Sixteenth and Seventeenth Centuries* (Oxford, 1973), 155–157; Lloyd Bonfield, "Affective Families, Open Elites, and Strict Family Settlements in Early Modern England," *Economic History Review*, XXXIX (1986), 343–344, 348; Clay, "Property Settlements," 29–34.

moneyed interests, especially if they had sired a brood of children from one or more previous marriages.[13]

Unlike the incentives to marry later and less often and to reduce the size of families, the pressure to shed kin, clients, and patrons was not uniformly felt throughout the landed class. Because their families were embedded within less extensive networks of kinship and clientage, the gentry faced fewer difficulties in severing these ties, and their more vigorous response to new commercial opportunities raised the stakes that they had in insulating their families from such obligations. As the major enclosers, the principal purchasers of land that the Tudor crown and the nobility unloaded on the market, and the leading investors in agricultural improvement, the gentry felt the need more strongly than the nobility to reduce the burden that kinship and clientage imposed on household finances. After the sixteenth-century crisis in aristocratic fortunes ended, a more conjugally centered family spread to the English nobility. The mounting financial difficulties of the aristocracy, together with failures in the male line and the Tudors' reluctance to ennoble new families led to a substantial reduction in the size and wealth of the peerage. This trend was reversed in the early seventeenth century when the Stuarts sold knighthoods and noble patents to prosperous merchants and gentleman farmers. The restocking of the peerage with the merchant elite and the gentry brought new wealth and a new vision to the operation of the aristocratic estate. At the same time, it disseminated a correspondingly new conception of the noble household, one that was limited more to the immediate family itself.[14]

Enterprise is also the key to understanding why the late sixteenth- and early seventeenth-century increase in domestic patriarchy was more keenly felt in the homes of the gentry and yeomanry. A willingness to experiment with new crops and new agricultural techniques, to enclose, to buy more land, to expand production, to invest in capital improvement and, above all, to take risks demanded that the gentleman farmer discipline himself

---

13 *Ibid.*, 34.
14 Tawney, "The Rise of the Gentry," *Economic History Review*, XI (1941), 12–18; Mingay, *The Gentry*, 40–50, 57–61; Stone, *Family*, 124–129, 655–661; *idem, The Causes of the English Revolution, 1529–1642* (London, 1972), 46–47, 73; *idem, Crisis of the Aristocracy*, 65–128, 177–189; *idem*, "The Inflation of Honours," *Past & Present*, 14 (1961), 48–59; Frederick C. Dietz, *English Public Finance, 1558–1641* (London, 1964), 86–92.

and his tenants, consume frugally, set aside income for savings, and carefully manage his estate. This changeover from the passive practice of enforcing the payments of rents and fines to the capitalistic administration of estates under turbulent and increasingly competitive markets was critical. Thrift and industry, the careful keeping of accounts, and entrepreneurship, all conducive to greater success in a volatile market, were carried into the home and profoundly influenced family life. Detailed accounting brought minute attention to the education and rearing of offspring. Resolve in dealings with tenants and hired hands carried over to the discipline and upbringing of family members. This transference of behaviors, produced by the juxtaposition of a rapidly expanding and volatile market beside a decaying feudal order, was, in our view, the principal factor behind the hardening of patriarchy.[15]

Besides paving the way for the onset of agrarian capitalism and the social rise of the gentry, enclosures had the long-term effect of eroding the solidarity of the peasant village. The varying impact of enclosures on freeholders, copyholders, and leaseholders, by the mid-seventeenth century, had considerably increased the amount of landed inequality within the peasant community. By itself, the widening of social divisions in the village was likely to produce some clashes of interest. More important, however, was the rise of freeholders and substantial copyholders into the ranks of the yeomanry. As small capitalist farmers and employers of village labor, they had every incentive to separate themselves from the tradition of village cooperation and the system of mutual aid which in the past had kept sinking peasant households afloat, and to plough back what capital they had amassed into improving their land. They also had a vested interest in regulating the religious and social behavior of their poorer neighbors to fashion a more tractable and disciplined work force, to lower their contri-

15   On improvements and the management of gentleman's estates in the sixteenth century, see Kerridge, *The Agricultural Revolution* (London, 1967); Tawney, "Rise of the Gentry," 6–25; Cliffe, *Yorkshire Gentry*, 23–48; Mingay, *The Gentry*, 39–53; Carolina Lane, "The Development of Pastures and Meadows during the Sixteenth and Seventeenth Centuries, *Agricultural History Review*, XXVIII (1980), 18–30; Thirsk, "Farming Techniques," in *idem* (ed.), *Chapters*, III, 15–53. On the growth, hazards, and turbulence of agricultural markets in the sixteenth and early seventeenth centuries, see Alan Everitt, "The Marketing of Agricultural Produce, 1500–1640," in John Chartres (ed.), *Chapters* (Cambridge, 1990), IV, 15–141.

butions to the poor rates, and to break away from customary agricultural usages and practices.[16]

The pressures of an ever-widening, increasingly competitive, and yet still unsteady market, in all probability, bore down more heavily on the yeomanry than on any other group. For the yeomanry, who lacked the financial cushion of a large estate and who had to make their farms profitable during a time of rising rents, keeping the books in the black was a task that took patience, care, hard work, a willingness to make capital improvements and to try new agricultural methods, and often necessitated restricting consumption and making other sacrifices. They demanded such a discipline of their poorer neighbors, as well. The new rigid moral discipline and work ethic that yeomen expected of the village were indicated by their withdrawal from the moral economy of the village, their frequent use of ecclesiastical and lay courts to redefine property rights and village social relations and to punish wayward neighbors, their accusations of witchcraft against neighbors who had the temerity to challenge their failure to abide by village customs, and their denunciations of the traditional work rhythm as mere frivolity and devilry. Their families were unlikely to escape the imposition of a similar regimen. Indeed, these arguments imply that patriarchy probably found its most exacting expression in the homes of the yeomanry.[17]

16 Wrightson and Levine, *Poverty and Piety in an English Village* (New York, 1979), 19–42; 173–185; Wrightson, *English Society*, 51–57, 134–139, 164–166; Croot and Parker, "Agrarian Class Structure and Economic Development," 43; Campbell, *The English Yeoman*, 156–220; Margaret Spufford, *Contrasting Communities* (Cambridge, 1974), 76–85.
17 The argument that follows is drawn directly from Hill, *Society and Puritanism*, 482–487, 134, 151, 443–454. In extending these arguments to the families of the yeomanry, we are aware that scant few records have survived and that we are veering from the path of current wisdom which claims that plebeian families were most likely organized very differently from the landowning and bourgeois families: see Wrightson, *English Society*, 67–88, 95–104, 130–132. Although Hill likens the running of a small property-holder's business to the running of his family, Puritanism plays the leading part in his explanation for the rise in patriarchy. On this score and that regarding the role of the authoritarian royal state, Stone borrows heavily from Hill: cf. *ibid*, 446–448, 461–465; Stone, *Family*, 152–156. On the breakdown of the village moral economy, see *ibid*, 148–149; Wrightson, *English Society*, 51–57; Spufford, *Contrasting Communities*, 76–85. On the rash of court cases before ecclesiastical and lay courts, see Wrightson and Levine, *Poverty and Piety*, 110–141; Wrightson, *English Society*, 162–173; Levine, "Production, Reproduction," 91–92; Stone, *Family*, 144–145. On the social interpretation of witchcraft, see Keith Thomas, *Religion and the Decline of Magic* (New York, 1971), 535–569; Alan Macfarlane, *Witchcraft in Tudor and Stuart England* (New York, 1970), 154–155, 205–206. For attacks on the agricultural work cycle, see Thompson, "Time, Work-Discipline and Industrial Capital-

Puritanism most likely reinforced the cupidity and patriarchy found in landed and bourgeois homes. But its appeal lay chiefly among those social groups that were more actively engaged in enterprise: shopkeepers, independent artisans, yeomen, and small to middling merchants. Further removed from the grimy, nerve-wracking, and exhausting work of making ends meet and turning a profit, the gentry and the upper bourgeoisie found substantially less meaning in Puritanism's spiritual exaltation of industry and thrift than did small property-holders. As rising social groups, the gentry and the upper bourgeoisie also could not help but look down with disdain on the meaner existence of small property-holders and gaze wistfully up at the grandeur and power of the titled nobility. For these reasons, the gentry and the upper bourgeoisie probably held onto Puritanism less as a religious commitment and more as a social and political convenience. Small property-holders' allegiance to Puritanism was much more direct and personal. It exhorted them onto greater efforts and thus greater spiritual glory and, at the same time, sanctified and dignified those efforts.[18]

The support of a large section of the gentry and certain well-placed members of the aristocracy was critical to both the spread of Puritanism and the general upswing in domestic patriarchy. The prestige, power, and wealth of the landed class brought respectability to both movements and, in the case of Puritanism, offered some protection against an often hostile church and crown. The landed class was also a valuable source of patronage for dissenting ministers. Neither social trend, however, would have had such a profound and lasting influence on English society without the widespread allegiance of small-property holders. Their numbers alone lifted Puritanism and increasing patriarchal

---

ism," *Past & Present*, 38 (1967), 77–78, 87–88; Hill, *Society and Puritanism*, 146–159; Keith Thomas, "Work and Leisure," 50–66.

18   Hill argues that "the economic transformation of our period did not revolutionize men's thinking overnight . . . It took time for these groups [the industrious sort of people] to realize their common interests, and that these interests were being formulated in a body of ideas and a disciplinary system by Calvin and others": *Society and Puritanism*, 222–223. Stone sees Puritanism as an independent force helping to create the restricted patriarchal nuclear family: *Family*, 135–142, 154–156, 133–134, 223, 240–241; Tawney, *Religion and the Rise of Capitalism* (Gloucester, 1962), 104–108, 240–246; Hill, *Puritanism and Revolution* 230–231; William K. Jordan, *The Development of Religious Toleration in England, 1603–1640* (Gloucester, 1936), 203.

dominance in the family from isolated, self-enclosed, and sectarian phenomena to social movements. As an upwardly mobile social group, they also brought the luster of rising economic success to both movements. Aware of who buttered their bread, itinerant preachers, ministers, and other moralists tailored their thinking and writing to fit the needs and aspirations of their most devout and numerous adherents.[19]

LANDOWNER HEGEMONY AND THE DECLINE OF PATRIARCHY   Following the Restoration, certain legal and social developments partly elevated the domestic status of women. Two important legal changes were the recognition by the courts that women had the limited right to bequeath property and wealth to their children, and the widespread use among the landed class of strict settlement under which wives were provided with inviolable annuities and younger sons and daughters with legally binding portions. Within the home, women began to be viewed by their husbands as respected partners, advisors, and closest friends. The resurrection of the libido in the eighteenth century also reflected the improved domestic status of women; in sexual matters as in business and other affairs, *helpmeets* were to be active, not disinterested participants. At the same time, middle- and upper-class parents increasingly took on the primary responsibility of raising their children. Child care was divested of servants for fear of their corrupting influence, and parents began to refer to the world of themselves and their children as their "little families." Education followed suit, as schools introduced reforms to keep in step with the new emphasis on domesticity. Parents sent their children to school less to teach them discipline and more to expose them to the culture that would make them polished and engaging members of the elite. And beginning in the late seventeenth century, marriages based on the free, romantic choices of children gradually began to replace traditional, arranged marriages.[20]

19 Hill, *Society and Puritanism*, 135–142.
20 Stone, *Family*, 243–244, 288–330, 424–444, 527–543; Randolph Trumbach, *The Rise of the Egalitarian Family* (New York, 1978), 97–113, 129–134, 197–281; Houlbrooke, *English Family*, 70–71; Lloyd Bonfield, *Marriage Settlements, 1601–1740: The Adoption of Strict Settlement* (Cambridge, 1983), 82–92; idem, "Affective Families, Open Elites, and Strict Family Settlements in Early Modern England," *Economic History Review*, XXXIX (1986), 341–354; idem, "Marriage Settlement, 1660–1740: The Adoption of Strict Settlement in Kent and Northamptonshire," in R. B. Outhwaite (ed.), *Marriage and Society* (New York,

The subsidence of patriarchy within the families of the landowning class following the Restoration was due primarily to the improving fortunes of the gentry and the aristocracy during the late seventeenth and eighteenth centuries. By the middle of the seventeenth century, the entire landed class was thoroughly versed in the workings of a competitive market system and the running of a commercial estate. The promotion of merchants and gentleman farmers into the peerage, and the survival of the noble lineages that had prospered during the Tudor agrarian revolution, recast the landed class—gentry and aristocracy alike—into a commercial, improvement-minded social class, better equipped financially and technically to weather and exploit shifting markets and changes in agricultural technology and organization than their Tudor predecessors.[21]

Politically, the abridgement of royal authority and the abolition of the royal courts also worked to shut down class mobility. Landowners now could enclose with impunity and, as a result, expand production and take advantage of new husbandry requiring larger holdings. Financially, Parliament's founding of the Bank of England and the National Debt created reliable and fairly lucrative financial opportunities for the landed class through investments in public debt. Bank notes, public securities, and stock in the East India and South Sea trading companies enabled the gentry and the aristocracy to live in part on invested income; the average return of 5 percent was significantly higher than the 3 to 4 percent normally obtained from the land.[22]

1981), 104–106. For an opposing view of strict settlement and affective relations in the family, see Ellen Spring, "The Strict Settlement: Its Role in Family History," *Economic History Review*, XLI (1988), 454–460; Bonfield, "Strict Settlement and the Family: A Differing View," *Economic History Review*, XLI (1988), 461–466.

21 On the landowning class' understanding of the workings of capitalism, see Habakkuk, "English Landownership, 1680–1740," *Economic History Review*, XIX (1940), 5, 10, 13–14.

22 On parliamentary enclosures between 1660 and 1815, see John Lawrence and Barbara Hammond, *The Village Laborer* (New York, 1967; orig. ed., 1911), 43–96; William Edward Tate, *The English Village Community and the Enclosure Movements* (London, 1967); Michael Turner, *English Parliamentary Enclosure: Its Historical Geography and Economic History* (Folkestone, Kent, 1980); idem, *Enclosures in Britain, 1750–1830* (London, 1984); Yelling, *Common Field and Enclosure*, 94–112, 134–144, 227–232. Jonathan D. Chambers and Mingay have remarked that "enclosure was by far the most profitable use of capital in connection with land": *The Agricultural Revolution, 1750–1880* (London, 1966), 84. On the development of new opportunities for investing savings, see Peter George M. Dickson, *The Financial Revolution in England* (London, 1967), 7, 39–75, 249–303; Clay, *Economic Expansion and*

Although land remained the keystone of social prestige, it became increasingly common for the gentry and aristocracy to round out their fortunes and to build the necessary capital to acquire more land by investing in public funds, especially when the price of land was rising. Investments in public funds also freed the family head from having to stipulate in marriage settlements that annuities and portions be raised through forced savings, the sale or mortgaging of land, or life tenures; instead, they could be underwritten with stocks and bonds, a device that bolstered the security of both the heirs and the testator and relations between the two.[23]

The outcome of these three developments was a marked improvement in the economic security of the landowning class. The nobility and gentry could devote more attention and time to the products and activities that money could buy. No longer was it necessary to be so zealously attentive to the details of estate management, and no longer was it necessary to be so disciplined, thrifty, and diligent in one's worldly affairs. In a sense, business, much more so than in the sixteenth century, took care of itself. This relaxation in the burdens of business produced, we believe, a corresponding relaxation in patriarchy.

The business of saving souls was conducted more leisurely as well. The discredit of Puritanism and the reinstatement of the episcopacy with the Restoration of 1660 shut down the religious ferment that had gripped England for nearly thirteen decades, and partially returned a monopoly of worship to the Church of England, but did little to restore its political and financial independence. The encroachments of the common law courts on ecclesiastical jurisdictions were not overturned; church government was further subordinated to parliamentary authority, and the bulk

---

Social Change, II, 274–280, idem, *Economic Expansion and Social Change*, I, 163–164; Hill, *The Century of Revolution* (New York, 1966), 270–274. On the different rates of returns from land and paper securities and the movement of landed income into securities, see Habakkuk, "Long-Term Rate of Interest," 26–45; Clay, "Price of Freehold Land," 184–187; idem, "Marriage, Inheritance, and the Rise of Large Estates in England, 1660–1815," *Economic History Review*, XXI (1968), 508–509, 513; P. J. Cain and Anthony G. Hopkins, "Gentlemanly Capitalism and British Expansion Overseas, Part I: The Old Colonial System," *Economic History Review*, XXXIX (1986), 511–515; Stone and Stone, *An Open Elite?*, 284.

23 On jointures and portions underwritten by debentures, see Dickson, *Financial Revolution*, 250, 256, 267–8, 281–3, 298–300.

of alienated clerical estates and appropriated tithes were left in the hands of the landed class. In short, the Anglican Church became even more dependent on the patronage of landed wealth. In the eighteenth century, this dependence became most evident at the level of the parish, where the Anglican clergy generally had to rely on the local gentry and magistracy to ward off dissent and to guarantee packed houses on the Sabbath. A working alliance between squire and parson emerged: the squire would bring in the flock, and the parson would extol the virtues of social deference and obedience. Once the gentry had wrested control of local affairs from the aristocracy and the economy had settled down, it desired not a religion that questioned the prevailing order as it had several decades earlier, but one that preached its inevitability and reasonableness.[24]

The triumph of agrarian capitalism not only improved women's position in middle- and upper-class homes, it also freed marriage from its traditional constraints. In the transition from feudalism to agrarian and then industrial capitalism, marriage among the gentry, the aristocracy, and the urban bourgeoisie continued to be arranged to preserve or to augment the lineage's wealth and political power; in fact, the stakes of marriage appreciated substantially from the sixteenth to the early eighteenth century, as dowries grew ever larger. What changed was the say that children had in their choice of mates.

In the past, when the perils and rigors of long-distance travel limited the geographic scope of marriage to the county, the number of potential mates for an eligible landed or moneyed person, given the small fraction of the population that the landed class and the urban bourgeoisie comprised, was abysmally low. With choice so circumscribed, parents were leery to let infatuation reign lest one of their children fall in love with a social inferior. Once children of the landed and bourgeois classes could freely meet and interact with their social peers, the odds that they would fall in love and want to marry others of their or near their own class should have risen dramatically. The more their romantic bents seemed to follow the rule of social endogamy, the more latitude

24 Stone, *English Revolution*, 99–103; Alan Gilbert, *Religion and Society in Industrial England* (London, 1976), 4–7, 12–14; Hill, *Century of Revolution*, 225, 242–245; Thirsk, "Restoration Land Settlement," 320–328; Habakkuk, "Landowners and the Civil War," 139–148; Roy Porter, *English Society in the Eighteenth Century* (Harmondsworth, 1982), 188–190.

in selecting a mate parents would be expected to grant their children. Such opportunities for children of landowners and moneyed interests to meet others of the same age and of similar social status only arose in greater force with the eighteenth-century advances in transportation, communication, and commerce, developments that not only expedited the flow of goods and the circulation of commercial traffic, but enabled the expanding middle class and the landed elite to follow the seasons as well. This increased geographical and commercial mobility had the indirect benefit of exposing the children of the middle and upper classes to a much wider slate of suitable mates, and with broader comparisons, middle- and upper-class children could form their sexual and social ideals, fall in love, and marry with less parental interference. The early stages of industrial capitalism created the mobility and the social opportunities for romantic love to become compatible with the principle of social endogamy.[25]

About this time, the long-term decline in the fertility of the English upper landed class, especially the aristocracy, was abruptly reversed. From the children of peers born during the first quarter of the eighteenth century to those born between 1775 and 1779, marital fertility rose from 3.8 to 5.0 children born per ever-married child, despite declines of 47 percent in infant mor-

---

25 Trumbach, *The Egalitarian Family*, 97–113; Stone, *Family*, 60–62, 270–274, 288–320; Nicholas Rogers, "Money, Land, and Lineage: The Big Bourgeoisie of Hanoverian London," *Social History*, IV (1979), 444–454; Lang, "Jacobean Merchants," 47. From the middle of the sixteenth century to the end of the eighteenth century, the rate at which the female children of the peerage practiced strict social endogamy never exceeded 41.3% and the rate of strict social endogamy practiced by male children of the peerage never surpassed 34.5%: Hollingsworth, "Demography of the Peerage," 9. During the eighteenth century, for which it is possible to distinguish between heirs and younger sons of the peerage, the percentage of heirs who married daughters of the peerage ranged between 33.3 and 47.1%. The percentage of younger sons who practiced social endogamy was much lower, varying between 22.6 and 30.5%. If the criterion for social endogamy is relaxed somewhat to include wives from untitled landowning families, then the rate of social endogamy for male children of the aristocracy rises to an average of about 57% for the eighteenth century, a figure very close to the 56% the Stones obtained from their sample. David Thomas, "Social Origins of Marriage Partners of the British Peerage in the Eighteenth and Nineteenth Centuries," *Population Studies*, XXVI (1972), 102, 107; Stone and Stone, *An Open Elite?*, 496. On eighteenth-century commercial developments, see Phyllis Deane, "Great Britain," in *Fontana Economic History of Europe*, Part I (Glasgow, 1973), IV, 165–174; John B. Owen, *The Eighteenth Century, 1714–1815* (New York, 1976), 315–316; Mingay, *English Landed Society in the Eighteenth Century* (London, 1963), 153–158, 187–201; Peter Mathias, *The First Industrial Nation* (London, 1983), 97–107; Stone and Stone, *An Open Elite?*, 222–225, 253–254, 315, 326; Porter, *English Society*, 72–73.

tality and 35 percent in child and adolescent mortality. Since both male and female nuptiality continued to increase one birth cohort later than marital fertility, the increase in generation replacement rates spanned four instead of three generations, climbing on the average from around 0.82 children born per noble child born between 1700 and 1724 to 1.39 per noble child born during the first quarter of the nineteenth century (Figs. 2–3). Such a robust increase was not displayed by the upper landed class in general, whose fertility only increased from 3.8 children to 4.2 children born per ever-married offspring between the two cohorts born during the eighteenth century (Fig. 1).[26]

Little of the increase in fertility rate can be attributed to a declining age at first marriage, since the median age at which male children of the aristocracy first married retreated by about five-sixths of a year; the median age at which female children first married increased by another two years (Figs. 2–3). Nor is declining adult mortality a likely cause. The mean number of years lived from age 20 for women of noble ancestry rose from only 27.8 years for the cohort born between 1700 and 1724 to 28.4 for those born between 1775 and 1799. A somewhat fitful increase in nuptiality, however, is partly responsible for the rise in fertility. Although the percentage of ever-married heirs remained essentially unchanged between 1720 and 1840, the percentage of younger sons who married rose from 58.6 percent for the cohort born between 1700 and 1719 to 73.0 percent for the cohort born between 1820 and 1839, while female nuptiality increased erratically from 73.3 percent of those born between 1700 and 1724 to 79.9 percent of those born during the period 1800–24 (Figs. 3–4).[27]

More important was a general rise in the speed at which married women bore children (Figs. 2–4). The generation of ever-married children of the peerage born during the last quarter of the eighteenth century exhibited a consistently higher average number of births for each five years of marriage than did the ever-married cohort born between 1700 and 1724. Fertility rose, then, not because children of the peerage were marrying earlier,

26 Stone and Stone, An Open Elite?, 468–470; Hollingsworth, "Demography of the Peerage," 20, 30–34, 62–63.
27 Ibid., 20, 25; idem, "Mortality in the Peerage," 327; Thomas, "Social Origins of Marriage Partners of the Peerage," 101.

or fewer wives were dying before their childbearing years were over, but because more aristocratic children were marrying, and wives were having children at a faster pace.[28]

By both broadening the slate of suitable spouses outside of landed circles and offering respectable and fairly lucrative careers to younger sons, the rapid growth during the eighteenth century in the numbers, wealth, and prestige of professional families—those tied to the military, the church, state administration, and the professions—was one reason for the increasing fertility and nuptiality of the peerage. Although the available information allows us to say only that sons of the upper landed class were marrying daughters of professional families with increasing frequency during the eighteenth century, as long as lesser heirs continued to wed mainly outside their class, the rise of professional families should have heightened competition on the elite marriage market and thus enhanced the overall marital prospects of noble children. On the other hand, younger sons became more marketable as suitors and more willing to suffer the financial inconvenience of raising a family, which by itself was likely to have raised the marital fertility of the peerage somewhat, as more and more of them entered the professions. No doubt, the pedigrees that they brought with them redounded favorably on the prestige of these positions and, in turn, on the social acceptance of marital alliances between aristocratic and professional families.[29]

Between 1700 and 1740, the landed class adopted a form of strict settlement that stipulated legally binding portions for younger sons and daughters, which also expanded marital opportunities. Guaranteed an endowment upon reaching majority, lesser heirs were in a better financial position to find spouses than they had been in the seventeenth century. The most common way that landowners set mandatory portions was to specify a fixed

28 Hollingsworth, "Demography of the Peerage," 20, 25, 30–34, 40, 54–55; idem, "Mortality in the Peerage," 327; Stone and Stone, An Open Elite?, 468–470.
29 On the growth of the professions, the social endogamy of younger sons and daughters, and intermarriage between professional and landed families, see ibid., 225–233, 247–249, 280–281, 491, 496; Hollingsworth, "Demography of the Peerage," 8–10; Thomas, "Social Origins of Marriage Partners," 99–111; Geoffrey Holmes, Augustan England: Professions, State and Society, 1680–1730 (London, 1982); idem, "The Professions and Social Change in England 1680–1730," Proceedings of the British Academy, LXV (1979), 313–354; Clay, Economic Expansion and Social Change, II, 26–27.

sum in the marriage settlement that was to be shared equally among all lesser heirs, rather than a variable sum, the value of which decreased as the number of children who survived declined. In this way, strict settlement also eliminated much of the disincentives that the inflation of portions had created for landowning families during the sixteenth and seventeenth centuries.[30]

Of greatest significance to marital fertility, however, was a marked improvement between 1720 and 1820 in the incomes of the landowning class. Some gains in income came from the favorable conjuncture of rising agricultural prices and increasing rents, rising land values, and lower interest rates and taxes that set in after 1720 (Fig. 5). Much larger gains were realized from enclosures and other investments in mining, canals, turnpikes, and urban property. During the eighteenth century, many of the greater landowners invested money in and earned substantial royalties from the exploitation of coal and other mineral deposits. Only those landowners whose holdings contained several mineral sites and whose income enabled them to underwrite large-scale operations were able to sustain a sizable income over several decades. But, countless other landowners made considerable windfall profits from the quick exploitation of open coal seams on their estates, profits which were often used to buy more land. Other landowners, sensing the press of people filling English cities, invested in urban property and housing developments on the outskirts of urban centers, which by the middle of the eighteenth century were yielding returns that rivaled the income of the wealthiest aristocrats. For the landed class as a whole, the most lucrative source of investment was enclosure. After 1730, enclosures could double a landowner's rents and yield returns as high as 15–20 perecent. The fact that 5 million or more acres were enclosed by parliamentary act between 1750 and 1830 suggests that a large share of the upper landed class benefited considerably from enclosing.[31]

30 Bonfield, *Marriage Settlements*, 107–151; Clay, "Property Settlements," 32–33.
31 On the upper landed class' investments in mining and in urban and suburban property, see John Towers Ward, "Landowners and Mining," in *idem* and Richard George Wilson (eds.), *Land and Industry: The Landed Estate and the Industrial Revolution* (New York, 1971), 63–116; Roy William Sturgess, "Landowners, Mining, and Urban Development in Nineteenth-Century Staffordshire," in *ibid.*, 173–204; Clay, *Economic Expansion and Social Change, II*, 70–71; *idem*, "Landlords and Estate Management," 318–320; David Cannadine, *Lords and Landlords: The Aristocracy and the Towns, 1774–1967* (Leicester, 1980), 21–93,

INDUSTRIAL CAPITALISM AND THE SECOND UPSWING OF PATRIARCHY

Toward the end of the eighteenth century, the position of women within the middle-class home began to deteriorate. No longer valuable and trusted partners whose assistance was vital to their husbands' businesses and public dealings, wives were instead relegated the socially limited task of creating a clean, comfortable, and quiet haven that had an atmosphere of gentility and was safely removed from the harsh, dirty, and frantic business of acquiring wealth. Only by preserving their innocence and purity could women fashion such a façade, and only if they were kept apart from the world of men, it was thought, could they retain their virtue. As a result, during the first half of the nineteenth century, social convention placed increasingly narrower boundaries on the spheres through which a proper woman was supposed to move. Travel, sexuality, business, finance, education, and informal mixed company all came to be regarded as activities at least potentially harmful to female innocence and purity.[32]

The relative permissiveness and indulgence of children that had characterized parent-child relations throughout much of the eighteenth century, too, gave way during the Romantic period to a stricter, more business-minded, and more punitive approach to

---

229–238. For enclosures and their potential to raise rental income, see Mingay, *English Landed Society* 182–183; Turner, *Parliamentary Enclosure*, 70–71, 94–105. The spate of ennoblements between 1750 and 1830, when some 249 new peers were created, affected the overall condition of aristocratic finances. Since neither Thomas nor Hollingsworth distinguished between recently ennobled families and older aristocratic families, it is impossible to say how their elevation influenced nuptiality and fertility within the peerage. However, the fact that 97 of them, or 39%, were promoted in recognition of their governmental service, makes it likely that the creation of new peers during this period generally deflated aristocratic wealth: Michael W. McCahill, "Peerage Creations and the Changing Character of the British Nobility, 1750–1830," *English Historical Review*, CCCLXXIX (1981), 259–261, 271. But it is also true that between 1750 and 1830 the upper landed class was most active in the building, renovation, and extension of its houses in Hertfordshire, Northamptonshire, and Northumberland, which was an indication of rising incomes: Stone and Stone, *An Open Elite?*, 508.

32 Porter, *English Society*, 323, 327–328; Stone, *Family*, 666–681; Steven Mintz, *A Prison of Expectations* (New York, 1983), 60–62; Deborah Gorham, *The Victorian Girl and the Feminine Ideal* (Bloomington, 1982), 3–12; Eric Hobsbawm, *Industry and Empire* (Harmondsworth, 1969), 84; Joan Perkins, *Women and Marriage in Nineteenth-Century England* (London, 1989), 10–31, 233–256; Catherine Hall, "The Sweet Delights of Home," in Michelle Perrot (ed.), *A History of Private Life: From the Fires of Revolution to the Great War* (Cambridge, Mass., 1990), IV, 47–93; Davidoff and Hall, *Family Fortunes*, 114–118, 166–192, 211–215, 234–240, 272–289, 331–335, 357–396, 403–415; Dorothy Marshall, *Industrial England, 1776–1851* (New York, 1973), 128–139.

parenting. Focus once again centered increasingly on the inherent willfulness of young children, whose sinful dispositions could only be forged into proper shape on the anvil of severe punishments. For middle-class Victorian children, locked closets, forced fasts, and the withdrawal of love became a common template on which their moral characters were carefully to be wrought. Zealous and intrusive parental supervision kept temptation at bay. Nonetheless, it stopped short of physical beatings. In fact, the founding of schools early in the nineteenth century by the middle class was motivated not only to equip their sons with a more practical education, one that supplemented classical studies with mathematics and the sciences, and to instill in them punctual and orderly habits, but also to remove their sons from the notorious brutal discipline of elite boarding schools.[33]

The industrial revolution had much to do with the intensification of patriarchy in middle-class homes after 1780. The accelerated pace of enclosures uprooted an increasingly greater number of smallholders, triggering and amplifying the marriage-driven population growth of the eighteenth century. The result was a larger pool of wage labor. Since the size of manufacturing concerns during the early stages of the industrial revolution generally remained at the level of the small shop, this rising supply was important not so much because it reduced the cost of labor, but because it created more opportunities for investments in new handicraft shops and innovations. Cotton and iron were the first, and are the best-known, industries to wed technical knowledge and wage labor. Not only cheap labor and technical breakthroughs, but also the need for only modest capital enabled the iron and cotton industries to overshadow developments in other areas. It took relatively little capital to get a small textile or iron works going, and even less to outfit it with the latest innovations. At least in their infancies, the iron and cotton industries were open to men of humble origins: many of the early iron and cotton entrepreneurs came from families of workers, yeomen, craftsmen, and minor merchants. The ease with which persons could enter manufacturing also meant that competition was fierce. The heady careers of Boulton, Peel, and Owen were revealing of the industrial revolution. Equally informative were the countless untold

33 *Ibid.*, 669–673; Davidoff and Hall, *Family Fortunes*, 234–240, 331–348.

stories of those who barely gained a foothold in a business, and those who lost their shirts.[34]

Early entrepreneurs faced more problems than stiff competition and unpredictable markets. Neither rural cottagers nor urban craftsmen and workers were familiar, let alone accustomed, to a regular, daily work routine. For craftsmen, the inconstancy of demand, poor communications, and periodic trade depressions, and for the cottager, climate and the seasonality of agriculture, prohibited the adoption of regular work rhythms. For generations, they and their ancestors had lived in a world that did not reward punctuality and deliberate, steady work habits, but had encouraged ways to fill the voids and to relieve the tension of an often fitful work cycle. Feasts, wakes, and other customary observances celebrated the communalism of the group, but were also frank recognitions of the natural order of work in a preindustrial society. These activities were in sharp contrast to the clocks, immobility, and thorough supervision that the early entrepreneurs tried to impose on their workers. During the initial stages of the industrial revolution, employers expended a great deal of energy trying to subordinate workers to a regular work schedule. Not until after the Napoleonic Wars were employers successful in regimenting workers.[35]

34 A declining average age at first marriage and a rising rate of nuptiality were the basis for population growth in the eighteenth century: see E. Anthony Wrigley and Roger S. Schofield, *The Population History of England, 1541–1871: A Reconstruction* (Cambridge, Mass., 1981), 248–269. Enclosures and proto-industrialization largely caused the shift in marital behaviors: see Levine, "Industrialization and the Proletarian Family in England," *Past & Present*, 107 (1985), 182–185; idem, "Production and Reproduction," 88; idem, *Reproducing Families*, 72–93. On the decline of real wages between 1740 and 1810, see Wrigley and Schofield, *Population History*, 642–644; John Rule, *The Experience of Labour in Eighteenth-Century English Industry* (New York, 1981), 68. On the technical strides made in the cotton and iron industries, their capital requirements, and the social origins of their founders, see Paul Mantoux, *The Industrial Revolution in the Eighteenth Century* (New York, 1961), 203–223, 271–299, 379–398; Marsall, *Industrial England*, 17–19; Porter, *English Society*, 339–3340; Reinhard Bendix, *Work and Authority in Industry* (Berkeley, 1974), 23; Davidoff and Hall, *Family Fortunes*, 86, 207–208. On the importance of coal to the industrial revolution, see Wrigley, *Continuity, Chance, and Change: The Character of the Industrial Revolution in England* (Cambridge, 1988), 28–30, 51–57, 77–78, 114–115.

35 Donald C. Coleman, "Labour in the English Economy of the Seventeenth Century," *Economic History Review*, VIII (1955), 289–291; Thompson, "Work-Discipline"; Thomas, "Work and Leisure"; Wrightson, *English Society*, 39–65; Bendix, *Work and Authority*, 46–115; Sidney Pollard, "Factory Discipline in the Industrial Revolution," *Economic History Review*, XVI (1963), 260–271; Rule, *Experience of Labour*, 204–206; Hobsbawm, *The Age of Revolution* (New York, 1962), 58–59; Davidoff and Hall, *Family Fortunes*, 360, 411–412.

We have come full circle. Facing highly competitive and unpredictable markets and stubborn work forces, the early industrialists like their late sixteenth- and seventeenth-century counterparts—the rising yeomanry and gentry—assumed the typical behavior of calculating, hard-pressed businessmen. Once again, the tenets of discipline, diligence, thrift, and responsibility came to the fore, and correspondingly, patriarchal dominance increased in middle-class homes.

Religious thought and its practice were in all probability strongly influenced by the sweeping social changes which the march of the industrial revolution left in its train. Any economic transformation that radically alters the institutional foundation of society is likely to shake up world views and elicit new solutions to humankind's proper positions and roles in the social order. Methodism and Evangelicalism fit that bill and, in slightly different ways, so did Quakerism, Unitarianism, and Independence—much as Tudor and Stuart Puritanism had a century earlier. The evangelical movement in England, by stressing that only through hard work, duty, and piety were the poor to remain on the straight and narrow and avoid temptation, gave industrial employers and their representatives the ideological ammunition and the missionary zeal to attack the preindustrial traditions of labor. It gave them a religious and social movement, the propaganda of which, despite its admonishment to the better-off to guide and reform the poor, championed the new industrial order in which the productivity of labor, although not materially well-rewarded, was spiritually well-recompensed. It gave them a spiritual justification and moral resolve for success in business, since riches often followed if one abided by evangelical precepts. It gave them a theological parapet from which to launch their attacks on the indolence, frivolity, and extravagance of the landed class.[36]

Evangelicalism's contribution to the rise of the industrial and professional classes was not limited to the ideological and spiri-

---

36 Anthony Armstrong, *The Church of England, the Methodists, and Society 1700–1850* (Totowa, N.J., 1973), 81–82, 88–89, 121; Gilbert, *Religion and Society*, 52–53; Thompson, *The Making of the English Working Class* (New York, 1966), 357–366; Bendix, *Work and Authority*, 60–86. Most of Methodism's faithful came from the working class, whereas Anglican Evangelicalism and other dissenting churches, such as the Independents (New Dissent) and the Unitarians and Quakers (Old Dissent) drew most of their support from merchants, manufacturers, professionals, and farmers: *Ibid.*, 73, 81–83, 77, 108–113, 158.

tual. To its members, the closed, cohesive community of evangelical churches offered comfort and protection against a world still hostile to the rule of capital. The courage for religious and economic "nonconformity" was more easily mustered when there were plenty of friends and relatives who were "nonconformists," too. The meshing of religious affiliations with business associations, friends, and kin often provided evangelical shopkeepers and professionals with ready-made clienteles and patrons, and evangelical manufacturers and bankers with sources of capital or credit. In bad times, the religious fellowship could also furnish loans to tie a family over until it restored its business to good health. As a result, banishment from a local church often spelled disaster for a middle-class family.[37]

Like the Tudor and Stuart small property-holders before them, the early entrepreneurs were simultaneously the inspiration for and the driving force behind the evangelical revival and the second upswing of patriarchy. Similar to the attraction of Puritanism and Elizabethan and Jacobean patriarchy before them, the widespread appeal of evangelicalism and Romantic and Victorian patriarchy depended heavily on the numbers and the financial support that the manufacturing and professional class provided.[38] Few, if any, world views, regardless of their intellectual and moral integrity, can be transformed into potent agents of social change without first gaining the support of a wide section of the population. Emerging ideologies will rarely attract a large body of followers without first addressing the social, political, and economic needs of a class or classes. Patriarchy and evangelicalism meshed well with the everyday needs of small manufacturers and professionals, and this fit gave each its social momentum.

CONCENTRATION OF INDUSTRY AND RELAXATION OF PATRIARCHY
Until 1850, the transition from dispersed artisanal manufacture to concentrated factory production remained slow, uneven, and piecemeal. The continued low fixed-capital requirements of manufacture, together with the cheapness of labor, made handicraft production in most fields the cost-effective technique, thereby impeding large-scale investment in heavy machinery and pro-

37 Ibid., 86, 99–106, 207–218, 246–252; Bendix, *Work and Authority*, 33–34.
38 Davidoff and Hall, *Family Fortunes*, 81–83.

moting instead a multiplication of small handicraft shops that could raise productivity by developing new tools or refining older techniques. As a result, the fierce competition that was characteristic of the early decades of the industrial revolution persisted well into the nineteenth century, although with steadily lessening intensity. This competition carried Victorian patriarchy along. The breakthrough to mechanization came with the great leap in railroad investment between 1845 and 1848. Thereafter, capital increasingly flowed into durable goods industries, especially coal, iron, and steel. Steam power and the factory rapidly replaced hand power and the artisan's shop as the dominant form of production. Rising wages in the half-century after 1850 further promoted investment in mechanization and accelerated the demise of small-scale production. For the remainder of the nineteenth century, industry continued to expand, largely through growing investments in machinery, while at the same time, the British state pursued an aggressive foreign policy to open markets for industrial products.[39]

The expansion of heavy industry and the accompanying contraction of handicraft manufacture dampened the frenetic competition that had been a defining feature of the industrial revolution's first century. As industry became more concentrated, and as the initial investment required to establish an industrial concern grew considerably beyond the means of ordinary persons, the composition of the middle class shifted from being a group of small- and medium-size entrepreneurs, whose incomes were ultimately tied to their ability to compete successfully on the market, to an occupational group of managers and professionals, whose status derived primarily from their educational attainments and whose incomes were derived principally from salaries and fees. Earning stable incomes, which were much less dependent

39 Levine, "Proletarian Family," 174–175, 185–187; C. Knick Harley, "Skilled Labour and the Choice of Technique in Edwardian Industry," *Explorations in Economic History*, XI (1974), 410; Hobsbawm, *The Age of Capital, 1848–1875* (New York, 1975), 27–47, 126–146; *idem, Industry and Empire*, 88, 112–118; Albert Edward Musson, *The Growth of British Industry* (New York, 1978), 242–246. For revisions of Deane's and William Alan Cole's estimates, *British Economic Growth, 1688–1867* (Cambridge, 1962), see Harley, "British Industrialization before 1841: Evidence of Slower Growth during the Industrial Revolution," *Journal of Economic History*, XLII (1982), 267–289; Nicholas F. R. Crafts, "British Economic Growth, 1700–1831: A Review of the Evidence," *Economic History Review*, XXXVI (1983), 177–199.

on market conditions, the middle class no longer needed to be so frugal, disciplined, diligent, and responsible in the discharge of work and domestic duties. Industrial employers, too, "felt rich and confident enough to be able to afford" less supervision and discipline of their workers. As a result, both evangelical religious fervor and domestic patriarchy declined.[40]

Religious practice assumed a more conformist and "institutional" form and, in the home, education replaced religion as a means of instilling morality and a world view into middle- and upper-class children. Wives and daughters were still regarded as symbols of virtue, innocence, and purity, yet their lives were less and less regimented to the task of creating an illusion of gentility and shielding fathers and husbands from the hectic and uncertain business of amassing wealth. Reflecting the shift in public opinion, which was becoming increasingly less tolerant of the control men exercised over their wives, Parliament passed a number of laws making it easier for women to escape from marriage and securing for them some rights over their property and earnings, their children, and their own bodies. Women also began to experience more freedom of movement in and out of the house, better educational opportunities, and greater acceptance of their rights to participate in social and recreational activities, formerly the exclusive preserve of men.[41]

40 Davidoff and Hall, *Family Fortunes*, 265–271; Charles Moraze, *The Triumph of the Middle Classes* (New York, 1968), 527–535; Musson, *British Industry*, 247–255; Hobsbawm, *The Age of Empire, 1875–1914* (New York, 1987), 171–181; idem, *Age of Capital*, 266–270. By professionals, we mean not only lawyers, doctors, and public servants, but also engineers, economists, and technicians, who rapidly increased in numbers with the concentration and expansion of heavy industry after 1850.

41 *Ibid.*, 302–305; idem, *Industry and Empire*, 123–124; idem, *The Age of Empire*, 202–207; Stone, *Family*, 680–681; Gorham, *The Victorian Girl*, 190; Perkins, *Women and Marriage*, 292–310.

Rudolph A. Zambardino

Mexico's Population in the Sixteenth Century: Demographic Anomaly or Mathematical

Illusion? The size of the pre-Conquest population of central Mexico and the extent to which this population declined during the first 100 years of Spanish rule are issues that have generated fascinating descriptions and passionate polemics. Since the late 1940s, however, new studies of all available contemporary documents have been carried out at the University of California. These studies, of unprecedented scope and sophistication, have reached revolutionary conclusions, which estimate figures for the pre-Conquest population of central Mexico and for its subsequent decline far higher than ever suggested before. The results of these studies were published first by Cook and Simpson and then, from the late 1950s, by Cook and Borah.[1]

The most recent and complete summary of the population figures estimated by Borah and Cook is as follows:

1518	25.2	million
1532	16.8	"
1548	6.3	"
1568	2.65	"
1585	1.9	"
1595	1.375	"
1603	1.075	"

The total surface area to which these figures refer is given by Borah and Cook as covering 514,000 square kilometers, equivalent to 200,000 square miles; the average population density in

Rudolph A. Zambardino is Principal Lecturer in Computing Science at the North Staffordshire Polytechnic, Stafford, England.

0022-1953/80/0101-27 $02.50/0

1   A recent and most comprehensive bibliography can be found in William M. Denevan (ed.), *The Native Population of the Americas in 1492* (Madison, 1977). Sherburne F. Cook and Lesley Byrd Simpson, "The Population of Central Mexico in the Sixteenth Century," *Ibero Americana*, XXXI (1948), 1–164; Woodrow Borah and Cook, "Conquest and Population: A Demographic Approach to Mexican History," *Proceedings of the American Philosophical Society*, CXIII (1969), 177–183.

1518 would be 125 people/sq.mi. or 49 people/sq.km. over the whole area, and 2,000–3,000 people/sq.mi. in the Valley of Mexico.[2]

Figures of such magnitude imply that central Mexico in the sixteenth century was an exceptional place both demographically and epidemiologically and they beg a reappraisal of many well-established views in several fields of study. This article has the dual purpose of considering such wider implications and of discussing in detail the cogency and reliability of these population estimates.

THE WIDER IMPLICATIONS

The population of Europe and Asia around 1500.

A recent analysis of the estimates of European population around 1500 arrives at a figure of 81.8 million for the total population of Europe, whereas the population estimated for the more heavily populated European countries is as follows:

Spain and Portugal	9.3	million
France	16.4	"
Germany	12.0	"
British Isles	4.4	"
Poland	3.5	"
Italy	10.5	"

This list is ordered according to the surface area of the various countries, and Mexico would be in third place. The population density of these countries ranges from about 30 people/sq.mi. (Poland) to 90 people/sq.mi. (Italy), as compared to 125 people/sq.mi. for central Mexico.[3]

A comparison with Asia seems much less relevant, considering the lack of substantial parallels in the subsequent demographic history of the Asian and American continents. However, it is interesting to contrast the central Mexican estimate with the

2 Cook and Borah, *Essays in Population History* (Berkeley, 1971), I, 8. Borah and Cook, "The Aboriginal Population of Central Mexico on the Eve of the Spanish Conquest," *Ibero Americana*, XLV (1963), 89–90.
3 Roger Mols, "Population in Europe 1500–1700," in Carlo M. Cipolla (ed.), *Fontana Economic History of Europe* (Glasgow, 1974), II, 38.

figures for the areas that had, in 1500 as at present, the largest concentrations of population:

Indian subcontinent	105	million
China proper	60–100	"
Indonesia	8	"
Japan	17	"

The estimated population density in central Mexico is more than double the values for China and India and 10 percent greater than in Japan, which appears to have been the most densely populated area of considerable size in the world. Comparison with earlier great civilizations is equally striking: the population of the Roman Empire at the time of Augustus is estimated at around 50 million, and Pharaonic Egypt had a population of about 5 million.[4]

The above figures show that the Borah and Cook estimates imply that central Mexico was the most densely inhabited sizable area in the world and, in terms of population, one of the largest political entities of the sixteenth century. All the dominions of Charles V in Spain, Italy, and Germany hardly reach the Aztec figure. As the sultanate of Delhi was disintegrating, only the Ming emperors of China were likely to have had a number of subjects greater than those attributed to Montezuma. Not being a historian, I cannot say whether these extraordinary characteristics are consistent with the general impressions and information conveyed by the contemporary documents. However, if the population estimates for pre-Conquest Mexico are correct, they obviously pose major problems in the context of the comparative study of history. Neither the size of central Mexico nor the magnitude of the 25 million estimated as its population would allow setting it aside as just an exception, as could be done for some relatively small island.

Of course, the European and Asian figures are not beyond

---

4 Colin McEvedy and Richard Jones, *Atlas of World Population History* (Harmondsworth, 1978), 170–174, 179–186, 196–200. The figures for China refer to China south of the Great Wall and without Turkestan and Tibet. For China see also John D. Durand, "The Population Statistics of China," *Population Studies*, XIII (1960), 209–256. For the Roman Empire a global figure of 54 million in A.D. 14 is given in William H. McNeill, *Plagues and Peoples* (Oxford, 1977), 104, quoting Julius Beloch. For a more detailed regional analysis of the Roman Empire and for Pharaonic Egypt see Marcel R. Reinhard and Andre Armengaud, *Histoire Generale de la Population Mondiale* (Paris, 1961), 22–25, 37–48.

doubt. The burden of disproving their order of magnitude, however, would be very heavy indeed, considering the broad comparability of the results reached by generations of scholars working in completely separate fields of study, and the fact that their estimates normally rest on contemporary written evidence that exceeds by several orders of magnitude what is available for Aztec and earliest Spanish Mexico.

It is also important to note that the 25 million population estimated for 1515 is remarkably high even by present day Latin American standards: only Guatemala, El Salvador, and several Caribbean islands exceed the 1518 density. In the same area of Mexico as covered by the 1518 estimate, comparisons are distorted by the growth of Mexico City, which in 1976 had 8.9 million out of about 38 million living in the area. However, even without any correction for Mexico City, the population of this area was only 20 million in 1960 (of which 5.4 was in Mexico City) and reached the 1518 figure only around 1969, in spite of half a century of "population explosion" during which Mexico has maintained one of the highest rates of population growth in the world.[5]

Epidemics

There is general agreement that a catastrophic collapse of population took place in central Mexico following the Conquest, and that a major reason was the spread of epidemics caused by the sudden contact with a stock of imported diseases against which the natives were defenseless. It seems relevant, therefore, to compare the Mexican experience with the effects of major epidemics in the Old World, for cases where numerical evidence is available.

One of the worst demographic disasters on record is the Black Death that engulfed Europe from 1346 to 1350, with recurrences in the 1360s and 1370s. There are abundant examples of the terrible death rates that occurred: small communities were

5 For the 1960 figures see Howard F. Cline, *Mexico* (London, 1962), 333. I have matched the states and territories for which the figures are given with the maps and lists of states published by Borah and Cook "Population on the Eve of the Conquest," 73, 157. For the other figures see U.N., *Statistical Yearbook 1977* (New York, 1978), 69–71; *Statesman Yearbook 1978/1979* (London, 1978), 842–843 (giving also 13 million as the 1975 estimate for the population of greater Mexico City).

wiped out; 60 percent of the population of Venice was killed within eighteen months; between 20 and 45 percent died in Britain at the onset of the plague; and between one quarter and one third of the European population was killed between 1346 and 1350. The global effects of the plague over a long period and for large areas show, for instance, that the population of England decreased from 3.7 million in 1348 to 2.1 million (i.e. 57 percent) in 1430, whilst the population of Europe fell from 73.5 million in 1340 to 43 million (60 percent) in 1380 and 50 million (70 percent) in 1450. Another relevant example is provided by the great epidemics that swept China in the fourteenth century, contributing to a decrease in population from 123 million in 1200 (before the Mongol invasion) to 65 million in 1393. There are also many examples of comparatively small communities that have been wiped out almost entirely by epidemics. For large areas and populations, however, these examples and other available figures indicate a loss of population of around 1 in 2 after about a century from the outbreak of the epidemics.[6]

The special circumstances of the European impact on the Americas, as well as the impressions and figures derived from contemporary sources, suggest that the population loss in central Mexico was much higher than in the other cases. However, as the population around 1600 was little more than 1 million, the population loss implied by the Borah and Cook estimate of over 25 million in 1518 is of 24 in 25. This is not just "much higher" than the previous maximum of 1 in 2: it represents a completely different order of magnitude.[7]

As McNeill has cogently explained, some general pattern can be recognized in epidemics widely separated in time and space, because germs have their own survival problems and must reach

6 Frederic C. Lane, *Venice* (Baltimore, 1973), 19; Lane also gives a death rate of one third for the epidemics of 1575–1577 and 1630–1631. J. C. Russell, "Population in Europe 500–1500," in Cipolla (ed.), *Economic History*, I, 36, 55; McNeill, *Plagues and Peoples*, 142, 163, 168; Durand, "Population Statistics of China," 228–230, 231–233.
7 Borah, in "America as Model," *Actas y Memorias XXXV Congreso Internacional de Americanistas* (Mexico City, 1962), 388–384, states that there is a parallel with the European impact on Oceania. However, apart from a vague statement about the New Hebrides, none of the examples refers to an original population above 500,000. Furthermore, for the areas with original population above 100,000 the residual population ranges from 1 in 2 (Fiji) to 1 in 4 (Australia) and 1 in 10 (New Zealand and Hawaiian Islands), all very far from the 1 in 25 postulated for Mexico.

some equilibrium, however unstable, with the host population, if they are to spread out and cause epidemics of considerable duration over wide areas. Once again, the 25 million estimate implies extraordinary processes that pose considerable problems for our understanding of the spread of diseases.[8]

ESTIMATING METHODS AND THEIR ACCURACY   The considerations in the previous sections are not intended to prove, or even to suggest that the 25 million population estimate is impossible: in practice hardly anything can be proved impossible. Those considerations, however, show that such a population would constitute an anomaly from different, albeit related, points of view. Such an anomaly may be possible, but before it can be accepted as historical fact, or even as a reasonable hypothesis, it is imperative that it be shown to emerge as the inescapable conclusion to be drawn from the available evidence. Since the estimates are the result of complex and sophisticated calculations, it is vitally important to assess the approximation level arising from the methods applied and from the data used.

Error bounds: their meaning and implications

The population figures derived by Borah and Cook are estimates and, as such, carry an intrinsic degree of approximation. They are symbolical of a range of values, all of which are compatible with the data and estimating methods used. The lowest and highest values of such a range are usually called the error bounds of the entity estimated.[9]

In our case, if such bounds were, say, 20 percent lower and higher than the published figures, then the validity of those figures would be beyond reasonable doubt and we ought to turn our attention to solving the problems arising from the demographic feat achieved by the Aztecs.

If, on the other hand, the error bounds were, say, ±75 percent, then the situation would be very different: if, for instance,

8 McNeill, *Plagues and Peoples,* 57–60.
9 A systematic account of error analysis will be found in J. H. Wilkinson, *Rounding Errors in Algebraic Processes* (London, 1963); this volume includes an extensive bibliography. In this article I have applied "standard errors" as defined and used by Borah and Cook; in many cases it would have been more appropriate to use "confidence intervals" and this would have increased the corresponding margins of error by a constant factor.

the 25 million figure was in reality symbolical of a range extending from 6 to 44 million, it would be unhelpful and misleading to use that figure at all. A very wide range of possible values is really an indication that the method used and/or the data available cannot lead to a meaningful quantitative result but only to a qualitative assessment. In our case, it would follow that instead of using the newly found figures to revise our ideas about past and present population densities, we would have to use such existing knowledge as an indicator giving greater credibility to the lower end of the estimated range.

The multipliers method

The contemporary sources on which Borah and Cook had to base their estimates are not anything like a modern census. They do not cover the whole country and the figures given can be the amount of tribute paid, the number of heads of family, and so on. In order to derive a population figure, such data must be multiplied by various factors, which are themselves the result of separate analyses and calculations.

In the simplest case, largely applicable for 1568, the basic data are the number of casados (married men)—indicated by C—given by or inferred from the sources. These numbers are then multiplied by a factor 3.3, which is itself the product of two other factors: $M_1 = 2.96$, expressing the ratio of persons over four years of age to casados, and $M_2 = 1.11$, expressing the ratio of total population to population above the age of four. Therefore, in this simple case: Population $= C\, M_1\, M_2$.

For the pre-1568 estimates the number of multipliers is considerably greater and the estimates are based on a calculation of the type:

$$\text{Population} = D\, M_1\, M_2\, M_3 \ldots M_n$$

where D represents the basic data derived directly from the sources (e.g. the tribute paid) and the various Ms represent the multipliers needed in order to arrive at a population figure (e.g. ratio of tributaries to amount of tribute paid). Each multiplier M, however, is not a physical constant but the result of a separate estimation and hence includes, inescapably, a margin of approximation. In other words, the true value of M can be anywhere in the range $M(1 \pm e)$, where e represents the estimated per unit error of this particular M; for example, if e = 0.1, the true value of M can be as low as 0.9 M or as high as 1.1 M. The expression given above for the population can therefore take any value in the range:

$$\text{Population} = D \ M_1(1 + e_1) \ M_2(1 + e_2) \ M_3(1 + e_3) \ \ldots M_n(1 + e_n)$$

The grave shortcoming of the multipliers method is, as shown by the above expression, that the errors multiply each other and can escalate rapidly to an unacceptable magnitude if the number of multipliers is more than a very few. If, for instance, the number of multipliers is 7 and all the margins of approximation are 10 percent (i.e., $n = 7$ and $e_1 = e_2 = \ldots = e_n = 0.1$) the population could be as low as $DM_1M_2 \ldots M_7(0.9)^7$ or as high as $DM_1M_2 \ldots M_7(1.1)^7$. But $(0.9)^7 = 0.478$ and $(1.1)^7 = 1.949$, so that the true value of the population could be less than half or almost twice the value assumed when ignoring the approximation inherent in the values of M, even when this approximation is as good as 10 percent. Many of the multipliers used by Borah and Cook have a much greater margin of error, due to their nature or to the paucity of the data from which they can be derived.

The justification for using the multipliers method is simply that there are no alternatives. However, the results obtained tend to become so inaccurate as to be meaningless if the number of multipliers increases and/or their approximation is poor. In such cases all the values in the range are possible and fully consistent with the data used. Although there may be compensation of errors, it would be misleading to try quantifying this possibility in terms of probability of the mean or of other values: with only a few numbers involved, using statistical theory largely amounts to whistling in the dark.

POPULATION ESTIMATES, 1518–1605

The 1568 population estimate

Borah and Cook estimate a value of 2.65 million and suggest a range of variation from 2.5 to 2.8 million. Due to the large amount of data available and to the tributary reorganization of the 1550s, the 1568 estimate is the most accurate in the whole period, and Borah and Cook use it as the reference point for most of the calculations applied to other years.[10]

The conversion from the categories listed in the sources to total population is achieved by a multiplier, taken as 3.3 for the population/casados ratio; other categories are converted into casados by other multipliers. As already mentioned, the value 3.3 is the product of two other multipliers M_1 and M_2.

The derivation of M_1 is very detailed and convincing. Borah and Cook derive six values ranging from 2.79 to 3.19, so that their average of 2.96 has a margin of error k_1 of about ±6 percent. The value of M_2 is related to the 1940 figure for Mexico of 11.4 percent for the population below the age of four, as well as to a similar value in a single report in the 1548 population survey. In 1940, however, the Mexican population was fast expanding, whereas in 1568 it had been collapsing for half a century. Therefore the proportion of infants could have been much lower, say as low as 5 percent, and is most unlikely to have been higher than 12 percent; the margin of error k_2 for this 1.11 multiplier can then be taken as from −5 to +2 percent. For 10 percent of the towns there are no data and their population is estimated by means of regional ratios applied to pre-1568 figures; the corresponding margin of error is likely to be within ±5 percent.

If we apply these three margins of errors[11] to the 2.65 million value estimated by Borah and Cook, we have:

Lower bound = 2.65 (1 − 0.05)(1 − 0.06)(1 − 0.05)
= 2.2 million
Upper bound = 2.65 (1 + 0.05)(1 + 0.06)(1 + 0.02)
= 3.0 million)

The 1568 population can then be expressed as:

2.6 ± 0.4 million.

10   Cook and Borah, "The Indian Population of Central Mexico 1531–1610," *Ibero Americana*, XLIV (1960), 37–39, 39–45, 47. Borah and Cook, "The Population of Central Mexico in 1548," *Ibero Americana*, XLIII (1960), 65, 75–102.
11   B. H. Slicher van Bath, "The Calculation of the Population of New Spain, especially before 1570," *Boletin de Estudios Latinoamericanos y del Caribe*, XXIV (1978), 67–95, considers in great detail the derivation of the population figures from data on casados, and shows that in *some* cases the term casado seems to have been applied individually to the husband and wife, rather than to the head of family. Slicher van Bath indicates that a consequent reduction of about 15% may need to be applied to the Borah and Cook figures. Since an accurate estimate would require a re-examination of the sources, I have not included this reduction factor in the figures derived in this article.

The post-1568 population estimates[12]

For 1580 Borah and Cook estimate a population of 1.9 million, by applying to the 1568 estimates regional ratios for the years 1580/1568, based on information available for 141 towns. Because the standard error for these ratios is not shown, we shall assume the same margin of error, ±15 percent as for similar ratios 1532/1568 discussed below. By introducing this other multiplier and by using the 1568 range derived above, the 1580 population can be expressed as:

1.9 ± 0.6 million

The 1595 population is estimated in the same fashion, using a sample of 294 towns. Since standard errors vary in inverse proportion to the sample size, the sampling margin of error applied for 1580 can be reduced to ±10 percent. The 1595 figure can then be expressed as:

1.4 ± 0.3 million

The 1605 estimate is based on a very small sample of forty towns that are in fact civil congregations of remnants of other towns and "give a distinctly biased sample." Therefore it seems proper to ignore this estimate, which in any case does not contribute much to the overall picture.

The 1548 population estimate

For 1548 Borah and Cook estimate a value of 6.3 million on the basis of an analysis of the contemporary population survey "Suma de visitas de pueblos" (compilation of the reports on the visits to the towns and villages). The population derived directly from the Suma data, by using the multipliers already discussed for the 1568 estimate, amounts to 1.366 million. For the towns not included in the Suma, later values are projected to 1548 by using regional ratios, which raises the overall estimate to 2.939 million. Borah and Cook, however, maintain that this total includes only the tributary population and they introduce two further multipliers, each equal to 1.5, to account for calpulli non-tributaries and for mayeques. The resulting figure of 6.6 million

12 Cook and Borah, "Population 1531–1610," 47–49.

is then reduced to 6.3 million by corrections for special areas and categories.[13]

The assumption that nearly *all* the Suma records referred only to tributaries is responsible for well over half of the estimated population, and the validity of this assumption is therefore of crucial importance. Borah and Cook justify their assumption with three main arguments:

(a) The Suma figures are too low, to the extent that "the population of most towns shows a substantial increase between 1548 and 1568."

(b) The Suma inspectors would have been instructed to count tributaries only; fuller counts were due to zeal on the part of some inspectors.

(c) Some Suma reports state that non-tributary groups are not included in the given figures.[14]

However, Borah and Cook, using unadjusted Suma data, derive a global 1548 population figure (2.939 million) which is 13 percent *higher* than for 1568, and calculate regional ratios for 1548/1568 which in nine regions out of ten show a *decrease* in the 1568 figures. Therefore argument (a) applies only to a minority of Suma data and suggests that there was lack of uniformity in the methods of counting used for the Suma. The general increase of all the Suma data by 225 percent, as applied by Borah and Cook, would simply magnify such inconsistencies.

Argument (b) is also unconvincing, since Borah and Cook show in their analysis of the genesis of the Suma that it originated with two separate royal orders and that whereas the order of April 10, 1546 issued by Prince Philip (later Philip II), acting that time as regent for Spain, was concerned with tribute assessment, the order signed by Charles V on April 12, 1546 was concerned with the assignment of encomiendas (grants of Indians for their tribute and/or labor) and required a survey of Indian population and indeed of "the Indian towns of New Spain and of their qualities." In fact the first thirty-four visita reports, out of nearly ninety, contained no statement concerning the tribute paid. In any case,

13 Borah and Cook, "Population in 1548," esp. Table 14, 58–62. The final value is corrected in Cook and Borah, "Population 1531–1610," 111. The non-tributary calpulli included administrators, nobles, and free Indians assigned to their service and to the churches. The mayeques were similar to the serfs of medieval Europe.

14 Borah and Cook, "Population in 1548," 55–57.

a general survey of population would have been of great relevance even from the strictly tributary point of view, since only a few years later the Suma payment of tribute was made practically universal. This extension not only must have been in the wind well before the Suma visits, but indeed was already taking place under the increasing tributary pressure.[15]

Argument (c) refers to twenty Suma reports and although it proves that in *some* cases only existing tributaries were counted, it does not lend support to the thesis that this was the recommended and/or normal practice of the Suma inspectors. In conclusion, the arguments put forward by Borah and Cook do not support the assumption that all Suma records covered only the tributaries, but they make a convincing case that this must have happened in a large number of cases.

Of the 1.366 million figure derived directly from the Suma data, about 18 percent was taken from records (classified by Borah and Cook as of types A and D) that specified numbers of persons, or of persons "sin los muchachos" (excluding the children). There are no obvious grounds for suspecting that the inspectors did not mean what they said and excluded the non-tributaries: to include women and children just because they belonged to the family of a tributary, while excluding able-bodied men just because they were not (yet) subjected to tribute, would make little if any sense. There is no reason for assuming that the Suma was an early example of bureaucratic stupidity.

Another 31 percent of the estimate related to records (types B and E) mentioning several categories of people. In many of these records the number of houses was also given and often the number of "muchachos" was specified, suggesting that most of these records covered all of the population. This impression is much strengthened by a comparison made by Borah and Cook between three groups of counts of tributaries made a few years after the Suma and the corresponding Suma data. The average change was −10 percent for the first group, −4 percent for the second and an enormous −34 percent for the third group. Further examination shows that all the towns in the first group and eighteen out of twenty of those in the second group were of type C (i.e., where Suma data mentioned only one category of people),

---

15 *Ibid.*, 12–16, 21, 63. Cook and Borah, "Population 1531–1610," Table 3B.

whereas all the four towns in the third group were of type B. The natural explanation for the anomalous -34 percent is that these type B Suma records must have included the non-tributaries, omitted in the later tributary count.[16]

The available evidence suggests therefore that all Suma records of type A and D, and most of those of type B and E covered all of the population, whereas most of the type C records (51 percent of the estimate) omitted non-tributaries. This implies that the 1.366 million estimate can be split into two practically equal groups of 700,000 each, with a correction factor M_t for including the non-tributaries being applied to one group only; i.e., the total can be expressed as 700,000 $(1 + M_t)$.

The inclusion of the towns not covered in the Suma can be based on the assumption that their population and that of the towns included in the Suma were in the same ratio as in 1568, when the ratio was 0.83. The error introduced by this assumption cannot be estimated accurately, but a margin of ± 20 percent seems reasonable, giving a range of 0.66 to 1.0 for the ratio.[17]

The multiplier M_t corresponds to the product of the two correction factors for non-tributaries, taken by Borah and Cook as $1.5 \times 1.5 = 2.25$. The first 1.5 implies that one third of the calpulli were tribute exempted and is based on Suma data for eleven towns. However, nine of these towns were in Nueva Galicia, a region with special characteristics and probably no mayeques; the corresponding data are consequently of doubtful relevance to other areas with different social structure and in any case are likely to be indicative of the global, rather than of the inter-calpulli ratio between tributaries and non-tributaries. The remaining two towns would give a factor of 1.38.[18]

As for the mayeques, the second 1.5 factor is based on just six towns, with data referring to years from 1551 to 1578 and giving a mean of 28 percent and a standard error of ± 8 percent for the ratio of mayeques to total population (i.e., a range from

16 Borah and Cook, "Population in 1548," 69–70, 146. The figures for the Mixteca Alta (Cook and Borah, "The Population of the Mixteca Alta," *Ibero Americana*, L (1968), Table 1, column III) show also a regular correlation between the values of the population ratios and the A, B, and C categories.

17 A similar method is applied by Borah and Cook for 1518. The data used are taken from Cook and Simpson, "Population in Sixteenth Century," *Ibero Americana*, XXXI (1948), Appendix I.

18 Borah and Cook, "Population in 1548," Table 8, 74.

1.2 to 1.5 for the correction factor); a global official estimate of 10 percent for this ratio, given in 1563 for the full area of the Audiencia of Mexico, is disregarded for no clear reason.[19]

The evidence on which the two Borah and Cook multipliers (accounting for 3.5 of their 6.3 million estimate) are based is both scanty and uncertain. We shall assume a range of 1.5 to 2 for the global multiplier M_t, as suggested by the figures derived above, with a warning that this range is probably on the high side and too narrow in relation to the quality of the evidence. The conversion coefficients M_1 and M_2 used for 1568 are also applied to the Suma data; the corresponding margin of errors k_1 and k_2 (±0.06 and from −0.05 to 0.02) should therefore be included, and the estimate will be:

Lower bound = 700,000 (1 + 1.5)(1 + 0.66)(1 − 0.06)(1 − 0.05)
= 2.6 million

Upper bound = 700,000 (1 + 2.0)(1 + 1.0)(1 + 0.06)(1 + 0.02)
= 4.5 million

The population for 1548 can then be expressed as:

3.6 ± 0.9 million

The 1532 population estimate

Borah and Cook have estimated for 1532 a population of 16.87 million. This value is obtained by projecting the 1568 population figures, using regional ratios for the 1532/1568 populations derived for 219 towns. Borah and Cook have evaluated also the standard error of these ratios, which vary over a wide range from 8 to 40 percent. The global margin of approximation of this method will be within this range, and we shall assume a rather

19 *Ibid.*, Table 9, 71–73. The ratios used by Borah and Cook for non-tributaries have been criticized recently by William T. Sanders, "The Population of the Central Mexican Symbiotic Region, the Basin of Mexico, and the Teotihuacan Valley in the Sixteenth Century," in Denevan (ed.), *Native Population*, 98–101. His conclusions are that the tax-exempt classes were likely to represent in 1548 only 20–30% of the tributaries. However, Sanders mentions data for Izucar where non-tributaries were 34.8% of the census (i.e. $M_t = 1.53$) and seems to accept a ratio of 40% (i.e. $M_t = 1.66$) for Cholula. As I have applied the correction to the C type records only, I do not feel there is sufficiently strong evidence for altering the suggested range $M_t = 1.75 \pm 0.25$. A change in line with Sanders to, say, 1.45 ± 0.2 would give a 1548 population range of 3.2 ± 0.8 million.

optimistic value of ± 15 percent, expressed by a factor $k_s = (1 \pm 0.15)$.[20]

The really vital element, however, is the accuracy of the 1532 population figures on which these ratios are based. These figures do not arise from any actual count of people, but are derived from statements about the goods and services assessed as tribute for these towns. Each item in these statements is converted into a monetary equivalent value, which also takes into account the inflationary price movements of that period. We shall indicate by k_m and k_p the factors expressing the margin of error introduced by the monetary conversion and by the inflationary correction. The monetary value of the tribute (derived by adding the individual items) is converted into a number of casados through division by a monetary value representing the average quota per casado, estimated by Borah and Cook for the various years in question. We shall indicate by k_t the factor expressing the margin of error due to the quota estimate. The number of casados is finally converted into a population figure by means of the multipliers M_1 and M_2, which introduce the margin of error factors k_1 and k_2, as in the 1568 estimate. The global variation of the figure of 16.8 million estimated by Borah and Cook will consequently be:

$$16.8 \; k_s \; k_m \; k_p \; k_t \; k_1 \; k_2$$

where $k_s = (1 \pm 0.15)$, $k_1 = (1 \pm 0.06)$, and k_2 varies from $(1 - 0.05)$ to $(1 + 0.02)$.

The calculation to which k_m refers aims at arriving at a global monetary value equivalent to the multitude of goods and services mentioned in the tribute statements, taking into account quality differences, local and seasonal price variations, etc. Such calculations are similar to those needed to estimate economic aggregates in sectors outside the monetary market (for example, subsistence agriculture) or where free market pricing does not apply (for example, defense expenditure in the Soviet Union or China). In these contemporary estimates the approximation can be expected to be comparatively optimal, due to the familiarity of the goods and to the existence of well documented parallel markets elsewhere; even in these cases, however, the margin of error is large

20 Cook and Borah, "Population in 1531–1610," 17–32, 40, 47.

and an approximation of ±50 percent would not be considered unreasonable. The Borah and Cook estimate is far from such optimal conditions, because the evidence available for the period before the middle 1530s is minimal in quantity and spans a wide range of values. Nevertheless, we shall assume the optimal value of ±50 percent, i.e., $k_m = (1 \pm 0.5)$, which really expresses the potential accuracy of the method rather than the much poorer level that could be achieved in this case.[21]

The difficulties of inflation accounting are, unfortunately, realities with which we have become very familiar. Furthermore, it seems unlikely that tribute assessment faithfully reflected the price variations of the goods involved. An accurate evaluation of the margin of error is not possible, and we shall assume (once again rather optimistically) a margin of ±15 percent, i.e., $k_p = (1 \pm 0.15)$.[22]

The average quota per family is estimated by Borah and Cook at 1.5 reales per family, exclusive of comida (provision of foodstuffs) and house service. The application of a single quota figure rests on the assumption that there was a sufficient degree of uniformity in the tribute levy and that the number of inhabitants represented the main factor on which taxation was based. Borah and Cook admit that there is conclusive evidence that in this period "there undoubtedly was great variation from town to town in the quotas paid by tributary families." But soon after

---

21 Borah and Cook, "Price Trends of Some Basic Commodities in Central Mexico, 1531–1570," *Ibero Americana*, XL (1958), 4–49. The evidence consists of records of individual transactions for various types of goods. The records listed for the period up to 1535 are:

maize: only 6 records, with prices from 0/0/6 to 0/4/1 and 1/0/0 (Fig. 1, Table 1);

wheat: 7 records, with prices from 0/2/0 to 0/6/0 (Fig. 5, Table 2);

cloth (mantas): 4 records, with prices from 0/0/1.25 to 0/0/4.125; also 20 records for 1536 from 0/0/0.9 to 0/0/8.33 (Fig. 8, Table 4);

labor: 1 case in 1524 (0/0/0.5) and 2 in 1535 (0/0/1.5 and 0/0/6) (Fig. 12, Table 13);

other goods: usually one single record per commodity (Tables 3, 5–10).

Borah and Cook have derived trend lines extending from the 1520s to the 1570s. These lines are really determined by the large number of records for the later periods; for the early decades they can be considered as proper and useful visual aids for conveying a general impression of price movements, but would be extremely unreliable as a source of specific figures for estimates.

22 The Borah and Cook calculations are very sensitive to price variation. Maize, for instance, is taken from 3.4 reales/fanega in 1555 to 1.5 r/f in the 1530s; cacao from 20 to 6 pesos/carga in the same period (Cook and Borah, "Population 1531–1610," Table 2, 28–31).

they conclude that "the amount of tribute that could be extracted from the individual family was small and the variation in the amounts over the country was within a fairly narrow range," adding that the Spaniards would probably exact the maximum tribute that their subjects could bear. Even if this were true, it would not account for the wide differences in climate, soil fertility, etc., which would cause great variations in the quota per family even in such conditions. In any case, Borah and Cook report that in the early period the Spanish administration took the tribute paid to Montezuma as the norm and applied small reductions in order to gain the loyalty of the Indians; as for the pre-Conquest tributes, these were negotiated in the course of the conquest of the town and were then doubled every time there was a rebellion.[23]

Due to the lack of tributary uniformity, the application of a single average quota to all of the towns involved is prone to error. However, the situation is made much worse because the determination of this single quota value is based on minimal evidence: Borah and Cook were able to use only five values and three of these refer to the *same* town, where the tributary quota changed from 0.47 reales in 1526 to 1.45 in 1527 and to 2.09 in 1528, highlighting the weakness of the assumption that a reasonable level of uniformity existed. Borah and Cook have plotted these five values together with much later values for the 1550s and 1560s, and have calculated (on the basis of the later points) a straight line that should indicate the value of the quota for the various years. However, if this line were prolonged it would show a nil tribute in 1523, indicating that the margin of error must point toward considerably higher values of the 1532 quota. The size of the margin of error range can be evaluated by referring to a table of tribute rates in 1548 covering 100 towns; if we were to assume that the spread (but not the magnitude) of these values was the same as for 1532, the approximation obtained by taking a random sample of between two and five towns would be of the order ±50 percent. Since the value 1.5 cannot be lowered any

23 Cook and Borah, "Population in 1531-1610," 20-32. This figure of 1.5 reales per family should also account for non-tributaries, but no details are given. The sources quoted in this section seem to be silent on this point and the assumptions interpolated by Borah and Cook are, of necessity, vague and doubtful. Borah and Cook, "Population on the Eve of the Conquest," 60-71.

further, we shall assume a range from 1.5 to 3, stressing that this range is narrower than implied by the sampling error as well as not making any allowance for the error due to using a single quota value; the corresponding value of the factor k_t will vary from $(1 - 0.5)$ to $(1 + 0.0)$. Therefore:

Lower bound = 16.8 $(1 - 0.15)(1 - 0.5)(1 - 0.15)(1 - 0.5)$
$\qquad (1 - 0.06)(1 - 0.05) = 2.7$ million.
Upper bound = 16.8 $(1 + 0.15)(1 + 0.5)(1 + 0.15)(1 + 0)$
$\qquad (1 + 0.06)(1 + 0.02) = 35$ million.[24]

With such a wide range of variation it would be meaningless to take the average or any other value. The conclusion to be drawn is that this method, with the data that are available, does not allow a meaningful quantitative estimate and can only indicate that the population in 1532 was of several million. In the absence of other evidence, such information would have been of some value, but since we have estimates of reasonable accuracy for 1548, 1568, and later years, an extrapolation from those figures will be far more accurate than the direct calculation that has been attempted.

The pre-Conquest, 1518, population estimate

Borah and Cook have made two separate estimates for 1518. The first is based on the pictographic records of the Triple Alliance and arrives at a figure of 25.2 million; the second derives a figure of 27.65 million by extrapolating the estimates for later years.

The derivation from tributes   The description of the historical background on which this method is based gives an unusually clear and fascinating picture of the pre-Conquest tributary system and of how it has been untangled. Unfortunately, the attempt to derive a population figure from this information is even more prone to intrinsic error than the 1532 estimate.[25]

To start with, this method is really applied to only four regions out of eleven. For three other regions Borah and Cook

24 *Idem,* "Population in 1548," Table 2; Cook and Borah, "Population in 1531–1610," Table 1.
25 Borah and Cook, "Population on the Eve of the Conquest," 72–88. Cook and Borah, "Population in 1531–1610," Table 6.

simply add 10 percent to the corresponding 1532 figures; not only is this arbitrary but it also makes little sense since the authors postulate a greater change of population in just the two years 1532–1534. For another two regions a figure is derived by assuming that the population ratio between them and Region I was the same in 1518 and 1568; the figures derived for the 1532 estimate, however, show changes of 33 and 15 percent in the corresponding 1568 and 1532 ratios. For the last two regions the figures for 1568 are projected to 1518 on the basis of tribute data for just one province; furthermore, the authors add a warning that the calculations for this province are even more doubtful than usual. In conclusion, for these six regions (which account for about 10 million out of 25.2) the estimate is based on assumptions that are either arbitrary or of very low accuracy.

The tribute method, applied to the remaining four regions, is based on the interpretation of the pictographic tribute records; the logical steps are as follows:

— Translation of the pictograms into quantities of goods. We indicate by k_a the factor embodying the corresponding margin of error.

— Conversion of the tribute items into a global monetary value. The corresponding error factor can be taken as the same $k_m = (1 \pm 0.5)$ already discussed for 1532.

— This result is multiplied by the number of payments per year. According to Borah and Cook, this is liable to a possible error $k_b = (1 - 0.06)$, if "every 80 days" means four times a year.

— This result is divided by the value assumed for the family quota of tribute. The factor taken for 1532, $k_t = (1 - 0.5)$, is even more optimistic for this case.

— Multiplication by the average family size. This is taken as the average of 4.0, assumed by Cook and Simpson, and 5.0, as for present-day Mexico. The error factor can then be taken as $k_c = (1 \pm 0.11)$.

— Multiplication by the regional ratio needed for including the towns not covered by the tribute lists. These ratios are based on 1568 values; the assumption that they were the same in 1518 implies another error factor, k_e.

— Multiplication by 1.5 to include the non-tributary calpulli. For Region I, with 70 percent of the population in this group of regions, the result is multiplied again by 1.5 to include the mayeques. The overall effect is the same as multiplying by 2 the grand total for this group of regions. If we use the 1.5 to 2.0 range discussed for 1548, the margin of error factor, k_f, will vary from $(1 - 0.25)$ to $(1 + 0)$.

Therefore the variation of the Borah and Cook figure can be expressed as:

$$15.34 \; k_a \; k_m \; k_b \; k_t \; k_c \; k_e \; k_f$$

If we assume a very high accuracy of 5 percent for k_a and k_e, then:

Lower bound = $15.34 \; (1 - 0.05)(1 - 0.5)(1 - 0.06)(1 - 0.5)$
$(1 - 0.11)(1 - 0.05)(1 - 0.25) = 2.2$ million.
Upper bound = $15.34 \; (1 + 0.05)(1 + 0.5)(1 + 0)(1 + 0)$
$(1 + 0.11)(1 + 0.05)(1 + 0) = 28$ million.

As we have seen already, the accuracy of the estimate for the other group of regions is even smaller than this; the range of variation for the overall figure will be, therefore, between 3 and 50 million. It should also be emphasized that in the discussion of both the 1532 and the 1518 estimates we have usually assumed margins of error much lower than warranted. The conclusion is the same as for the 1532 estimate: the method used cannot provide a quantitative estimate when the multipliers involved are so many and so uncertain.

The Borah and Cook extrapolation   A major purpose of this extrapolation was to provide confirmation, by means of an independent method, for the 1518 figure derived from the tribute lists. However, as we have already pointed out, a large proportion of the 1518 results is derived from the 1532 and 1568 figures. Furthermore, even for the remaining portion, the calculation performed is essentially the same as for 1532 and most of the multipliers are either identical or similar to those derived for 1532 and 1548. In other words, the two methods are not fully independent but are closely related. Furthermore, Borah and Cook perform the extrapolation in a complex way, using a coefficient of population change ω. From its variation over short periods, its behavior in other periods can be estimated and used for the extrapolation. The margin of error of this method is very high even in the best conditions. In this case, very strangely, Borah and Cook have used this method on a sequence of values of ω derived not from actual data (which do not exist) but from numbers that they themselves have generated joining the 1532, 1548, and 1568 points with curves of their own choice. In conclusion, the credibility of the 1518 estimate is not increased by the apparent convergence of two estimates that are closely related and carry a margin of error that is unacceptably high.[26]

Extrapolation based on the new figures   The figures suggested in this article for the 1548–1595 population are plotted on a log-arithmic scale in Figure 1, together with the estimated values of

Fig. 1   Extrapolation to 1518 of the Post-Conquest Population Values Defined in this Article.

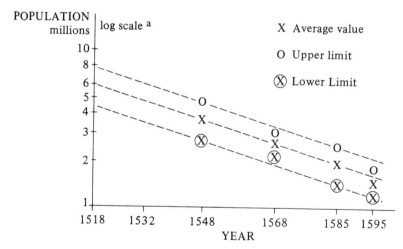

a   On a log. scale equal ratios are represented by equal distances. For example, in Fig. 1, the distance from 2.5 to 5 is the same as the distance from 5 to 10, since population doubles in both cases. On a log. scale a variable declining at a constant rate is represented by a straight line.

26   *Idem, Essays,* I, 73–118. I have already commented on these techniques in Zambardino, "Critique of David Henige, 'On the Contact Population of Hispaniola'," *Hispanic American Historical Review,* LVIII (1978), 706–707.

their upper and lower error bounds. The broken lines define a band of possible values, which when extrapolated to 1518 suggest a population in that year of around 6 million, with variation from 4.5 to over 8 million. As the process of extrapolation has an inherently wide margin of error, it would be acceptable to express the range of variation in rounder figures as: 5 to 10 million.

Extrapolation is always a dangerous and inaccurate technique, particularly when extended over a time span almost equal to the period for which data are available, and when the entity considered is likely to vary exponentially, rather than linearly, with respect to time. Even so, and provided that the large degree of variation of 2 to 1 is kept in mind, I have no doubt that the extrapolated figure of 6 million with range from 5 to 10 million has a far better level of intrinsic reliability than tribute derived figures for 1532 and 1518, and that it matches the evidence gathered and presented by Borah and Cook far more accurately than their estimate of 25 million. In what follows this new estimate is related to other evidence.

Alonso de Zorita's estimate   Alonso de Zorita, who served as a judge of the Audiencia of Mexico from 1556 to 1566, represents a contemporary source consistently supporting the Indians and highly critical of Spanish exactions. Borah and Cook quote him extensively and, in particular, they quote but do not take into account his statement, in 1566, that the population at that time was not one third of what it had been at the time of the Conquest. As the population estimated for 1568 is about 2.6 million, this statement implies a 1518 population of about 8 million, well within the range of 5–10 million.[27]

Clerical and military contemporary evidence   The available clerical evidence consists of estimates of baptisms by friars, whereas the military evidence is based on estimates of the strength of enemies and allies during the Conquest. Cook and Simpson made a detailed analysis of all the available evidence of these two types and derived a figure of 9 million for the pre-Conquest population. The range of variation inherent in this figure implies a wide overlap with our 5–10 million range.[28]

27 Borah and Cook, "Population in 1548," 5 (note 15). Alonso de Zorita, *Breve y sumaria relacion de los señores de la Nueva España* (Mexico City, 1942), 136.
28 Cook and Simpson, "Population in Sixteenth Century," 20–30, 30–38. Cook and

The 1957 Cook and Borah estimate In an article published in 1957, Cook and Borah considered sixty-four towns for which two population figures within the period 1552–1570 could be derived; the interval between the two figures varied from one to fifteen years. The raw average of all the depopulation rates was 3.8 percent; by applying this average rate to the Cook and Simpson 1565 estimate, Borah and Cook derived a figure of 25.3 million for 1520, adding however "the calculation is of theoretical significance only, and is presented simply as one possible way of approaching the problem." Furthermore, both the method and the reference figures used are superseded by the later works of Borah and Cook; in particular their revision of the population/tributaries ratio from 4 to 2.8 would imply a direct reduction from 25 to 17 million. Rather strangely, none of this is mentioned by Dobyns, who quotes extensively from the article.[29]

However, the figures for the sixty-four towns offer the opportunity for an independent check on the 1548 and 1518 esti-

---

Simpson concluded by accepting a figure of 11 million, but this was based on a comparison method with 1565 figures which Borah and Cook later found to be too high by 40 percent (Borah and Cook, "Population in 1548," 102). For a recent critique of the Cook and Simpson estimates, see Sanders, "Population of Symbiotic Region," 101–103, Table 4.1. Sanders maintains that estimates of this type tend to be too high. If the 9 million figure must be considered as an upper limit, this would make the agreement with the 5–10 million range that we have suggested very close indeed.

29 Cook and Borah, "The Rate of Population Change in Central Mexico, 1550–1570," *Hispanic American Historical Review*, XXXVII (1957), 463–470. Borah and Cook, "Population in 1548," 102. Henry F. Dobyns, "Estimating Aboriginal American Population," *Current Anthropology*, VII (1966), 396, 407. This article has been influential and it is unfortunate that its section on tribute payers' methods should have been based so heavily on the 1957 Cook and Borah estimate (which had been superseded by their later published studies) and on their 1963 article ("Population on the Eve of the Conquest") which, as we have shown, embodies their methodologically weakest estimate. It is also strange that Dobyns should find it surprising that the mortality figures over 40 years given by Bartolomè de Las Casas in 1541 exceed the aboriginal contact population estimated by Kroeber and Rosenblat. Alfred L. Kroeber, "Cultural and Natural Areas of Native North America," *University of California Publications in American Archeology and Ethnology*, XXXVIII (1939), 166; Angel Rosenblat, *La Poblacion Indigena y el Mestizaje* (Buenos Aires, 1954), I, 102. Apart from any considerations on the reliability of Las Casas (see: David Henige, "On the Contact Population of Hispaniola," *Hispanic American Historical Review*, LVIII [1978], 222–225), the life expectancy for a stable population could be defined as the number of years over which the aggregate number of deaths is equal to the size of the population. A life expectancy of 40 years would not be unreasonable for the sixteenth century even without the massive epidemics that swept the American continent. Therefore the number of deaths in the 40 years after the Conquest can be expected to be considerably larger than the original population.

mates. The raw average of depopulation rates used by Borah and Cook would be appropriate only if these rates had remained constant over the full period for all of the towns considered: this is most unlikely. If for each year we consider, instead, only the towns for which the data include that year, and estimate by interpolation the corresponding population, it is possible to arrive at a figure for the depopulation rate in each year. These rates cover a full cycle: from 5 percent in the early 1550s to around zero in the early 1560s, increasing again to 5 percent in the late 1560s. The average over the whole period is 2.8 percent. If this rate is applied to the 2.6 million estimated for 1568, we obtain 9.1 million for 1518 and 4.4 million for 1548, both within the ranges proposed in this article but well outside the Borah and Cook estimates.[30]

Other recent analyses and estimates   Sanders has presented a detailed criticism of the Borah, Cook and Simpson estimates in which he focuses on the historical validity of many of their premises and data. We have concentrated on the numerical methods applied by Borah and Cook, complementing their work by the introduction of appropriate margins of error. As these two studies were carried out independently and from different points of view, it is interesting to note the considerable measure of agreement in their conclusions: criticism of the direct link between tribute and population, abandonment of the 1532 and 1518 estimates, and reduction of the 1548 estimate. Similar observations apply to the criticism of the Borah and Cook estimates published recently by Henige, and on which I have commented elsewhere.[31]

30 The interpolation was carried out separately for each town, assuming a constant rate of change from the initial to the final population over the corresponding period. The data could yield even more information by more sophisticated processing and it is hoped to make this the subject for another article. Another set of calculations for checking the 1518 estimate is published in Cook and Borah, "On the Credibility of Contemporary Testimony on the Population of Mexico in the Sixteenth Century," *Homenaje a Roberto J. Weitlaner* (Mexico City, 1966), 229–239. The data used, however, cannot be considered as contemporary evidence as they consist of answers to a questionnaire returned as late as 1577–1585. Furthermore, the method of comparison applied by Borah and Cook is only one of the many that could be pursued. If, for instance, we were to compare the global figures tabulated by the authors, instead of comparing the average of the individual differences, the new figure would be 30 percent higher than the Borah and Cook estimate instead of 8.6 lower, as they claimed.

31 Sanders, "Population of Symbiotic Region," 77–150, esp. 122–123 for the main

Sanders followed his critique with an estimate of the population of a "Central Symbiotic Region" around the Basin of Mexico. This estimate was based largely on an undated census document giving two population figures for each district. With two exceptions, one set of figures was approximately double the other. Sanders has assumed that the smaller figures refer to the 1550s and the larger ones to the 1530s. Thus he arrived at a figure for 1519 of 2.6 to 3.1 million, as against 6.4 million estimated by Borah and Cook. Although the assumption made by Sanders was reasonable, it seems risky to base so much of the estimate on it. I found the regularity reported by Sanders in the ratio of the two sets of figures somewhat strange, since population figures show wider and wilder variations even over relatively small areas. At any rate, if the Sanders reduction of the Borah and Cook figures were to be applied throughout central Mexico, the global 1519 population would be 10.2 to 12.2 million.[32]

The population figures that have emerged from our discussion of the Borah and Cook estimates are as follows:

1518	5	to	10	million
1548	3.6	± 0.9		"
1568	2.6	± 0.4		"
1585	1.9	± 0.6		"
1595	1.4	± 0.3		"

These figures are based *exclusively* on the evidence used and published by Borah and Cook. They are not based on any new data or on a re-examination of primary sources. The range of variation of the results is an essential component of the result itself. Unless this range is reasonably small, the meaningfulness and usefulness of a calculated result taken in isolation is minimal; indeed, such an isolated value could be very misleading and lead to completely unwarranted conclusions.

If we compare our figures with those estimated by Borah and Cook, it is clear that there is hardly any difference for the 1568–1595 period; the small ranges of variation enhance the reli-

---

assumption, Table 4.9, Fig. 4.4 for the summary of results. Henige, "On the Contact Population of Hispaniola," 217–237; for my commentary and Henige's reply, *Hispanic American Historical Review*, LVIII (1978), 700–712.

32 Sanders, "Population of Symbiotic Region," 122–123, 132–136.

ability of the Borah and Cook estimates. The first large difference appears for 1548 and it is due to a more restricted application of the original hypothesis by Borah and Cook that the Suma reports omit non-tributaries. Without this hypothesis the Suma would have remained almost useless; our alteration consists of applying this hypothesis selectively to a specific category of Suma data, using the categorization introduced by Borah and Cook. The major result of our discussion of the Borah and Cook estimates is the abandonment of their 1532 and 1518 figures: a method of calculation producing a range of 15 to 1 is obviously useless for a quantitative estimate. Our discussion underlines the unreliability of the multipliers method for any calculation involving more than very few and very accurate multipliers.

Finally, we can consider the new estimates for the pre-Conquest population. The rate of depopulation implied by the 5–10 million estimate for 1518 is about 2 ± 0.5 percent per year over the sixty-seven years to 1585. Since there must have been violent oscillations, corresponding to outbreaks of epidemics and to partial recovery, the depopulation rate must have been much higher at various times and places. If we consider that the present day population explosion refers to a worldwide rate of population increase of about 2 percent per annum (U.N. estimate for 1963/1972), the depopulation of central Mexico in the sixteenth century can still be considered as a population implosion of catastrophic magnitude and duration. The 25 million estimate implies the doubling of this already enormous average rate of depopulation, raising this demographic catastrophe to a level that is almost beyond our grasp, where depopulation of cataclysmic intensity has become a normal process lasting nearly a century. Furthermore, the 25 million figure implies that this extraordinary depopulation was preceded by another extraordinary demographic feat that pushed the population density to levels higher than anywhere else at that time. Such a sequence of extraordinary events is possible, but the evidence would need to be beyond reasonable doubt before it could be accepted. I think the discussion developed in this article shows that this cannot be the case.

The range of 5 to 10 million suggested in this article is nothing more than an extrapolated range from the 1548–1595 estimates. Hence, it suffers from the pitfalls of any extrapolation, particularly from its dependence on the assumption that trends observed in a given period continued unchanged over another time stretch of similar duration. New evidence could show that such an assumption was entirely false. Until this happens, however, this range of values represents, in my opinion, the best estimate that it is possible to derive from the available data for central Mexico.

Francis J. Brooks

Revising the Conquest of Mexico: Smallpox, Sources, and Populations

Embedded in the received story of the "Conquest of Mexico" are two questionable assertions. The first is that the population of central Mexico in 1519 was approximately 25 million people. The second is that these people were struck in 1520 by smallpox and, possibly, by other diseases; and that as a result perhaps one-third of them died. The first assertion has been questioned without noticeably affecting the confidence of those who continue to make it. The second has not been questioned although there are indications that historians are not too happy about it.

The two assertions are not unrelated. If the population in 1519 were five times larger than it had once been thought to be, then our perceptions of the strength and complexity of the Aztec polity should be fundamentally restructured as well. More crucial, however, is the dimension of the demographic collapse revealed in the proportion between the figures of c. 25 million in 1519 and c. 1 million in 1600. A 96 percent drop in so large a population was, literally, unheard of and, if true, is unique in the history of the world. No merely human slaughter could account for such a catastrophe, even allowing that the killing was abetted by anomie and loss of the will to live on the part of the victims. Some visitation or affliction of God or of Nature must be invoked to account for such wholesale mortality. Smallpox—Macaulay's "most terrible of all the ministers of death"—seems precisely to fit the case.[1] If smallpox did attack large groups of indigenous

Francis J. Brooks is Senior Lecturer in History, Flinders University, Adelaide, South Australia. He is the author of "Disease and Population in the Conquest of Mexico: Twenty-Five Years of Scholarship," in *idem* and Martin J. Scurrah (eds.), *Iberia and Latin America: The Last Twenty-Five Years, 1966–1991* (Adelaide, Australia, 1992), 45–61.

The author acknowledges the financial assistance of the Flinders University Research Board. He thanks Philippa Mein Smith, Robin Haines, Ralph Shlomowitz, Greg Tobin, John Mallon, David Arnold, Kerry Cox, Bill Thorpe, Pauline Brooks, Eric Richards, Brian Dickey, and Hanna Law for their intellectual assistance.

1   Thomas Babington Macaulay, *The History of England from the Accession of James the Second* (1849; London, 1889), II, 498.

people, who were unprepared and nonimmune, we have been led to expect that millions of them would have died. The plausibility of the total story is rounded out by invoking the devastating impact of smallpox to explain first, why the Conquistadores were not annihilated after their expulsion from Tenochtitlan in 1520 and second, why so few Spaniards were able to conquer so many Aztecs.

Almost every element of this received account is false, epidemiologically improbable, historiographically suspect, or logically dubious. The population of Mexico in 1519 was almost certainly nowhere near as large as 25 million. Smallpox was present but at what time it was introduced is problematical and some of the descriptions, which are supposedly of smallpox, are either imaginary or of some other disease. Accounts of the course of the disease are difficult to square with its known epidemiology. Some of the sources have extraneous reasons for describing the disease which imposes great caution in interpreting them. Others, purporting to be original, either copy earlier sources or are unwittingly influenced by them. Some have internal contradictions. Finally, many of the inferences made from this somewhat problematical material are logically flawed.

Up to the end of World War II, most estimates of the preconquest population of Mexico—they were in only the widest sense "calculations"—were in the range of 3 million to 6 million. In 1948, Cook and Simpson calculated that the preconquest population of Central Mexico was 11 million. Subsequent revisions by Borah and Cook, based on calculations derived from censuses of the mid-sixteenth century and from tribute records of the preconquest period, settled on a figure for 1518 of 25.2 million. In 1948 the size of the Indian population at its nadir was estimated by Cook and Simpson to be about 2 million. By 1963, Borah and Cook had revised that figure downward to around 1 million in 1600 (See Table 1).[2]

2 Alfred L. Kroeber, *Cultural and Natural Areas of Native North America* (Berkeley, 1939), 166; *idem*, "Native American Population," *American Anthropologist*, XXXVI (1934), 1–25; Angel Rosenblat, *La población indígena de América desde 1492 hasta la actualidad* (Buenos Aires, 1945); Julian H. Steward, "Native Populations of South America," in *idem* (ed.), *Handbook of South American Indians* (Washington, D.C., 1949), V, 656; Sherburne F. Cook and Lesley B. Simpson, *The Population of Central Mexico in the Sixteenth Century* (Berkeley, 1948); Woodrow Wilson Borah and Cook, *The Aboriginal Population of Central Mexico in 1548* (Berkeley, 1960); *idem, The Indian Population of Central Mexico, 1531–1610* (Berkeley,

Table 1   Estimate of Population of Mexico, 1518–1603

YEAR	POPULATION IN MILLIONS
1518	25.2
1532	16.8
1548	6.3
1568	2.65
1585	1.9
1595	1.375
1603	1.075

SOURCE   Woodrow Wilson Borah and Sherburne F. Cook, *Essays in Population History: Mexico and the Caribbean* (Berkeley, 1971), I, xiii.

Fig. 1   Extrapolation to 1518 of the Post-Conquest Population

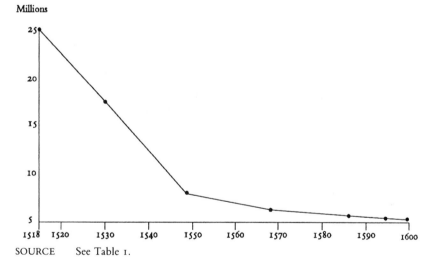

SOURCE   See Table 1.

In 1966, Dobyns, taking the work of the Berkeley historical demographers as proven, reviewed the available techniques and then estimated that the continental population in 1492 was be-

1960); *idem, The Aboriginal Population of Central Mexico on the Eve of the Spanish Conquest* (Berkeley, 1963).

tween 90 million and 112 million. In 1971, Borah and Cook turned their attention to Hispaniola. In the most skeptically received of all their essays in demographic history, they argued that there was firm evidence and sound logic which pointed to a figure of 8 million in 1492. Given that most earlier historians were extremely skeptical even of Bartolomé de Las Casas' apparently absurd estimate of 3 million, this was grandstanding in the great tradition.[3]

There have since been a number of studies of other areas which have uncovered evidence of large-scale depopulation throughout the course of the sixteenth century. Yet, in two respects the Borah and Cook figures for central Mexico have taken on a life of their own. First, they have sometimes been discounted by as much as 50 percent and still retained considerable authority. As Denevan comments: ". . . scholars who will not accept 25,000,000 find figures between 10,000,000 and 15,000,000 not unreasonable." Notwithstanding the degree of "más o menos," they continue to be taken by some historians as a firm analog for discussions of historical demography elsewhere. Second, the whole exercise has been remarkably unproductive of any advances in our knowledge of either preconquest or postconquest society. Given the enormous differences in the order of magnitude between these conclusions and earlier estimates, we would have expected that all previous notions about the impact of colonial rule, about the deculturation of the indigenes, and about the relative blame to be attached to labor, land-grabbing, disease, and anomie would have been reexamined and fundamentally recast. Enormous advances have been made in the past thirty years in our understanding both of Aztec society and of Indian life under early colonial rule. But the only new conclusions that have been reached as a direct result of the Borah and Cook figures have been concerned with virgin soil populations and the epidemiology of infectious diseases in nonimmune populations. It is these that must be questioned. In contrast, the conclusions of the physical anthropologists, derived from the carrying capacity of the available

3 Henry F. Dobyns, "Estimating Aboriginal American Population: An Appraisal of Techniques with a New Hemispheric Estimate," *Current Anthropology*, VII (1966), 395–416; Cook and Borah, *Essays in Population History: Mexico and the Caribbean* (Berkeley, 1971), I, 376–410; Bartolomé de Las Casas, *Apologética Historia* (Madrid, 1958), III, 65; *idem, Historia de las Indias* (Madrid, 1957), II, 217; III, 51–52.

agricultural technology, still point stubbornly to a total figure for Mexico in 1500 in the 5 to 10 million range.[4]

Not only has the whole edifice proven less than productive but its very foundations have been vigorously challenged. The mathematical methods by which the figure for 1548 was calculated, it has been suggested, involved unjustified assumptions and problematic multipliers. In a detailed analysis of both the evidence and the mathematical methods used by Borah and Cook, Zambardino argues that their figure of 6.3 million should more realistically be somewhere between 2.6 million and 4.5 million, or in precise statistical terms, 3.6 million ±0.9 million. Sanders, from the perspective of a physical anthropologist, reaches a similar conclusion. "The weakest argument in the studies conducted by Borah and Cook on sixteenth-century demography lies in their statistical manipulations to arrive at a figure for the tax-exempt population in 1548."[5]

The earlier estimates for 1532 and 1518 are even more problematical. The 1532 figure was based on statements about goods and services assessed for tribute in 219 towns. These goods and services are given an equivalent monetary value which is then adjusted for inflation during the period 1532–1568. This total monetary value is divided by the average quota per *casado* (married men who were liable to tribute) to give a total number of tributaries for these towns. Further multipliers are used to turn tributaries into population by a factor for each tributary household and a further factor to take account of nontributary population. Finally, the total population is calculated from the sample of 219 towns.

---

4 The literature has been comprehensively reviewed by Linda A. Newson, "Indian Population Patterns in Colonial Spanish America," *Latin American Research Review*, XX (1985), 41–74. See also *idem, The Cost of Conquest: Indian Decline in Honduras under Spanish Rule* (Boulder, 1986); *idem, Indian Survival in Colonial Nicaragua* (Norman, 1987). Cf. Dean R. Snow and Kim M. Lanphear, "European Contact and Indian Depopulation in the Northeast: The Timing of the First Epidemics," *Ethnohistory*, XXXV (1988), 15–33; William M. Denevan in *idem* (ed.), *The Native Population of the Americas in 1492* (Madison, 1976), 80; William T. Sanders, "The Population of the Central Mexican Symbiotic Region, the Basin of Mexico, and the Teotihuacan Valley in the Sixteenth Century," in Denevan (ed.), *The Native Population*, 85–150.
5 Rudolph A. Zambardino, "Mexico's Population in the Sixteenth Century: Demographic Anomaly or Mathematical Illusion?" *Journal of Interdisciplinary History*, XI (1980), 1–27; Sanders, "The Population," 99.

The possible margin of error for each of these multipliers is discussed by Zambardino and in each case he adopted a conservative estimate. The conclusion of his analysis was that the lower bound of the population in 1532 was 2.7 million and the upper, 35 million. Obviously, any average is meaningless. His conclusion was that "this method, with the data that are available, does not allow a meaningful quantitative estimate." The figure for the 1518 population, derived from preconquest tribute assessments, yields a similar result: somewhere between 3 million and 50 million. This conclusion gives added point to Sanders' comment on Borah and Cook's procedures. "Their discussion of the use of this material to arrive at population estimates is particularly puzzling since the authors provide us with a detailed and excellent analysis of all the problems and objections to such use. Their own analysis leads the reader to the almost inescapable conclusion that it cannot be done!"[6]

In the thirteen years since Zambardino's article appeared, there has been no serious attempt to reconsider the demographic and epidemiological history of the conquest period in Mexico in light of these extraordinary criticisms. Typically, all that is allowed is that there is some controversy over the Borah and Cook figures but that, nevertheless, everyone agrees that there was a sharp drop in the population. If, however, we were to follow Zambardino's suggestion and extrapolate from the 1568 and later figures (which are much more complete and reliable) back to 1518 we reach a figure within the 5 to 10 million range (See Figure 2). This number matches the results suggested by more traditional historical demographers such as Rosenblat and it is compatible with the reconstructions by physical anthropologists based on the known agricultural technology and carrying capacity of the land. All of these suggest a figure within the 5 to 10 million range, with the lower figure more probable than the higher. Given the absence of wheels, beasts of burden, and iron implements, this downward adjustment does not seem unwarranted.

Zambardino's revisionism is supported by Sanders. The estimate for 1548, although flawed, is probably not completely awry. Much more unlikely is "the extraordinary steepness of the curve between 1519 and 1540." It is the early and catastrophic

6 Zambardino, "Mexico's Population," 18; Sanders, "The Population," 112.

Fig. 2 Population of Mexico, 1518–1603

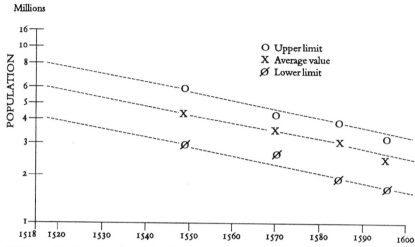

NOTE   Based on Borah and Cook's estimates of population for 1595, 1585, 1568, and Zambardino's adjusted figure for 1548 with upper and lower limits; drawn on a logarithmic scale.

SOURCE   Rudolph A. Zambardino, "Mexico's Population in the Sixteenth Century: Demographic Anomaly or Mathematical Illusion?" *Journal of Interdisciplinary History*, XI (1980), 21.

collapse of the population to which it is so difficult to give credence. Such a collapse is "all the more surprising since the first major epidemic occurred in the 1540s and an equally severe one occurred in the 1570s. One would expect a slow decline between 1519 and 1540 and then a rapid increase in the curve between 1540 and 1595." Yet catastrophe is precisely what the large estimates of aboriginal population must invoke. It was that catastrophic collapse which caught the imagination of historians in the 1960s. It is catastrophe which was at the core of the anti-Columbus polemic in 1992.[7]

Criticisms of the assertion of sudden and massive collapse leave intact the reality of depopulation over the duration of the century. From 5 million to 1 million is still an 80 percent drop. But such criticisms do raise the question of what we are to make

7   *Ibid.*, 120.

of the accounts of massive mortality, of 50 percent or more, in a smallpox pandemic starting in 1520. From Motolinía, Gómara, and Bernal Díaz through Clavijero, Prescott, and Bancroft to Dobyns, Crosby, Hopkins, and MacNeill, the unquestioned assertion is that smallpox killed millions of nonimmune indigenes, and that the conquest of Mexico was achieved by the *orthopoxvirus, variola major* to a degree which makes the role of the Conquistadores almost incidental. "The disease exterminated a large fraction of the Aztecs and cleared a path for the aliens to the heart of Tenochtitlan and to the founding of New Spain. . . . The miraculous triumphs of [the] *conquistador . . .* are in large part the triumphs of the virus of smallpox."[8]

The newly imported disease was no ordinary infection. According to Prescott, it rampaged through the country "sweeping over the land like fire over the prairies, smiting down prince and peasant." It bestrode the continent from Atlantic to Pacific "leaving its path strewn with the dead bodies of the natives, who, in the strong language of a contemporary, perished in heaps like cattle stricken with the murrain." The contemporary was Toribio de Benavente, a Franciscan known as Motolinía, a key figure in the historiography of smallpox in Mexico. Bancroft's prose is less elegant than Prescott's, but on smallpox he is no less graphic. He also introduced a theme of racial superiority into his account. He was neither the first nor the last to do so.

> At hand even now, coming to the assistance of the magnificent Cortés, civilization's pride and pet for the moment, is another ally of civilization, more terrible than horses, bloodhounds, gunpowder or steel. At the time of Narváez' departure for Cuba [*sic*], smallpox was raging. . . . The terrible force of the first attacks of epidemics is well known, and it has been advocated, with apparent truth, that the diseases of a strong people fall with particular force on weaker races. [The disease crossed from the Atlantic to the Pacific] smiting high and low, rich and poor. For sixty days, according to the native records, the *hueyzahuatl,* or great pest, raged here with such virulence as to fix itself a central point in their chronology. In most

8 Bernal Diaz del Castillo (trans. Alfred Percival Maudslay), *The True History of the Conquest of New Spain* (London, 1912), 218–219; Alfred W. Crosby, *Ecological Imperialism: The Biological Expansion of Europe, 900–1000* (Cambridge, 1986), 201; William H. McNeill, *Plagues and Peoples* (London, 1979), 192.

districts, says Motolinía, over half the population died, leaving towns almost deserted and in others the mortality was appalling.[9]

The key to a plausible explanation for these almost incredible reports is Bancroft's remark about "the terrible force of the first attacks of epidemics," which strike what modern historians of epidemiology call "virgin soil populations." Virgin soil epidemics are defined by Crosby as "those in which the populations at risk have had no previous contact with the diseases that strike them and are therefore immunologically almost defenseless. . . . In theory, the initial appearance of these diseases is as certain to have set off deadly epidemics as dropping lighted matches into tinder is certain to cause fires."[10]

The logic which moves the argument from the given fact of 10 to 30,000 years without contact between two groups of the human race to a massive mortality rate once contact has occurred has three strands of unequal cogency. The first is evolutionary. Over the millennia pathogens and their human hosts have necessarily arrived at a balance such that neither eliminates the other. Immunity or, at least, enhanced capacity for resistance is inherited, it is argued, by new generations. Infants and children with genes that make them more susceptible are more likely to die. Over time, this enables the host species to breed offspring more capable of sustaining an attack of the disease, and hence of developing an immunity to subsequent attacks. These offspring may then pass on, if not acquired immunity, at least the capacity to develop one's own immunity.

The evolutionary argument has that cogent elegance one recognizes in the essays of Gould. The World Health Organization (WHO) report, *Smallpox and Its Eradication,* is impressed by it. "It seems likely that a disease as lethal as smallpox must have exerted some selection for more resistant genotypes within populations in which it has been endemic for centuries." However, its authors are forced to conclude that experiments done to determine a genetic effect were "unconvincing" although they "do not exclude

9   William Hickling Prescott, *History of the Conquest of Mexico* (1843; New York, 1970), bk. IV, chap. VI, 482; Hubert Howe Bancroft, *History of Mexico* (San Francisco, 1883), I, 541–542.
10   Crosby, "Virgin Soil Epidemics as a Factor in the Aboriginal Depopulation in America," *William and Mary Quarterly,* XXXIII (1976), 289–290.

the possibility that a selection of more resistant genotypes had indeed occurred."[11]

Differences in susceptibility to some diseases between different racial groups are well-known. The WHO report points to case-fatality rates in India which were significantly higher than those typically found in southeast Asia, southern Africa, and South America. In principle, therefore, it is possible that the aboriginal inhabitants of America were more susceptible to smallpox than were Europeans, Africans, or Asians. Yet, while possible, it cannot be assumed. The empirical foundation on which such an assumption might be based is not strong. What evidence there is suggests "that native Americans have no special susceptibility to Old World diseases that cannot be attributed to environmental influence and probably never did have." As Newman puts it: "there is mounting evidence that American Indians were no more susceptible to most of these infectious disease imports than other populations where these diseases had not struck within the lifetime of the people." What led epidemiologists to suggest "that the Amerindians, an unexposed population when smallpox was first introduced into the Americas, were more susceptible than unvaccinated whites or negroes" was the conclusions not of epidemiology but of historians. Both Dixon and the authors of the WHO report cited the accounts of the first epidemic in Mexico as evidence that an inexperienced population did suffer significantly higher mortality than does one where the disease has previously occurred. The judgment of such expert epidemiologists is not lightly to be ignored. Yet the sources they cited—Stearn and Stearn, Crosby, and Hemming—ultimately rely not on modern epidemiology but on sources such as Motolinía and Díaz whose reliability it is precisely the purpose of this paper to call into question. The conclusions of the historians are problematical. Assertions by twentieth-century epidemiologists about sixteenth-century epidemics when they are based on those problematical conclusions must themselves be no less moot. Thus, historians who draw conclusions from "present day knowledge of the impact of smallpox . . . on people without previous immunities"

---

11 Stephen Jay Gould, *The Flamingo's Smile: Reflections in Natural History* (New York, 1985); *idem, The Panda's Thumb: More Reflections in Natural History* (New York, 1980); Frank Fenner et al., *Smallpox and Its Eradication* (Geneva, 1988), 195; Murdo MacLeod, *Spanish Central America: A Socioeconomic History* (Berkeley, 1973), 41.

are in danger of committing a concealed but very dangerous form of *petitio principii*.[12]

The second strand of the logic connecting virgin soil populations to massive mortality on the first impact of a new infectious disease is the argument that since all of the population is susceptible all will get the disease at the same time. In contrast to groups which have experienced the disease before, all ages will be infected, young vigorous adults no less than infants and the aged. The third strand is the observed phenomenon that in some new infectious diseases it is precisely the strongest group, the young adults, who succumb in disproportionate numbers. Both of these arguments concern the functions of the adult providers in the

12 Crosby, "Virgin Soil Epidemics," 291; Marshall T. Newman, "Aboriginal New World Epidemiology and Medical Care, and the Impact of Old World Disease Imports," *American Journal of Physical Anthropology*, XLV (1976), 671; Fenner et al., *Smallpox*, 195. One cannot rule out the possibility for the sixteenth century of devastating epidemics with unusually high mortality rates. Historians, however, are concerned not with what might have occurred but with what did occur, or, rather, what the evidence suggests did occur. It is illuminating to notice the precise reasons for which the leading experts on smallpox accept the stories of massive mortality in sixteenth-century America. "In the early outbreaks in Mexico and other countries, it was stated that about one-half of the population died . . . ," Cyril W. Dixon, *Smallpox* (London, 1962), 325. "Although racial differences in susceptibility probably did exist, they were never convincingly demonstrated . . . However, it is impossible to read the accounts of smallpox among the indigenous inhabitants of the Americas (North America: Stearn and Stearn, 1945; Mexico: Crosby, 1967; Peru: Hemming, 1970; Brazil: Hemming, 1978) without suspecting that the Amerindians, an unexposed population when smallpox was first introduced into the Americas, were more susceptible than unvaccinated whites or Negroes," Fenner et al., *Smallpox*, 195. E. Wagner Stearn and Allen E. Stearn, *The Effect of Smallpox on the Destiny of the Amerindian* (Boston, 1945); Crosby, "Conquistador y Pestilencia: The First New World Pandemic and the Fall of the Great Indian Empires," *Hispanic American Historical Review*, XLVII (1967), 321–343; John Hemming, *The Conquest of the Incas* (London, 1970); *idem, Red Gold: The Conquest of the Brazilian Indians* (London, 1978); Diaz, *True History*, 218–219.

Their evidence is the historical record, not modern epidemiology. Yet, even the worst of modern epidemics are orders of magnitude less than what is asserted to have happened in Mexico. One of the most explosive occurred in Bangladesh in 1972 and 1973. The population was about 70 million, the density, 486 per square kilometer. The 25 million people who are claimed to have been living in Mexico in 1519 were at the most about 30 persons per square kilometer, or more than 16 times less dense than was the population in Bangladesh in 1972. In 1972 and 1973 it is estimated that 91,415 and 81,906 cases, respectively, occurred. It is impossible to know the number of susceptibles, but it was probably between 10% and 20% (15% of the total population is about 10 million). Hence less than 1% of the susceptible population was infected in 1972 and in 1973, and about 0.16% of the susceptible population died of smallpox in each year (0.16% of the putative 25 million in Mexico in 1520 is about 40,000, not 3.5 million). Fenner, et al., *Smallpox*, 812, 824, 847.

community. They are, however, logically distinct and need to be examined separately.

Smallpox is not a cloud of infection that descends from on high. It is caused by a virus and there is no other carrier than the human smallpox victim. Only persons in the eruptive stage of the disease can infect others. Since such persons are likely to be immobile, and even recumbent, they cannot carry the disease very far. The virus is attached to droplets coughed, sneezed, breathed, or spat out by sick persons. Anyone in the same room as a smallpox victim will breathe in the virus and many, if they are not immune, are likely to contract the disease themselves. Other routes of infection, such as the conjunctiva, skin lesions (other than direct inoculation), or infected food, are not important. The WHO report concluded: "There is no evidence that infection ever occurred via the alimentary tract in smallpox." The virus can adhere to clothes and to scabs shed from dried-up pustules, but will not infect someone else unless breathed in. As the virus organisms tend to fall to the ground, they are a real potential source of new infection but an extremely inefficient one. Aside from droplets breathed in, infection is possible but it has a probability of less than 1 percent.[13]

As a result, and despite all the exaggerated language of it whip-sawing up and down the continent, spreading like wildfire, or going on the rampage, smallpox in the real world tends to infect only people who are in the same house or in the same hospital. Millar, a member of the WHO Smallpox Eradication Campaign Executive Committee wrote: "The communicability of smallpox is relatively low in comparison to other common viral infections such as measles and chickenpox. Perhaps this relates to the rapid settling of the relatively large infective particle." Clearly, that settling is one of the reasons for the slow spread of the disease. A further factor must be the behavior of infected persons, which distinguishes smallpox from milder eruptive fevers like measles and chickenpox. Persons infected with measles can usually move around and infect others for a significant time, making schools and other public places such efficient propagators

13 On the modes of infection and their limitations, see Dixon, *Smallpox,* 170–186; Fenner, et al., *Smallpox,* 183.

of the disease. Persons with smallpox usually do not, and often, cannot move around.[14]

For this reason, in a closely knit community, one, for instance, that shares a common dwelling, everyone might well catch the disease at the same time. In such a case no one would be healthy enough to nurse the sick or even to gather food. When this happens mortality might be high not just from the disease but from secondary infections and hunger as well. In a larger population, however, even a village with multiple dwellings, the spread of the disease through the community may be slow enough to allow the first victims to recover well before everyone caught it. The experience of the WHO eradication team was that "smallpox sometimes took several generations of infection to spread through quite small populations." In such cases continuity of food supply would be much less problematical.[15]

There are hazards in trying to determine the behavior of smallpox in sixteenth-century Mexico on the basis of knowledge acquired in the eradication campaign in the twentieth. In that campaign, in all communities where epidemiological patterns were observed, there were always a number, and probably a frequently underestimated number, of people with immunity acquired from vaccination, variolation, or an earlier attack of the disease. Within closed communities the disease surely spread more quickly in sixteenth-century Mexico than it did in twentieth-century Ethiopia. Yet, what is at issue is not so much the small communities as the total population. In order to demonstrate the likelihood of a rapid and extensive spread, we would have to show the mechanisms by which the disease was carried rapidly from one community to another. Bathing would have been important only in the immediate community. There were no customs such as showing off the diseased child to relatives or handling the diseased corpse. By definition, there were no cultural customs in Mexico in 1520 connected with smallpox. Again, just as a putative greater susceptibility is possible but cannot be assumed, its rapid spread across the whole population must be

14 J. Donald Millar, "Smallpox, Vaccinia and Cowpox," in Paul D. Hoeprich (ed.), *Infectious Diseases* (Hagerstown, 1972), 815–823.
15 Fenner, et al., *Smallpox,* 201.

demonstrated by means of evidence and not simply inferred from a modern epidemiological pattern.

The third element of the argument adds a possible immunological quirk that needs to be examined. In some new infectious diseases young adults succumb in disproportionate numbers. Burnet observed that in the great influenza epidemic of 1918/19 the graph of age-specific mortality showed an unexpected bulge for fifteen to twenty-five year olds and twenty-five to thirty-five year olds. He concluded: "The young adult in full physiological vigour is less easily infected and deals rapidly with local infections, but in the absence of a pre-existing immunity is liable to be overwhelmed by his own too vigorous reactions to general infections." This unusual pattern of age-specific mortality was picked up by Crosby. He asserted that it was the fate of the Arawaks in 1493 and 1495 that "all or almost all of these victims seem to have been young adults, usually the most resilient members of our species—except in the case of unfamiliar infections." Unfortunately, Crosby gave no evidence for his assertion and it is difficult to imagine what evidence there could be. If the principle were generally true and not just an aberration of the influenza pandemic, it would be important for our understanding of the effect of infectious diseases on nonimmune populations. However, what we do know of the age-specific mortality of smallpox suggests that it adheres to the norm, namely that the highest mortality occurs in the zero to one age bracket, the next highest in the one to five group, the lowest in the bracket five to fifteen, the next lowest in fifteen to twenty-five year olds, and thereafter it becomes progressively higher for each succeeding decennium.[16]

The following points summarize the salient elements of the virgin-soil epidemic thesis as it applies to smallpox. First, in a small population there will be very widespread infection and high mortality is likely. Second, in larger populations smallpox spreads fairly slowly and both morbidity and mortality rates should be reconstructed empirically rather than inferred from some assumed general principles applying to virgin-soil populations. Third, there is no empirical evidence for a relatively higher mortality

---

16 Frank Macfarlane Burnet and David O. White, *Natural History of Infectious Disease* (Cambridge, 1972; 4th ed.), 100; Crosby, *Ecological Imperialism,* 199; Fenner, et al., *Smallpox,* 176, 195–196.

among the fifteen to twenty-five (young adult) age-group and there is evidence that smallpox age-group mortality approximates that of most other virulent infectious diseases.

The virgin-soil epidemic thesis is based on an indisputable fact. For diseases in which immunity is acquired by surviving contact with them or by being vaccinated against them, a population with no previous contact of any kind will be 100 percent susceptible. All of its members are likely to be infected. If all are infected at the same time, all will experience the full course of the disease with greater or lesser virulence. As a model, then, it has considerable significance for the history of first contacts between peoples. Inferences may reasonably be made from otherwise incomplete evidence. Extrapolation from the known to the unknown becomes much more respectable. General patterns may be assumed. Analogies between one region where there is relatively complete documentation and other regions and times which are less well documented become almost cogent. This drawing of analogies enlarges the significance of the case of smallpox in Mexico. It is important also for early-contact historiography in other regions. In Mexico, the argument goes, there was massive and documented depopulation that was primarily caused by epidemic diseases, particularly smallpox. It was smallpox that made possible the conquest of Mexico. If it happened in Mexico, it could also have happened in other parts of America, in Oceania, in Australia, or anywhere a population had lived for many generations in isolation from a particular pathogen. If there are hints and suggestions that it did happen elsewhere, then those hints are very probably correct.[17]

What arguments are there against the presumed massive and rapid depopulation of Mexico by smallpox in 1520? The first is that smallpox does not actually spread fast or far. When the number of susceptible persons in casual contact with cases was still large, the spread of the disease would halt. "Even among household contacts smallpox was not highly contagious; prolonged or intimate exposure was usually necessary."[18]

17 Borah, "Mexico as Model: The Demographic Impact of European Expansion upon the Non-European World," in *Actas y Memorias, XXXV Congreso Internacional de Americanistas* (Mexico, 1964), III 379–387; on Mexico as a model for the impact of smallpox on Aborigines in Australia, see Judy Campbell, "Smallpox in Aboriginal Australia, 1829–31," *Historical Studies*, XX (1983), 539.
18 Fenner, et al., *Smallpox*, 204.

The second argument is that the virulence of smallpox varies so much that "there is no such thing as a typical smallpox. The wide range, severity and variation in signs and symptoms is characteristic of the disease and depends on the reaction of the host to the virus attack." There are two separate kinds of variation. The first is that, virologically and epidemiologically, at least two strains of the *variola* virus have been distinguished: *variola major* and *variola minor*. A number of characteristics distinguish the one from the other. The most important is that the case fatality rate for *variola major* can be as high as 100 percent and is typically in the 10 to 20 percent range, whereas for *variola minor* it is only 1 or 2 percent. The second is that both types show large variations—within their typical ranges—of virulence and mortality.[19]

Variola minor was not identified until the end of the nineteenth century. It may or may not have existed before then; there is simply no way of knowing. What is certain is that some mild cases of smallpox did occur in the past. The assumption, then, of Crosby and Hopkins, that *variola minor* "did not appear until late in the nineteenth century" is not only virologically unprovable but is historically irrelevant. Crosby quoted Hopkins: "I shall always be referring to the often fatal *variola major* smallpox." It was often fatal, but how often in any epidemic before the twentieth century is completely indeterminable. What is important and what is borne out by the empirical evidence is that historically, as Dixon made clear, mild forms of smallpox were common even in the seventeenth and eighteenth centuries when the disease was most feared.[20]

In sixteenth-century Europe mild cases appear to have been the norm. Apart from the case of smallpox in the New World, historians have paid little attention to the occurrence of the disease until the seventeenth century. Creighton knew that it was not feared in England. Most writers thought of it not as a disease at all, but rather as the expulsion of a poison with which all people

19 Dixon, *Smallpox*, 2.
20 Most of our systematic knowledge of the historical virulence of smallpox derives from treatises written by medical professionals. What they describe happened for the most part in clinical situations. But, Dixon pointed out, "exceedingly mild smallpox in the unvaccinated had been observed by many of the older writers. Such cases . . . rarely find their way into the hospitals," *Smallpox*, 2. Crosby, *Ecological Imperialism*, 343; Donald R. Hopkins, *Princes and Peasants: Smallpox in History* (Chicago, 1983), 5–6.

are born. Treatises on smallpox often described it as a form of measles.[21] Since this view was held in Europe, we can only speculate that there was a transmutation of the virus in its passage across the Atlantic, although there is no convincing reason in epidemiological theory why there should have been. Microorganisms do mutate and they can behave differently in different environments. But to argue from the general evolutionary possibility to the fact of a disease with very different characteristics would be logically valid only if it were supported by empirical evidence.[22]

Apart from Mexico, the most fully documented case of massive mortality from smallpox as a result of the first contact of indigenes with Europeans was made by Dobyns for Florida in the years after 1500. In two devastating book reviews, Henige systematically cut the ground away from Dobyns' evidence. Dobyns argued that the population of Florida in 1500 was about 700,000. Most previous historians suggested a figure from one-tenth to one-thirtieth of that figure. Henige showed that some of Dobyns' sources were spurious, misleading, or misquoted (on

21   Samuel X. Radbill and Gloria R. Hamilton, "Measles in Fact and Fancy," *Bulletin of the History of Medicine*, XXXIV (1960), 430; Ann G. Carmichael and Arthur M. Silverstein, "Smallpox in Europe before the Seventeenth Century: Virulent Killer or Benign Disease?" *Journal of the History of Medicine*, XLII (1987), 147–168; Charles Creighton, *A History of Epidemics in Britain* (London, 1965; 2d ed.). A curious case of historians voting with their feet appears in the number of items listed for each of the four diseases: leprosy, plague, smallpox, and syphilis in the four chronological divisions: Ancient (to 500), Medieval (500–1500), Renaissance (1500–1700), and Modern (after 1700) in the *Bibliography of the History of Medicine, 1964–1984* (Bethesda, 1965–1985), 4 v.

	ANCIENT	MEDIEVAL	RENAISSANCE	MODERN
Leprosy	18	61	12	133
Plague	27	117	176	162
Smallpox	5	4	6	304
Syphilis	4	6	43	115

22   The speculation about the change in the character of the smallpox virus needs emphasizing. It is taken to be "undoubted fact" that a virulent smallpox destroyed "within a generation or two from one-third to one-half of the indigenous population." (It will be observed that what is actually asserted is that from one-third to one-half of the population died in a few weeks or, at most, a few months.) The destroyer "may have been the more benign European form of the disease that was carried to the Americas, followed by an early mutation there which exposed a more virulent agent to the Amerindian population . . . The relatively inbred Amerindian population . . . might hyper-respond to even the mild European strain of the disease . . . ," Carmichael and Silverstein, "Smallpox in Europe," 165, 167. The subject seems to breed subjunctives.

one occasion 7,000 in one original document becomes 70,000 in translation). His case for any smallpox epidemic, let alone a catastrophic pandemic, was shredded.[23]

The history of smallpox seems to attract dubious stories. Henige detailed the slipshod methods of those who discovered a nonexistent epidemic of smallpox on Hispaniola in 1507. Unfounded conjectures abound. "It has been speculated that the malady came with the Spaniards in 1511." "Such is the communicability of smallpox and other eruptive fevers that any Indian who received news of the Spaniards could also have easily received the infection of European diseases." Assertions were made on the basis of dubious epidemiology. "Given present day knowledge of the impact of smallpox or plague on people without previous immunities, it is safe, indeed conservative, to say that a third of the Guatemala highland populations died during this holocaust." More careful historians have been content to note the anomalies. "Oddly, no Spanish observer commented on the tell-tale pockmarks." Again and again the *deus ex machina* is invoked. Smallpox jumps in front of European advance and the earliest massive mortality occurs before any records are kept and before any European observes it.[24]

No report of smallpox exists in the record of the New World before 1518. Some historians have mistakenly believed there was one. They relied on the authority of August Hirsch, a nineteenth-century German whose misreading of an English account led him

23 David Henige, "Primary Source by Primary Source? On the Role of Epidemics in New World Depopulation," *Ethnohistory*, XXXIII (1986), 293–312; *idem*, "If Pigs Could Fly: Timucuan Population and Native American Historical Demography," *Journal of Interdisciplinary History*, XVI (1986), 701–720. Both are reviews of Dobyns, *Their Number Become Thinned: Native American Historical Demography* (Knoxville, 1983).
24 Anomalies abound in the smallpox story. Hopkins' *Princes and Peasants*, 1–3, opens with an account of Queen Elizabeth I having an attack of smallpox in 1562. The only authority for this story is F. E. Halliday, "Queen Elizabeth and Dr. Burcot," *History Today*, 5 (1955), 542–544. The story in this article is based on the *Memoirs* of Richard Carew, son of the Richard Carew who wrote *The Survey of Cornwall* (London, 1602). Carew the younger, writing some time after 1628, recounts a lively dinner party at his father's house, "perhaps in 1610," where he heard his father and three of his kinsmen "retail riotous stories about the life and times of the famous doctor." As an authority for an otherwise unreported attack of smallpox on the Queen of England in 1562 it seems thin. Henige, "When did Smallpox Reach the New World (And Why Does It Matter)?" in Paul E. Lovejoy (ed.), *Africans in Bondage* (Madison, 1987), 11–26; Crosby, "*Conquistador y Pestilencia*," 328, 331; MacLeod, *Spanish Central America*, 41; Inga Clendinnen, *Ambivalent Conquests: Maya and Spaniard in Yucatan, 1517–1570* (Cambridge, 1987), 19.

to assert that there had been a severe epidemic in Hispaniola in 1507. From there, it was claimed, the disease spread to other islands, to the mainland, to the Isthmus of Panama, and to the Yucatan. No sound contemporary evidence exists for any such assertion.[25]

The first unequivocal reports are contained in a letter written in early 1519 by the Jeronymite friars who were the governors, *pro tem,* of the Spanish colonies in America. At the time, Hernan Cortés was preparing his expedition and would set out from Cuba the following month. The gist of the letter was that so many Indians were dying of smallpox that the Crown would have to grant licenses to individual merchants and colonists permitting them to import slaves to do the work of which the Indians were no longer capable. In other words, the letter was not a simple report of the epidemic. It was part of a campaign to persuade the Crown to allow African slaves to be imported as a labor force into America.[26]

In April 1519, Cortés landed at Vera Cruz. By July, he had decided to invade the Aztec Empire with 500 men. The decision took three forms. He announced his intention in a letter to the King. He effectively threw off his allegiance to Diego Velázquez, the governor of Cuba, by appealing directly for royal approval; and he "burned his boats," that is, he scuttled them—although the myth that he "burned" them survives in popular parlance. In November he arrived in Tenochtitlan. In April or May, 1520, an expedition to arrest Cortés sent by Diego Velázquez and led by Pánfilo de Narváez, landed in Mexico. This expedition was said to have been accompanied by a black man infected with smallpox. From this beginning the disease is said to have spread over the whole country and, eventually, over the whole continent. Several itineraries and chronologies for the epidemic have been asserted by historians. None has any contemporary evidence to support it.

25 Henige, "When Did Smallpox," 11–26.
26 "Al Rey—Los Padres geronimos.—De Santo Domingo á 10 de Enero de 1519," "Al Rey é Reina por mano del Secretario Cobos.—El licenciado Figueroa.—De Sevilla á 7 de Abril de 1519," "Memorial de Hernando de Gorjón, acerca de la despoblación de la Isla Española," *Coleccion de documentos inéditos, relativos al descubrimiento, conquista y organización de las antiguas posesiones españolas de América y Oceania* (Madrid, 1864), I, 366–368, 368–370, 428–429; Henry Raup Wagner (with Helen Rand Parish), *The Life and Writings of Bartolomé de Las Casas* (Albuquerque, 1967), 25–34, 22–23.

Cortés marched with about half his men from Tenochtitlan to the coast, successfully neutralized Narváez and annexed his followers. While he was absent, the Aztecs revolted against the remainder of his men. When he returned in late June, he found the Spaniards' position in the Aztec capital had become untenable. On the night of June 30, the *Noche Triste,* the Spaniards fought their way out of the Aztec capital. They were pursued around the lake as far as Otumba where they turned and fought a pitched battle against the Aztec army, more or less victoriously. Thereafter the Aztecs withdrew, leaving the Spaniards to crawl back to their allies in Tlaxcala, where they were able to recuperate. In the uprising, Montezuma was killed and was succeeded by Cuitlahuac, who died (of smallpox, say many historians without evidence; of unspecified causes, say the sources that report his death) either sixty or eighty days later, the end of August or of September.

In Tlaxcala and the new town he founded, Segura de la Frontera, Cortés composed a letter to the King, the second of his *Cartas de Relación* signed October 30, 1520. He makes no mention of smallpox. By December 1520, he was ready. He first secured the allegiance or neutrality of all the towns and cities in the vicinity of the lake and, in May 1521, initiated the siege of Tenochtitlan which ended with virtually the total destruction of the city in August 1521. In May 1522, Cortés wrote his third letter to the King giving his version of the events of the conquest. In that letter he mentions that his friend, Maxixca, one of the rulers of Tlaxcala, had died of smallpox and that he, Cortés, had ratified the succession of his son in the name of Charles V. Several chiefs in Cholula had also died of smallpox and he had appointed successors to those as well. Both episodes serve the function, central to Cortés' overall purpose in writing to the King, of demonstrating that he was acting in the name of Charles V. His purpose was to build up his claim to postfactum ratification by Charles in order to validate his position which, at the time, was technically one of rebellion against his lawful superior, the governor of Cuba.[27]

There are a few minor mentions of smallpox, mostly in Cortés' *residencia* of 1529, which are largely repetitions of his own

27 Hernán Cortés (ed. and trans. Anthony Pagden), *Hernán Cortés: Letters from Mexico* (New Haven, 1986), 164, 165.

statements. The next description of smallpox, and the one which really determined the whole historiography, occurs in Motolinía's *History of the Indians of New Spain,* written in the late 1530s and finished in either 1541 or 1543.

> The first plague was an epidemic of smallpox. It broke out in this manner. Hernando Cortés was Captain and Governor at the time when Captain Pánfilo de Narváez landed here. On one of his ships came a Negro stricken with smallpox, a disease that was unknown in this land. New Spain was very thickly populated at this time. When the smallpox began to infect the Indians, there was so much sickness and pestilence among them in all the land that in most provinces more than half of the people died, whereas in others the number was somewhat smaller. The Indians did not know the remedy against smallpox. Besides, they were accustomed, the healthy and the sick, to bathe frequently; and, because they did not cease doing this, they died like flies. Many succumbed also to hunger because, all taking sick at the same time, they were unable to assist one another. There was no one to give them bread or anything else. In many places it happened that all of the same household died. Since it was impossible to bury all the dead in order to remove the offensive odor that came from the corpses, their houses were thrown over them and thus their house became their sepulcher. The Indians called this sickness the great leprosy because the pocks, being so large, covered the Indians in such a way that they resembled lepers. Today, on some of the persons who survived the sickness this is quite apparent from the marks they bear; they are full of pockmarks.[28]

The *Historia* is not the only place where Motolinía described the smallpox epidemic. There is a somewhat longer account in the corresponding location in the *Memoriales* where he developed the analogy with the story of the ten plagues in Exodus and Revelation. The Biblical themes in this version reveal his overall purpose even more clearly than in the *Historia* and provide useful signposts for interpreting his meaning. A further account, toward

---

28 "Probanza de Hernán Cortés, 1529," *Colección de documentos,* XXVI, 355–512; XXVII, 5–77, 301–455; Toribio de Benavente (or Motolinía, a name he adopted when he arrived in Mexico) (trans. Francis Borgia Steck), *Motolinía's History of the Indians of New Spain* (Washington, D.C., 1951; orig. ed., 1858), 87–88.

the end of the *Memoriales,* needs to be read alongside the more frequently quoted one.[29]

With very few differences the *Memoriales* follows the *Historia* word for word up to "they resembled lepers." In the *Memoriales,* Motolinía then added: "*y aparecía esta enfermedad significarles las tribulaciones y plagas que por todo y en toda parte se habían de seguir* [and this sickness seemed to them to symbolize all the tribulations and plagues that for all of them everywhere had to ensue]." He then developed the similarities between smallpox and the first of the ten plagues of Egypt, in which the waters were turned to blood and stank.[30]

Motolinía's description of smallpox in the *Historia* is the basis (to say no more) of the accounts of both Gómara and of Díaz. Gómara not only read Motolinía but he incorporated *verbatim* much of the friar's material on Aztec culture into his own account. He added a few humanistic flourishes. "This war cost Diego Velázquez a great deal of money, Pánfilo de Narváez his eye and the Indians many dead, who died, not of wounds but of disease . . . The corpses stank so horribly that no one would bury them" (a nosewrinkling *delicatesse* which inverts cause and effect in Motolinía). Smallpox, in Motolinía a symbol of the Aztecs' greater tribulation, becomes for Gómara (as it does for Bancroft) the epochal event from which later they counted their years—about as psychologically plausible as saying one is reminded of World War I because it happened just before the influenza epidemic of 1918/19. By 1552, when he was writing his history, Gómara had read Fracastoro and knew about contagion. "It seems to me that this is how they were repaid for the *bubas* [syphilis] which they gave our men." The facts are identical. Only the style distinguishes Gómara's account from Motolinía's.[31]

Díaz, who knew Motolinía, was even more completely dependent on him, although it is possible that he extracted the gist from Gómara's version. All that he added of his own was a typically earthy comment about "a very black affair it was for New Spain" when a black man brought smallpox there. Char-

29 Motolinía (ed. Edmundo O'Gorman), *Memoriales o Libro de las casas de la Nueva España y de los naturales de ella* (Mexico, 1971; orig. ed., 1903), 10–11, 294.
30 *Ibid.,* 11.
31 Francisco López de Gómara (trans. Simpson), *Cortés: The Life of the Conqueror by His Secretary* (Berkeley, 1965), 204–205.

acteristically, his attempt at an elegant summary just misses the point: "dark as was the lot of Narváez, still blacker was the death of so many persons who were not Christians." If, indeed, Díaz was copying either Motolinía directly or Gómara's paraphrase— and a comparison of the three texts points to that conclusion—it is likely that he had not even seen smallpox in Mexico let alone been a witness of an epidemic.[32]

Where Gómara and Díaz adapted Motolinía to their own style, Mendieta, his younger confrère, simply copied him. A comparison of the texts reveals an identical structure in the accounts and, largely, identical phraseology as well. The one detail in Motolinía that Mendieta omitted was the pockmarked survivors. It is unlikely that he had himself seen them. Whereas he could readily copy Motolinía's account of the actual epidemic, his silence on pockmarks suggests that he had not himself observed the one piece of evidence which, had they been present, he would have seen.[33]

We have no way to be certain that Gómara and Díaz had any knowledge of a smallpox epidemic in Mexico in 1520 other than what they had read in Cortés' third letter and in Motolinía. Mendieta is even less an independent witness. Indeed, for historians to cite Mendieta on smallpox, even to cite him in addition to Motolinía, is to show that they have not taken the elementary critical step of comparing the accounts. Motolinía, and only Motolinía, is the sole source we have for asserting that there was a widespread epidemic and that "half the population died."

Yet his account is suspect. In the first place it is unclear that he was certain in which year the epidemic had occurred. The *Historia* and the corresponding account in the *Memoriales* date it firmly in April or May 1520, with the arrival of Narváez. Yet, in chapter 70 of the *Memoriales,* while he ruminated on the hidden judgments of God who sent his scourges for our sins, he wrote that it happened in 1521.

In it [the year 1521] happened the greatest mortality and scourge which were ever seen in this New Spain. These were the three first

32 Díaz, *True History,* II, 218–219.
33 Motolinía, *Historia de los indios de la Nueva España* (Barcelona, 1914), 14–15; Gerónimo de Mendieta (ed. Joaquín García Icazbalceta), *Historia eclesiástica indiana* (Mexico City, 1945; orig. ed., 1870), Lib. IV, 514.

and principal plagues of which we spoke in Part One, Chapter Two. The first was the conquest of Mexico; the second the Indians called *huei zahuatl,* which means the great pestilence of smallpox, from which died innumerable people because at the time the land everywhere seethed with people. In many provinces and pueblos half or more of the people died, in others a little less than half, or the third part. The third was hunger as in the said chapter of the plagues was related. After these three massacres of war, pestilence and famine, which are the major scourges with which God punishes the world, there followed many other of these plagues.[34]

Two questions arise from this passage. The first concerns the date of the arrival of smallpox in Mexico. All later accounts date the epidemic in the first half of 1520. It is practically certain that Gómara and Díaz copied both the date and the details about Narváez and his infected black from Motolinía. It is certain that Mendieta did. Yet Motolinía himself, later in the *Memoriales,* categorically dated the smallpox in 1521. We must conclude that he did not know (or, at least, was not sure) when smallpox reached Mexico and, hence, that the connection with Narváez and his black man is no less problematical.

The second question concerns the plausibility of the story of Narváez' black slave. That anyone would remember such a person between 1520 and the late 1530s is intrinsically unlikely. No one in 1520 thought of smallpox as a communicable disease. All descriptions attribute it to a virus (Latin: poison) acquired in the womb which then needed to be ejected in childhood. This etiology accounted for it being considered a virtually universal experience, for its comparative mildness when it occurred in childhood, and for it often being more serious when it occurred later in life since the poison had had a chance to fester and burrow much deeper into the body. Even Fracastoro thought smallpox was an innate infection.[35] Indeed, the idea of contagion was largely limited to the Biblical case of leprosy, although by the 1540s,

---

34 Motolinía, *Memoriales,* 294.

35 Girolamo Fracastoro, *De Contagione et contagiosis morbis et curatione libri III* (Venice, 1546), quoted in Arthur M. Silverstein and Alexander A. Bialasiewicz, "A History of Acquired Immunity," *Cellular Immunology,* LI (1980), 156. The authors add the comment that Fracastoro "could still refer to smallpox in Italy as an essentially benign and almost beneficial process, apparently ignorant of its lethal effects upon the Mayan and Incan civilizations from 1518 on." Fracastoro had not read Motolinía.

Fracastoro, as well as most other people in Europe, had recognized the all-too-apparent contagiousness of syphilis.

How the fact that a particular black who had smallpox would have been recorded in the Narváez expedition or anywhere else is hard to imagine. Even if he did exist and he were infectious, he could not have infected more than the very few who came in contact with him while he was immobile, if not actually recumbent. Those so infected would themselves not show symptoms until ten or twelve days later. Whether anyone would or could connect these symptoms to the Narváez black seems unlikely. The whole process is so improbable that we could well dismiss the account out of hand. Hence, that the story surfaces without explanation of its provenance some twenty or so years after the events it purports to describe is sound basis for saying that it is an invention.

What are we to make of Motolinía's story and its circumstantial details? Unlike Mendieta, Motolinía does not make a great deal of Cortés as the new Moses. The implication, nonetheless, is there. The setting of his extended metaphor of the Ten Plagues is precisely the exodus of the Indians' souls, held for so long like the Israelites in captivity by Pharaoh/Satan, now released and led out into the Promised Land of the Church. In this narrative, the ideal secondary agents of this first plague (God is the primary cause) were the sworn enemies of Cortés/Moses, Pánfilo de Narváez and his Ethiopian slave.[36] As etiology it is improbable, unrecorded in the sources and virtually unrecordable. As mythopoesis, however, it is perfect. It evokes not only the story in Exodus, but many of the associations attached to the same story recounted in Psalms 78 and 105—chanted each week in choir by the friars—in the Book of Wisdom, [Song of Solomon] and as explicitly cited by Motolinía, in the Book of the Apocalypse [Revelations].

The fractions of the population which he says died came from the Apocalypse. No count could have been made or record kept of the catastrophe that his figures imply. No source uninfluenced by his own account reports them. But they are the levels

36 Motolinía, *History*, 87. The corresponding passage in the *Memoriales* is more explicit. "*Hirió Dios esta tierra con diez plagas muy crueles por la dureza é obstinacion de sus moradores, y por tener cautivas las hijas de Sion, esto es, sus propias ánimas so el yugo de Faraon,*" Motolinía, *Memoriales*, 10.

of mortality wreaked by the Four Horsemen of the Apocalypse—Fire, Pestilence, and Famine, the first three who accompany the fourth, War (or Conquest). Motolinía's contagionist views derive not from any theory of etiology but from the notions of clean and unclean, of uncleanness caused by contact with what is ritually impure, gleaned from the Book of Leviticus. His understanding of pestilence comes from Exodus and Revelations.[37]

It would be anachronistic to criticize sixteenth-century diagnoses in light of twentieth-century medical science. In two respects, however, such comment is useful. First, all of the sources declare more or less patronizingly that the Indians did not know the remedy for smallpox. But the Spaniards did not know the remedy for smallpox. We do not know the remedy for smallpox. We can prevent it. We have eradicated it. But we still cannot cure it. Second, to translate the Nahuatl *huey zahuatl* as leprosy is simply misleading. Hansen's Disease did not exist in precontact America. The Biblical ritual construct *tsara'th* which became "lepra" in Greek and "leprosy" in English translation is simply inapplicable. To speak of leprosy is a commentary on the friars' understanding, not on that of the Indians. It even suggests that Motolinía was not familiar with smallpox, a disease that does not cover the whole body. Its characteristic form is precisely centrifugal, tending to appear on the extremities—the face and limbs—and to be thinly spread on the trunk.[38]

The final comment regards the stench. Those who experienced it described it in terms which are inescapably real. Any feel for the authenticity of personal experience in historical documents makes it impossible to doubt that the stench was real and that it was foul. Cortés told the king that it was unendurable. "Because it was now late, and we could no longer endure the stench of the dead bodies that had lain in those streets for many days, which was the most loathsome thing in all the world, we returned to our camps." He clearly convinced Gómara. "[The defenders] were numerous; they suffered from hunger and had to drink salt water; they slept among the dead and lived in a perpetual stench, for which reason they sickened or were struck down by the pestilence, in which an infinite number died. . . . Cortés had great fires

---

37 Rev. 8:6–13.
38 Dixon, *Smallpox*, 180–181.

lighted in the street to celebrate and to get rid of the suffocating stench." But it is Díaz who rubs our noses in the fetid filth. "When the city was free of [the survivors moving out], Cortés went to examine it and we found the houses full of corpses and there were some poor Mexicans, who could not move out, still among them, and what they excreted from their bodies was a filth such as thin swine pass which have been fed upon nothing but grass."[39]

What they are describing is not an epidemic of smallpox but the destruction of the city of Tenochtitlan. And that is the problem with Motolinía. He evoked apocalyptic images from the Bible, but what he described fit the Conquest in 1521, not the days of uncertainty in mid-1520. He would have us believe that a third to a half or more of the population died inside two months in 1520. Yet, nowhere in Cortés, Gómara, or Díaz are there any hints, still less any statements, that half the Indians—allies it must have been as well as enemies—died in a few short weeks. Rather, all the accounts of the numbers on both sides of the final siege are at pains to emphasize just how many fought and just how very many died. The catastrophe was war. Smallpox was incidental.

The final source which must be mentioned is Sahagún. The greatest of the ethnographers, he systematically interviewed Aztec survivors on all aspects of their culture. He also had his informants piece together their own account of the Conquest which forms Book XII of his great *The Florentine Codex: The General History of the Things of New Spain*. That account is interesting both for its similarities to Motolinía's and for its differences.

> But before the Spaniards had risen against us, first there came to be prevalent a great sickness, a plague. It was in Tepeilhuitl that it originated, that there spread over the people a great destruction of men. Some it covered [with pustules]; they were spread everywhere, on one's face, on one's head, on one's breast, etc. There was indeed perishing; many indeed died of it. No longer could they walk; they only lay in their abodes, in their beds. No longer could they move, no longer could they bestir themselves, no longer could they stretch themselves out on their sides, no longer could

39 Cortés, *Letters from Mexico*, 262; Gómara, *Cortés*, 293; Díaz, *Conquest of New Spain*, IV, 185, 187.

they stretch themselves out face down, no longer could they stretch themselves out on their backs. And when they bestirred themselves, much did they cry out. They was much perishing. Like a covering, covering-like, were the pustules. Indeed many people died of them, and many just died of hunger. There was death from hunger; there was no one to take care of another; there was no one to attend to another.

And on some, each pustule was placed on them only far apart; they did not cause much suffering, neither did many of them die of them. And many people were harmed by them on their faces; their faces were roughened. Of some, the eyes were injured; they were blinded. At this time this plague prevailed indeed sixty days— sixty day-signs—when it ended, when it diminished; when it was realized, when there was reviving, the plague was already going toward Chalco. And many were crippled. It came to be prevalent in Teotl eco, and it went diminishing in Panquetzaliztli. At that time the Mexicans, the brave warriors were able to recover from the pestilence.[40]

Sahagún shared the Franciscan image of the Conquest as Exodus. As he recounted it, the timing of the plague, the description of the symptoms, the people dying of hunger unable to care for one another all suggest Motolinía's influence. The remainder of his account, however, looks much more like smallpox as we know it to be. "No longer could they walk; they only lay in their abodes." But Sahagún's informants noticed what no one else did: there were a significant number of mild cases and the brave warriors were able to recover.

Sahagún's informants had heard the Franciscan account. But they had also experienced the disease themselves. They had been there. There can be no doubt that there had been an epidemic of smallpox in the city of Tenochtitlan, details of which were later recalled by the survivors. Yet, it is reasonable to credit their collective memory with knowledge that not many died. Therefore, reporting that many died of it must be the influence of the Franciscan myth.

40 Bernardino de Sahagún (trans. Arthur J. O. Anderson and Charles E. Dibble), *The Florentine Codex: The General History of the Things of New Spain* (Santa Fe, 1975), bk. XII, 83. Several historians quote the first part of Sahagun's description. I cannot recall one who quotes the qualifications in the second paragraph.

It is apparent that in the memory of many of the surviving Indians—as in Motolinía's—smallpox in 1520 and conquest in 1521 became conflated. Their descriptions of the disease take on many of the characteristics, which if literally true would be epidemiologically improbable, of the siege and the defeat. In that version half the population succumbed to the disease long before the Spaniards' final attack. What Sahagún's informants remembered of smallpox is more real and less melodramatic. It is also like the contemporary experience of smallpox in Europe.

For the Franciscans in the sixteenth century, the massive pestilence initiated by a black man, who would be the agent of the devil, fit into the Biblical apocalyptic strain that runs through so much of their writing and thinking. In the eighteenth and nineteenth centuries, Robertson, Humboldt, Hirsch, Prescott, and Bancroft all saw the colored races as weaker and more susceptible to diseases that were resisted by white races.

Diseases that caused massive mortality of indigenous peoples may have cleared the way for later Western European empires overseas. Yet, a critical reading of the texts suggests that it does not explain what happened in Mexico in 1520 and 1521. Cortés' brief references, the logic of the Aztec account in Sahagún, the total absence before Motolinía of any reference to massive mortality, and even after Motolinía of any reference in Gómara or Díaz other than in the single chapter or paragraph lifted in their essentials from the *Historia,* point inescapably to a mild attack of smallpox, such as occurred in contemporary Europe with some suffering, some deaths, and little further effect.

In the West Indies and Mexico, where smallpox was first carried from Euro-Asia-Africa to the rest of the world, a detailed examination of the historical sources calls into question the melodramatic stories of prairie-fire epidemics killing off the majority of the population in no more than a few years.

What we know about smallpox suggests that these criticisms are well-founded. There is no reliable evidence of a massive pandemic of smallpox in Mexico in 1520. Many, certainly thousands, perhaps 100,000 people died during the siege of 1521. Nothing in the historical record allows us to feel confident that one-third to one-half of the Aztec population died of smallpox in 1520. No such catastrophe actually occurred.

Michael Craton

Changing Patterns of Slave Families in the British West Indies

. . . any Attempt to restrain this Licentious Intercourse between the Sexes amongst the Slaves in this Island in the present State of their Notions of Right and Wrong, by introducing the Marriage Ceremony amongst them, would be utterly impracticable, and perhaps of dangerous Consequence, as these People are universally known to claim a Right of Disposing themselves in this Respect, according to their own Will and Pleasure without any Controul from their Masters.[1]

Writers on the West Indies have echoed the negative statements of Alexis de Tocqueville and E. Franklin Frazier on slave and modern black families in the United States.[2] In this vein, Simey, Henriques, and Goode exaggerated the matrifocality and instability of modern Caribbean families as "deviant" results of an alleged absence of family life in slavery, while Smith and Patterson confidently backed up their analyses of modern family with assertions that "the women normally acted as the sole permanent element in the slave family, whether or not the male partner was polygynous," and that "the nuclear family could hardly exist within the context of slavery."[3]

Michael Craton is Professor of History at the University of Waterloo. He is the author of *Searching for the Invisible Man: Slaves and Plantation Life in Jamaica* (Cambridge, Mass., 1978).

This article is the revision of a paper presented at the Organization of American Historians meeting, 1978. Grateful thanks are expressed for help in the compilation of data to Gail Saunders, Archivist of the Bahamas, and her staff in the Public Records Department, Nassau; to Louis Arruda and Geoffrey Dunlop for preliminary work on the twenty-six Bahamian holdings and Burton Williams' slaves; to Stanley Engerman for some of the Trinidad data and useful comments on an earlier draft; to Colin Clarke and David Lowenthal for material on Barbuda; to Barry Higman and Arnold Sio for sharing ideas and information; and to Gary Brannon for the execution of the map and figures.

1 John Quier, "Report of the Jamaican House of Assembly on the Slave Issues," in Lt. Gov. Clarke's no. 92, Nov. 20, 1788; Public Record Office, London, C.O. 137/88, Appendix C.

2 Herbert G. Gutman, *The Black Family in Slavery and Freedom, 1750–1925* (New York, 1976), xxi.

3 Thomas S. Simey, *Welfare and Planning in the West Indies* (Oxford, 1946), 50–51, 79; Fernando Henriques, *Family and Colour in Jamaica* (London, 1953), 103; William J. Goode,

In work published since 1973, Higman has proved these assertions to be wrong and thus has reopened the whole study of the West Indian family and its roots. Although concentrating on sugar plantation colonies and the period of slave amelioration and registration (1807-1834), he has shown that family life—even in patterns recognizable to Europeans—was then the norm for British West Indian slaves. Although polygyny and other African practices persisted, the nuclear, two-headed household was extremely common among the African-born as well as Creole slaves. More remarkably, single-headed maternal households were in a minority in every area studied by Higman, save for the towns. The frequency of matrifocal families and the general disruption of slave families had become exaggerated, he suggested, because of the practices of those slaves with whom whites were most familiar: domestics and urban slaves.[4]

The purpose of this present paper is fourfold. It adds to Higman's evidence by using material chiefly from the Bahamas, a non-sugar, largely non-plantation colony. It also summarizes the evidence hitherto gathered, sketches the varieties of slave family from place to place and time to time, and, finally, discusses developmental models. Despite great variations according to location, employment, and ownership (not to mention the difficulties presented by fragmentary and uneven evidence) a consistent pattern does emerge. This suggests both the place that the rediscovered West Indian slave family of the late slave period occupies in the continuum between West African roots and modern West Indian black family, and some of the ways in which the dynamics of West Indian black family have differed from those of the United States and Latin America.

As Stephen noted as early as 1824, slave conditions in the

"Illegitimacy in the Caribbean Social Structure," *American Sociological Review*, XXV (1960), 21-30; M. G. Smith, *The Plural Society in the British West Indies* (Berkeley, 1965), 109; H. Orlando Patterson, *The Sociology of Slavery* (London, 1967), 167.

4 Barry W. Higman, "Household Structure and Fertility on Jamaican Slave Plantations: A Nineteenth-Century Example," *Population Studies*, XXVII (1973), 527-550; *idem*, "The Slave Family and Household in the British West Indies, 1800-1834, "*Journal of Interdisciplinary History*, VI (1975), 261-287; *idem, Slave Population and Economy in Jamaica, 1807-1834* (Cambridge, 1976). Higman's "Family Property: The Slave Family in the British Caribbean in the Early Nineteenth Century," unpub. paper (1976) is now largely superseded by his "African and Creole Slave Family Patterns in Trinidad," paper delivered at the Tenth Conference of Caribbean Historians (1978). See *ibid.*, 12.

Bahama Islands were at the benign end of a scale on which the sugar colonies further south—particularly the newly acquired colonies of Trinidad and Guyana—represented the opposite extreme. An influx of Loyalist planters after 1783 had changed the tone and pace of the archipelagic colony, doubling the white population and trebling the number of slaves; but the population density remained a twentieth of that of Jamaica and a fiftieth of that of Barbados, while the ratio of black slaves to white freemen and the average size of slave holdings remained among the lowest in the British West Indies.[5]

Most of the Loyalist emigrés settled their slaves on Bahamian "Out Islands" until then unpopulated, attempting to replicate the plantation conditions they had left behind in the Carolinas, Georgia, and Florida. They found the climate ideal for growing sea island cotton, but the exhaustion of the thin soil and the depredations of the chenille bug left them unable to compete with American cotton once Whitney's gin became effective after 1800. Although a local planter, Joseph Eve, invented a wind-powered variant of the gin, Bahamian cotton production had almost faded away by 1820. Plantations were turned over to stock or the growing of grains and other provisions, and many of the slaves had to fend for themselves.

Those planters who could sold up and migrated once more. Many of them attempted to transfer their slaves to the old colony of Jamaica or the new sugar plantations in Trinidad and St. Vincent, where fresh slaves were at a premium after the African supply had been cut off by the abolition of the Atlantic slave trade in 1808. Although slaves were registered in the Crown Colony of Trinidad as early as 1813, this opportunistic trade was not revealed until the first returns under the Bahamian Slave Registration Act of 1821 reached London, after which it was effectively scotched by the abolitionists under Stephen Lushington in 1823. By then, perhaps 2,000 Bahamian slaves (a fifth) had already been transferred.[6]

5 James Stephen, *The Slavery of the British West India Colonies Delineated* (London, 1824), I, Appendix III, 454–474. The Bahamas, with almost exactly the same total land area as Jamaica (4,400 square miles), had approximately 10,000 slaves against 300,000 in Jamaica. Barbados, with only 166 square miles, had 65,000 slaves. In 1800, the ratio between blacks and whites in the Bahamas was about 4:1; in Barbados it was 8:1; in Jamaica 12:1.
6 David Eltis, "The Traffic in Slaves between the British West Indian Colonies, 1807–1833," *Economic History Review*, XXV, (1972), 55–64. Perhaps through a misunderstand-

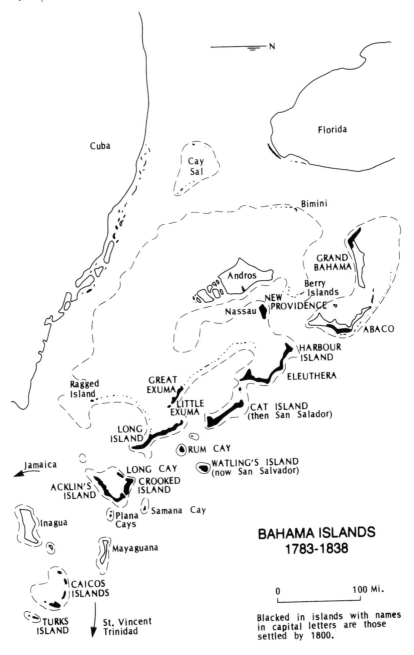

N

Florida

Cuba

Cay
Sal

Bimini

GRAND
BAHAMA

Andros

Berry
Islands

NEW
PROVIDENCE

Nassau

ABACO

HARBOUR
ISLAND

ELEUTHERA

Ragged
Island

GREAT
EXUMA

LITTLE
EXUMA

CAT ISLAND
(then San Salador)

LONG
ISLAND

RUM CAY

Jamaica

LONG CAY

WATLING'S ISLAND
(now San Salvador)

CROOKED
ISLAND

ACKLIN'S
ISLAND

Plana
Cays

Samana Cay

Inagua

Mayaguana

BAHAMA ISLANDS
1783-1838

CAICOS
ISLANDS

TURKS
ISLAND

St. Vincent
Trinidad

0   100 Mi.

Blacked in islands with names
in capital letters are those
settled by 1800.

Fig. 1 Population Pyramids, Rolle Slaves and 26 Bahamian Holdings, 1822.

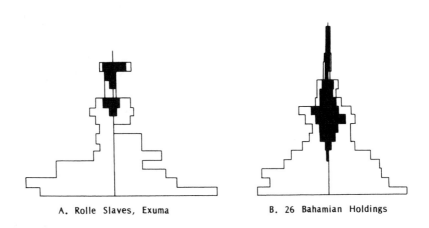

A. Rolle Slaves, Exuma   B. 26 Bahamian Holdings

trasts between the Bahamian slave population and those in sugar plantation colonies further south, but also point up the typicality of the only Bahamian slave group previously studied, that of the slaves owned by John, Lord Rolle on the island of Exuma.[8]

Ten times the size of the Rolle holding, this widespread fourth of the Bahamian slave population exhibited almost as balanced, "modern," and "unslavelike" a demographic pattern, with a broad base of youngsters and a fair number of elderly slaves. The sexes in the fertile age ranges were almost as equally balanced as Rolle's slaves, and the only features reminiscent of slave populations further south were a slight "bulge" in the age range from forty to fifty-four, representing in this case survivors from the migration of Loyalists' slaves in the 1780s, and a substantial remnant of Africans, 18.8 percent of the total. Unlike the Rolle holding, there also was evidence of considerable miscegenation,

8 Craton, "Hobbesian or Panglossian? The Two Extremes of Slave Conditions in the British Caribbean, 1783–1834," *William and Mary Quarterly,* XXV (1978), 324–356; *idem, Searching for the Invisible Man: Slaves and Plantation Life in Jamaica* (Cambridge, Mass., 1978), 60–118.

The meticulous triennial returns of British West Indian slaves produced by the registration laws were of great value to the emancipationists, who were able to prove the persistence of "natural decrease" as well as to end the intercolonial trade. Modern demographers, however, can put them to much wider use, reconstituting and comparing whole colony populations by age, sex, African or Creole birth, mortality, fertility, and life expectancy. In at least two colonies, Trinidad and the Bahamas, it is also possible to discover and compare patterns of slave family. Unlike the Trinidadian instructions, the Bahamian law did not require the listing of slaves' families or households-by-name. But approximately a quarter of Bahamian slaves were voluntarily listed by their owners in such a way as to indicate family relationships, though with limits on the range of family types identifiable. Comparison between the original lists of 1821 and 1822 and those of 1825, 1828, 1831, and 1834, moreover, allows both for corroboration of relationships and the testing of their permanence.[7]

In all, it has proved possible to analyze twenty-six slave holdings in the first Bahamian census of 1821–22 in which owners listed slaves in family groups, rather than by alphabetical order, age, sex, or any other method. This sample comprised 3,011 out of a Bahamas grand total of about 12,000, an average of 116 slaves per holding, but with a range between 20 and 840, drawn from eleven different islands. The findings not only illustrate the con-

---

ing, there was a partial census of Bahamian slaves in 1821. Most of these were relisted in 1822, but not all. The 1822 census book gives a grand total of 10,808 slaves, but this seems to omit the slaves listed in 1821 and not relisted in 1822. The intercolonial migration was at its peak between 1821 and 1822; its volume may never be known with complete accuracy.

7 Archives of the Bahamas, Nassau; Register of Returns of Slaves, Bahama Islands, 1821–1834. It was fortunate that the Bahamas Registration Act of 1821 required the listing of all slaves every three years, not just an initial census and subsequent triennial increases and decreases as in most other colonies. The Act specified what information should be given but not the order of the lists. Despite this, there seems to have been a remarkable uniformity in the method used by those owners who chose to list their slaves in family and household groups. An absolutely certain distinction between family and household was scarcely possible, but a comparison of the data on slaves transferred from the Bahamas to Trinidad (where the registration returns gave fuller details), and corroboration between the triennial Bahamian censuses, suggested that although extended families were understated, the listings concentrated on families rather than mere cohabitation, and the groups listed were almost invariably cohabiting families, rarely mere "housefuls."

Table 1 Household Patterns, Rolle Slaves, and 26 Bahamian Holdings, 1822

FAMILY TYPE	ROLLE SLAVES, EXUMA				26 BAHAMIAN HOLDINGS			
	TOTAL SLAVES	NUMBER OF UNITS	MEAN SIZE OF UNITS	PERCENT OF TOTAL IN TYPE	TOTAL SLAVES	NUMBER OF UNITS	MEAN SIZE OF UNITS	PERCENT OF TOTAL IN TYPE
1. Man, Woman, Children	110	26	4.23	46.6	1,629	308	5.29	54.1
2. Man, Woman	14	7	2.00	5.9	178	89	2.00	5.9
3. Woman, Children	40	12	3.33	16.9	377	95	3.97	12.5
4. Man, Children	11	2	5.50	4.7	16	3	5.33	0.5
5. Three-Generation Groups	29	5	5.80	12.3	358	46	7.78	11.9
6. Men Alone, or Together	11	—	—	4.7	264	—	—	8.8
7. Women Alone, or Together	9	—	—	3.8	173	—	—	5.8
8. Children Separately	12	—	—	5.1	16	—	—	0.5
Totals	236	—	—	100.0	3,011	—	—	100.0
A. Nuclear Family (1,2,5)	153	38	4.03	64.8	2,165	443	4.89	71.9
B. Denuded Family (3,4)	51	14	3.64	21.6	393	98	4.01	13.0
C. No Family (6,7,8)	32	—	—	13.6	453	—	—	15.1

Table 2 Bahamas, 26 Slave Holdings, 1822—Average Ages of Mothers at Births and Child Spacing

WHICH CHILD	NUMBER OF MOTHERS	PERCENT TOTAL MOTHERS IN EACH GROUP	AVERAGE AGES AT BIRTHS	AVERAGE SPACING (YEARS)
1st	479	100.0	22.37	
2nd	356	74.3	26.53	3.36
3rd	244	50.9	30.00	2.93
4th	170	35.5	32.60	2.93
5th	105	21.9	33.38	2.42
6th	59	12.3	35.22	2.81
7th	31	6.5	40.10	2.95
8th	8	1.7	43.46	2.67
9th	2	0.4	38.75	1.87
10th	1	0.2	38.00	1.00
Averages			34.84	3.02

Besides these basic statistical findings, a study of the Bahamian returns allows for some general observations and analysis along lines followed by Gutman and other scholars of slavery in the United States. First, important implications concerning the incidence of endogamy and exogamy—or at least of in-group and out-group mating—arose from the tendency of slave families to appear most clearly in the records of the larger and more isolated holdings, which were mainly in islands distant from Nassau, the colonial capital.[11] In contrast, on New Providence (Nassau's is-

11 Of the 26 holdings analyzed, 20 were established in the further islands, with a total of 2,643 slaves, an average of 132 per holding. Six were established in New Providence and Eleuthera, with a total of 367 slaves, an average of 61. In 1834 (the only year for which figures have been tabulated), 481 of the 730 Bahamian holdings of 5 or less slaves, and 692 of the 1,088 of 20 or less, were in New Providence and Eleuthera (including Harbour Island), but only 26 of the 107 Bahamian holdings of more than 20 slaves: Archives of the Bahamas, Nassau; Register of Returns of Slaves, Bahama Islands, 1834. The 1834 tabulation has been made by Gail Saunders.

land) and the nearer, long-established settlements of Harbour Island and Eleuthera, conjugal patterns seem to have been more disrupted. Many of the holdings were too small to include whole families and this clearly contributed to the custom of choosing mates from other holdings. But there were other factors. Among a heavily creolized population (with some slaves six generations removed from Africa), in small units, marital mobility was not only possible but probably seen as desirable to avoid too close a consanguinity. Miscegenation was also rather more common in New Providence and Eleuthera than further afield, those slaves listed as mulatto or yellow constituting 8 percent of the few holdings analyzed, and probably more than 10 percent overall.[12]

In general, it seems that these conditions led not to familial cohesion but the reverse, with many male mates absent or even temporary. Female-headed families were most common in the listings for New Providence (where almost a quarter of all Bahamian slaves lived), not only in the several holdings that consisted solely of slave mothers and their children, but also in such groups as the thirty-seven slaves of Elizabeth Mary Anderson, where nine men aged from twenty-two to sixty were listed together but separately from five female-headed families averaging five children each. Only in the exceptional holding of William Wylly at the isolated western end of New Providence were families distinct and clearly permanent.

In the distant, more recently established settlements, populations were on the average larger, more isolated, and, perhaps of necessity, more cohesive. The choice of mates was limited, and thus relationships were likely to be not only well-known but also more permanent. In relatively large populations, consisting in most cases primarily of first and second generation Creoles, such enforced in-group mating would not yet come into conflict with any customary ban on cousin-mating that may have existed (whether derived from Africa or Europe). In all, it is possible that conditions in the Out Islands, which Nassauvians, both white and black, might consider primitive, were more conducive to stable family formation than those closer to the colonial centre. Certainly, in modern times, Otterbein has documented a greater

12 The figure for 1834 was 9.6%, but by that date a considerable number had been manumitted.

awareness of the value of stable families in "primitive" Andros Island than that to be inferred in the less affluent sections of modernized Nassau, which include large groups of displaced Out Islanders. Yet these conditions seem to have also obtained in slavery days, a conclusion that runs counter to Gutman's contention that the dislocating effects of urbanization postdated emancipation, at least in the United States.[13]

The listings of families headed by single females may disguise the existence of serially shifting, or even polygynous, relationships. But in the series of five censuses spread over twelve years (1822–1834) there is very little positive evidence of serial monogamy, and only rare and equivocal evidence of polygyny.[14] Naming practices were very little help in tracing family patterns. Bahamian slaves did not universally adopt surnames before emancipation, and then it is by no means certain that surnames were patronymics in the modern style.[15] The practice of taking the surname of the former owner tends to exaggerate consanguinity as well as to confuse relationships—the most extreme case being Lord Rolle's 372 slaves, all of whom took the surname Rolle in order to share common rights in their former master's land. The discernment of immediate relationships was aided, however, by the frequent practice of naming a male child after his father or grandfather, and the occasional custom of naming a female after her grandmother.[16]

13 Keith F. Otterbein, *The Andros Islanders; A Study of Family Organization in the Bahamas* (Lawrence, Kansas, 1966). There is as yet no scholarly study of family in New Providence, or of the huge migration that has concentrated more than half the Bahamian population in the capital. Gutman, *Black Family*, 444–445, 489–491.

14 In the 1822 sample of 26 holdings, 5 possible cases of polygyny occurred. One such was Jack Stewart, a mulatto slave aged 66 belonging to James Moss at Acklin's Island, who appeared to live with Phoebe, an African aged 55, Kate, a Creole aged 37, and 10 children aged between 1 and 15, all listed as mulattoes.

15 Permanent mates and their children generally shared a surname, but in female-headed families and transient unions a practice common later in the Bahamas may have been followed; children went by their mother's surname until they were 21 and then adopted their father's surname.

16 Craton, "Hobbesian or Panglossian?" 19. Today there are thousands of Rolles in the Bahamas, including, it is said, two thirds of the population of Exuma. Male children often had a prefix or suffix added, as with Young Bacchus, Jack Junior, Little Jim, or the African-sounding Jim Jim, son of Jim. Males were often named after their fathers, females more rarely after their mothers. Out of the 67 family units of the Williams group of slaves transferred to Trinidad there were 22 males named after their fathers and at least one after a grandfather; four females were named after their mothers, at least 3 after a grandmother, and 1 after a mother's sister.

Such three-generation links sometimes allowed for the identification of extended family units, but the positive evidence of wider kinship links was disappointingly meager, and the direct evidence from the records of related families living close together in clusters of huts or "yards" was non-existent, although such groupings are known to have been a feature of Out Island life in later times. However, the frequent listing of a young girl with her first child in the household of her parents, or mother, does permit some inferences about sexual customs. Few girls under twenty cohabited with their mates; few mothers over twenty lived with their parents, and most, as we have seen, lived with mates. Nearly all girls who bore their first children in their mothers' households began separate cohabitation at, or shortly before, the birth of their second children. It therefore seems likely that premarital sex was not uncommon, and even that virginity at marriage was not excessively prized; but that separate cohabitation in a nuclear household was the accepted norm for couples over the age of twenty.[17]

The evidence proves the vigorous existence of families among Bahamian slaves during the registration period and, indeed, points to the existence of types of family classified as "modern" by Europeans among the least modernized groups of slaves. It remains to be decided, though, whether this was a social pattern chosen by the slaves themselves—and thus likely to have existed before the recorded period—or one determined, or at least encouraged, by the Eurocentric, pro-natalist, or publicity-conscious masters.

Strong evidence for the latter conclusion is found in the case of the slaves of William Wylly, Attorney-General of the Bahamas. An ardent Methodist who arranged for a minister to preach regularly to his slaves, he came to be regarded as a crypto-emancipationist by his fellow planters because of a legal decision made in 1816, and was at the center of a bitter wrangle between the plantocratic Assembly and three successive governors, lasting until 1820. Close examination of the evidence, however, shows that Wylly was a strict paternalist, and suggests that if he wished to

17 In the populations studied, 28 young mothers lived with their parents, their average ages being 18 years and 9 months. Only 5 were over 20 years old, and the average age at the birth of their first children was 17 years and 8 months. Only 1 of the 28 had a second child.

turn his slaves loose it was because they were no longer profitable.[18]

By 1818, Wylly's three adjacent estates in western New Providence had ceased to grow cotton, Tusculum and Waterloo being turned over to stock raising and Clifton, the largest, being devoted to growing provisions for the slaves and the Nassau market. The Attorney-General's many enemies accused him both of allowing his slaves more time to work for themselves than laid down by Bahamian law, and of supplying them with less than the provisions specified. In response, Wylly produced convincing proof of the degree to which his slaves were self-supporting, and stated, "My principal object has been, to accustom them to *habits of Industry and Oeconomy*—which I am convinced, never will be found to exist among any Slaves, in this part of the World, who are victualled by their Masters."[19]

At the same time, Wylly forwarded a revealing set of regulations for his slaves which he had caused to be printed and published in Nassau in 1815. Apart from his concern for religious instruction and regular prayers, and details of clothing, feeding, work, and punishment regulations, these clearly illustrated his views on slave marriage, sexual continence, and motherhood. "Every man, upon taking his first wife," read the seventh article of the regulations, "is entitled to a well built stone house, consisting of two apartments, and is to receive a sow pig, and a pair of dunghill fowls, as a donation from the proprietor."[20]

"In cases of Adultery," read Article XI, "the man forfeits his hogs, poultry, and other moveable effects; which are to be sold, and the proceeds paid over to the injured husband. Both offenders are moreover to be whipt; their heads to be shaved, and they are to wear *Sack cloth* (viz. gowns and caps made of Cotton bagging) for the next half year; during which time they are not to go beyond the limits of the plantation, under the penalty of being whipt."

With far less Mosaic severity, Article XIX enjoined that, "On working days, the children are to be carried, early every morning, by their mothers, to the Nursery, where proper care

---

18 Michael Craton, *A History of the Bahamas* (London, 1962), 173–174, 194–196.
19 William Wylly to President W. V. Munnings, Aug. 31, 1818, C.O. 23/67, 147.
20 *Regulations for the Government of the Slaves at Clifton and Tusculum in New Providence,* Printed at the Office of the New Gazette, 1815, enclosed in *ibid.*

will be taken of them during the day; and their mothers are to call for them when they return from their work in the afternoon. Women who have children at the breast, are never to be sent to any distance from the homestead."

Predictably, Wylly's slave lists in the registration returns disclose a neat pattern of families and a healthy natural increase. Since his regulations were published and his views on slave management became well known, it is possible that they became normative. The very decision to list slaves according to families and households may indicate owners who shared Wylly's concerns. Certainly, the other two Bahamian owners known to have engaged in correspondence on the management of their slaves, Lord Rolle of Exuma and Burton Williams of Watling's Island, demonstrated an awareness of the value of stable families in producing healthy, fertile, and contented slaves.[21]

It is likely, though, that such planters as Wylly, Rolle, and Williams were self-deluding if not self-serving. The widespread incidence and consistent form of slave families suggest customary choice on the part of the slaves rather than the dictates of the masters. Few plantations were owner-managed, especially in the Out Islands, and it seems strange that orderly patterns of slave family should be more common the further from Nassau (where slaves were commonly under the daily scrutiny of their owners), unless this was the slaves' own choice. Nor can the growing influence of Christianity be given unequivocal credit. The established Anglican Church, which held a monopoly on formal weddings until 1827, did not proselytize the slaves, and the few sectarian missionaries concentrated on Nassau and the nearer islands. The underground "Native Baptists," who were active among the Loyalists' slaves in Nassau as early as in Jamaica, may have had more widespread influence. But they were known to be tolerant about informal marital ties, being regarded by whites as hardly Christians at all. Indeed, the common impression held by the whites of the mass of the slaves was that those who were not

21 Of Wylly's 67 slaves in 1821, as many as 53 lived in 8 two-headed households (in 2 of which the family included a teenage single mother), with 1 female-headed family and a maximum of 9 slaves living alone, averaging 49 years old and including 6 elderly Africans. Almost certainly, 3 of the household units at Clifton were the extended family of Jack, the African under-driver, and his wife Sue. Twenty of the 67 slaves were under the age of 10 in 1821. See below, 19–23; C.O. 295/66, 53–59; 295/67, 219; 295/71, 26–35; 295/78, 233–265.

heathen practisers of *obeah* were infidel "followers of Mahomet."[22]

This at least suggests strong African cultural retentions, particularly in the Out Islands. Numerically the Africans were few by the registration period but, as elderly survivors, seem to have been highly respected members of the slave community. Indeed, it became clear on further analysis of the twenty-six holdings that the African slaves had influence out of all proportion to their numbers, and even that they were dominant in shaping family life in the Bahamas. Although most of the African-born slaves were grouped together toward the end of the rolls, in more than a third of the slave holdings analyzed an African couple was at the head of the list. This usually indicated that the owner had chosen the most prestigious married African as head driver.[23]

As in all slave communities the role of such leaders was ambivalent. They were chosen for what was termed "confidentiality"—fidelity, reliability, and respectability. But they were known to be effective because they commanded respect and "reputation," among Creoles as well as African blacks. For example, Wylly's African head driver and under-driver, Boatswain and Jack, practically ran his estates. Strong family men, they were expected to lead prayers at Sunday services and conduct funerals. Boatswain at least was literate, and was paid for each slave taught to read; both were rewarded with twelve guineas a year, the right to own and ride a horse, and the power to inflict punishment on their own initiative up to twelve stripes. But did their authority, ultimately, stem from their paternalistic master, or from their position as family heads and from African roots? And what did the family pattern at Clifton, Tusculum, and Waterloo owe, respectively, to memories of Africa, the examples of Boatswain and Jack, and the encouragement of Wylly?

Strong clues emerged from the discovery that, when African-headed families—those in which both parents, either parent, or the only parent were African-born—were separated from purely

22 D. W. Rose, reporting on the slaves of Exuma, 1802; Craton, *History of the Bahamas*, 183.

23 Besides 10 African couples, there were 3 holdings in which an African male headed the list with his Creole mate. In these 13 holdings (half of the total) there were 187 Africans out of a total of 805 slaves or 23.2%, not significantly more than the overall average, 18.8%.

Creole families, it became obvious that Africans were considerably more inclined toward family formation than Creole slaves. Of the Africans, 65.3 percent lived in couples, compared with less than 60 percent of the Creoles over the age of twenty. Of all African-headed families, 61.0 percent were of the simple nuclear type, with an additional 9.4 percent indicated as extended family households. This compared with 48.4 percent in nuclear units and 14.4 percent in extended households among Creole families. Only 11.9 percent of Africans lived alone, compared with 16.7 percent of adult Creoles.

By a Bahamian law of 1824, owners were forbidden to separate slave husbands from wives by sale, gift, or bequest, or to take their children away from them before they were fourteen years old. Although the act did not expressly forbid the splitting of families by shifting slaves from island to island, or the separation of children from single parents, it would seem to have provided owners with a motive for discouraging rather than encouraging slave families. Yet the evidence strongly suggests that masters were not only forced to acknowledge slave marital arrangements and to sell or transfer slaves only in families, even before 1824, but also to consider carefully the social consequences before they shifted slaves from their customary houses, plots, and kin at all.[24]

Wylly, although an alleged emancipationist, only manumitted three of his slaves after 1822 and did not scruple to scatter them by sale and transfer between 1821 and his death in 1828. Families, however, were carefully kept together. In another case, Rolle proposed an ingenious scheme in 1826 to shift all of his slaves to Trinidad, where they were to work to earn their freedom in the Spanish style. Fortunately for the slaves, the project was vetoed by the Colonial Office. But the word must have filtered down to Exuma, for in 1828 when Rolle's agent set about transferring some slaves to Grand Bahama, all of the slaves, fearing a move to Trinidad, became so mutinous that troops had to be sent down to keep order. Two years later, when they heard that the agent planned to ship them from Exuma to Cat Island, forty-four slaves (five men, eight women, and their families) actually re-

---

24 Act of 4 Geo. IV, c. 6; *Acts of the Assembly of the Bahama Islands* (Nassau, 1827), V, 227–228.

Table 3 Bahamas, 26 Slave Holdings, 1822 Comparison between African–Headed and Creole Families

FAMILY TYPE	A. AFRICAN HEADED FAMILIES[a]				B. CREOLE FAMILIES			
	TOTAL SLAVES	NUMBER OF UNITS	MEAN SIZE OF UNITS	PERCENT OF TOTAL IN TYPE	TOTAL SLAVES	NUMBER OF UNITS	MEAN SIZE OF UNITS	PERCENT OF TOTAL IN TYPE
1. Man, Woman, Children	830[a]	154	5.39	61.0	799	154	5.19	48.4
2. Man, Woman	138[a]	69	2.00	10.2	40	20	2.00	2.4
3. Woman, Children	91	21	4.33	6.7	278	72	3.86	16.8
4. Man, Children	11	2	5.50	0.8	5	1	5.00	0.3
5. Three-Generation Groups	128[a]	19	6.73	9.4	238	29	8.21	14.4
6. Men Alone, or Together	114	—	—	8.4	150	—	—	9.1
7. Women Alone, or Together	48	—	—	3.5	125	—	—	7.6
8. Children Separately	—	—	—	—	16	2	8.00	1.0
Totals	1,360	—	—	100.0	1,651	—	—	100.0
A. Nuclear Family (1,2,5)	1,096	242	4.53	80.6	1,077	203	5.31	65.2
B. Denuded Family (3,4)	102	23	4.43	7.5	283	73	3.88	17.1
C. No Family (6,7,8)	162	—	—	11.9	291	—	—	17.7

a African-Headed Families were taken to be those in which both parents, either parent, or the single parent were of African birth. Thus in categories 1, 2, and 5 in Section A mixed couples were included.

belled. Under the leadership of a slave called Pompey they first fled to the bush, then seized Rolle's salt boat, and sailed to Nassau to put their case to Governor Smyth, who was widely thought to be a friend of the slaves. The fugitives were thrown into the workhouse and the leaders flogged (including the eight women). But Smyth was angry when he heard about it and none of the slaves in the end were sent to Cat Island; it can be said that Pompey and his fellows won the principle that Bahamian slaves could not with impunity be shifted against their will.[25]

The largest single transfer of slaves had been the shipment in 1823 of most of the 840 slaves of James Moss from Acklin's Island and Crooked Island to Jamaica, where their fate remains obscure. Yet the most interesting of all Bahamian transfers was that to Trinidad between 1821 and 1823 of the majority of the slaves of Burton Williams of Watling's Island and his family, since it allows for comparisons between the fortunes of those transferred and other slaves in Trinidad, and between all those and the slaves left behind in the Bahamas.

Early in 1825, after he had been in Trinidad three and half years, Williams gave evidence to the Trinidad Council about his slaves. He claimed that in "30 odd" years of Bahamian residence he had seen the group of seven slaves inherited and "about 100" bought augmented by 224 through natural increase. This remarkable growth (as rapid as that indicated for Rolle's slaves, and sustained over a longer period) was attributed by Williams to his own residence among the slaves, to firm management, and to the encouragement of marriage "by giving a feast to the Gang when they come together and a sharp punishment when they part."[26]

Certainly, the 450 Williams slaves found in the Bahamas in 1821 exhibited an even healthier demographic balance and a higher incidence of family formation than the Bahamian average, as is shown in Figure 4 and Table 4. The proportion of young children was higher, there were only two thirds as many Africans, and yet

25 Archives of the Bahamas, Manumissions Index; Register of Returns of Slaves, 1825, 1828, 1831, 1834; Public Record Office, London; Register of Returns of Slaves, St. Vincent, 1822, 1825. Craton, "Hobbesian or Panglossian?" 19–20; C.O. 295/67, 219; 295/71, 26–35; 295/78, 233–265; Governor James Carmichael Smyth to Lord Stanley, Oct. 27, 1830, C.O. 23/82, 368–420.
26 Evidence given on Jan. 18, 1825, C.O. 295/66, 53–59. A population of 107 increasing at the Rolle rate for 1822–1834, 34.5 per thousand per year, would have reached 331 in the thirty-fourth year.

Fig. 4   The Burton Williams Slaves, 1822 and 1825, compared with Bahamas and Trinidad Slaves, 1825; Population Pyramids.

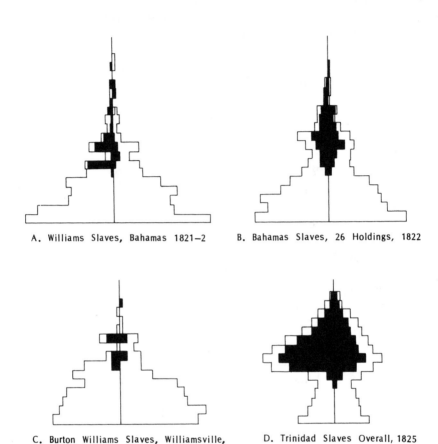

A. Williams Slaves, Bahamas 1821–2

B. Bahamas Slaves, 26 Holdings, 1822

C. Burton Williams Slaves, Williamsville, Trinidad, 1825

D. Trinidad Slaves Overall, 1825
(Hypothetical Reconstruction)
Shaded Area = African Slaves

a fair number were very elderly slaves. The proportion of slaves in nuclear families, 55.8 percent, was some 2 percent higher than the average for the twenty-six holdings analyzed earlier, and the total in some kind of family more than 5 percent higher, at 90.2 percent. Yet, by Williams' account, the situation in the Bahamas had become economically and demographically critical by 1821,

Table 4 Bahamas, Family Formation, Williams Slaves 1822 and 1825 compared with 26 Holdings, 1822

FAMILY TYPE	A. WILLIAMS SLAVES, 1822				B. WILLIAMS SLAVES, BAHAMAS, 1825				C. 26 BAHAMIAN HOLDINGS, 1822			
	TOTAL SLAVES	NUMBER OF UNITS	MEAN SIZE OF UNITS	PERCENT OF TOTAL IN TYPE	TOTAL SLAVES	NUMBER OF UNITS	MEAN SIZE OF UNITS	PERCENT OF TOTAL IN TYPE	TOTAL SLAVES	NUMBER OF UNITS	MEAN SIZE OF UNITS	PERCENT OF TOTAL IN TYPE
1. Man, Woman, Children	251	47	5.34	55.8	103	20	5.15	46.0	1,629	308	5.29	54.1
2. Man, Woman	28	14	2.00	6.2	10	5	2.00	4.5	178	89	2.00	5.9
3. Woman, Children	45	10	4.50	10.0	38	14	2.71	17.0	377	95	3.97	12.5
4. Man, Children	2	1	2.00	0.5	0	0	—	—	16	3	5.33	0.5
5. Three-Generation	80	9	8.88	17.8	25	4	6.25	11.2	358	46	7.78	11.9
6. Single Men	15	—	—	3.3	22	—	—	9.8	264	—	—	8.8
7. Single Women	14	—	—	3.1	8	—	—	3.5	173	—	—	5.8
8. Separate Children	15	—	—	3.3	18	5	3.60	8.0	16	—	—	0.5
Totals	450	—	—	100.0	224	—	—	100.0	3,011	—	—	100.0
A. Nuclear Family (1,2,5)	359	70	5.13	79.8	138	29	4.75	61.6	2,165	443	4.89	71.9
B. Denuded Family (3,4)	47	11	4.27	10.4	38	14	2.71	17.0	393	98	4.01	13.0
C. No Family (6,7,8)	44	—	—	9.8	48	—	—	21.4	453	—	—	15.1

so that he could neither clothe nor feed his slaves adequately, although he owned 13,000 acres of land. Taking advantage of the inducements offered by Trinidad, he therefore transferred 324 of his slaves in five cargoes between 1821 and 1823.[27]

Although one or two couples were split and an unknown number of extended family members separated, Williams clearly attempted to transfer his slaves predominantly in family units. Comparison of the slaves settled at Williamsville, his new estate in Naparima, in the Trinidadian returns of 1825 with those left behind listed in the Bahamas returns of the same year, indicates also that the majority of the elderly and Africans were left behind, and that rather more young females were carried than young males. The transferred population therefore exhibited many characteristics sharply different from those of the generality of Trinidadian slaves. Only 5.3 percent of the Williamsville slaves were African-born, compared with the Trinidadian average of over 40 percent, and females outnumbered males by 7.8 percent, more than reversing the general Trinidadian pattern. Whether using the categories used elsewhere in this paper or those employed by Higman, the contrast in family formation is even more noticeable. Because of the greater detail given in the Trinidadian registration returns more types could be differentiated, but the total of Williamsville slaves in some type of family was as high as in the Bahamas sample, and almost twice as high as the Trinidadian average indicated by Higman. The percentage in simple nuclear households, 57.3 percent, was slightly higher than in the Bahamas, and three times as high as the Trinidadian average. Mothers

27

		MEN	WOMEN	BOYS	GIRLS	INFANTS	
July	1821	27	43	7	5	23	
February	1822	9	11	6	4	24	
July	1822	6	11	3	3	14	
March	1823	10	10	7	5	33	
June	1823	6	11	6	7	33	
		58	86	29	24	127	324

This compilation was made on Sept. 27, 1823. By that time, 19 children had been added to Williams' slaves by birth, and only 7 of the total had been lost by death. This indicated a crude annual birth rate of 29 per thousand and a death rate around 11 per thousand. However, of 3,239 slaves imported into Trinidad from all sources between 1813 and 1822 (1,678 being males and 1,561 females), 232 males and 156 females had died, 388 in all, against only 236 births; C.O. 295/59, 252, 255.

living alone with their children accounted for only 6 percent of the Williamsville slaves, half of the Bahamas figure, and little more than a quarter of that for Trinidad as a whole.

As a consequence of the division of the Williams slaves, those left behind in the Bahamas were less well-balanced in composition than the Bahamian average and therefore increased in number rather less rapidly after 1823. Yet those transferred were less healthy than those left behind and increased even more slowly. However, they did increase, in contrast to Trinidadian slaves in general, who suffered an alarming depeletion throughout the registration period. By the end of 1826, thirty-three of Williams' Trinidadian slaves had died, while fifty-seven were born (forty-nine having been sold and two manumitted), an annual rate of natural increase of roughly sixteen per thousand. This was half the Bahamian rate, and compared with an annual net decrease at least as high for Trinidadian slaves on the average.[28]

Although his 1825 evidence was twisted to justify the transfer, Williams had to admit that the health and morale of his slaves had suffered in the first three years—the seasoning period. "Fevers and Agues and bowel Complaints," as well as unfamilar "Sores," although not great killers, were common among the transferred slaves. These ills Williams attributed to his having arrived in the middle of the wet season, settling in a wooded and marshy area, and being forced to feed his slaves on plantains and saltfish rather than their customary guinea corn (millet or sorghum). He deplored the laxity of Trinidadian morals and the effects on family life of the disparity in the sex ratio. He also pleaded that the demoralizing effects of Colonial Office regulations would encourage the idleness of slaves and limit the powers of correction of their masters. Against the evidence, he denied that the work required of slaves was harder than in the Bahamas, and claimed that slaves had more opportunity in Trinidad to dispose of the surplus food that they grew on their own allotments. However, he remarked that most of the slaves would have returned to the Bahamas if they had been given the choice.[29]

28 "Return showing the number of Negroes imported into this Island by Burton Williams Esq.," enclosed in Governor Sir Ralph Woodford to William Huskisson, March 7, 1828, C.O. 295/77, 33-49.
29 C.O. 295/66, 57.

Table 5 Family Structure, Williams Trinidadian Slaves, 1825 compared with Trinidadian Total, 1813 (Higman, 1978)[a]

FAMILY TYPE	A. WILLIAMS SLAVES, 1825				B. TRINIDADIAN SLAVES TOTAL, 1813			
	TOTAL	UNITS	MEAN SIZE	PERCENT IN TYPE	TOTAL	UNITS	MEAN SIZE	PERCENT IN TYPE
Man, Woman, Children	142	24	5.9	57.4	4,675	1,162	4.0	18.3
Man, Woman	6	3	2.0	2.4	1,036	518	2.0	4.0
Woman, Children	15	3	5.0	6.0	5,690	2,066	2.8	22.2
Man, Children	0	0	—	—	357	138	2.6	1.4
Polygynists	0	0	—	—	31	7	4.4	0.1
Three-Generation and Extended[b]	47	8	5.9	18.9	445	97	4.6	1.7
Siblings	14	4	3.5	5.7	} 547	197	2.8	2.1
Siblings, Children	9	2	4.5	3.6				
Man, Woman, Cousins	5	2	2.5	2.0	0	0	—	—
No Family[c]	10	—	—	4.0	12,892	—	—	50.2
Totals	248	—	—	100.0	25,673	—	—	100.0

a Data from Public Record Office, London, T. 71/513 (1825); T. 71/501–503; Higman, "Family Patterns in Trinidad," 32.
b In the Williams Population: Man, Woman, Children, their Children (8); Man, Woman, Children, Man's Sister, her Children (7); Man, Woman, Children, Woman's Brother, his Spouse (6); Man, Woman, Child, Man's Brother, his Spouse (5); Man, Woman, Man's Sister, her Child (4); Woman, Children, Spouses (5). In the Higman Total: Woman, her Children, her Grandchildren (227); "Extended" (218).
c In the Williams Population, Men and Women living alone, unrelated separated Children.

The research undertaken so far not only indicates a far wider existence of family in slave society than hitherto expected, but has also clarified the varieties of family within the range of West Indian slave communities in the late slave period. At one end of the scale were the virtual peasants of the Bahamas, Barbuda and, perhaps, the Grenadines, with locational stability, a small proportion of African slaves, natural increase, and a relatively high incidence of nuclear and stable families. At the opposite pole were the overworked slaves of new plantations such as those of Trinidad, Guyana, and St. Vincent, with a high rate of natural decrease, a majority of slaves living alone or in "barrack" conditions, and a high proportion of "denuded," female-headed families. In between came the mass of West Indian slaves, all but 10 percent living on plantations of one sort or another, with a wide range of demographic patterns but a generally declining rate of natural decrease and a rapidly dwindling African population, and varying degrees of practical exogamy, miscegenation with whites, and family formation.[30]

Unfortunately, statistical information on West Indian slave families is practically limited to the registration period, 1813–1834, after the slave trade with Africa had ended, when all plantations were starting to decline, amelioration measures were being applied, and missionaries were beginning to make their influence felt. It remains to be seen whether a morphology of slave family during the entire period of slavery can be inferred, or projected, from this material alone; what additional light is shed by the white-produced literary sources from an earlier period; and, finally, what other arguments can be adduced, including the incorporation of West African material.

Earlier speculation led the present writer and Higman to postulate, and then to refine to the point of dismissal, two successive models. First, if one took the nuclear two-headed family as the quintessentially modern family form, it was beguilingly easy to propose its different incidence during the registration period as relating to the degree of maturation, creolization, or modernization of each slave unit, and thus to suggest a historical progression from some aboriginal African form of family. Such

30 Craton, "Hobbesian or Panglossian?" 19–21; Colin Clarke and David Lowenthal, "Barbuda; the Past of a Negro Myth," in Vera Rubin and Arthur Tuden (eds.), *Comparative Perspectives on Slavery in New World Plantation Societies* (New York, 1977), 510–534.

a progression initially seemed borne out by the closer parallels among the modern Jamaican rural communities analyzed by Edith Clarke and the Exumian slaves of Rolle, as compared with Jamaican slave plantation examples, and by the highly developed family patterns traced by Colin Clarke and Lowenthal among the completely creolized peasants of Barbuda in 1851.[31]

However, the discovery by Higman, amply corroborated by the Bahamian material examined here, that Africans were at least as likely as Creoles to form nuclear families, modified the original model. This revision, coupled with the likelihood that the registration records largely concealed the existence of extended families, and the apparent paradox that Creole men were more likely to be polygynous than Africans, led Higman to a second developmental model, based on the seemingly progressive differences between Trinidad, Jamaica, and Barbados.[32] By this formulation, the establishment of "elementary nuclear families" was the primary response of the displaced Africans in the first slave generation. This was the stage of fictive kin such as the "shipmate" relationship described by Edwards. Owing to high mortality, the further shifting of slaves, and a high male ratio, families were small and impermanent, and only a few privileged slaves were

31 The argument is proposed in Craton, "Hobbesian or Panglossian?" which was first delivered at the conference on Comparative Perspectives in New World Plantation Societies, New York, 1976. Edith Clarke, *My Mother Who Fathered Me* (London, 1957).

Barbuda Household Types, 1851

HOUSEHOLD TYPE	NUMBER OF UNITS	NUMBER OF PERSONS	PERSONS PER UNIT	PERCENT TOTAL PERSONS PER UNIT TYPE	
1. Man, Woman, Children	76	425	5.59	67.57	
2. Man and Woman	14	28	2.00	4.45	
3. Woman and Children	12	50	4.17	7.95	
4. Man and Children	1	6	6.00	0.95	
5. Three Generations (i.e. Two Women and Children)	18	90	5.00	14.31	(95.23)
6. Men Alone	7	7	1.00	1.11	
7. Women Alone	10	10	1.00	1.59	
8. Women Together	6	13	2.17	2.07	(4.77)
	144	629	4.73	100.00	

Colin Clarke and Lowenthal, private correspondence (Codrington records, Gloucester County Record Office, England).

32 What follows is the argument proposed by Higman, "Family Property," now superseded by his "Slave Family Patterns in Trinidad," 1977. The change was based on the analysis of the full 1813 slave population of 25,673 (a quarter of whom lived in Port of Spain), rather than the rural sample of 1,296 previously used.

able to practice polygyny. A second slave generation began to establish extended families based on the formation of virilocal "yards" within single plantations; but, because mortality remained high and fresh Africans were continually arriving, the elementary family continued the dominant norm. At this stage polygyny may actually have increased, as an index of status and property. In subsequent generations, kinship networks expanded as slaves increasingly practiced exogamy. This occurred earliest and most rapidly where holdings were small annd contiguous, and the proportion of Creoles high. The process tended toward matrifocality rather than the nuclear family, especially where lack of slave-controlled provision grounds, money, and property deprived slaves of the chance of "marriage strategies."[33]

It was clearly right to de-emphasize the normative role of the slaveowners and to stress that slaves largely determined their own family arrangements. Higman's schematic formulation also properly recognized that a wide variety of family types coexisted in all periods, since different islands and sectors developed at different rates and in different ways. A closer study of the Bahamian materials, however, suggested that it was the Bahamas rather than Barbados which represented the forward extreme of slave family development. Higman's most recent analysis of the 1813 registration returns also suggested that Trinidad was a more special case than previously thought: an area directly supervized and rapidly expanding on the eve of emancipation and changing technology, rather than a frontier area exactly analogous to Barbados in 1650 or Jamaica in 1720. In particular, his scrutiny pointed up three conclusions apparent or latent in the Bahamian material considered here: the critical importance to slave family development of plantation size; the effects of urbanization; and the difficulty of tracing simple cultural transfers from Africa. Even more critically, Higman's earlier model underestimated the formative changes that occurred over the century and a half before the slave trade ended. These included great changes in the intensity of the plantation system and the gradual evolution of systems of slave management aimed at greater efficiency in general, and thus at increasing slave fertility as well. Perhaps most important of all was

33 Bryan Edwards, *The History, Civil and Commercial, of the British Colonies in the British West Indies* (London 1801), II, 155.

Table 6 West Indian Family from Slavery to the Present; A Comparison of Trinidad, Jamaica, and the Bahamas in Slavery Days with Barbuda immediately after Slavery, and with Modern Rural Jamaica, 1813–1955

FAMILY[a] TYPE	A. TRINIDAD, 1813				B. MONTPELIER, JAMAICA, 1825			
	TOTAL SLAVES	NUMBER OF UNITS	MEAN SIZE OF UNITS	PERCENT OF TOTAL IN TYPE	TOTAL SLAVES	NUMBER OF UNITS	MEAN SIZE OF UNITS	PERCENT OF TOTAL IN TYPE
1	4,675	1,162	4.0	18.3	204	50	4.1	25.1
2	1,036	518	2.0	4.0	76	38	2.0	9.3
3	5,690	2,066	2.8	22.2	328	70	4.7	40.3
4	357	138	2.6	1.4	0	0	—	—
5	445	97	4.6	1.7	24	6	4.0	2.9
6								
7	12,892	—	—	50.2	182	—	—	22.4
8								
Others	578	204	2.8	2.2				
	25,673	—	—	100.0	814	—	—	100.0
A	6,156	1,777	3.5	24.0	304	94	3.2	37.3
B	6,625	2,408	2.8	25.8	328	70	4.7	40.3
C	12,892	—	—	50.2	182	—	—	22.6

a   1 = Man, Woman, Children; 2 = Man, Women; 3 = Woman, Children; 4 = Man, Children; 5 = Three-Generation Groups; 6 = Men Alone, or Together; 7 = Women Alone, or Together; 8 = Children Separately;

the filtering down into the West Indies of evolving concepts of the "modern" family, which gradually gained hold in the practice of creolized slaves, as well as in the minds of white masters.

It is notable that the two most important early writers on British West Indian slavery gave sympathetic accounts of the slaves' society and customs. Ligon (1657) and Sloane (1707) described the early slaves as having a great sense of decorum. Unlike Europeans, they were not ashamed of nakedness and, though with a healthy sex drive, fastidiously avoided public displays of "wantonness." They married when they could, and had a rigorous distaste for adultery. "They have every one his Wife," wrote Sloane, "and are very much concern'd if they prove adulterous, but in some measure satisfied if their Masters punish the Man who does them the supposed injury, in any of his Hogs, or other small wealth. The care of the Masters and Overseers about their Wives, is what keeps their Plantations chiefly in good order,

	C. BAHAMAS, 26 HOLDINGS, 1822			D. BARBUDA, 1851				E. RURAL JAMAICA, 1955[b] 1. "SUGARTOWN" 2. "MOCCA"	
TOTAL SLAVES	NUMBER OF UNITS	MEAN SIZE OF UNITS	PERCENT OF TOTAL IN TYPE	TOTAL POPULATION	NUMBER OF UNITS	MEAN SIZE OF UNITS	PERCENT OF TOTAL IN TYPE	PERCENT OF TOTAL POPULATION IN TYPE	PERCENT OF TOTAL POPULATION IN TYPE
1,629	308	5.3	54.1	425	76	5.6	67.7	} 46	41
178	89	2.0	5.9	28	14	2.0	4.5		
377	95	4.0	12.5	50	12	4.2	8.0	16	17
16	3	5.3	0.5	6	1	6.0	0.7	3	3
358	46	7.8	11.9	90	18	5.0	14.3	18	30
264	—	—	8.8	7	7	1.0	1.1	} 17	9
173	—	—	5.8	10	10	1.0	1.6		
16	—	—	0.5	13	6	2.2	2.1		
3,011	—	—	100.0	629	144	4.7	100.0	100	100
2,165	443	4.9	71.9	543	108	5.0	86.3	65	71
393	98	4.0	13.0	56	13	4.3	8.6	19	20
453	—	—	15.1	30	23	1.3	3.1	17	9

A = Nuclear Family (1,2,5); B = Denuded Family (3,4); C = No Family (6,7,8).
b   Edith Clarke, *My Mother Who Fathered Me* (London, 1957), 191–194.

whence they even buy Wives in proportion to their Men, lest the Men should wander to neighbouring Plantations and neglect to serve them." The males appeared to be dominant and the practice of polygyny by no means uncommon, being enjoyed, "by certain brave fellows . . . of extraordinary qualities," from the earliest days. In contrast to later reports there was a strong bond of affection between parents and children, particularly between mothers and infants, who, in African fashion, were carried to work in the fields and not weaned for two years or even longer. Great respect and care were shown for the aged, whether or not they were actual kin.[34]

34   Richard Ligon, *A True and Exact History of the Island of Barbadoes* (London, 1657), 47; Hans Sloane, *A Voyage to the Islands Madera, Barbados, Nieves, S. Christophers and Jamaica* (London, 1725), II, xlviii; Stanley L. Engerman, "Some Economic and Demographic Comparisons of Slavery in the United States and the British West Indies," *Economic History Review*, XXIX (1976), 258–275.

Ligon and Sloane wrote with exceptional objectivity before the plantation system was intensified, and also in a period when extended families were more important than nuclear families in Europe itself, and modern ideas of childhood and parental affection were still relatively strange. Besides, during Ligon's period in Barbados and Sloane's in Jamaica miscegenation had not yet become institutionalized because there was still a sizeable proportion of whites of both sexes in the laboring population, and the majority of the blacks were unacculturated Africans.

Echoes of Ligon and Sloane could still be heard in later writings, but most gave a far less sympathetic account of the slaves. As Barbados, followed by the Leeward Islands and Jamaica, became dominated by sugar plantations, the planters became more callous and indifferent to slaves' social arrangements. Wedded to the plantations, the slave trade also intensified, and now men imported outnumbered women by three to two. Meanwhile, bourgeois social values increasingly added insult to injury. As far as they were concerned at all, planters disparaged as natural faults characteristics in their slaves for which the whites themselves were chiefly to blame, and often similarly guilty. Thus, although marriage and family life were practically discouraged and forcible miscegenation was rife, planters condemned the slaves' "promiscuity," "polygamy," and apparent indifference to their children, or even to having children at all.

Behind the planters' ignorance and exaggeration, however, lay the undoubted truth that the quality of slave life had nearly everywhere deteriorated seriously. In this phase, West Indian families were probably at a low point of integration—before extended new kinships had been built up and laws passed forbidding the separation of husbands and wives, and mothers and children. Except for the polygynous favors enjoyed by privileged slaves like drivers—the slaves' "worst domestic tyrants"—conjugal unions were rare and impermanent, and the majority of infants lived with single mothers or grandmothers—up to 10 percent of whom were, or had been, the casual mates of plantation whites.

In the last phase of slavery, as the profits of plantations dwindled, the price of slaves rose, and in 1808, the supply of fresh Africans was cut off and the West Indian slaveowners came under economic constraints at the same time as they were coming under pressure from metropolitan philanthropists. Writers on slave society attacked or defended plantation customs, or proposed methods of raising the dismal level of slave fertility. The encouragement of Christianity and family life were seen by some as methods for making slaves contented, peaceable, and fertile. Some measure of local reform would, moreover, vitiate the arguments of the emancipationists and undermine the sectarian missionaries, who shared none of the establishment's reluctance to proselytize the slaves and promote respectable marriage. Accordingly, in the 1820s, plantocratic Assemblies passed acts ostensibly encouraging slave marriage and actually authorizing fees to Anglican ministers for slave baptisms.

Few writers, though, acknowledged the slaves' own motives. Since all slaves yearned chiefly to be free, if adherence to the Church and its formulas were conditions of freedom, a growing number of slaves would aspire to baptism and formal marriage, with their official registrations, as potent indicators of improving social status. Most writers also ignored the degree to which slaves actually possessed property and virtual tenure of houses and plots, which they were able, in custom if not in law, to bequeath to whomever they wished. Long before emancipation, a fair proportion of West Indian slaves had ample reasons, on the grounds of respectability and conformability to the laws of inheritance, to adopt the familial norms of the master class.

But nearly every commentator, from Ligon and Sloane to "Monk" Lewis and Mrs. A. C. Carmichael, did share two absolute certainties: that as to marriage, whatever the masters did, the slaves always had and always would (in the words of the Jamaican, John Quier) "claim a Right of disposing of themselves in this Respect, according to their Own Will and Pleasure without any Controul from their Masters"; and that within certain obvious constraints these voluntary arrangements were African rather than European. "We restrain their Actions sufficiently, to our conveniences," wrote Lindsay, Rector of St. Catherine's, Jamaica, "tho' we inslave not the Inclinations of the Heart, against their Natural Habits and Native Customs, which may well be injoy'd separately from their Obedience to us."[35]

35 Quier, "Report," 492; Lindsay, "A Few Conjectural Considerations upon the Creation of the Human Race, Occasioned by the Present Quixottical Rage of setting the Slaves from Africa at Liberty," unpub. ms. dated Spanish Town, July 23, 1788, British Museum, Additional Mss. 12439.

Few Africans carried their children with them into slavery, and fewer still accompanied marital partners from West Africa into West Indian plantations, let alone the members of the extended family and kinship groups which were of prime importance in West African society. The ethnic mixing which was standard plantation policy meant additionally that the legacies of Africa were transmitted in a haphazard or generalized way. Yet the impress of Africa was indelible, and African patterns were replicated where possible, and reconstituted as soon as possible where not, surviving slavery itself in modified forms.

On large plantations there were sometimes sub-cultural groups—such as "Ibo" or "Congo"—and some forceful cultural traditions, particularly the Akan (or "Coromantee"), seem to have been normative. Yet the very variety of West African roots allowed for creative syncretism, or the choice of alternative customs—for example, concerning the role of women, and the acceptability of cousin-mating and premarital intercourse—as the slaves made the necessary adjustments to the new environment, the dictates of the plantation system, and the shifting demographic conditions.[36]

Some features of the plantation system, such as the expectation that women would work in the fields, that men would monopolize the skilled and privileged roles, and that slave drivers and other elite slaves such as head craftsmen would be likely to practice polygyny, actually facilitated the continuation of West African customs. Other continuities were of necessity more covert, having to exist in the narrow scope of private life left to the slaves by the master class: rites of passage, courtship and premarital negotiations, marriage ceremonies and celebrations, and the role of elderly slaves as "councils of elders" to determine custom and settle domestic disputes. While the slave trade lasted, direct links with Africa were never cut, native Africans being brought in groups to expand plantations or, more commonly, arriving in ones and twos to make up the shortfall in slave fertility.

36 Higman, "Slave Family Patterns in Trinidad," 14–18, 33–35. This strongly stressed the melding effect of the African slave trade to Trinidad. Only among the Ibo was there a recognizable transfer of specific African family patterns, and this was attributed to their high numbers and comparatively even sex ratio. When the African slaves were broken down by 7 general regions of origin there were no really significant variations in the proportions of family types recreated in Trinidad.

As Edwards testified, these Africans were welcomed into family units, especially those of their own tribe and language.[37]

From the simple pairings which were all that the planters provided for, the slaves built up extended family relationships beyond the masters' ken or concern and, in the course of generations, whole new kinship networks based on the cohesive "village" of a single plantation holding but gradually extending beyond the plantation's bounds into nearby groups. In Barbados, a small island covered with small contiguous plantations, the process of social diffusion had gone on longest; but even there, as in Africa, the primary allegiance remained the village, the birthplace, the home and burial-place of closest family, kin, and ancestors.

In 1808 the direct connection with Mother Africa was cut, but by that time the area of social autonomy had significantly expanded for most slaves. Slaves owned their own property (in some colonies even in law), bequeathed and inherited houses and land, and in some islands virtually controlled the internal market system. On declining plantations they were encouraged to be as nearly self-sufficient as possible, and on decayed plantations were left almost entirely to their own devices. Yet, contrary to the masters' pessimism, the young and the aged were better cared for than under more rigorous slave regimes, and the unfavourable ratio between deaths and births began to reverse. In the phrase of Sidney Mintz, the most fortunate British West Indian slaves were proto-peasants long before slavery ended, and made an easy transition into "full freedom" in 1838.[38]

Four influences militated against the continued development of peasant lifestyles and family systems: the breakup of the old slave quarters and the consequent "marginalization" of many ex-slaves; the persistence of plantations in a more impersonal form; an accelerated urbanization; and the spread of the canons of respectability. The closing down of the slave cantonments after emancipation, as plantations decayed or turned to less intensive forms of agriculture (particularly, grazing "pens"), or ex-slaves who refused to work on the planters' terms were evicted from houses and plots, was as traumatic a change as the cutting of the

37 Edwards, *British West Indies*, II, 155.
38 Sidney W. Mintz, *Caribbean Transformations* (Chicago, 1974), 151–152.

African link or the ending of formal slavery itself. The more fortunate ex-slaves were able to form their own villages and develop a healthy peasant society; but many others without land of their own were forced into a marginal existence, depending on the increasingly mechanized plantations for wages, but competing with each other, and with newly imported indentured laborers, in a cruelly seasonal economy. Far fewer women worked as plantation laborers, and most of the men became transients, living in barracks or strange villages during crop-time and being unable to form permanent or stable attachments while women provided the only permanence and stability for children. A similar continuation of the worst features of the slave period occurred among the poor of the towns, which burgeoned after emancipation. The new towns had a high proportion of migrants from the countryside, a disproportionately high ratio of women, and thus a majority of impermanent, fractured, and matrifocal families.

As we have noticed, many slaves in the last phase of slavery were attracted by the apparent advantages of respectable, European-type families. After emancipation these became the norm among the small emergent middle class, many of the members of which were the colored descendants of domestic slaves who had engaged in miscegenous relationships. Under the growing influence of the churches, a far wider spectrum of the ex-slaves continued to subscribe outwardly to the canons of respectability, especially in islands like Barbados where the Anglican Church was deeply entrenched and conditions were unfavourable for true peasant development. Yet, as Wilson has plausibly argued, the subscription to respectability is superficial among the majority of British West Indian blacks. Far more deeply engrained are the tenets of "reputation": those elements of custom which place greater stress on community, kinship, and extended family, and place greater value on social worth, than on introspective family forms, bourgeois manners, and material wealth. In this analysis, reputation provides a continuous thread of tradition passing back through slavery to Africa itself.[39]

39 Peter J. Wilson, *Crab Antics: The Social Anthropology of English-Speaking Negro Societies of the Caribbean* (New Haven, 1973).

Therefore, in assessing the nature of slave family and its place in the continuum we emphasize not the ways that slavery destroyed or distorted family, but the ways in which the slaves' own forms of family triumphed over adversity. In this light, we evaluate slavery not by the manner in which it controlled and shaped slaves' destinies, but by the degree to which it allowed slaves to make family lives of their own.

Robert Y. Eng and Thomas C. Smith

Peasant Families and Population Control
in Eighteenth-Century Japan

After expanding rapidly in the seventeenth century, total Japanese population grew slowly, if at all, from the first national census in 1721 to the last census in the Tokugawa period in 1846. Surprisingly, unless the evidence has been badly misread, this was a period when the economy was expanding through improvements in farming, the spread of rural industry, and the growth of internal trade.[1] Per capita income must therefore have been rising as well, and the rise by lifting income per head to an unspecifiable but critical "threshold" level and inducing institutional and attitudinal changes may have been a necessary condition of Japan's subsequent industrialization.

It has been thought that population was held in check between 1721 and 1846 by high mortality as the result of periodic food crises and a rather high level of urbanization. But recent studies of local records similar to the parish registers of Europe call this inference into question. Though few in number these studies by Hanley, Hayami, and others consistently show low mortality and low fertility.[2] Our

Robert Y. Eng is a graduate student in history at the University of California at Berkeley. Thomas C. Smith is Professor of History at the University of California at Berkeley and the author of *The Agrarian Origins of Modern Japan* (Stanford, 1959) and *Political Change and Industrial Development: Government Industry in Japan 1850–1880* (Stanford, 1955).

The authors wish to express thanks to the following colleagues for criticism and advice at various stages of work: Gary Allinson, Sei'ichi Ando, James Bartholomew, Sydney Crawcour, Jan de Vries, Ronald P. Dore, Eugene Hammel, Robert Lundy, Byron Marshall, Irwin Scheiner, Etienne van de Walle, Ann Waswo, and James White; and for financial aid from the Center for Japanese and Korean Studies and the Institute of International Studies at the University of California at Berkeley, and from the National Science Foundation.

1 From 1721 on, all jurisdictions were required to make a periodic register of the commoner population by sex, age, and family relationship; this was usually done annually but in some places at longer intervals. Also at regular intervals population by sex had to be reported up the administrative hierarchy to the central government in Edo (Tokyo), where it was aggregated by province. It is this periodic nationwide administrative count which we refer to as a "Census." Sekiyama Naotarō, *Kinsei Nihon no jinkō kōzō* [The Population Structure of Tokugawa Japan] (Tokyo, 1957), 95–96, 123. Nakamura Satoru, "Hōkenteki tochi shoyū kaitai no chiikiteki tokushitsu" [Regional Characteristics of the Dissolution of Feudal Landownership], *Jimbun gakuhō* [Journal of Humanities], XIX (1964), 130–152.

2 The most comprehensive fertility and mortality data are crude birthrates and death rates (unadjusted for "infant mortality") for a group of villages in Suwa county in Nagano Prefecture between 1670 and 1860, based on a total population of more than

own study of the population of a small farming village in central
Japan, which we call Nakahara, confirms these findings. We intend
to report elsewhere in detail on mortality in Nakahara and the reliability of the documentation.[3] Here we are concerned with marital
fertility and why it was low.

Our views are based on analysis of the annual registers of population for the village in the period 1717–1830, which are complete
except for thirteen scattered years that are missing. Births in the gap-
years are recoverable, however, when the child lived until the next
registration. Population registers in Nakahara were made up in the
sixth month of each year; they listed all residents by name, age, sex,
and relation to family head, and during the year notations were made
of changes in the population through birth, death, and migration.
Unfortunately births were not normally entered until the infant's
first new year's celebration; consequently, children born after one new
year who died before the next never appeared in the record. We call
these omissions "infant mortality," a term not strictly accurate, and
estimate their number at about 20 percent of all births.[4]

THE QUESTION OF FERTILITY CONTROL   Table I compares age-specific
marital fertility in Nakahara and in a number of other contemporaneous
Japanese villages and European parishes for which there are estimates.
To make the estimates as nearly comparable as possible, we have

---

15,000 at the end of the period. See also age-specific estimates (later referred to) for
Yokouchi village, in Hayami Akira, *Kinsei nōson rekishino jinkō-gakuteki kenkyū* [A Demo-
graphic Historical Study of the Tokugawa Village] (Tokyo, 1973), 218. There are interesting crude rates for urban populations in Sasaki Yōichiro, "Tokugawa jidai kōki
toshi jinkō kenkyū" [A Study of Town Population in the Late Tokugawa Period],
Shikai [History], XIV (1967), 31 ff.; *idem*, "Hida no kuni Takayama no jinkō kenkyū"
[Study of the Population of Takayama in Hida Province], in Hayami Akira (ed.),
Keizai shi ni okeru jinkō [Population in Economic History] (Tokyo, 1969), 95–118. Crude
and age-specific birthrates and death rates for a number of scattered villages are to be
found in Susan B. Hanley, "Fertility, Mortality, and Life Expectancy in Premodern
Japan," *Population Studies*, XXVIII (1974), 131–135, (Tables 2–4).
3 Life expectancy in Nakahara at age 1 was 50.7 years for females and 46.9 for males.
4 It is not clear from internal evidence whether all infants born during the year and
alive at registration in the sixth month were registered then, or only infants born prior
to the first day of the calendar year. In the former case, the average age at registration
would be 6 months; in the latter case, 12 months. We have assumed the latter in making
estimates of the loss through "infant mortality" by fitting life tables for age 1 or older
in Nakahara to the most appropriate Coale-Demeny model life tables ("North" and
"East"). Our estimate would be much too high if the former case conformed to the
actual practice.

Table 1 Age-Specific Marital Fertility in Selected European and Japanese Communities (No. of Births/1000 Woman-Years)

PLACE AND PERIOD OF FORMATION OF MARRIAGE	AGE GROUP							TOTAL FERTILITY[a]
	15–19	20–24	25–29	30–34	35–39	40–44	45–49	
England								
Colyton, 1647–1719	500	346	395	272	182	104	020	6.6
Colyton, 1770–1837	500	441	361	347	270	152	022	8.0
France								
Crulai, 1674–1742	320	419	429	355	292	142	010	8.2
Le Mesnil-Beaumont, 1740–99	452	524	487	422	329	135	017	9.6
Thézels-St. Sernin 1700–92	208	393	326	297	242	067	000	6.6
Meulan, 1660–1739	585	519	507	503	379	157	014	10.4
Meulan, 1740–89	492	493	477	403	294	111	015	9.0
Germany								
Anhausen 1692–1799	n.a.	472	496	450	355	173	037	9.9
Japan								
Yokouchi, before 1700[b]	204	382	358	266	264	164	028	7.3
Yokouchi, 1701–50[b]	168	275	240	232	146	071	026	5.0
Yokouchi, 1751–1800[b]	188	205	226	161	116	078	010	4.0
Yokouchi, after 1800[b]	306	264	231	202	092	042	011	4.2
Kando-shinden, after 1800[b]	471	531	351	269	225	138	016	7.7
Nishijo, 1773–1835[b]	321	399	356	315	251	121	032	7.4
Nakahara, 1717–1830	214	326	304	300	221	122	034	6.5

a Computed from ages 20 to 49.
b Birth cohorts of mothers.
SOURCES: E. A. Wrigley, "Family Limitation in Pre-industrial England," *Economic History Review*, XIX (1966), 89; Etienne Gautier and Louis Henry, *La population*

inflated the figures for the Japanese villages (all of which had essentially the same system of late registration of births) in each group in order to adjust for births lost through "infant mortality" at an estimated rate of 20 percent.

Two things stand out in Table 1. First, fertility in Nakahara was about the average for the Japanese communities; second, even after adjustment for infant mortality, it was distinctly low compared with all of the European parishes with two exceptions: Colyton in 1647–1719, where there is strong evidence that some form of family limitation was in force; and Thézels-St. Sernin, in the region of puzzlingly low fertility in southwestern France.[5]

Fertility was much lower in Nakahara than in any of the other European communities, including Colyton at a later date. This can be seen in the column entitled total fertility on the far right, which shows the number of children which a woman would have if she lived in marriage from age 20 to 49 and bore children on the schedule shown by the age-specific rates.[6] Using Nakahara's total fertility as an index of 100, the ratio was 123 for Colyton in 1770–1837, 126 for Crulai, 148 for Le Mesnil-Beaumont, 152 for Anhausen, and 160 for Meulan in 1660–1739 and 138 in 1740–89.

The general contrast is brought out graphically by Fig. 1, which compares age-specific marital fertility in Nakahara and in two French

---

de Crulai, paroisse normande (Paris, 1958), 105; Jean Ganiage, Trois villages d'Ile-de-France au XVIIIᵉ siècle (Paris, 1963), 82; Pierre Valmary, Familles paysannes au XVIIIᵉ siècle en Bas-Quercy (Paris, 1965), 120; Marcel Lachiver, La Population de Meulan du XVIIᵉ au XIXᵉ siècle (Paris, 1969), 152; John Knodel, "Two and a Half Centuries of Demographic History in a Bavarian Village," Population Studies, XXIV (1970), 369; Hayami, Kinsei nōson, 218; idem, "The Demographic Analysis of a Village in Tokugawa Japan: Kando-shinden of Owari Province, 1778–1871," Keio Economic Studies, V (1968), 78; idem, "Jinkō gakuteki shihyō ni okeru kaisōkan no kakusa" [Class Differences in Demographic Indices], Tokugawa rinseishi kenkyusho [The Tokukawa Institute of Forestry History] (ed.), Kenkyū kiyō [Research Annals] (1973), 182.

5   On the comparatively low levels of age-specific fertility in southwestern France, see Valmary, Familles paysannes, ch. 6; L. Henry, "Fécondité des mariages dans le quart sud-ouest de la France," Annales, XXVII (1972), 612–640, 977–1023, esp. 985, 991, 1001–1005; Pierre Goubert, "Legitimate Fecundity and Infant Mortality in France during the 18th Century: A Comparison," Daedalus, XCVII (1968), 593–603, esp. 597–599.

6   It is standard practice to omit the 15–19 age group in computations of total fertility because inclusion of that group would introduce a serious bias for two main reasons: (1) adolescent sterility would greatly reduce the actual fertility of the 15–19 age group if all women marry at 15, but in fact the rate attributed to the whole group is usually computed from a few women who marry around age 18 or 19; (2) in many communities early marriers are exceptionally baby-prone because of forced marriages.

Fig. 1 Age-specific Marital Fertility in Nakahara and Two French Parishes

Age-specific marital fertility
(number of births / 1000 woman-years)

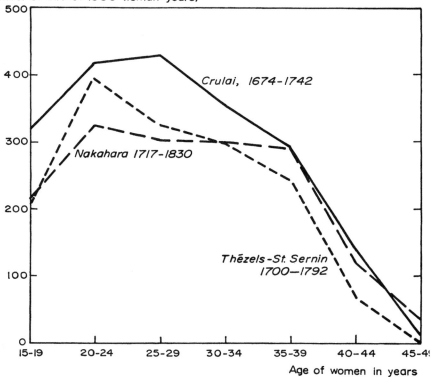

parishes representing cases of relatively high and low fertility for that country. The Nakahara curve, it will be seen, is at about the same general level as Thézels-St. Sernin (low fertility) and much below Crulai (high fertility).

It seems unlikely that Nakahara's comparatively low marital fertility is to be explained by the practice of any form of birth control since the shape of its fertility curve is of the kind usually associated with the absence of such limitation. In these circumstances the woman's age is the preponderant factor in fertility which is independent of the length of marriage and declines slowly at the early ages, and then more rapidly as fecundity declines and the proportion of infertile couples increases. This gives a convex curve. When birth control is widespread, however, couples tend to concentrate childbearing in the early years of marriage, stopping procreation when they reach the usually small number of children desired. Thus, fertility declines with the length of

Fig. 2 Marital Age-specific Fertility in a Community Practicing Family Limitation

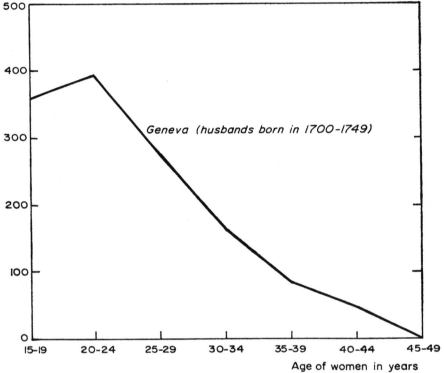

Age-specific marital fertility
(number of births / 1000 woman years)

Geneva (husbands born in 1700-1749)

Age of women in years

marriage and may be quite low even when the woman is still young, since couples who marry young tend to bear the desired number of children at an early age. Age-specific fertility therefore falls steadily with increasing age, tending to flatten out at the late ages, and this gives a concave curve (Fig. 2).[7]

It is well known, of course, that great differences in marital fertility exist among different populations in the absence of birth control. This is probably due to the different spacing between births as a result of variations in the waiting period between birth and the resumption of sexual relations, the length of suckling, and physiological differences governing the reappearance of ovulation after confinement.[8]

7 Louis Henry, *Manuel de démographie historique* (Geneva, 1970), 89–90; E. A. Wrigley, "Family Limitation," 91.
8 Louis Henry, "Some Data on Natural Fertility," *Eugenics Quarterly*, VIII (1961), 90–91.

Fertility in Nakahara may have been low partly in consequence of some combination of these factors; we have no way of knowing. But it was almost certainly low in part because of infanticide.

There is an immense amount of legal and literary evidence of abortion and infanticide in the country at large, though none to our knowledge places either practice specifically in Nakahara.[9] *Daimyo* governments repeatedly prohibited infanticide and abortion in the eighteenth century, attributing to these practices the stagnation of population. Moralists railed against both infanticide and abortion, frequently running these distinct terms together, as if they had a common significance. Abortion was apparently more widely practiced in the towns where there were skilled specialists; but both practices were found in rural and urban locales and, also, seemingly among all classes. Contemporary writers were inclined to be lenient with the poor, whose circumstances presumably drove them to these acts; their special wrath was saved for families in comfortable circumstances—samurai and merchants as well as substantial farmers—who were said to limit children merely to increase their own ease or to improve the prospects of the children whom they chose to raise.

Infanticide is consistent, in theory at least, with the Nakahara fertility curve. If the act occurred at birth, as contemporary writers said, the victims would never appear in the registers; if it also occurred frequently, registered fertility would be extremely low through the combined effects of eliminated births and the sterile periods of pregnancy associated with them, and at the same time the fertility curve would in all probability be convex. Infanticide is the only form of birth limitation—to equate that term with a form of abortion—which permits control over the sex of offspring, an advantage that probably no society which adopted it would forego entirely. As a result of eliminating children of the unwanted sex in various circumstances, one would expect extremely long average intervals between births. As long as there were not too many very small families, childbearing would be widely spread over the fertile years of marriage; fertility would therefore tend to vary with the woman's age rather than with the length of marriage, and so describe a convex curve.

There is no way to detect abortion specifically in the Nakahara registers, but infanticide, being sex-selective, has left many traces. What follows is an analysis of this evidence, which lead us to believe

9 The most comprehensive study of this sort of evidence is the massive work by Takahashi Bonsen, *Nihon jinkōshi no kenkyū* [Studies of Japanese Population History] (Tokyo, 1941–62), 3v.

that infanticide was widely practiced in the village and, moreover, practiced less as part of a struggle for survival than as a way of planning the sex composition, sex sequence, spacing, and ultimate number of children. As the evidence is complex and unfamiliar, it may be helpful to summarize the main points in advance:

1. There were few very large or very small completed families; distribution clustered heavily around the mean.
2. Small land-holders had fewer children than large; and early stoppers (last child born before mother reached age 38) had fewer children than late stoppers.
3. But late-stopping small holders had larger families than early-stopping large holders.
4. The smaller the family, the younger the mother at the birth of the last child, and the more likely the last child to be male.
5. Families tended, beginning with the third child, to have a next child of the sex of which they had fewer.
6. There is evidence that children were spaced for the convenience of the mother.
7. There is also some evidence of the avoidance of an unlucky sex in the next child under specifiable circumstances.

SEX BIAS   We initially thought infanticide was practiced exclusively or mainly against females and that evidence to this effect would be found in the sex ratio at birth. We soon discovered that this was not the case. A sex ratio of 114 males per 100 females in 658 births could not be considered abnormally high. We observed, however, certain variations in sex ratio by birth order which, in time, led to the inference that infanticide was practiced against both sexes and, further, that married couples had a marked tendency to have a next child of the sex underrepresented in their present family.[10]

This tendency was evident only after the second birth; there

10 As may be seen below in the distribution of births by sex for births 3–10 in all first marriages, almost invariably from the third birth on, odd birth orders showed an excess of males and even birth orders either no bias or a slight excess of females:

BIRTH ORDER	M	F	SEX RATIO
3	53	43	123
4	39	40	98
5	35	18	194
6	19	19	100
7	11	10	110
8	3	6	50
9	2	1	200
10	0	1	0

seems to have been no general sex preference before then. The sub-sequent preference can be seen both in complete first marriages—first marriages for both partners which lasted through the wife's age 45—and in all first marriages, in the following way. Consider each married couple as a distinct case of marriage at each birth of a child when two or more previous children are registered in the household. Thus, a couple with six children all living and registered at home would appear four times as four different families in the sample, once at each birth after the second. Now divide these statistical families into three groups according to the sex of the previous children registered at home: those with predominantly male children (*PM*), those with predominantly females (*PF*), and those with an equal number of both sexes (*M* = *F*). Then for each group calculate the sex ratio of the next children born. Table 2 shows the results of this test for complete first marriages.

Table 2 Distribution of the Sex of the Next Child Relative to the Sex Composition of Living Sibling Sets of Two or More Children (All Complete First Marriages)[a]

SEX COMPOSITION	SEX OF NEXT CHILD		
OF SIBLING SET	M	F	SEX RATIO
PM	30	45	67
M = *F*	31	21	148
PF	38	19	200

a Includes all living siblings residing in the family and all of those away as hired servants but registered with the family at the time of birth of the next child; one case of births of fraternal twins of opposite sex is excluded.

If the sex of the next child in these families was independent of that of the previous children, the ratio of male-to-female births ought to have been about the same in each group of families. The ratios in the various groups, however, differ significantly from one another; and the chances of differences of this magnitude occurring inde-pendently of the sex of previous children is considerably less than 1 in 100. Also, the sex ratio in two of the groups, *PM* and *PF*, is significantly different from normal (102).[11] We must suppose, therefore, that the

11   We can test for homogeneity of the three groups by applying the χ^2 test to a 3 × 2 contingency table consisting of the distribution of the sex of the next child of the three groups; the null hypothesis is that births are independent of each other and of the composition of the existing sibling set. Four degrees of freedom are lost in our assumption

sex of the next child was to some extent a matter of choice, enforced by infanticide, and that families tended to eliminate infants of the sex which they had more of, and to eliminate girls somewhat more often than boys. Otherwise, it is quite inexplicable that families with predominantly male children tended to have females in the next child by a ratio significantly different from normal; that those where females predominated tended to have males by a ratio significantly different from normal; and that those with an equal number of both sexes, though tending to have more males than females, did *not* do so by a significant margin.

Table 3 Distribution of the Sex of the Next Child Relative to the Sex Composition of Living Sibling sets of Two or More Children (all first marriages)[a]

SEX COMPOSITION	SEX OF NEXT CHILD		
OF SIBLING SET	M	F	SEX RATIO
PM	47	65	72
M = F	42	25	168
PF	55	32	172

a Includes all living siblings residing in the family and all of those away as hired servants but registered with the family at the time of birth of the next child; one case of births of fraternal twins of opposite sex is excluded.

Table 3 shows that the results are similar when the sample is enlarged to include all first marriages. This sample gives a less smooth rise in sex ratio from *PM* to *M=F* to *PF*; the proportion of male

that the true probability of a male birth equals the observed proportion of male births in the sample (0.54), and that the expected frequency of births in each class of sibling composition equals the observed frequency. We get a χ^2 of 10.6, significant at the 0.006 level on 2 degrees of freedom.

If the sex ratio at birth was 105, the expected sex ratio at age 1 (registered birth) would be 102 by Model North of the Coale-Demeny life tables (which most closely resembles the Nakahara life tables for mortality at age 1 or older). We can test for sex bias in any distribution of sex by applying the χ^2 test on the null hypothesis that the true sex ratio at (registered) birth is 102. The results for the three groups are as follows:

	χ^2	DEGREES OF FREEDOM	LEVEL OF SIGNIFICANCE
PM	3.4	1	0.07
M = F	1.9	1	0.17
PF	5.7	1	0.02

births in the two latter groups was nearly identical. But in all groups the sex ratio of the next child was significantly different from normal (102), and again, the differences in sex ratio among all three groups were statistically significant ($p < 0.004$).[12] It seems likely, therefore, that parents with both complete and incomplete marriages tended to keep or "return" (as the euphemism had it) newborn babies, depending in part upon the sex of the infant and on that of previous children.

SEX OF THE NEXT CHILD AFTER THE DEATH OF A CHILD   If parents in fact selected the sex of infants generally in order to get approximately the sex mix in offspring that they wished, then with the death of a child, one would suppose that they would have a next child of the same sex as the deceased. To our astonishment, there was a significant tendency for the next child to be the opposite sex of the deceased, as the "Total" column of Table 4 shows.[13] Even controlling for the sex of the surviving siblings, this tendency holds. Hence, families losing a male and left with predominantly female children nonetheless tended to have a female next, and vice versa. Perhaps replacement by a child of the same sex was thought challenging or offensive to the powers who had taken away the deceased, but this is the purest speculation.[14] What is certain is that this surprising behavior went against the general tendency to

12   Applying the test for sex bias as described in 11, we get:

	χ^2	DEGREES OF FREEDOM	LEVEL OF SIGNIFICANCE
PM	3.6	1	0.06
M = F	3.8	1	0.05
PF	5.6	1	0.02

Applying the test for homogeneity as described in note 11, we get a χ^2 of 11.2, significant at 0.004 level on 2 degrees of freedom.

13   Applying the χ^2 test to the 2 × 2 contingency table corresponding to all cases regardless of living sibship composition, on the null hypothesis that the sex of the deceased child was unrelated to the sex of the next child and with the assumptions that the true probability of a male birth equals the observed frequency in the sample (0.49) and that the expected frequencies of births in both classes of deceased child equal the observed frequencies, we get a highly significant χ^2 statistic of 10.7 (0.001 level) on 1 degree of freedom. Moreover, for both classes of deceased child, the sex ratio of the next birth deviates significantly from 102 (0.02 level).

14   The objection has been made that this assumes an absurdity, namely, that a child of the wrong sex was killed in order to preserve it from harm. But presumably infanticide was never committed primarily in the interest of its victim but of someone else—family, mother, siblings, etc. Also it is not necessarily absurd to think of an infant being killed to protect it; one of the modern arguments for abortion is that the victim is better off than if raised as an unwanted child.

balance sexes, and otherwise this tendency would have been still stronger.[15]

Table 4 Distribution of Sex of Next Child Born after Death of a Child (All First Marriages)[a]

SEX OF DECEASED CHILD	SEX COMPOSITION OF LIVING SIBLING SET AT BIRTH OF NEXT CHILD[b]							
	PM		M = F		PF		TOTAL	
M	2	3	3	9	4	10	9	22
F	6	3	8	2	4	1	18	6
	M	F	M	F	M	F	M	F

SEX OF NEXT CHILD

a Includes all cases where two or more children of the same sex died before the next birth but excludes three cases where two or more children of different sex died before the next birth.

b Unlike Table 3, the groups here include sibling sets of one or no child, null sibling sets being counted in the M = F group; the reason is that we are here primarily interested in the relationship between the sex of a deceased child and the sex of the next child, and introduce sibship composition only as a control variable. Eliminating sibling sets of one or no child does not alter the general picture:

SEX OF DECEASED CHILD	SEX COMPOSITION OF LIVING SIBLING SET OF TWO OR MORE CHILDREN AT BIRTH OF NEXT CHILD							
	PM		M = F		PF		TOTAL	
M	2	3	2	9	1	2	5	14
F	5	3	4	1	4	1	13	5
	M	F	M	F	M	F	M	F

SEX OF NEXT CHILD

15 If we remove from the pool of families those with a child dying before the next birth, the sexual preferences shown in Table 3 become stronger for the *PM* and *PF*, though not for the M = F, groups. This can be seen in the proportion of male births in the three groups:

	COMPOSITION OF SIBLING SETS OF 2 OR MORE LIVING CHILDREN		
	PM	M = F	PF
All first marriages	0.42	0.63	0.63
All first marriages eliminating cases where birth was preceded by death of a previous child	0.40	0.63	0.68

Fig. 3 Distribution by Completed Family Size (Complete First Marriages)

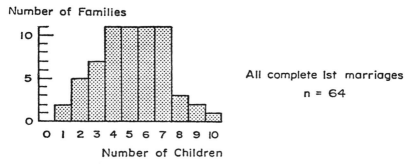

Number of Families

All complete 1st marriages

n = 64

Number of Children

LIMITATION OF FAMILY SIZE   Sex selection in the next child was probably not the unique aim of infanticide. An equally important aim, no doubt, was family limitation. Mean family size for complete first marriages was notably small, 5.1 children;[16] but by itself this fact tells us little since the small mean may have been the result of family limitation or, alternatively, of such factors as sex selection, infant mortality, and low fecundity. Some light is thrown on the subject, however, by the distribution of completed families by size.

As Fig. 3 shows, there was a heavy bunching around the mean, with few families of less than four or more than seven children. The extreme bunching of this distribution can be brought out by a comparison of Nakahara with Meulan in France, using only complete marriages with the wife aged 30 or younger, a restriction explained in note 16. Only 10 percent of complete families in Nakahara had eight or more children compared with 57 percent in Meulan in a period of no family limitation (1660–1739); and only 8 percent of complete families in Nakahara had two or less children compared with 33 percent in Meulan in a period of family limitation (1790–1839).[17]

"Infant mortality," for which we have made no adjustment in the

16 International comparison is complicated by the fact that the median age at first marriage of women in Nakahara was 18.5 years, about five or more years younger than in most West European parishes. However, if we restrict ourselves to cases in which the wife was younger than age 30 at the time of marriage, the mean family size for complete first marriages in Nakahara was 5.2 children, as compared with 6.1 children and 8.0 children for complete marriages in Crulai (1675–1744) and Meulan (1660–1739), respectively. (Calculated from figures in Gautier and Henry, *La population de Crulai*, 126; Lachiver, *Meulan*, 171.) Only two complete first marriages in Nakahara, each producing three children, are eliminated because of this restriction.
17 The proportions for Meulan are computed from data in Lachiver, Meulan, 171–172.

above comparison, obviously cannot account for the rarity of small or the complete absence of childless families in Nakahara. With the means at hand to achieve such families, their rarity must have been intentional. The avoidance of childless families is especially clear. As about 4 percent of any human population may be expected to be sterile, merely letting matters take their course would almost certainly have produced some childless families. But matters were not allowed to take their course: infertile brides were sent home early, as is evident from the fact that ten of thirteen divorces in the village ended childless marriages after an average of 3.0 years of conjugal living. In other words, childless marriages never became complete marriages.

Although the small proportion of large families in Nakahara, as compared with Meulan, is obviously accounted for partly by "infant mortality," a substantial difference remains even when the Nakahara figure is generously adjusted upward for "infant mortality."[18] Was the relatively small proportion of large families in Nakahara partly intentional, too?

One piece of evidence concerns the age of mothers at the birth of the last child (*MALB*), which for obvious reasons is a meaningful datum only when marriages are complete. The mean *MALB* in complete first marriages in Nakahara was 37.5.[19] This is rather early for a population not practicing family limitation. In this case it may be accounted for by "infant mortality," i.e., infants dying, unregistered, of natural causes (after the last registered birth); and, possibly, the early

18   To test the hypothesis whether "infant mortality" accounted for the low proportion of large families in Nakahara, we inflated the size of each completed family by assigning through random drawing an unregistered infant mortality rate to each family so that:

$\frac{1}{4}$ of the families would have a mortality rate of 100‰
$\frac{1}{2}$ of the families would have a mortality rate of 200‰
$\frac{1}{8}$ of families would have a mortality rate of 300‰
$\frac{1}{8}$ of families would have a mortality rate of 400‰.

The size of each family was then adjusted upward according to the mortality rate assigned, with decimals rounded off to the nearest whole number. Note that the procedure implicitly assumes an overall infant mortality rate of 213‰, which may be far too high; moreover, some of those infants "recovered" in this way might have been eliminated by infanticide rather than through natural death. Even so, the proportion of families of 8+ children in Nakahara rises only to 45%, still considerably lower than 57% as found in Meulan.

19   This is earlier than one would expect if there were no limitation of births; in eighteenth-century European communities practicing little or no family limitation, mean *MALB* is about 40 or 41. On the other hand, the differential between Nakahara's *MALB* and the European norm would be narrowed or perhaps even eliminated if we could take into account infants born after the mother's last registered birth and dying unregistered of natural causes in the first year of life.

age of marriage for females enabled subfecund couples, who in a late-marrying population would be childless, to have one or two children, presumably at an early age. However, if we divide the mothers into two nearly equal groups of early stoppers ($MALB \leq 37.0$) and late stoppers ($MALB > 37.0$), we almost rule out these possibilities for the critical early group. The early stoppers, whose average $MALB$ was 33.0 as compared with 41.2 for late stoppers, ended by a ratio of 2.6 to 1 with a male child. Late stoppers on the other hand ended about as often with a female as a male (see Table 5). Thus, much of the early stopping was apparently deliberate; if it had been involuntary, say the result of infecundity or "infant mortality," the sex of the last child would have been randomly determined and not skewed in favor of males.

Table 5   Sex of the Last Child by $MALB$ in Complete First Marriages

	M	F	SEX RATIO
$MALB \leq 37.0$	21	8	262
$MALB > 37.0$	19	16	119

Significantly, though not surprisingly, early stoppers had fewer children than late. The mean completed family size of the two groups, respectively, was 4.0 and 6.1; although only 10 percent of early stoppers had as many as 6 children, an astonishing 71 percent of late stoppers did. No part of this difference is attributable to differential duration of marriage: the average age of marriage for the two groups of women was nearly identical—19.4 and 19.6—and all members of both groups were married through age 45. The smaller sized families were due mainly to early stopping, a good deal of which we have just seen must have been deliberate to account for the heavy predominance of males as last children.

This leaves open the possibility that late stoppers did not practice infanticide. After all, they stopped with one sex about as often as another and had about as many female as male births in total, and abstention from infanticide would account for the late $MALB$ of the group, and the normal sex ratio of both the last birth and all births.[20] But they were not abstainers. This fact appears when late stoppers are

20   There was an exactly equal number of boys and girls among the 212 children born to late stoppers.

Fig. 4 Distribution of the Sex of the Next Child relative to the Sex Composition of Living Sibling Sets of Two or More Children (Complete First Marriages with *MALB* > 37.0)

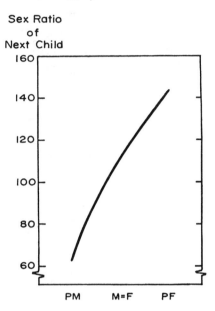

divided into *PM*, *M* = *F*, and *PF* groups, as all families were earlier, on the basis of the sex of two or more children registered at home, and the sex of the next child observed for each group. As Table 6 and Fig. 4 show, the probability of a male birth increased by large and nearly uniform jumps from *PM* to *M* = *F* to *PF* families.[21]

Table 6 Distribution of the Sex of the Next Child Relative to the Sex Composition of Living Sibling Sets of Two or More Children (*MALB* Groups in Complete First Marriages)

	SEX COMPOSITION OF LIVING SIBLING SET								
	PM			*M* = *F*			*PF*		
MALB ≤ 37.0	9	11	82	12	4	300	15	3	500
MALB > 37.0	21	34	62	19	17	112	23	16	144
	M	*F*	sex ratio	*M*	*F*	sex ratio	*M*	*F*	sex ratio

SEX OF THE NEXT CHILD

21 Carrying out the test for homogeneity as described in note 11, we get a χ^2 of 4.6, significant at the 0.10 level on 2 degrees of freedom.

It would therefore appear that late stoppers continued child-bearing to a relatively late age *despite* the practice of infanticide; that by infanticide they tended to keep offspring sexually balanced from one birth order to another after the second; and that the large size of completed families among them would not generally have been due to a need to continue procreation to a late age in order to correct a severe sex imbalance among early children. Assuming that these statements are warranted, we may add another. Both sex balance and larger-than-average family size were in all probability intentional: Late stopping was the necessary means of achieving these goals.

FARM SIZE AND FAMILY SIZE   We come now to another kind of evidence for family limitation. Although there is no direct information on farm size, we have a reasonable proxy in estimates of the normal productivity of holdings in rice equivalents (*kokudaka*) of all holdings in the village, identified by holder, at ten scattered dates (1716, 1727, 1738, 1746, 1764, 1780, 1792, 1802, 1812, and 1823).[22] The accuracy and currency of these evaluations, which were made for purposes of taxation, are uncertain; they also tell us nothing about how land was distributed for farming as opposed to how it was held for purposes of taxation (roughly, ownership); nor do they reveal anything about the non-agricultural income of families. Nevertheless, we have found these data relevant in analyzing mortality in Nakahara.[23] We use them here to divide all complete first marriages into above

22   *Kokudaka* expressed the productivity of a unit of land and was usually arrived at by averaging yields, estimated just before the harvest, over a period of years. Adjustments were often made to take account of differential costs, distance from market, and other factors that varied from one piece of land and one village to an other. To assign a *kokudaka* to an individual field, it was necessary not only to estimate the yield per *tan* of land, but also to measure the field. To estimate the yield and to survey for size all of the plots in a village, which often ran to several hundred, was an immensely difficult and politically sensitive job. It is not surprising, therefore, that assessments were not kept current.

Assessments in Tokugawa villages, it is known, tended to get out of date through a combination of changes in productivity and infrequent and piecemeal reassessment. Also, assessments covered only land held in Nakahara, though some families might have held land in neighboring villages. For these reasons assessments can be regarded as reflecting real farm income, at best, only approximately; see Thomas C. Smith, "The Land Tax in the Tokugawa Period," *Journal of Asian Studies*, XVIII (1958), 3–19.

23   Using 12 *koku* as the dividing line, the expectation of life at age 1 for large holders and small holders is 52.5 and 47.8 years, respectively, for females, and 49.4 and 43.9 years, respectively, for males.

and below median holding families, which we hereafter call large and small holder.[24]

Table 7 Economic Status and Fertility in Complete First Marriages

LANDHOLDING GROUP	NO. OF FAMILIES	WIFE'S MEAN AGE AT MARRIAGE	MEAN *MALB*	MEAN NO. OF CHILDREN
Below median	32	20.5	36.1	4.5
Above median	32	18.5	37.9	5.7

Table 7 shows that completed family size was significantly different for the two groups: large holders had an average of 5.7 children, small 4.5. This was partly because large holders' wives married two years younger on average than small holders' and ended procreation 1.8 years older. Size of holding, however, did not affect the spacing of children; if we divide the mean number of children by the difference between mean *MALB* and mean wife's age at marriage, we get 0.29 children per year for both the large and the small holders. Thus, farm size affected family size through the age of marriage and the age of stopping, not through the spacing of children.

It is interesting that both large and small holders break down almost evenly into early and late stoppers, and that size of holding and *MALB* together determine family size to a greater degree than either alone. This can be seen in Fig. 5, where we divide completed families into four groups based on a combination of holding size and *MALB*. We arrange the four groups down the page in descending order of average family size and show for each group the distribution of families by size. Notice that the order turns out to be alternately large and small holders. Each group has a strongly marked, modal family size which accounts for one-third to more than one-half of the families, and the mode decreases neatly as we move down the page. Also, smallest family size and largest family size for the various groups

24 First, for each family during its period of existence, we construct a function of farming income in *kokudaka* vs. time by straight line interpolations between registration dates, and by horizontal interpolations forward and backward for the first and last dates, respectively. We then calculate for each complete first marriage the average annual income of the couple's family over the time interval from the beginning of the marriage through the end of the wife's fecundity (age 45). Finally, we divide these marriages equally into above and below median landholding classes.

Fig. 5 Distribution of Completed Family Size in Groups by Landholding and Mother's Age at Last Birth (Complete First Marriages)

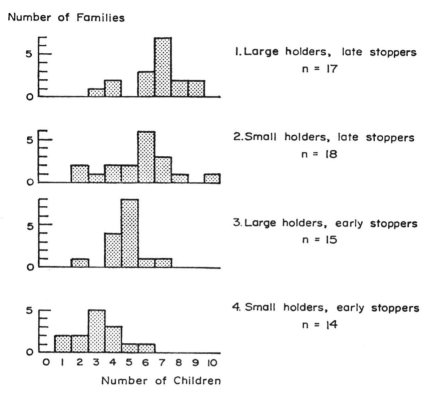

Number of Families

1. Large holders, late stoppers
   n = 17

2. Small holders, late stoppers
   n = 18

3. Large holders, early stoppers
   n = 15

4. Small holders, early stoppers
   n = 14

Number of Children

decrease in the same order, though a bit less smoothly. These groups, defined by holding size and *MALB*, seem, therefore, to have distinct fertility characteristics.

Average family size is clearly related to holding size. Early stopping large holders had larger families than early stopping small holders; and late stopping large holders had larger families than late stopping small holders. This was probably because large holders wanted more children. They could better afford them and could use the additional labor more efficiently in farming. On the other hand, large holders' wives may have been more fertile than small holders', owing to their better nutrition and shelter and less crowded quarters. In any case, holding size was not the only determinant of family size because late or early stopping, which was independent of holding size as already noted, was an equally or almost equally important factor. This can be seen in the fact that late stopping small holders had more children than early stopping large holders, but whether accidentally or intentionally, we cannot guess.

SEX SELECTION AND FAMILY SIZE   One of the difficulties a family would have in achieving a preferred number of children was the concurrent desire for a particular sex mix and sequence of children. These objectives must have obstructed one another. Accepting or annulling births because of the sex of the infant would tend to defeat plans about completed family size, and vice versa. It is surprising, therefore, that a clear relation emerges between completed family size and the sex ratio of children. The larger the family, generally speaking, the more evenly balanced the sex of children; the smaller the family, the higher the proportion of boys. We must qualify this statement before exploring possible explanations.

Families of the smallest size used in testing the relationship—one to three children—had in fact an almost even number of boys and girls. But dividing this group into early and late stoppers (Table 8) reveals that early stoppers had nearly twice as many boys as girls, while the few late stoppers had nearly all girls. This difference may be due to sampling error, as the number in each group is small. But another explanation is also possible since late stoppers with three children or fewer had long intervals between births; this raises the suspicion that they may have tried repeatedly for males, failed to get them and after annulling a number of births, finally settled for females. If so, the early stoppers, who were much the more numerous group, would more accurately reflect the intentions of small families.

Table 8   Complete First Marriages with Three Children or Less

	NO. OF FAMILIES	ALL CHILDREN		MEAN BIRTH INTERVAL (YR.)
		M	F	
$MALB \leq 37.0$	10	15	8	3.8
$MALB > 37.0$	4	2	8	6.1

With the qualification then that a few small families ended up unintentionally with a high proportion of girls, the statement holds that the sex ratio of children was high in small completed families, and converged to normal as family size increased. This is shown in Table 9 (where we use early stoppers only for families with one to three children).

Table 9 Sex Ratio and Family Size (Complete First Marriages)

FAMILY SIZE	ALL CHILDREN BORN		
	M	F	SEX RATIO
1–3[a]	15	8	188
4–5	56	43	130
6+	101	94	107

a Excluding late stoppers.

One naturally wonders to what extent the relation between family size and sex ratio was the outcome of different family strategies, and to what extent due to factors beyond anyone's control. It will be obvious to the wary reader that we cannot really hope to answer this question, but some observations relevant to an answer are possible.

Three partial explanations hinging on unintentional factors can probably be rejected. One turns on the wife's age at first marriage. The earlier the age of marriage, as Table 10 shows, the larger the mean completed family size tended to be. Now *if* couples also tended first to have a certain number of males and then—in the event that they had more children—females, the earlier the marriage the larger the completed family would be and also the lower the sex ratio of the children. But this does not seem to have been the case. Eighty-six percent of all complete first marriages for women occurred before age 22, and the mean age of marriage for women with four-five and six or more children ever (Table 11) was nearly identical—18.7 to 18.4. So age of marriage would seem to have no influence on family size *after* three children and, hence, none on the difference in sex ratio between families of four-five and six or more children.

Table 10 Wife's Age at Marriage and Completed Family Size (Complete First Marriages)

WIFE'S AGE AT MARRIAGE	NO. OF FAMILIES	MEAN FAMILY SIZE
18 –	33	5.7
19–21	22	4.7
22 +	9	3.8

Table 11 Completed Family Size and Wife's Age at Marriage (Complete First Marriages)

NO. OF CHILDREN	NO. OF FAMILIES	WIFE'S AGE MEAN AT MARRIAGE	MEAN *MALB*
1–3	14	22.9	33.4
4–5	22	18.7	36.0
6+	28	18.4	40.8

Another possible explanation concerns the effects of mortality on completed family size. As large families had proportionately more deaths among children before birth of the last child than small families had, the desire to replace deceased children conceivably prompted these families to continue procreation longer than they would have otherwise, and also to accept more female births.[25] However, when we examine the case more closely, it is by no means certain that large families really had a disproportionately high child mortality in terms of person-years of risk. Rather, they may have suffered more deaths before the birth of the last child merely because childbearing continued longer.

If we count the proportion of children born and dying before the mother's age 38, the figure in families of one to three children is 7 percent, while it is 13 percent in families of four-five and 14 percent in families of six or more. Although there may be a real difference between very small families and the others, there is none among families with more than three children. Further, if we eliminate deceased children in computing mean family size (Table 12), we still find a significant difference among the groups. Thus, child replacement would seem to account, at best, only marginally for differences in completed family size and sex ratio.

Table 12 Child Mortality and Family Size (Complete First Marriages)

NO. OF CHILDREN	NO. OF FAMILIES	MEAN FAMILY SIZE[a]	MEAN FAMILY SIZE WITH CHILDREN DYING BEFORE THE LAST BIRTH EXCLUDED[a]
1–3	14	2.4 (34)	2.2 (37)
4–5	22	4.5 (64)	4.1 (69)
6+	28	7.0 (100)	5.9 (100)

a Relative index in parentheses.

25 For complete first marriages, the proportion of children who died before the birth of the last child is 17% in families of 6 or more children, 12% in families of 4–5 children, and 11% in families of 1–3 children.

The third explanation has already been rejected in another context: that, although small families practiced infanticide in favor of males, large families rarely resorted to infanticide and so ended inadvertently with approximately the same number of males as females. This line of reasoning, however, does not square with the facts summarized in Table 13, namely, that by dividing the group of large families according to the sex of two or more previous children registered at home, the probability of the next child being female rises from 0.38 for *PF* families, to 0.41 for *M = F*, and to 0.62 for *PM*. This suggests that large families were intentionally large and intentionally sex balanced.

Table 13 Distribution of the Sex of the Next Child Relative to the Sex Composition of Living Sibling Sets of Two or More Children (Complete First Marriages with 6 + Children)

SEX COMPOSITION OF SIBLING SET	SEX OF NEXT CHILD		SEX RATIO
	M	*F*	
PM	22	36	61
M = F	19	13	146
PF	23	14	164

AN HYPOTHESIS ON THE RELATION BETWEEN FAMILY SIZE AND THE SEX OF CHILDREN   We can only speculate as to why family size and the sex of children were linked. Our guess is that all families wanted at minimum one or two male children on account of their value as labor and as male heir and replacement heir in case of need. Small families were predominantly male, therefore, because they accepted male children, tended to eliminate females, and stopped procreation early. But few families wanted many more than the minimum number of males for fear of causing future competition for the family headship, and creating pressure to divide property or problems of providing for non-inheriting sons. After the minimum number, therefore, female children were as desirable as males or more so, since they raised none of these problems and could perform tasks in the house and on the farm that were unsuitable for males. They were also valuable as a means of affiliation with other families and could inherit in the event of the failure of the male line or be used to recruit an adoptive heir through marriage. Consequently, the greater the number of children a family had, the higher the proportion of girls was likely to be. This is not meant to imply that large families first assured themselves of the minimum number of males, then added females at the higher birth orders. On the contrary, large families tended to keep the sexes in balance as they went along, which suggests an approximate notion of ultimate family size from the start.

SPACING CHILDREN   If we may cautiously conclude that infanticide sometimes enabled families to approximate the number and sex of the children that they wanted, we must then ask whether it was also of help in spacing children conveniently. Table 14 shows for complete first marriages the mean (registered) birth interval, in years and fractions of years, for intervals 0-1 (marriage to first child) to 4-5 and also for the penultimate and ultimate intervals.[26] If we keep in mind comparable data from European parishes, three features of the table stand out. First, the intervals tend to be very long; second, after the 1-2 interval they show no decided tendency to lengthen until the last interval; and third, the 1-2 interval is much longer than subsequent intervals, whereas in European parishes it seems invariably shorter.[27]

26 For most demographic events in Nakahara we have only the year of the event's occurrence; in computing birth intervals we have assumed that births were distributed evenly through the months of the year and occurred on average at mid-year. This assumption can entail a maximum error of 0.5 year in dating a particular birth, but we can expect the error to be substantially reduced on average: For those births which can be dated by the month we found a possible error of no more than 1 month by our assumption. A more serious source of error arises from our inability to account for "infant mortality," which would add to the length of the birth intervals. Thus, our birth intervals are less accurate than and not strictly comparable with conventionally measured intervals for which exact dates of birth are available.

At first sight, the 0-1 interval looks suspiciously long as compared with the European norm of about 1.5 years or less. However, 70% of the brides in complete first marriages married before age 20; 39% before age 18. As the following table shows, the mean first birth interval decreases as age of marriage increases:

AGE OF MARRIAGE	NO. OF CASES	MEAN FIRST BIRTH INTERVAL
16 or younger	15	3.4
17–19	30	2.6
20 or older	19	1.9

Thus, it seems probable that adolescent sterility, in conjunction with "infant mortality" and some infanticide, could well account for the length of the 0–1 birth interval.

27 For example, for complete marriages between 1740 and 1789 at Meulan, the mean second birth interval is 1.5 years, as compared with 1.7 years for the third birth intervals, 1.8 years for the fourth birth intervals, and 2.1 years for the fifth birth intervals (Lachiver, *Meulan*, 184).

Table 14 Registered Birth Intervals in Complete
First Marriages (Years)[a]

BIRTH INTERVAL	NUMBER	MEAN	STANDARD DEVIATION
0–1	64	2.6	2.3
1–2	57	4.4	2.3
2–3	50	3.3	1.5
3–4	39	3.2	0.9
4–5	28	3.5	1.8
Penultimate	57	3.9	1.9
Last	62	4.2	2.4

a   First birth intervals are not counted in penultimate
or last birth intervals; and any interval for birth orders
2–5 that also happened to be the last birth of the mother
is counted only in the tabulation for the last birth interval.

The length and uniformity of the Nakahara intervals (except the
first two) would seem to result from a combination of "infant mortality" and infanticide for purposes of family limitation and sex selection, independently of considerations of spacing. This is suggested by
the fact that, at almost every interval, the distribution ranges from short
to extremely long with no pronounced mode. If families were spacing
for convenience, their standards of convenience were too various to be
perceptible.

But the 1–2 interval may be an exception. Its length is so idio-
syncratic yet consistent, standing out clearly in every subset of families,
that one suspects that there was some deliberate prolongation of this
interval in some families. We speculate that the second child might
differ from all others in a way affecting its timing as follows. The first
child had to come as soon as possible after marriage to prove the
fertility of the bride. Beginning with the third child, given average
spacing, there would be one or more older children in the house to
care for the new arrival. Thus, the first child would be age 7 at the
birth of the third child and in a many ways able to care for himself
and help with the baby. At later births the existing children would be
still older and the mother's situation easier. But her situation might
be difficult at the second birth, when with normal spacing the first
child would be only 4.4, that is, unable to care for himself, let alone
help with another child. Also at this time, through the decease or aging
of the husband's parents, the mother's responsibilities in the house and
on the farm might become heavier. She and her husband might

consequently be tempted to defer the second birth until the first child was somewhat older. The deferral would be less likely, however, if the husband's mother were still alive, an unmarried sister at home, or some other adult female in the house.

We therefore divided all complete first marriages into families in which another adult female was present at the time of the second birth, and those in which there was none, excluding families in which the first child died or departed before the birth of the second. The mean 1-2 interval was significantly different ($p < 0.05$) between the two groups—3.5 and 5.1 years, respectively.[28] Only 18 percent of intervals in the first group were five years or more and only 5 percent were seven years or more, whereas the corresponding percentages for the second group were 47 percent and 28 percent. We suspect, therefore, some deliberate spacing for the convenience of the mother at the second birth, and possibly also at other births though for reasons which we are unable to discern.

The data on spacing bring us back to a point that we mentioned earlier: age-specific fertility in Nakahara shows a convex curve of the kind usually associated with unrestricted births, not the concave curve associated with birth control. The reasons for the shape of the curve in Nakahara, where births were limited by infanticide, would seem to be the following. First, infanticide gave rise to a pattern of births different from other forms of limitation because, being sex-selective, some children of unwanted sex were eliminated at every birth order in the population, which created exceptionally long intervals between registered births. Second, the smaller the completed family the more sex selection was likely to have taken place and, therefore, as seen in Table 15, the longer the mean interval between births was likely to be. Third, Nakaharans had fewer very small and childless families than populations that limit births generally have. The result of these three factors together was to spread childbearing over the fertile years of marriage, instead of concentrating it in the early years; hence, the major factor in difference in fertility between one age group and another was declining fecundity with age and the increasing proportion of infertile women, which tends to give a convex curve.

On the other hand, if infanticide was practiced without sex selection, presumably it would not be used until families reached the

---

28 The number of families in each group was 22 and 32 respectively. A test of the difference in means yields a t statistic of 2.3, significant at the 0.05 level on 52 degrees of freedom.

Table 15 Completed Family Size
and Mean Birth Intervals
(Complete First Marriages)

NO. OF CHILDREN	MEAN BIRTH INTERVAL (YEARS)
1–3	4.4
4–5	3.8
6+	3.2

desired size; then it would be vigorously enforced. This would make the average birth interval relatively short and give fertility a concave curve. But it seems most unlikely that any population would accept infanticide as a normal means of family limitation, yet ignore its use to control the sex composition of sibling sets.

Infanticide, common in the past in both East and West, has been seen by historians mainly as a product of social demoralization and the struggle of parents to keep themselves and favored progeny alive.[29] This may be justified generally, though it is obviously a view based mainly on literary and legal evidence with a strong moral and class bias. But it fits the Nakahara case badly. Infanticide seems to have been widely practiced there by the most respectable and stable part of the population: married couples who, at a time when divorce and early death were common, lived together through the wives' fecund years, a term completed by no more than 59 percent of first-married couples. Also, infanticide seems to have been practiced by large holders as well as, though somewhat less frequently than, small, and by all holders as often in good as in bad growing years. At any rate, we find no difference in registered births per thousand of population in years when rice was dear and when it was cheap, though the marriage rate differs significantly for these groups of years (Table 16).[30]

29 William L. Langer, "Infanticide: A Historical Survey," *History of Childhood Quarterly*, I (1974), 353–365; Barbara A. Kellum, "Infanticide in England in the Later Middle Ages," ibid., 367–388; Hélène Bergues et al, *La prévention des naissances dans la famille* (Paris, 1960), esp. ch. 6: "Exposition, abandon d'enfants, infanticides." For Japan, Takahashi, *Nihon jinkō*, and Sekiyama, *Kinsei Nihon*.

30 Prices are spring and fall rice prices for the Mitsui main store in Kyoto, over a hundred kilometers away. Mitsui bunkō [Mitsui Archives] (ed.), *Kinsei kōki ni okeru shuyo bukka no dōtai* [Commodity Price Movements in the Late Tokugawa Period] (Tokyo, 1952), 67ff. Prices and demographic events were not matched by chronological years but offset to take account of the normal lag between an occurrence and its recording at the end of the registration year, and the fact that the registration year and calendar year overlapped by six months.

Table 16 Price, Births, and Marriages

PRICE YEARS	BIRTHRATE (NO. OF BIRTHS PER 1000 PERSON-YEARS)	MARRIAGE RATE (NO. OF MARRIAGES PER 1000 PERSON-YEARS)[a]
Upper third	29.1	33.7
Middle third	26.7	46.7
Lower third	27.4	60.1

a Population base taken to be unmarried adults, ages 15-45 only.

Among the apparent objectives of infanticide in Nakahara were: overall family limitation; an equilibrium of some sort between family size and farm size; an advantageous distribution of the sexes in children and possibly, also, the spacing of children in a way convenient to the mother; and the avoidance of an unlucky sex in the next child. These goals required foresight and the ability to carry out long-range plans; qualities not usually associated with demoralized or desperate people. What proportion of families through the practice of infanticide sought some or all of these goals which tended to overlap, we cannot say. Given the degree of agreement in subgroups on completed family size, the percentage may have been substantial. Most important, we do not know how common in Tokugawa society this pattern of infanticide was. It cannot be emphasized too strongly that Nakahara was a village with a population that never exceeded 300, one of thousands of that size, and possibly highly deviant. No general significance can be attributed to our findings until, in some respects at least, they have been duplicated elsewhere.

But at a time when the design of spades and mattocks differed from one village to the next, it would be folly to expect in villages practicing infanticide that the patterns of family limitation and sex selection would be everywhere closely similar. It does not seem improbable, for example, that there were villages which discriminated overall against males in about the same degree that Nakahara discriminated overall against females. Nor is it unlikely that the sex bias changed from one period to another in the same village; or that different strata in the same village discriminated against different sexes, or against the same sex in significantly different degree. It will be important in looking for patterns, therefore, to disaggregate data as much as possible to prevent contrary tendencies from cancelling one another to give an overall appearance of normality.

And if such differences may be reasonably expected within and between villages, we should not expect continuity from one region, historical background, ecology, or economic structure to others. If variety on the basis of these variables was as great as we believe, assuming infanticide to have been widespread, it will take a great amount of ingenuity and patience to uncover it; and at every stage efforts will be hampered by the small size of villages. But if in time systematic differences do appear, we may begin to be able to identify various kinds of reproductive behavior and their social correlates in pre-industrial Japan, and possibly to fashion a test of some general use in distinguishing types of groups and communities.

Daniel H. Kaiser

Urban Household Composition in Early Modern

Russia   In the introduction to the landmark *Household and Family in Past Time,* Laslett observed that many conclusions that had been advanced about family life in the past depended upon sources which, whatever their value otherwise, could not describe the actual size and configuration of household structure. Therefore he and his associates at the Cambridge Group for the History of Population and Social Structure employed household inventories and local parish records to establish the average sizes and configurations of households in the past. The results indicated that the norm for early modern Europe was the simple family household with an average size of about five persons.[1]

Critics soon complained that the records on which Laslett depended to ascertain the sizes and structures of households were misleadingly static, thereby missing important developmental processes in family structure, and the social links which extended beyond the household door. Others observed that the so-called "demographic approach" to family history ignored important differences in family structure between classes. However, even among those who disputed the methods developed by Laslett and others, there was widespread agreement that the usual household in Western Europe after about 1600 "was not an extended family

Daniel H. Kaiser is Professor of History and Professor of Social Studies at Grinnell College. He is the author of *The Growth of the Law in Medieval Russia* (Princeton, 1980); editor of *The Workers' Revolution in Russia, 1917: The View from Below* (New York, 1987); editor and translator of *The Laws of Rus'* (Salt Lake City, 1991).

The author thanks the John Simon Guggenheim Memorial Foundation, the American Council of Learned Societies, the Woodrow Wilson International Center for Scholars, and Grinnell College (Joseph F. Rosenfield Chair in Social Studies) for funds. He also thanks Phillips Wolf, Peyton Engel, Brenda Horrigan, and Darrel Mullins for computer assistance.

1   Peter Laslett, "Introduction: The History of the Family," in *idem* with Richard Wall (eds.) *Household and Family in Past Time* (New York, 1972), 1–89. See also *idem, Family Life and Illicit Love in Earlier Generations* (New York, 1977), 1–11,

of kin, relatives, or several married generations . . . but the familiar isolated nuclear family of parents and children."[2]

More recently, consensus on this conclusion too has broken down. Following the lead of Hajnal, Laslett proposed that Western Europe might well have developed a household dynamic which distinguished it from household patterns elsewhere in the world. In Western Europe, he observed, late marriage, high mortality, and the prohibitive cost of founding a new household had conspired to make simple family households dominant, whereas the evidence then available indicated that elsewhere, especially in Eastern Europe and parts of Asia, early marriage and different financial constraints had combined to generate and sustain extended and multiple family households which played important, if not dominant, roles in household organization.[3]

Several studies have since disputed the accuracy of Laslett's characterization, not only for its applicability outside Europe but also as an adequate description of Western European households. For example, Kertzer found among sharecroppers in central Italy in the mid-nineteenth century both late marriage and a high proportion of multiple family households, leading Kertzer not only to dissent from Laslett's typology of household distribution but also from the demographic determinacy explicit in Laslett's logic.[4]

---

2 Lutz K. Berkner, "The Use and Misuse of Census Data for the Historical Analysis of Family Structure," *Journal of Interdisciplinary History*, V (1975), 721–738; Michael Anderson, *Approaches to the History of the Western Family 1500–1914* (London, 1980), 27–38; Louise Tilley and Miriam Cohen, "Does the Family Have a History? A Review of Theory and Practice in Family History," *Social Science History*, VI (1982), 131–179; Tilley, "Demographic History Faces the Family: Europe Since 1500," *Trends in History*, III (1985), 45–68. Laslett responded to a number of these criticisms in "The Character of Familial History, Its Limitations and the Conditions for its Proper Pursuit," *Journal of Family History*, XII (1987), 263–284. See also Wall, "Introduction," in *idem* with Jean Robin and Laslett (eds.), *Family Forms in Historic Europe* (New York, 1983), 1–63; Lawrence Stone, "Family History in the 1980s," *Journal of Interdisciplinary History*, XII (1981), 62.
3 John Hajnal, "European Marriage Patterns in Perspective," in David V. Glass and David E. C. Eversley (eds.), *Population in History: Essays in Historical Demography* (Chicago, 1965), 101–143; Laslett, *Family Life and Illicit Love*, 12–49.
4 Laurel L. Cornell, "Hajnal and the Household in Asia: A Comparative History of the Family in Preindustrial Japan 1600–1870," *Journal of Family History*, XII (1987), 143–162; David I. Kertzer, *Family Life in Central Italy, 1880–1910* (New Brunswick, 1984), 57–85; *idem*, "The Joint Family Household Revisited: Demographic Constraints and Household Complexity in the European Past," *Journal of Family History*, XIV (1989), 1–15.

HOUSEHOLD COMPOSITION IN RUSSIA   The impact of this debate on the study of household composition in Russia is still limited. In Russia, as in much of the rest of Europe, historians have long been interested in family history and household organization. And, as in Western Europe, the suspicion has been that large, complex households have dominated Russian family life, at least until the advent of industrialization.

So far, however, only a few studies of widely dispersed estates have applied to the Russian Empire the methods suggested in *Household and Family in Past Time*. In general they have confirmed Laslett's conclusions. Plakans, for example, has examined several Baltic estates where, because of the complicating factor of large numbers of resident farmhands, the average farmstead proved very populous. But even when these farmsteads are sorted out to discover units roughly comparable to Western European households, it appears that mean household size (MHS) was much higher than that reported for preindustrial Western Europe. Furthermore, among the farmstead heads' own families, multiple family households were in the majority. On the Linden estate in southeastern Kurland in the period between 1797 and 1826, multiple family households accounted for about 59 percent of the total, and another 10 to 18 percent of the farmsteads represented extended family groups (although by 1858, the number of multiple family households had fallen to 23 percent, extended households making up another 23 percent). In 1797 in Spahren, another of the communities Plakans studied, multiple family households (excluding the coresident farmhands) represented 39.2 percent of all households, and another 11.7 percent were extended households.[5]

---

5 Andrejs Plakans, "Peasant Farmsteads and Households in the Baltic Littoral, 1797," *Comparative Studies in History and Society*, XVII (1975), 2–35; *idem*, "Familial Structure in the Russian Baltic Provinces: The Nineteenth Century," in Werner Conze (ed.), *Sozialgeschichte der Familie in der Neuzeit Europas* (Stuttgart, 1976), 346–362; *idem*, "Identifying Kinfolk Beyond the Household," *Journal of Family History*, II (1977), 3–27; *idem*, "The Familial Contexts of Early Childhood in Baltic Serf Society," in Wall, Robin, and Laslett, *Family Forms in Historic Europe*, 167–206; *idem*, "Serf Emancipation and the Changing Structure of Rural Domestic Groups in the Russian Baltic Provinces: Linden Estate, 1797–1858," in Robert McC. Netting, Richard R. Wilk, and Eric J. Arnould (eds.), *Households: Comparative and Historical Studies of the Domestic Group* (Berkeley, 1984), 245–275; *idem*, "Ties of Kinship and Kinship Roles in an Historical Eastern European Peasant Community: A Synchronic Analysis," *Journal of Family History*, VII (1982), 62.

Studies of central Russia make much the same point, even more forcefully. Czap has studied serf households in Mishino, a Gagarin estate in Riazan' province. Here during the late eighteenth and early nineteenth centuries the "perennial multiple family household" prevailed, accounting for between 62 to 85 percent of all serf households. As a consequence, MHS was large, varying from 8.0 to 9.7. Hoch, who studied another estate which belonged to the same landlord, found that in Petrovskoe (Tambov province) serf households were also generally large. MHS varied from 7.7 to 9.0, and multiple family households represented 60 to 78 percent of the total before 1856, when a significant drop occurred. Melton found similarly high populations among serf households in Rastorg, a Kursk province estate belonging to the Sheremetevs. Among well-off peasant families early in the nineteenth century, average household size was 9.8 persons; households of poorer families numbered on average just 5.1 persons.[6] These studies, valuable as they are, have, however, only initiated the study of household composition in the vast territory of the Russian Empire. Before these findings can be extended to eighteenth- and nineteenth-century Russia as a whole, many more local studies will be necessary.

The study of early modern Russian households is even less developed. As in the later imperial period, studies of the early modern Baltic region have anticipated similar studies in central Russia. Palli reports that in one Estonian parish (Karuse) early in the eighteenth century, MHS was no more than 5.7, rising to 8.0 by the end of the century. Household structure was almost evenly divided between simple family households (48.0 percent) and other more complex households (extended family households accounting for 13.2 percent and multiple family households representing 38.8 percent).[7]

6 Peter Czap, "Marriage and the Peasant Joint Family in Russia," in David Ransel (ed.), *The Family in Imperial Russia* (Urbana, 1978), 118–119; idem, "The Perennial Multiple Family Household, Mishino, Russia, 1782–1858," *Journal of Family History*, VII (1982), 5–26; idem, "A Large Family: The Peasant's Greatest Wealth: Serf Households in Mishino, Russia, 1814–58," in Wall, Robin, and Laslett, *Family Forms in Historic Europe*, 122–135; Steven Hoch, "Serfs in Russia: Demographic Insights," *Journal of Interdisciplinary History*, XIII (1982), 233–235; idem, *Serfdom and Social Control in Russia: Petrovskoe, a Village in Tambov* (Chicago, 1986), 79–81; Edgar Melton, "Proto-industrialization, Serf Agriculture and Agrarian Social Structure: Two Estates in Nineteenth-Century Russia," *Past & Present*, 115 (1987), 97.
7 Heldur Palli, "Estonian Households in the Seventeenth and Eighteenth Centuries," in

Studies of household structure in early modern central Russia suffer from the inadequacy of available sources. Until recently, prescriptive sources have dominated the discussion, giving rise to generalizations that have exceptionally weak documentation. Some years ago on the basis of slim evidence, Smith allowed that the so-called nuclear family was the dominant form of household organization in Muscovy. More persuasive was Hellie's examination of slave families in the late sixteenth and early seventeenth centuries, the reconstruction of which depended upon slavery sale contracts. According to Hellie, "the nuclear family predominated . . ." among those who sold themselves into slavery, accounting for 95 percent of those whose records Hellie retrieved.[8]

But self-selecting populations of this sort are hardly ideal for determining population-wide patterns. Census reports or parish-level vital statistics promise conclusions with broader applicability. Early modern Russian population inventories, however, present significant problems. Designed primarily to count taxable households, almost all the inventories from the period before 1700 identify only adult males. Therefore, most attempts at determining household size and structure in the sixteenth and seventeenth centuries depend upon the dubious method of doubling reported males. The results, uncertain as they are, indicate that in peasant communities in early modern central Russia households generally held from about 2.5 to 3.9 males, suggesting a MHS of between 5 and 8 persons, generally increasing over time.[9] Because Soviet

Wall, Robin, and Laslett, *Family Forms in Historic Europe*, 207–216; Juhan Kakh, Palli, and Halliki Uibu, "Peasant Family and Household in Estonia in the Eighteenth and the First Half of the Nineteenth Centuries," *Journal of Family History*, VII (1982), 76–88.

8 Robert E. F. Smith, *Peasant Farming in Muscovy* (New York, 1977), 80–83; Richard Hellie, *Slavery in Russia, 1450–1725* (Chicago, 1982), 418.

9 Vadim A. Aleksandrov, "Tipologiia russkoi krest'ianskoi sem'i v epokhu feodalizma," *Istoriia SSSR*, XXXV (1981), 78–96 [translated into English as "Typology of the Russian Peasant Family in the Feudal Period," *Soviet Studies in History*, XXI (1982), 26–62]; O. B. Kokh, "Krest'ianskii dvor i krest'ianskaia sem'ia na Dvine v nachale XVIII v.," in *Agraryne otnosheniia i istoriia krest'ianstva Evropeiskogo Severa Rossii (do 1917 g.)* (Syktyvkar, 1981), 86–92; idem, "Krest'ianskaia sem'ia," in *Agrarnaia istoriia Severo-Zapada Rossii XVII veka (Naselenie, Zemlevladenie, Zemlepol'zovanie)* (Leningrad, 1989), 55–62; Iaroslav E. Vodarskii, "K voprosu o srednei chislennosti krest'ianskoi sem'i i naselennosti dvora v Rossii v XVI–XVII vv.," in *Voprosy istorii khoziaistva i naseleniia Rossii XVII v. Ocherki po istoricheskoi geografii XVII v.* (Moscow, 1974), 117–130; idem, *Naselenie Rossii v kontse XVII–nachale XVIII veka* (Moscow, 1977), 46–49; Irina V. Vlasova, "Struktura i chislennost' semei russkikh krest'ian Sibiri v XVII–pervoi polovine XIX v.," *Sovetskaia etnografiia*, L (1980), 37–50.

historians normally apply to household structure categories which do not correspond directly to those employed in most Western studies, precise parallels are difficult to establish. Nevertheless, it would appear from fragmentary results that simple family households dominated the seventeenth-century rural communities that have been studied so far.

Much less has been written on urban households in early modern Russia. Chechulin and other prerevolutionary historians attempted to calculate MHS for a series of sixteenth- and seventeenth-century Russian towns by employing inventories which listed only adult males. The tentative conclusions indicated that mean household size varied from about 4 to 6. More recently, Vodarskii has examined similar sources with only slightly different results. A study of Siberian households early in the eighteenth century found that rural peasant households were 70 percent, 84 percent, even 90 percent simple (or, in Soviet historical parlance, "small") family households. The average number of males per household ranged from 2.7 to 4.1, suggesting a MHS ranging from about 5 to 8. Siberian townsmen evidently operated even smaller households. In places like Tiumen', Turinsk, and Tara, more than 90 percent of all urban households were "small," and "the typical size of families [in the towns of western Siberia] in the eighteenth century was 1–3 males."[10]

SOURCES   Early in the eighteenth century, largely as part of an effort to accumulate resources—both financial and human—with which to conduct war, the Russian state undertook to inventory the population of its towns. The shape of the Petrine censuses was slow to emerge, several isolated inventories preceding the first general "revision" enacted in 1718. But in February 1710, in connection with the introduction of a new system of provincial government, Czar Peter Alekseevich (Peter the Great) ordered

10   Nikolai D. Chechulin, *Goroda Moskovskogo gosudarstva v XVI veke* (St. Petersburg, 1889), 26–31; *idem*, "K voprosu o naselennosti posadskogo dvora v XVII veke," *Zhurnal ministerstva narodnogo prosveshcheniia*, CCLXXIV (1891), 18–19; Vodarskii, "Chislennost' i razmeshchenie posadskogo naseleniia v Rossii vo vtoroi polovine XVII v.," in *Goroda feodal'noi Rossii. Sbornik statei pamiati N. V. Ustiugova* (Moscow, 1966), 271–297; Nina A. Minenko, "Gorodskaia sem'ia zapadnoi Sibiri na rubezhe XVII–XVIII vv.," in *Istoriia gorodov Sibiri dosovetskogo perioda (XVII–nachalo XX v.)*. (Novosibirsk, 1977), 175–195; *idem*, *Russkaia krest'ianskaia sem'ia v zapadnoi Sibiri (XVII–pervoi poloviny XIX v.)* (Novosibirsk, 1979), 42–57.

local governors ". . . to count individually, male and female, all serfs and working people in your provinces by households." To judge from some of the instructions subsequently issued to the data gatherers, the government set about the count seriously, threatening with death anyone who overlooked ". . . even a single child." In contrast to the seventeenth-century inventories, the 1710 census broadened considerably the social layers to be counted, including the various categories of peasants and townsmen as before, but adding the lowest layer of town servitors as well as all military men headquartered in towns. Although the original legislation had envisioned that the census would be complete in 1711, still in 1714 many totals had not yet found their way to the capital. More importantly, to the dismay of the sovereign and his officials, the 1710 census did not yield the expected population increase.[11]

Despite the difficulties, the shortfall encouraged the government to try again, and a decree of 10 December 1715 called for a new census. As the preface of one of these inventories indicates, the intention was to have local officials (*landratty*) collect precise information on all of Russia's taxable citizens, male and female, young and old.[12]

The surviving records are arranged mainly according to the towns' topography. The 1715 inventory of Tula begins with the few households within the fortress ("stone city"), then moves on

11 For a survey of the first local Petrine censuses, see Mikhail Klochkov, *Naselenie Rossii pri Petre Velikom* (St. Petersburg, 1911), 1–19. Although these inventories, like those discussed in more detail below, considered both males and females, the so-called "first revision" of 1718–1721 reverted to the old practice, and counted only males. See Vladimir M. Kabuzan, *Narodonaselenie Rossii v XVIII-pervoi polovine XIX v.* (Moscow, 1963), 50–59. For the 1710 legislation, see *Polnoe sobranie zakonov Rossiiskoi imperii*, (St. Petersburg, 1830), IV, no. 2253. Klochkov notes that the published legislation erroneously identified as targets of the count household servants (*dvorovye liudi*) rather than tradespeople and working people (*delovye liudi*), *Naselenie Rossii pri Petre*, 28. See also, 33–34, 37, 43–71. Kokh contradicts the conventional wisdom about the shortfall, attributing it not to errors or to deception, but rather to population migration, the result of Petrine military and labor recruitment, and flight to escape the growing financial and labor burdens ("K voprosu o dostovernosti perepisnykh knig 1710 g.," *Vspomogatel'nye istoricheskie distsipliny*, XVI [1985], 154–66). But Vodarskii, in reexamining this problem, correctly observes that those who fled, unlike those who died, must have gone somewhere; consequently, although flight and recruitment may have affected some areas, it is impossible to attribute the overall population decrease to these causes (*Naselenie Rossii v konste* 184–191).

12 *Polnoe sobranie zakonov Rossiiskoi imperii*, V, no. 2964; *Maloiaroslavets: Materialy dlia istorii goroda XVII i XVIII stoletti* (Moscow, 1884), 10–11.

to the "wooden town," listing in turn households of clerics, government officials, and others, before identifying households along certain streets (Kochemarov Alley, Chernikov Alley, Il'in Street, and so forth). The household record itself normally begins with the eldest male resident, after which follows his wife, sons, daughters, and then any other coresidents, including affines, grandchildren, or other relatives, together with any unrelated coresidents. The record also specified an age for each household resident. The 1715 Tula census contains the following record: "The household of Perfilei Fedorov syn Kachemarov, 48 years old; he has a wife, Anna, 44, and they have [the following] children: Stepan, 22; Pankrat, 20; a daughter, Nastas'ia, 18; Stepan also has a wife, Dar'ia, 21, and they have a son, Kondratei, 4 years old."[13]

Normally the census takers also had in their possession a copy of a previous inventory, and officials were invited to compare their results with the earlier figures, still another indication of the government's desire for a complete, accurate count. But this census, too, suffered reverses, chief among which was the slow pace at which officials compiled and reported the results. Despite repeated entreaties and threats, the tally sheets for many regions never appeared, so that finally in September 1721 the Senate gave up, the government already having embarked upon a new attempt at inventorying the population.[14]

As a result, these inventories never served the government's intentions, and have remained, for the most part, beyond the attention of historians as well. Some of the inventories were published late in the nineteenth century as part of a series devoted to Russian urban history. But students of family life in Russia have made scant use of these materials. Part of the explanation is that demographers have concentrated their attention on the aggregated data, with a view to determining total population and the dynamics of population change. And, as several scholars have noted, the aggregate figures recorded in inventories of the period contain significant errors, sometimes on the order of 20 percent.[15]

13 *Tula: Materialy dlia istorii goroda XVI–XVIII stoletii* (Moscow, 1884), 133.
14 Klochkov, *Naselenie Rossii pri Petre*, 341–352.
15 Those employed in the present study are: *Belev: Materialy dlia istorii goroda XVII i XVIII stoletii* (Moscow, 1885), 40–96; *Borovsk: Materialy dlia istorii goroda XVII i XVIII stoletii* (Moscow, 1888), 129–145; *Maloiaroslavets: Materialy dlia istorii goroda XVII i XVIII*

But only a few scholars have employed the household-level data from these inventories.

In 1970 two historians who lived in Ustiuzhna published one of these inventories, made in 1713 for the north Russian city of Ustiuzhna-Zheleznopol'skaia, but they made little attempt to evaluate or study the data. A few years later, Rabinovich used this source to analyze family structure, in the process examining a number of important related questions (age at birth of first child, age differential between spouses, and so forth). According to Rabinovich, in Ustiuzhna, households were considerably smaller than rural households of the late eighteenth and nineteenth centuries. Rabinovich also reported that the "two-generation family" was most usual in Ustiuzhna-Zheleznopol'skaia, suggesting that the simple family dominated. However, Rabinovich's method of analysis obscures some households which, although two-generational, were extended. More recently, Kokh has turned to the 1710 census to determine the demographic history of the Russian North, but the results of her work have only just begun to appear. Several other scholars have examined the household data from these inventories, principally for rural areas.[16]

The present essay analyzes household structure for early modern Russia on the basis of twelve population inventories compiled between 1710 and 1720 in ten towns of European Russia.

stoletii (Moscow, 1884), 10–18; Riazan': Materialy dlia istorii goroda XVI–XVIII stoletii (Moscow, 1884), 125–136; Toropets: Materialy dlia istorii goroda XVII i XVIII stoletii (Moscow, 1883), 16–48; Tula: Materialy dlia istorii goroda XVI–XVIII stoletii (Moscow, 1884), 119–175; Uglich: Materialy dlia istorii goroda XVII i XVIII stoletii (Moscow, 1887), 6–120; Viatka: Materialy dlia istorii goroda XVII i XVIII stoletii (Moscow, 1887), 57–117; Zaraisk: Materialy dlia istorii goroda XVI–XVIII stoletii (Moscow, 1883), 51–69; see also n. 16; Pavel N. Miliukov, Gosudarstvennoe khoziaistvo Rossii v pervoi chetverti XVIII veka i reforma Petra Velikogo (St. Petersburg, 1892), 660; Klochkov, Naselenie Rossii pri Petre, 71–79; Kabuzan, Narodonaselenie, 48; and Vodarskii, Naselenie Rossii v konste, 52–53, who estimates the undercount at about 25%.

16 N. I. Balandin and V. P. Cherviakov, "Perepisnaia landratskaia kniga Ustiuzhny-Zheleznopol'skoi 1713 g.," in Agrarnaia istoriia Evropeiskogo Severa SSSR = Voprosy agrarnoi istorii Evropeiskogo Severa SSSR (Vologda, 1970), 111, 195–252; Mikhail G. Rabinovich, "Russkaia gorodskaia sem'ia v nachale XVIII v.," Sovetskaia etnografiia, XLVIII (1978), 96–108 [translated into English as "The Russian Urban Family at the Beginning of the Eighteenth Century," Soviet Studies in History, XXI (1982), 63–87]; idem, Ocherki etnografii russkogo feodal'nogo goroda (Moscow, 1978), 189–191; Kokh, "K voprosu o dostovernosti," 154–166. For example, Elena N. Baklanova, "Perepisnaia kniga 1717 g. kak istochnik po istorii krest'ianskoi sem'i v Vologodskom uezde," Severnyi arkheograficheskii ezhegodnik, I (1970), 170–181; idem, Krest'ianskii dvor i obshchina na russkom Severe konets XVII–nachalo XVIII v. (Moscow, 1976), 10–46.

THE TOWNS   As Figure 1 makes clear, these towns occupied rather different locations. Most are clustered to the south of Moscow along the Oka River basin. Towns situated along the forest-steppe frontier—Tula, Zaraisk, Riazan', Borovsk, Belev, and Maloiaroslavets—had to contend with the military exigencies of their location. Almost all of them fell to the Mongols or to Mongol successors who operated in the area, and therefore each played a role in the defense lines erected by Moscow in the sixteenth and seventeenth centuries. The towns with a more western orientation—especially Toropets—had similar problems. Toropets began to suffer from Lithuanian raids as early as 1206, and eventually fell to Lithuanian conquerors under Grand Prince Olgerd, only to be recaptured by Muscovite armies in 1499. Belev, too, was under Lithuanian control for much of the fifteenth century.

But even after Moscow had brought these towns safely within the borders of the Moscow principality, location continued to affect their history. Towns along the southern frontier also had

Fig. 1   Central European Russia: Early Eighteenth Century

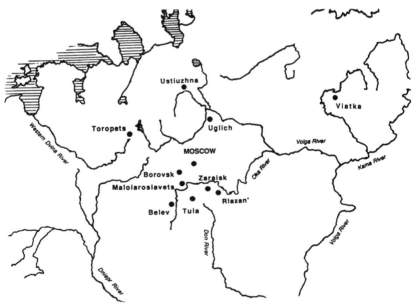

SOURCE   Adapted from *Atlas SSSR* (Moscow, 1983), 22–23.

a part in the social disturbances which characterized the first decade of the seventeenth century. Tula played an especially visible role in the struggle with pretenders to the Muscovite throne. Made into a special fortress in the middle of the sixteenth century as protection against the Crimean Tatars, Tula nevertheless recognized the first False Dmitrii (the name given to pretenders to the throne) in 1605, and in 1607 Bolotnikov occupied the city, whereupon the armies of Czar Vasilii Shuiskii besieged Tula for more than three months. Maloiaroslavets and other towns also found themselves between the various contending forces during the Time of Troubles, the period from 1598 to 1613 when famine, civil war, and foreign intervention plagued Russia.[17]

None of these towns was especially large. Although exact comparisons are impossible to establish, it appears that all the towns increased their populations after the last census of the seventeenth century. Toropets, in 1678, reported 290 households occupied by townsmen (*posadskie liudi*), and in 1710 counted 369. In Tula data gatherers in 1678 counted 351 townsmen households, a number which grew to 524 in 1715.[18] By the early eighteenth century, Tula was the most populous of the cities examined here, numbering just over 5,300 taxable inhabitants; Uglich followed close behind. Viatka and Belev occupied the next ranks, each counting more than 4,000 inventoried inhabitants. Toropets had more than 3,000, and Zaraisk counted just under 3,000. Maloiaroslavets was the smallest, boasting fewer than 1,000 taxable inhabitants at the time of its census in 1715 (see Table 1).

The sex ratios among the inventoried populations indicate some irregularity (see Table 2). Although females outnumber males, as might be expected, in most of these towns the ratio substantially exceeds the normal distribution. The sex ratio for these towns as a whole resembles that reported more recently for populations devastated by World War II. Petrine Russia was then fighting a war, and the inventories not infrequently specify missing soldiers whose wives remained behind. But the war does not

17   *Entsiklopedicheskii slovar' Brokgauza-Efrona* (St. Petersburg, 1890–1904), XXXIV, 493, LXVI, 641, LIV, 528–529, VII, 731, LXVII, 39, IX, 179, XXIII, 296, VII, 431, XXXVI, 490, XXXV, 59.
18   Vodarskii and V. V. Pavlenko, "Svodnye dannye o kolichestve podatnykh dvorov Evropeiskoi Rossii po perepisi 1678 g.," *Sovetskie arkhivy*, VI (1971), 69–70. See also Vodarskii, "Chislennost' i razmeshchenie posadskogo naseleniia," 282–290.

Table 1 Urban Household Inventories Employed

TOWN	DATE OF INVENTORY	POPULATION	NUMBER OF HOUSEHOLDS
Belev	1718	4110	841
Borovsk	1719	2399	335
Maloiaroslavets	1715	976	156
Riazan'	1718	1589	220
Toropets	1710	3674	839
Tula	1715	5309	916
Tula	1720	3022	502
Uglich	1717	5089	877
Ustiuzhna	1713	2277	417
Viatka	1710	4368	724
Viatka	1717	2387	394
Zaraisk	1715	2980	498
TOTALS		38180	6719

SOURCES   *Belev: Materialy dlia istorii goroda XVII i XVIII stoletii* (Moscow, 1885), 40–96 (hereafter cited as *MDIG*); *Borovsk: MDIG* (Moscow, 1888), 129–145; *Maloiaros-lavets: MDIG* (Moscow, 1884), 10–18; *Riazan': MDIG* (Moscow, 1884), 125–136; *Toropets: MDIG* (Moscow, 1883), 16–48; *Tula: MDIG* (Moscow, 1884), 119–175; *Uglich: MDIG* (Moscow, 1887), 6–120; *Viatka: MDIG* (Moscow, 1887), 57–117; *Zaraisk: MDIG* (Moscow, 1883), 51–69; N. I. Balandin and V. P. Cherviakov, "Perepisnaia landratskaia kniga Ustiuzhny-Zheleznopol'skoi 1713 g.," in *Agrarnaia istoriia Evropeiskogo Severa SSSR = Voprosy agrarnoi istorii Evropeiskogo Severa SSSR* (Vologda, 1970), III, 195–252.

suffice to explain all of the reported sex imbalance. Labor conscription, widely used in Peter's reign, especially to build the new capital, also undoubtedly affected sex ratios, at least locally. Occasionally the inventories used here identify men sent off to Petersburg to work. Even beyond direct mentions, however, it is clear that labor conscription was widespread. One recent study points out that mobilized labor sometimes amounted to 10 percent of the counted population; furthermore, many of the migrant laborers never returned home, either because they died at their work or could find no means or desire to return. Still others, frightened at the prospect of military or labor recruitment, fled.[19]

19   Henry S. Shryock and Jacob S. Siegel, *The Methods and Materials of Demography* (Washington, D.C., 1971), I, 191, 192 which reports the sex ratio of postwar Austria as 87.3 and postwar USSR as 81.9. The 1713 Ustiuzhna census records the household of the soldier Grigorii Petrov syn Chernavin, who was inducted into the army the preceding year, and whose wife, Katerina, remained at home alone, "fed in Christ's name" (Balandin and Cherviakov, "Perepisnaia landratskaia kniga," 247). The Belev inventory identifies

Table 2 Sex Ratio in Towns of Early Modern Russia (Males per 100 Females)

Belev	89.1
Borovsk	94.1
Maloiaroslavets	88.8
Riazan'	95.2
Toropets	99.3
Tula/1715	91.9
Tula/1720	97.5
Uglich	82.9
Ustiuzhna	94.8
Viatka/1710	81.6
Viatka/1717	80.7
Zaraisk	94.5
ALL TOWNS	90.0

SOURCE   See Table 1.

Normally scholars have advanced labor migration not as an explanation for sex ratio irregularities, but rather to explain and justify the apparent overall decline in population since the 1678 count. Critics are correct to point out that labor migration cannot explain the overall declines. Fleeing laborers had to have been living and working somewhere, and, if the count were reasonably conscientious, they must have entered the totals somewhere. In one district, at least, males did outnumber females: the 1717 inventory of the Kuben' district reported 117.7 males for every 100 females.[20] Consequently, even if it cannot explain fully the decline in population reported in the totals, labor conscription, and the mobility which it implied, had a detectable impact upon local, especially urban, populations, making the shortfall among males in these inventories less astonishing.

---

the household of Iakov Stepanov syn Davydov, who in 1718 was "serving in the Kievan garrison" while his wife, Praskov'ia, remained home alone (*Belev: Materialy dlia istorii goroda*, 76). Kirilo Nikitin was sent in 1712 from his home in Ustiuzhna to work in St. Petersburg, leaving behind his 52-year-old wife, Solomanida, who was dependent upon charity (Balandin and Cherviakov, "Perepisnaia landratskaia kniga," 247); P. A. Kolesnikov, "K istorii naselennykh punktov i dvizheniia sel'skogo naseleniia Evropeiskogo Severa v XVII–XIX vv.," *Ezhegodnik po agrarnoi istorii Vostochnoi Evropy 1966 god* (Tallinn, 1971), 189–190.

20   Vodarskii, *Naselenie Rossii v konste*, 191; Baklanova, *Krest'ianskii dvor*, 18–20.

The eighteenth-century inventories testify to substantial age-heaping. Population pyramids constructed for Uglich and Tula (1720) illustrate the extremes (see Figures 2–3). Reported age preference is not unusual among populations where illiteracy and low levels of education prevail, as they almost certainly did in eighteenth-century Russia.[21] However, indexes of age accuracy

Fig. 2   Uglich 1717

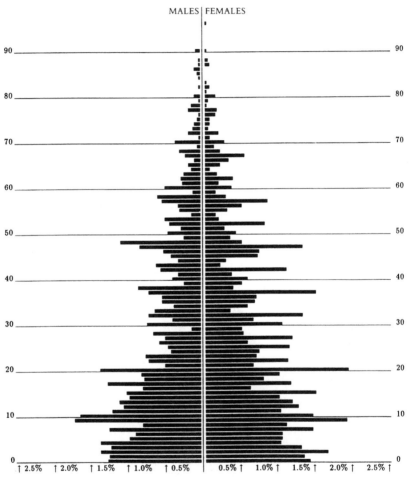

SOURCE   *Uglich: Materialy dlia istorii goroda XVII i XVIII stoletii* (Moscow, 1887), 6–120.

21   Shryock and Siegel, *Methods and Materials of Demography*, 204.

Fig. 3 Tula 1720

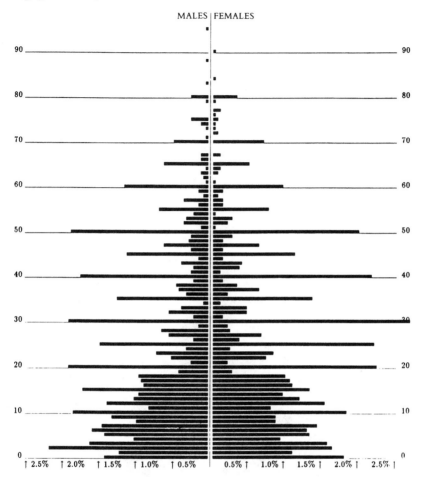

SOURCE   *Tula: Materialy dlia istorii goroda XVI–XVIII stoletii* (Moscow, 1884), 152–75.

demonstrate that age-heaping was not usual among the youngest respondents, but normally came to prevail only among the oldest population cohorts (see Table 3). Furthermore, composite indexes of age accuracy show considerable variability, both between sexes and among the towns. Almost everywhere female ages proved less reliable than male ages, and in Maloiaroslavets, Toropets, Tula (1715), Ustiuzhna, and Viatka (1710) reported age in general

Table 3 Age-Ratios for Populations of Selected Towns in Early Modern Russia

Cohort Age[a]	5	10	15	20	25	30	35	40	45	50	55	60	65
Belev													
Male	110.0	93.7	94.3	106.4	84.2	112.4	87.2	109.5	96.0	105.9	102.6	107.5	61.7
Female	95.7	107.1	82.9	115.5	84.0	119.1	76.8	125.2	83.7	134.3	57.1	154.7	53.1
Borovsk													
Male	104.7	108.4	92.2	104.1	83.9	112.7	81.9	109.4	99.3	94.7	112.8	94.1	104.0
Female	102.3	107.7	74.0	130.8	82.3	106.4	82.3	113.7	94.2	114.9	78.6	135.9	64.5
Maloiaroslavets													
Male	96.0	117.5	100.6	75.6	103.7	108.4	71.9	76.5	147.5	73.9	126.7	74.8	113.8
Female	125.5	98.2	85.7	112.0	81.6	116.1	83.0	118.2	76.2	127.8	104.9	51.5	123.3
Riazan'													
Male	91.2	89.0	112.0	94.3	102.9	89.6	118.8	83.9	108.4	94.1	114.3	83.9	77.8
Female	111.7	86.3	99.6	100.0	111.3	95.0	95.7	90.2	113.5	91.4	108.0	111.1	63.0
Toropets													
Male	105.0	99.4	91.9	91.4	99.4	106.0	86.8	119.6	82.3	140.8	53.0	160.3	40.2
Female	101.4	95.4	89.0	102.4	89.5	128.0	77.9	129.7	70.0	136.8	58.2	166.7	39.2
Tula/1715													
Male	96.7	107.5	90.9	96.9	94.1	120.5	74.3	136.9	75.5	139.6	60.4	151.6	50.3
Female	97.9	102.3	95.3	104.7	83.2	123.4	69.5	145.2	71.4	136.6	46.9	180.2	46.2
Tula/1720													
Male	100.2	102.3	100.2	95.6	92.0	107.0	92.8	104.3	92.4	127.9	72.7	117.1	85.7
Female	82.3	112.4	93.3	100.2	94.0	112.5	83.1	116.9	86.3	124.0	78.0	114.0	69.2
Uglich													
Male	93.2	110.5	97.0	105.0	77.2	106.7	109.1	80.1	132.1	79.1	110.8	102.6	82.1
Female	102.4	101.3	94.2	109.1	90.4	101.9	110.1	76.5	136.5	72.4	123.8	74.3	132.7
Ustiuzhna													
Male	105.2	99.4	97.5	91.6	93.5	116.2	78.9	133.8	70.3	151.2	46.7	163.0	60.8
Female	109.4	90.6	102.4	109.3	78.6	137.9	59.5	154.9	53.7	175.1	43.9	155.0	53.5
Viatka/1710													
Male	100.4	106.9	85.8	102.7	88.9	118.5	78.3	137.5	69.2	145.8	47.5	163.9	57.5
Female	97.6	95.3	129.7	75.0	88.4	132.3	55.6	173.1	46.3	183.9	29.2	218.8	21.7
Viatka/1717													
Male	94.7	106.0	99.4	95.6	103.5	100.0	92.2	108.2	99.4	104.1	93.1	96.0	79.6
Female	92.2	104.2	91.5	119.4	84.8	108.1	87.0	107.7	102.8	103.9	87.8	109.7	83.3
Zaraisk													
Male	103.4	102.1	100.0	85.4	109.3	98.8	94.4	96.5	102.0	113.4	78.8	131.6	75.9
Female	103.2	99.4	100.9	97.7	97.6	104.0	92.6	109.4	83.9	125.6	78.3	130.2	64.7

NOTE Age ratios measure the "ratio of the population in the given age group to one-third of the sum of the populations in the age group itself and the preceding and following groups, times 100." (Henry S. Shryock, Jacob S. Siegel, and associates, *The Methods and Materials of Demography* [Washington, D.C., 1971], I, 218).

[a]Numbers indicate the first year of five-year cohorts, so that 5 represents the cohort 5–9, and so on.

SOURCE See Table 1.

was less accurate than in Borovsk, Riazan', Tula (1720), Uglich, Viatka (1717), and Zaraisk (see Table 4). When specific ages are blended into five-year cohorts, however, many of the age irregularities disappear, giving the population pyramids a rather unsurprising shape (see Figures 4–5).

Because the population inventories were intended to assist the government in allocating tax, labor, and military duties, they do not represent a complete count of the urban populations. Data gatherers did not include households of the gentry, who, having been exempted from tax liability, were the chief beneficiaries of czarist taxation policy. Although no firm figures are available, scholars estimate that the gentry constituted about 4 to 6 percent of the total population, probably even less in urban settlements.[22]

Table 4 Mean Age Accuracy Index by Sex, Towns of Early Modern Russia

TOWN	MALE	FEMALE
Belev	10.6	24.1
Borovsk	8.7	18.1
Maloiaroslavets	21.2	19.4
Riazan'	11.0	10.3
Toropets	22.1	26.6
Tula/1715	24.4	29.4
Tula/1720	9.8	14.9
Uglich	12.9	16.2
Ustiuzhna	25.4	31.5
Viatka/1710	26.8	48.4
Viatka/1717	5.5	9.9
Zaraisk	10.2	12.2

NOTE   The reported figures equal the sum of deviations from 100 of age ratios divided by the number of age groups. The lower the number, the greater the accuracy of age data. For discussion of the method of calculation and the meaning of these figures, see Henry S. Shryock and Jacob S. Siegel, *The Methods and Materials of Demography* (Washington, D.C., 1971), I, 218–219.
SOURCE   See Table 1.

22 Several of the inventories do not survive complete, the printed text noting that some specified section is missing. When processing the households, I discovered that sometimes the printed text introduces an obvious error, perhaps conflating names from two households. I did not include in the data base any of these obvious erroneous cases, nor could I process the missing households. The inventory data as reported here should not be considered complete representations of the town populations of that time. Vodarskii, "Naselenie Rossii v kontse XVII–nachale XVIII veka (problemy, metodika issledovaniia, resul'taty)," in *Problemy istoricheskoi demografii SSSR. Sbornik statei* (Tallinn, 1977), 57–58; idem, *Naselenie Rossii v konste*, 192.

Fig. 4 Uglich 1717

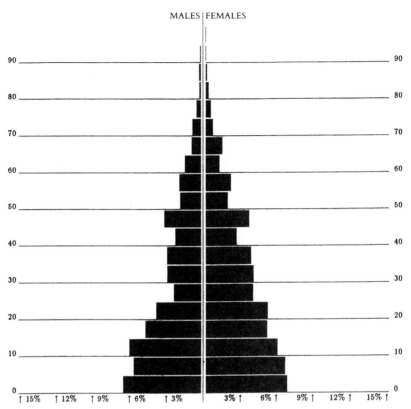

SOURCE   *Uglich: Materialy dlia istorii goroda XVII i XVIII stoletii* (Moscow, 1887), 6–120.

Their absence from the inventories, then, would not significantly affect the overall population.

Also missing were the peasants. Mainly settled in rural areas rather than towns, peasants (including privately-held serfs and state peasants) represented 80–90 percent of the total population early in the eighteenth century. Consequently, the inventories employed in the present study can say little about households situated outside town borders. At the same time, in many of these towns some peasants did live and work. The so-called landless

Fig. 5 Tula 1720

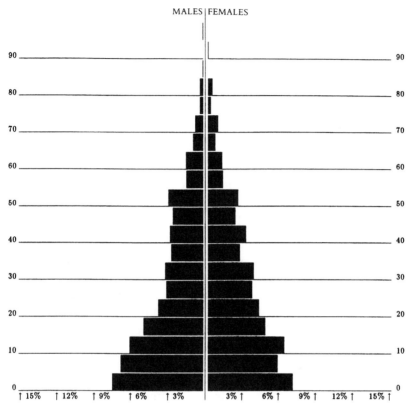

SOURCE   *Tula: Materialy dlia istorii goroda XVI–XVIII stoletii* (Moscow, 1884), 152–75.

peasants (*bobyli*) often took up residence in town at the initiative of their lords, who encouraged them to practice crafts or trade in town.[23] As the records demonstrate, rarely were these households prosperous or large. But whether the household profile of these

23   *Ibid.*; Mikhail T. Beliavskii, "Sosloviia i soslovnyi stroi," in *Ocherki russkoi kul'tury XVIII veka* (Moscow, 1985/87), II, 29. On the origin and history of *bobyli*, see Aleksandr L. Shapiro, "Bobylstvo v Rossii v XV–XVII vv.," *Istoriia SSSR*, III (1960), 49–66. On the process by which these peasants took up urban residence and crafts, see Arkadii G. Man'kov, "Bor'ba posada s feodalami vo vtoroi polovine XVII v.," *Istoricheskie zapiski*, LXIV (1959), 217–232.

newly-urbanized peasants reflects the rural reality of the time will require separate demonstration.

Among those who were inventoried for the census, townsmen (*posadskie liudi*) unsurprisingly represented the overwhelming majority. In Belev, townsmen accounted for 77.2 percent of the total. Clergymen and -women added another 4.1 percent. Scribes and other chancellery officials and their households accounted for 2.8 percent of the whole. Because of its location, Belev also sheltered a garrison, the soldiers' households of which represented 8.5 percent of the population; cannoneers accounted for 2.6 percent and musketeers another 1.4. The remainder came from household servants of townsmen (2.5 percent), treasury blacksmiths, concierges, and other smaller groups. In Borovsk, the census takers were to count households of "all tax-paying townsmen, the poor, soldiers, and widows," although the surviving record seems not to distinguish these categories, grouping most respondents simply as townsmen. Elsewhere, too, townsmen made up the bulk of the counted population, with clergy, chancellery officials, landless peasants, and others rounding off the whole. That the records identify social and occupational groups permits comparisons of households by social identity, as some students of family life have recommended.[24]

MEAN HOUSEHOLD SIZE   In these towns MHS was not nearly so large as that reported for peasant communities in imperial Russia.

24 For a thorough discussion of the position of townsmen in seventeenth-century Russia, see Richard Hellie, "The Stratification of Muscovite Society: The Townsmen," *Russian History*, V (1978), 119–175. The urban estates, of which townsmen were the overwhelming majority, constituted 3–4% of the entire population of the Russian Empire in the eighteenth century (Vodarskii, "Naselenie Rossii v kontse," 58; Irina V. Vlasova and Dmitrii N. Shanskii, "Poseleniia," in *Ocherki russkoi kul'tury XVIII veka*, 1, 305). It is widely thought that after the musketeer rebellion of 1698 the government disbanded all musketeer regiments, but the process was not so prompt or thorough as once thought. Apparently the government decided simply to rename many musketeer regiments, instantaneously converting them into the new-style regiments, and employing them directly in the northern war. According to Moisei D. Rabinovich, as early as 1704 the Toropets musketeers experienced this reorganization ("Strel'tsy v pervoi chetverti XVIII v.," *Istoricheskie zapiski*, LVIII [1956], 297). As Rabinovich himself notes, in Sevsk in 1711 and in Belev in 1718 there were still musketeer households (*ibid.*, 301–302). Tilley and Cohen, "Does the Family Have a History," 147–157, 164. In the successor volume to *Household and Family in Past Time*, Wall responded to criticism of it by stating that the authors intended "to look in more detail at all the constituent parts of the household and to place the household within the broad economic and social context," Wall, Robin, and Laslett, *Family Forms in Historic Europe*, 1.

As Table 5 indicates, the totals varied considerably. Whereas in Mishino and Petrovskoe in the nineteenth century, MHS sometimes reached 9.7 or 9.0 and never dipped below 7.7, nowhere in these early eighteenth-century towns did MHS exceed 7.2. Those at the lower end of the distribution revealed a MHS much closer to the figure reported for early modern England, and the overall mean is only slightly larger than the long-term English mean.

Like the Petrine government, historians have not credited the censuses, maintaining that czarist taxation policy, which until late in Peter's reign depended upon the household rather than the population within it, encouraged deception and the formation of large households as a means of escaping taxes.[25] Household size in these cities indicates that this logic did not have general application. In the cities of the early eighteenth century, household size on average was not large, and in many places was small. So that if rural Russian households did in fact grow to lessen tax liability, that dodge apparently had little application in the towns of early eighteenth-century Russia.

Poverty seems to have played a much more influential role in determining household size. Because the census takers often

Table 5 Mean Household Size in Early Modern Russia

TOWN	MEAN HOUSEHOLD SIZE	RANGE
Belev	4.9	1–21
Borovsk	7.2	1–24
Maloiaroslavets	6.3	1–18
Riazan'	7.2	2–30
Toropets	4.6	1–25
Tula/1715	5.8	1–41
Tula/1720	6.0	1–19
Uglich	5.8	1–20
Ustiuzhna	5.3	1–17
Viatka/1710	6.0	1–39
Viatka/1717	5.8	2–18
Zaraisk	6.0	1–21
MEAN	5.7	1–41

SOURCE   See Table 1.

25   Evgenii V. Anisimov, *Podatnaia reforma Petra I* (Leningrad, 1982), 36; Rabinovich, *Ocherki etnografii*, 182.

distinguished between those who could pay taxes and those who, for reasons of disability or family situation, were freed from tax obligations, it is possible to compare household size between taxpayers and the tax-exempt. In Toropets the data gatherers identified a whole set of townsmen (about 25 percent of all town households) "who, because of poverty, do not pay taxes, and who are fed in Christ's name."[26] Typically, such households were headed by widows (forty-eight of ninety-two) or by males who were maimed or otherwise seriously disabled.

Exceptional cases make clear why a given household was exempted from taxes. For example, at the time of the 1710 inventory the widow Tat'iana Kondrat'eva was thirty-five, but was responsible for six young children. Densely populated and short on adult hands, the widow's household desperately required relief. But most households headed by widows or the disabled were not so populous. Avdot'ia Antonova, another widow, was forty in 1710, and had two young sons; Avdot'ia Svechnikova was thirty-five and her two sons were also minors. These households were small and poor for obvious reasons. It is hardly surprising that the tax-exempt had a much lower MHS (see Table 6).

In Borovsk, the census takers recorded only townsmen households, but they did distinguish the tax-exempt (*beztiaglye*) and the poor (*nishchie*), both of whom paid no taxes. Normally the record does not provide a reason for tax exemption; for example, Evsegnei Ipatov syn Avchinnikov was described as "poor," but why his household was poor is not evident; from the outside it appeared little different from any taxpaying household. At age forty-nine Evsegnei was not elderly, and in any case not only was his wife still living, but also living with them were their

Table 6   Mean Household Size, Toropets 1710

SOCIAL CATEGORY	NUMBER OF HOUSEHOLDS	MHS	RANGE
Taxpaying Townsmen	277	6.5	2–25
Tax-Exempt Townsmen	92	3.6	1–9

SOURCE   *Toropets: Materialy dlia istorii goroda XVII i XVIII stoletii* (Moscow, 1883), 16–48.

26   *Toropets: Materialy dlia istorii goroda,* 39–40.

twenty-four-year-old son, their daughter-in-law, and their one-year-old grandson. It appears that able hands did exist. All the same, Evsegnei paid no taxes.

The case of Fetin'ia Guliaeva is clearer. Although not formally a widow, she was a soldier's wife (*soldatka*), a fate often likened to widowhood.[27] Apparently Guliaeva's husband had been long absent, since at the time of the census she was living with her only daughter, Dar'ia, who was sixteen. Whatever the circumstance, Guliaeva's household was evidently impoverished and naturally small. Consequently, although MHS for Borovsk as a whole was reasonably large (7.2), among the tax-exempt and poor MHS was much lower (4.4 and 4.5, respectively).

The same pattern is apparent in Ustiuzhna (see Table 7). The households of the tax-exempt, whether townsmen, peasants, or other urban dwellers, were invariably smaller than those of regular taxpayers. In Riazan' the data gatherers distinguished between households of the first merchant guild (*gostinnaia sotnia*), ordinary townsmen, and the impoverished (or, as the inventory put it, "those people who did not have their own house, were destitute, or paid little [taxes]").[28] Although not identical to the social distinctions observed in inventories cited above, the Riazan' categories reflect a similar impact on MHS: households in the merchant guild were large, averaging nine persons; townsmen, generally not quite so well-off as guild members, dwelt in households smaller than those of guild members, but still well above the town average. The poor occupied much smaller households (see Table 8).

In the towns of early eighteenth-century Russia smaller households prevailed among the poor; only the better-off could sustain large households.

Even among those who paid taxes there is little evidence that taxation policy was central to household size. On the contrary, the evidence indicates that social estate strongly influenced house-

27 See Gregory L. Freeze, "Bringing Order to the Russian Family: Marriage and Divorce in Imperial Russia, 1760–1860," *Journal of Modern History*, LXII (1990), 725, who quotes a *soldatka*: ". . . having not heard from [my] husband, a soldier, for fourteen years, [I] considered him deceased and married [another peasant]." On the miserable fate of the *soldatka* as recorded in later times, see Beatrice Farnsworth, "The Soldatka: Folklore and Court Record," *Slavic Review*, XLIX (1990), 58–73.
28 *Riazan': Materialy dlia istorii goroda*, 134.

Table 7 Mean Household Size, Ustiuzhna-Zheleznopol'skaia, 1713

SOCIAL CATEGORY	NUMBER OF HOUSEHOLDS	MHS	RANGE
Townsmen	41	7.7	2–16
Tax-Exempt Townsmen	8	4.6	2–8
Landless Peasants	106	6.3	2–17
Tax-Exempt Landless Peasants	75	4.7	1–10
Armament Masters	10	5.2	3–9
Clergy	57	3.9	1–13
Soldiers	6	1.7	1–2
Chancellery Officials	14	5.5	2–13
Other Taxable	58	5.6	1–13
Other Tax-Exempt	42	4.0	1–11
TOTAL	417	5.4	1–17

NOTE   The figures reported here differ from those reported by N. I. Balandin and V. P. Cherviakov, "Perepisnaia landratskaia kniga Ustiuzhny-Zheleznopol'skoi 1713 g.," *Agrarnaia istoriia Evropeiskogo Severa SSSR = Voprosy agrarnoi istorii Evropeiskogo Severa SSSR* (Vologda, 1970), III, 195–252, who seem to have relied upon the subtotals reported in the inventory rather than upon a calculation based on individual households. Mikhail G. Rabinovich, too, provides a slightly different distribution ("Russkaia gorodskaia sem'ia v nachale XVIII v.," *Sovetskaia etnografiia*, XLVIII [1978], 98.

Table 8 Mean Household Size, Riazan' 1718

SOCIAL CATEGORY	NUMBER OF HOUSEHOLDS	MHS	RANGE
1st Merchant Guild (*gostinnaia sotnia*)	32	9.0	3–17
Household-Owning Townsmen	155	7.3	2–30
Poorer Townsmen	33	5.2	2–10

SOURCE   *Riazan': Materialy dlia istorii goroda XVI–XVIII stoletii* (Moscow, 1884), 125–136.

hold formation, leading to significant differences in households among different social groups, all of whom paid taxes. In Toropets, for example, where there was, in addition to the usually sizable townsmen population, a considerable number of other town residents, MHS varied considerably across the population (see Table 9).

Table 9 Mean Household Size by Occupation, Toropets, 1710

SOCIAL CATEGORY	NUMBER OF HOUSEHOLDS	MHS	RANGE
Townsmen	369	5.8	1–25
Clergy	11	5.2	3–8
Landless Peasants	142	4.7	2–12
Scribes, Officials	6	3.0	1–5
Musketeers	263	3.2	1–7
Cannoneers	28	4.1	1–10
Concierges (*dvorniki*)	20	2.8	1–7
TOTAL	839	4.6	1–25

SOURCE   *Toropets: Materialy dlia istorii goroda XVII i XVIII stoletii* (Moscow, 1883), 16–48.

None of these groups had extremely large households, although, as might be expected, MHS among townsmen was highest, exceeding the town-wide mean; households headed by concierges trailed far behind. Most notable in this breakdown is the relationship of military households to those of ordinary townsmen in Toropets. The latter generally had far more populous households than did the former, who nevertheless made up a significant proportion of the population in Toropets. Military servitors, soldiers, cannoneers, and others generally lived in smaller households than did their civilian counterparts.

Priests, deacons, sextons, and other churchmen who served parishes in these towns also lived in smaller households than did ordinary townsmen. In Viatka, for example, townsmen households averaged 7.2 persons in 1710, but the clergy averaged just over 6 persons per household. When Viatka was next inventoried, mean household size among townsmen had slipped to 6.4; but clergymen's households also shrank, dropping to 4.7. In Tula, too, households of townsmen and clergy maintained the same relationship: in 1715 townsmen (including the poorer townsmen) averaged 6 persons per household, but the households of priests, deacons, and other clergy averaged 5.7 persons.

As Table 9 demonstrates, in Toropets scribes, clerks, and other officials did not dominate other social strata in household size. Elsewhere, however, these officials exceeded the city-wide MHS. Maloiaroslavets is an exceptional case; here scribes and investigators occupied only four households altogether, but they were large households, averaging almost 10 persons. In Belev, clerical households averaged 7 persons, more than 40 percent above the city-wide mean. And in both counts of Viatka, scribes and other officials averaged more than 7 persons per household, well above the mean for townsmen.

Consequently, although in all these towns MHS was relatively low, there was also considerable variation. In general, households of the poor were significantly smaller than households of townsmen or scribal officials. Clergy in these towns generally occupied households slightly more modest than townsmen, and military households were smaller still. This variability indicates that no single strategy about taxes governed household formation in these towns. On the contrary, household size in the towns of early modern Russia depended much more upon social station and wealth.

HOUSEHOLD TYPE   In the towns of early eighteenth-century Russia simple family households predominated (see Table 10). About half (50.7 percent) of all households inventoried were simple, and in six of the twelve populations simple family households accounted for at least half the total. On the other hand, complex households were hardly exceptional in these towns. Extended family households made up a small, but fairly constant, proportion of the total (12 percent), and multiple family households accounted for about a third (33.8 percent) of all households, very unevenly distributed among these several towns. As a result, simple family households and complex family households nearly equaled one another (see Table 11).

Since social station proved to be so closely tied to MHS, it is hardly surprising that social station should also be strongly associated with household composition. In Toropets, for example, where MHS was low for all strata of the inventoried population, simple family households prevailed among all social groups, representing just over half of townsmen households to more than three-quarters of musketeer households. Extended family households were unusual; even among townsmen no more than a tenth of the households were extended. But multiple family households had a greater attraction, at least among some elements of society. Roughly a third of all townsmen and clergy households were

Table 10 Household Types in the Towns of Early Eighteenth-Century Russia (Percent)

TYPE	BELEV	BOROVSK	MALOIAR.	RIAZAN'	TOROPETS	TULA/1715	TULA/1720	UGLICH	USTIUZHNA	VIATKA/1710	VIATKA/1717	ZARAISK
MHS	4.9	7.2	6.3	7.2	4.6	5.8	6.0	5.8	5.4	6.0	5.8	6.0
IA	3.3	0.3	0.0	0.0	0.1	0.4	0.0	1.0	2.2	5.8	1.0	2.2
IB	0.6	0.0	0.6	0.0	1.8	0.9	0.2	0.2	1.2	3.2	1.3	0.2
2A	0.4	0.0	0.0	0.0	2.0	0.1	0.2	0.5	1.0	0.1	1.0	0.2
2BC	0.5	0.0	0.0	0.0	0.0	0.6	0.0	0.5	0.2	0.5	0.8	1.2
3A	4.8	1.8	1.3	4.1	8.3	4.6	2.8	3.9	7.4	6.4	7.9	3.0
3B	36.0	25.7	32.1	34.1	44.0	38.3	36.5	28.5	34.5	34.1	32.5	33.1
3C	0.8	0.0	1.9	0.0	0.5	0.8	0.0	0.2	0.0	0.1	0.3	0.6
3D	14.0	5.1	7.7	0.0	13.0	6.6	6.6	9.2	9.6	8.1	7.6	9.4
3E	1.5	0.6	1.3	0.0	1.5	1.1	0.8	0.7	1.2	2.1	2.0	0.8
4	12.4	9.0	12.8	11.4	7.9	11.9	11.6	13.1	8.9	15.3	16.5	12.7
5	25.7	57.6	42.3	50.5	20.9	34.7	41.4	42.2	33.8	24.2	29.2	36.5
6	0.0	0.0	0.0	0.0	0.0	0.0	0.0	0.0	0.0	0.0	0.0	0.0

NOTE   Key to Household Types (Modified from Peter Laslett, "Introduction: The History of the Family," in *idem* and Richard Wall (eds.), *Household and Family in Past Time* [New York, 1972], 28–32; Eugene A. Hammel and Laslett, "Comparing Household Structure Over Time and Between Cultures," *Comparative Studies in Society and History*, XVI [1974], 73–99.)

1A: Solitary, Widowed
1B: Solitary, Single, or Unknown Marital Status
2A: No Family, Coresident Siblings
2BC: No Family: Coresident Relatives of Other Kinds or Persons Evidently Not Related
3A: Simple Family Household: Married Couples Alone
3B: Simple Family Household: Married Couples with Children
3C: Simple Family Household: Widowers with Children
3D: Simple Family Household: Widows with Children
3E: Simple Family Household: Single, Non-Widowed with Children
4: Extended Family Households
5: Multiple Family Households
6: Indeterminate

SOURCE   See Table 1.

Table 11   Composite   Figures   on
             Household Type

TYPE	NUMBER	PERCENT
1A	109	1.6
1B	66	1.0
2A	36	0.5
2BC	28	0.4
3A	340	5.1
3B	2351	35.0
3C	28	0.4
3D	606	9.0
3E	82	1.2
4	803	12.0
5	2270	33.8
6	0	0.0
TOTAL	6719	100.0%

NOTE   For key to household types see
Table 10.
SOURCE   See Table 1.

multiple family, but among the poorest taxpaying citizens of
Toropets, multiple family households were exceptional: 7 percent
of musketeer households and 5 percent of *concierge* households
were multiple family ones. Cannoneers and trading peasants
showed a greater inclination to conglomerate families within a
single dwelling (14.3 percent and 19.7 percent respectively), but
these rates trailed far behind frequencies registered by townsmen
and clergy. In other words, just as with mean household size, the
dynamics of household composition indicate that among taxpayers there was no single, general move toward complex households
as a means of escaping taxation. Instead, social station seems to
have played the more decisive role in household formation.

Because the Riazan' inventory is more selective, it presents a
somewhat different picture which, all the same, sustains the contention that in the cities of early modern Russia complex household organization prevailed not among the poor but rather among
the richer elements in town. As noted above, in Riazan' the census
distinguished between households of the first merchant guild,
ordinary townsmen, and the impoverished. Among the first two,

more financially secure strata, more than half of all households were multiple family, and only about a third were simple family households. Furthermore, household servants were also present in many of these households. Those who had fallen on hard times, however, were more likely to be found in simple family households (48.5 percent); exactly a third populated multiple family households (see Table 12).

The same point emerges from comparison of the taxable and tax-exempt. In Ustiuzhna, the census takers divided several social categories on the basis of their tax liability. In each case, tax-exempt households tended to be found in smaller, less complex forms of household organization. Among the landless peasants who pursued crafts and trade in the city, taxpaying peasants lived in multiple family households about twice as often as did tax-exempt peasants; about the same ratio governed extended households. And more than 70 percent of all tax-exempt peasants lived alone or in simple family households, whereas only about 40 percent of all taxpaying peasants lived in those kinds of households.

Townsmen in Ustiuzhna exhibited a similar household behavior. About a quarter of all tax-exempt townsmen lived in multiple family households, but more than six-tenths of taxpaying townsmen lived in such arrangements, and another tenth lived in extended-family households. None of their poorer parallels lived in extended-family households; fully three-quarters of the total lived in simple family households, more than doubling the percentage of this group among taxpaying townsmen. Other households, for whom the Ustiuzhna census provides no specific social category, replicate this pattern: among taxpayers more than 40 percent occupied multiple family households, whereas among the

Table 12 Household Type By Social Group, Riazan'

SOCIAL GROUP	NUMBER OF HOUSEHOLDS	% SIMPLE FAMILY	% EXTENDED FAMILY	% MULTIPLE FAMILY
1st Merchant Guild	38	34.4	12.5	53.1
Townsmen (All)	155	36.8	9.7	53.5
Poor Townsmen	33	48.5	18.2	33.3

SOURCE   See Table 8.

tax-exempt just over a tenth of all households were complex. By the same token, 43.1 percent of the taxpaying households were simple but more than 78 percent were of the tax-exempt.

In other words, the poorer strata in these towns more often occupied simple family households than did their betters. It might be argued that these figures confirm that taxation considerations did play a vital role in forming households. Widows, the poor, and the disabled had little reason to consolidate families within one household, inasmuch as they already received special consideration for their taxes. Households headed by able-bodied males, on the other hand, had every reason to extend families or aggregate them, thereby multiplying the able hands and decreasing the taxation per capita.

The available evidence, however, contradicts that logic. Some households may well have expanded in order to diminish the effect of taxation, but other more powerful factors determined tax liability. For example, the Shishkin brothers were both townsmen, and shared a dwelling in the Nikol'skoi district in Ustiuzhna. Mikhailo, fifty-two, was married, and had three children: Andrei (twelve), Anna (seventeen), and another Anna (thirteen). Petr, forty-four, was Mikhailo's younger brother. At the time of the inventory, he was apparently already widowed, but his son Matvei (sixteen) was married to a twenty-year-old woman, and all three shared the household with Mikhailo's family. The two brothers also sheltered their maiden sister, Arina (sixty-two), and the widowed bride of a deceased brother, Ivan. This woman, thirty-seven, also brought into the household her seven-year-old son. Consequently, the multiple family household numbered eleven persons, and stretched laterally to include the families of four siblings and vertically for two generations. The tax burden (*tiaglo*) on this household was a staggering 100 rubles, well over the average for Ustiuzhna's townsmen and peasants (about 8 rubles per household). And although the populous household included many able hands, it is also clear that the brothers were providing relief to their elder spinster sister and to the widow of their youngest brother. Exceptional in the size of its tax burden, this household is typical of the general effect on taxation of grouping families within one household: aggregation brought no tax relief.

When looked at more systematically, the household data reveal the same lesson. In general, complex households in Ustiuzhna brought little respite from taxes, and in many categories raised per capita taxation (see Table 13). Among the worst paid townsmen and peasants, those who performed manual labor (*chernaia rabota*) and those who tilled the land, taxes per household were low: 2.8 rubles for manual laborers and 3.3 rubles for farmers. Approximately 40 percent of all households among these two groups were multiple family, but per capita taxation showed little difference between the simple family households and their larger parallels. Aggregation here had little evident effect upon taxation. Among the better-off occupations the situation was more dramatic. Here larger households in general paid a higher per capita tax. Traders (*torgovye*) in Ustiuzhna on average paid 16.4 rubles per household, which amounted to about 2.3 rubles per household

Table 13 Taxation Among Townsmen and Peasants, Ustiuzhna-Zheleznopol'skaia, 1713

LABOR SPECIALTY	MHS	TAX/HOUSEHOLD (RUBLES)	TAX/CAPITA (RUBLES)
Manual labor (all; n = 39)	6.6	2.8	0.42
Multiple Family	8.7	3.2	0.36
Farmers (all; n = 19)	6.1	3.3	0.54
Multiple Family	8.1	4.8	0.59
Smiths (all; n = 15)	7.3	6.5	0.89
Multiple Family	8.9	7.0	0.79
Bakers (all; n = 11)	6.2	3.7	0.52
Multiple Family	8.7	5.3	0.61
Painters (all; n = 9)	5.7	6.6	1.16
Multiple Family	9.0	5.3	0.58
Salt, meat merchants (all; n = 5)	6.8	7.4	1.09
Multiple Family	10.0	11.5	1.15
"Traders" (all; n = 46)	7.1	16.4	2.31
Multiple Family	9.7	26.3	2.71

NOTE   Calculations depend upon 144 townsmen and peasant taxpaying households.
SOURCE   N. I. Balandin and V. P. Cherviakov, "Perepisnaia landratskaia kniga Ustiuzhny Zheleznopol'skoi 1713 g.," in *Agrarnaia istoriia Evropeiskogo Severa SSSR = Voprosy agrarnoi istorii Evropeiskogo Severa SSSR* (Vologda, 1970), 111, 221–234.

inhabitant. Traders who formed multiple family households paid a considerably higher tax per household, 26.3 rubles; on a per capita basis these multiple family households paid 2.7 rubles tax, more than the overall mean. Consequently, household aggregation did not lead to tax savings.

In the towns of early eighteenth-century Russia, then, no "Eastern European" household type prevailed. Rather than a large, multiple family household, one finds in these towns mainly simple family households of modest size the configuration of which was not much distinguished from those once championed as unique to Western European history. At the same time, extended and multiple family households, if not dominant and perennial as they seem to have been in later Russian peasant society, nevertheless represented a substantial proportion of all households. Found most often among the higher and more financially secure social orders, complex and densely populated households were rare among the poor and the lower social orders.

These data also indicate that the dominant generalization about household formation in Russia before Peter the Great is in need of revision. Although consideration of taxes may have played a part in organizing townsmen's households, data from these towns indicate that taxes were not influential in decisions governing household composition. The considerable differences in household size and structure among social groups confirm that occupational and social differentiation was far more significant in shaping households in early modern Russia. As a rule, the largest, most complex households were found among the richest members of town society; townsmen, scribes, and other officials, and even the clergy were more likely to inhabit populous and structurally complex households. The poor—especially those exempted from taxation because of illness, disability, or other catastrophe—occupied households of modest dimensions, their inhabitants most often belonging to a single biological family.

These population inventories, then, significantly supplement the history of households so far written. On the one hand, they demonstrate that early in the eighteenth century Russian experience was not much different from that which prevailed elsewhere in Western Europe, thereby further undermining the hypothesis about a distinct Western European experience. On the other hand, household organization in these towns did differ dramatically from the pattern discovered in rural Russian peasant communities of a later time. Instead of the large, multi-generational families evidently characteristic of serf society, townsmen households early in the eighteenth century generally were neither large nor complex in composition.

Finally, it is worth emphasizing that these household inventories also leave some important questions unanswered. As others have already observed, household counts do not permit us to know how kinship networks, which extended beyond the household, affected family life. As Laslett observed some years ago in commending household study to the profession, the sources for which he was champion do not permit the study of kin relations outside coresident domestic groups. By the same token, these inventories cannot fully represent the developmental process of domestic social organization in Russia. Framed on either side by censuses which excluded females and minors, these inventories provide no more than a glimpse—a snapshot—of domestic life. The developmental course of domestic organization remains out of view. Only if additional local nominal data can be matched with census materials will a more dynamic picture of household organization in Russia emerge.[29]

29 Laslett, *Household and Family in Past Time*, 1. The likelihood that such records survive for the early eighteenth century is not great. See Freeze, "Bringing Order to the Russian Family," 716.

W. R. Lee

Bastardy and the Socioeconomic
Structure of South Germany
According to Davis, the bastard ". . . is a living symbol of social irregularity, an undeniable evidence of contramoral forces."[1] Although the problem of bastardy, in its various forms (whether adulterous, incestuous, or violating caste endogamy), has traditionally faced many different types of society in which the act of marriage was an integral norm of socialization, its magnitude increased considerably in certain areas of Europe in the late eighteenth and nineteenth centuries. This development has been described as part of the thawing process of the "great iceberg" of sexuality in traditional society, culminating in a veritable "sexual revolution" and involving a growth of transvestism and prostitution, as well as rising illegitimacy rates.[2]

Certainly in Bavaria profound changes had occurred during the period from 1750 to 1850. In the late eighteenth century illegitimacy was no real social problem. By the 1820s, however, the situation was different. A priest in Ruprechtsberg claimed that few single women had not given birth to illegitimate children. "A Virgin! Rara Avis."[3] The two bulwarks of innocence, fear of God and modesty, had been breached. The seriousness of the situation cannot be doubted (Table 1). Only two other areas in Germany and Austria had higher illegitimacy rates (Table 2). Furthermore the preeminence of Bavarian bastards in the whole of Western Europe was still as severely pronounced in 1865–1870 (Table 3). Single women were conceiving five to six children each. In the parish of Gremertshausen ". . . morality and religiosity [were] . . . in such a bad condition, that deteriorations were daily visible."[4] The picture of moral decay would seem to be complete: a sexual

W. R. Lee is Lecturer in the Department of Economic History, University of Liverpool.

1 Kingsley Davis, "Illegitimacy and the Social Structure," *American Journal of Sociology*, XLIV (1939), 215.
2 Edward Shorter, "Illegitimacy, Sexual Revolution, and Social Change in Modern Europe," *Journal of Interdisciplinary History*, II (1971), 237.
3 Ordinariats-Archiv München (O.A.M.) Ruprechtsberg. Visitation 1823. Cited by Fintan Michael Phayer, *Religion und das Gewöhnliche Volk in Bayern in der Zeit von 1750–1850* (Munich, 1970), 114.
4 O.A.M. Gremertshausen. Visitation 1822.

Table 1   Illegitimacy Rates and Birth Rates in Bavaria (1825/6–1874)

	ILLEGITIMATE BIRTHS PER 100 BIRTHS	BIRTH RATE PER 1,000 POPULATION
1825/6–29/30	19.6	
1830/1–34/5	20.4	
1835/6–39/40	20.8	36.4
1840/1–44/5	20.6	35.7
1845/6–49/50	20.5	35.1
1850/1–54/5	20.8	33.7
1855/6–59/60	22.8	35.3
1860/1–64/5	22.8	37.2
1865/6–69/70	19.4	39.6
1871 –1874	13.9	40.4

revolution had taken place, disrupting the equilibrium of traditional peasant behavior norms and replacing them with greater freedom in sexual activity. But how viable is such a hypothesis in the case of South Germany? To what extent were the general causative factors found in other parts of Europe present in Bavaria? Was there really a "sexual revolution," which could be regarded as marking a fundamental change with preindustrial social and sexual codes?

South Germany, and specifically Bavaria, had a social and economic factor endowment which should have militated against a radical revolution in behavior patterns. Despite increasing acceptance of the Reformed Church, Catholicism remained a semi-official religion to which 92 percent of the population belonged even in 1902. Social control is often institutionalized in religion as an adjunct to secular mechanisms and specifically in Catholicism, which rigidly maintained the "principle of legitimacy." Significantly the Catholic Church was to take a harder and more conservative line on the "social question," with hierarchical pronouncements such as the encyclical Rerum Novarum (1891). In Bavaria the Church's position in the late eighteenth century appeared strong. Of all peasant families, 50.5 percent were tenants of ecclesiastical foundations. In 1776 Upper and Lower Bavaria boasted 120 monastic foundations. A rural chaplain claimed in 1797 that ". . . no more than 10 from 1,000 parishioners failed to attend Sunday Mass" and nineteenth-century figures reveal no evidence of a cataclysmic change and certainly nothing compara-

Table 2 Illegitimacy in German and Austrian Territories (c. 1840)

TERRITORY	ANNUAL FREQUENCY OF ILLEGITIMATE BIRTHS	
	ILLEGITIMATE BIRTHS PER LEGITIMATE BIRTHS	ILLEGITIMATE BIRTHS PER INHABITANTS
Austria below the Ems	3.77	131.50
Steiermark	3.66	142.06
Bavaria	3.98	144.00
Baden	5.61	172.41
Saxony	6.15	184.58
Austria above the Ems	4.71	196.14
Carpathia and Krain	4.95	197.62
Bohemia	6.63	201.42
Hessen	5.71	210.03
Mecklenburg-Schwerin	6.50	222.35
Silesia and Moravia	8.02	228.49
Württemberg	7.69	242.66
Saxony-Weimar	7.10	242.67
Hanover	9.62	308.12
Mecklenburg-Strelitz	10.86	335.80
Galicia	14.06	366.26
Prussia	13.49	392.95
Tyrol and Vorarlberg	19.20	655.98
Lombardy	25.16	660.98
Oldenburg*a*	11.33	748.26
Venetian territory	31.38	832.39
Dalmatia	27.38	952.15

a   without Kniphausen

SOURCE: F. Rivet, "Ueber die ausserehelichen Geburten, insbesonders in Baiern," *Archiv der politischen Oekonomie und Polizeiwissenschaft,* I (1843), 44–45.

ble to the low church attendance rates in parts of the United Kingdom revealed by the 1851 census. In Hohenkammer, average attendance rates in 1843–1848 still stood at 97.9 percent. It is against this backcloth that the "revolution" in social behavior is supposed to have taken place.[5]

5   Wolfram Fischer, "Social Tensions at Early Stages of Industrialization," *Comparative Studies in Society and History,* IX (1966), 70. Joseph Hazzi, *Statistische Aufschlüsse über das Herzogtum Baiern* (Munich, 1802), II, 123. Phayer, *Religion,* 30. K. Inglis, "Patterns of Religious Worship in 1851," *Journal of Ecclesiastical History,* XI (1960), 79. According to Horace Mann ". . . the masses of our working population . . . are never or but seldom seen in our religious congregation." H. Mann, "On the statistical position of the religious bodies in England and Wales," *Journal of the Statistical Society,* XVIII (1855), 141.

Table 3 Illegitimacy Rates per 100
births (1845/50–1865/70)

COUNTRY	1845/50	1865/70
Bavaria	20.5	19.3
Saxony	14.8	15.1
Württemberg	11.8	15.7
Denmark	11.4	10.8
Austria	11.3	14.7
Scotland	9.8	9.6
Norway	8.3	9.2
Sweden	8.8	9.3
Belgium	8.1	7.2
France	7.4	7.6
Prussia	7.5	8.3
England	6.7	6.3
Netherlands	4.8	4.0
Spain	–	5.8
Italy	–	5.0
Sardinia	2.1	–

Local kinship factors were also important throughout the period 1750–1850. Although extended families seldom existed, couples rarely had a neolocal residence completely independent of existing kinship connections. The strong identity of separate rural regions, visible in traditional costume styles, also meant that family contacts with a specific region remained strong. Godparents, for example, often came from within a radius of 5–10 km. and within individual families there was a strong element of continuity in choice. Community ties, often of crucial importance as mechanisms of social control, were reinforced by the pattern of settlement. Average population per village in Oberbayern (1808) fluctuated from 23.5 (Landgericht Miesbach) to 93.5 (Landericht Freising) and settlements of only one–two holdings were predominant near the Alps. The small, decentralized settlement pattern should have made the implementation of kinship and neighborhood sanctions more effective than in other parts of Europe, even if the result were simply to retard social change.

Demoralization in the Hegelian sense implies the loss of identity between the objective societal order and the subjective will of the individual, and both industrialization and urbanization are traditionally regarded as causative factors in this process. Certainly even prominent liberals, such as Gottfried Ludolf Camphausen and Gustav von Mevissen, stressed the power of urban life (and the development of a market economy) to weaken primal solidarities. Bavaria, however, was minimally affected by these disequilibriating macrodevelopments. The first mechanical cotton-spinning factory was not established until 1837. The question of industrial employment only became problematic after the 1850s. In the whole of the Landgericht Freising, with a total population of over 14,000 in 1830, apart from eighteen small-scale breweries there was only one factory employing one spinner and three part-time workers. Throughout the nineteenth century the agrarian sector in Bavaria remained predominant. Even as late as 1890 only 23 percent of the population lived in towns; there were only twenty-nine urban centers of more than 10,000 inhabitants. It is therefore doubtful whether the multiplier effect of urbanization on the infrastructure of rural society would have been significant. The development of a market economy was also slow and tentative, and it is difficult to see this factor as ". . . the most corrosive of the traditional communitarian order." In 1810 only 168 market centers existed in Altbayern and no additions were made until 1840. With an average population of 945, the smallest being Essing (Niederbayern) with only 317 inhabitants, it is not surprising that the economic role of these market centers in the nineteenth century was limited. In the Landgericht Freising only 28.5 percent of the annual grain crop and 0.2 percent of the region's sheep came up for sale. The development of inter-regional trade was also retarded by the fall in grain prices in the 1820s and 1830s. The whole of the Isarkreis in the early nineteenth century had only 457 registered merchants, whose turnover was officially described as not being "particularly favourable."[6]

Despite the absence of dramatic economic changes, an explosive upswing did take place in early nineteenth-century illegitimacy rates. How then is this phenomenon within a preindustrial

6 Donald G. Rohr, *The Origins of Social Liberalism in Germany* (Chicago, 1963), 9. Wolfgang Zorn, "Gesellschaft und Staat im Bayern des Vormärz," in Werner Conze (ed.), *Staat und Gesellschaft im deutschen Vormärz, 1815–1848* (Stuttgart, 1962), 119. Staatsarchiv für Oberbayern (St.A.ObB.), Regierungs Akten (R.A.) 1123/15702. Jahres-Berichte, Landgericht Freising, 1827–30. Shorter, "Illegitimacy," 249. Roman Mauerer, *Entwicklung und Funktionswandel der Märkte in Altbayern seit 1800* (Munich, 1971), *passim*. St. A.ObB. R.A. 1103/15676.

242 | POPULATION HISTORY AND THE FAMILY

society to be explained? How valid are existing interpretations within the general European framework to the specific case of South Germany and Bavaria? Closer analysis will reveal many of their deficiencies.

It is impossible that increasing illegitimacy rates can be attributable to improved registration. Local priests were particularly assiduous in listing all illegitimate births in the eighteenth century and the maintenance of special burial plots for bastard children reinforced the need for careful differentiation.

The hypothesis relating changes in social patterns to the growth of rural industry provides a further possible explanation. Even if Bavaria had not industrialized in the period under consideration, rural industry already exercised an important role in the economy. In 1771 in the Pfleggericht Kranzberg, 21.7 percent of listed families depended to some extent on income from crafts and manufacturing. By 1788 restrictions on the spread of rural industry had been lifted and by 1809 182,216 individuals, with 70,539 apprentices and assistants were occupied in this sector.[7] Linen production was particularly noted in Upper Frankonia, shoe-making in the Palatinate, and wood-carving in Oberbayern. The disequilibriating effect on peasant society could have been considerable.

If primary social functions are normally linked to a system of occupational status, the growth of rural industry may have stimulated the emergence of new social behavior norms, as envisaged by von Benekendorf. Claims have been made of a positive correlation between the extent of rural industry and the rate of illegitimacy and it is perhaps significant that the settlement pattern associated with rural industry tended to differ slightly from that of traditional agricultural holdings, being associated with small-holdings and reduced family size. Significantly, the lowest family size located in Germany of 1.82 individuals per family related to small-holders in Calenberg-Göttingen and Grubenhagen in 1689. If it is argued that the nuclear family, despite its positive attributes in meeting the demands of primary groups, being face-to-face, permanent, effective, and noninstrumental, encountered difficulties in handling crucial tension management problems where the source of difficulty lay within the family (as in the case of illegiti-

7 Rudolf Braun, *Industrialisierung und Volksleben* (Zurich, 1960). St. A.ObB. General Register (G.R.) 290/1. St. A.ObB. R.A. 1103/15676.

mate offspring of family dependents), then the societal repercussions of rural industry may well have been adverse: the smaller nuclear family was even less likely to be able to cope with deviations from the norm.[8]

The applicability of this hypothesis to the case of Bavaria, however, remains doubtful. The growth of rural industry was a cumulative process which had probably reached its peak in individual sectors before the end of the eighteenth century. In many areas optimum distribution of small-holdings had been achieved by 1760 (Table 4). If this factor had been causative, why are explo-

Table 4   Percentage Distribution of Small Holdings (1/6–1/32) in Bavaria, 1760

ADMINISTRATIVE AREA	NUMBER OF HOLDINGS	NUMBER OF SMALL HOLDINGS	% OF SMALL HOLDINGS
Moosburg	2557	1359	53.1
Mering	701	550	78.9
Friedberg	1524	1078	70.7
Starnberg	1285	800	62.2
Weilheim	2217	1468	67.0
Benediktbeuren	559	302	54.0
Ettal	947	804	84.8
Mainburg	571	301	52.7
Neustadt	259	230	91.8
Vohburg	1326	872	65.7
Traunstein	1652	1026	62.1
Trostberg	804	407	50.6
Pfaffenhofen	3008	1682	56.0
Dachau	3402	2148	63.1
Kranzberg	2335	1361	58.6
Aichach	2620	1749	67.5
Landsberg (Landkreis)	3233	2349	75.7

SOURCE: P. Fried, "Historisch-statistische Beiträge zur Geschichte des Kleinbauerntums (Söldnertums) im westlichen Oberbayern," *Mitteilungen der Geographischen Gesellschaft in München*, II (1966), 19.

8 Werner Conze, "Vom 'Pöbel' zum 'Proletariat'. Socialgeschichtliche Voraussetzungen für den Sozialismus in Deutschland," in H.-U.Wehler (ed.), *Moderne Deutsche Sozialgeschichte* (Köln, 1966), 114. A. Beelitz, G. Ostermuth, H. Schlegel, and H. Pohl. "Unterschiedliche Fortpflanzung in den Fürstentumern Calenberg-Göttingen und Grubenhagen auf Grund der Kopfsteuerbeschreibung von 1689," *Archiv für Bevölkerungswissenschaft und Bevölkerungspolitik*, XI (1941), 311. Eugene Litwak and Ivan Szelenyi, "Primary Group Structures and their Functions: Kin, Neighbors and Friends," *American Sociological Review*, XXXIV (1969), 419.

sive illegitimacy rates not found prior to the nineteenth century? By 1800 other areas of Germany had extensive rural industries and a settlement distribution pattern with an equal emphasis on small-holdings, and yet this fact alone did not stimulate illegitimacy rates as dramatically as it did in South Germany and Bavaria.[9]

High illegitimacy rates have also been regarded as a consequence of the reintroduction of restrictive marriage and settlement legislation, which "narrowed the range of economic opportunities open to those wanting to establish a family."[10] In states where this type of legislation was adopted in the early nineteenth century, including Bavaria, Hannover, Wurttemberg, Baden, Hessen-Nassau, Hessen-Darmstadt, Mecklenburg-Schwerin, and Hohenzollern, influenced perhaps by such neo-Malthusians as Rau, von Mohl, and Weinheld, it is believed that a considerable number of legitimate births suppressed through marriage restrictions accounted for the large number of illegitimate conceptions. Legislation of 1818 and in particular of 1825 in Bavaria did indeed reduce marriage prospects, but certain weaknesses remain in this hypothesis.

First, the changes in Bavarian illegitimacy rates do not fit the chronological pattern of legislation. Significant changes in illegitimacy can be found in the 1780s and 1790s (Table 5), and as early as 1812–1813 the rate in Freising already stood at 19.7 per 100 births, a figure typical of other areas (Table 6).[11] Even after the lifting of marriage restrictions in the 1850s, Bavarian illegitimacy rates remained far above the average for the German Empire. In 1901 the rate for Oberbayern stood at 18.9 per 100 births and 25.3 in Munich.

Second, many of the important demographic indices connected with marriage and nuptiality remained constant for the period 1750–1850. For the constituent parishes of the Hofmark Massenhausen, for example, the overall proportion of female children eventually marrying rose from 29.5 percent in 1750–1799 to

9 Friedrich-Wilhelm Henning, "Die Betriebsgrössenstruktur der mitteleuropäischen Landwirtschaft im 18. Jahrhundert und ihr Einfluss auf die ländlichen Einkommensverhältnisse," *Zeitschrift für Agrargeschichte und Agrarsoziologie*, XVII (1969), 171–193.

10 John Knodel, "Law, Marriage and Illegitimacy in Nineteenth-Century Germany," *Population Studies*, XX (1967), 280.

11 St. A.ObB. R.A. 1105/15680.

Table 5 Decennial Illegitimacy Rates per 100 Live Births (1750–1849)

DECADE	HOFMARK MASSENHAUSEN	HOFMARK THALHAUSEN
1750–9	4.09	3.94
1760–9	3.84	3.40
1770–9	4.69	3.15
1780–9	8.55	8.77
1790–9	7.47	13.41
1800–9	7.69	11.11
1810–9	14.03	12.17
1820–9	18.04	25.53
1830–9	16.41	22.97
1840–9	15.28	55.29

34.3 percent in 1800–1849. The mean age at first marriage for women did rise, but only marginally, from 26.9 years in 1750–1799 to 27.1 in 1800–1849. On the Hofmark Thalhausen there was an equally marginal fall in this important index from 31.1 to 29.3 years. It is not surprising to find, therefore, that little change took place in the overall proportion of unmarried individuals to total

Table 6 Early 19th Century Illegitimacy Rates in Administrative Areas of Bavaria

DISTRICT	YEAR	ILLEGITIMACY RATE (PER 100 BIRTHS)
Bez. Ingolstadt	1810/11	24.0
Isarkreis	1810/11	17.0
Aichach	1811/12	12.1
Altötting	1811/12	15.5
Burghausen	1811/12	13.4
Isarkreis	1811/12	16.6
Erding	1812/13	14.5
Rosenheim	1812/13	14.5
Munchen	1812/13	18.9
Dachau	1812/13	10.1
Freising	1813/14	20.0
Rosenheim	1813/14	15.3
Starnberg	1813/14	11.3
Trostberg	1813/14	10.4
Weilheim	1813/14	7.4

population. In the Landgericht Freising 37.1 percent were listed as unmarried in 1840. If this figure is adjusted according to age-group, it corresponds closely to the late eighteenth-century figure of just over 33 percent.[12] Indeed, although the marriage rate in Bavaria in the 1820s and 1830s was lower than that pertaining to other German territories with minimal marriage restrictions, the difference only accounts for a small proportion (c. 15 percent) of the additional illegitimate births recorded.

Third, if factors affecting the ease of marriage are viewed as influencing illegitimacy rates, then an inverse correlation should be expected between the variable rates of marriage or total births and illegitimacy. This was not usually the case. In 1813–1814 both the number of solemnized marriages and illegitimate births rose. During the late 1840s a similar parallel is found, with illegitimacy rates falling at a time when total births fell at a faster rate.[13] To this extent the restrictive marriage legislation of 1825 does not appear to have had a decisive effect on relative rates of illegitimacy.

It has also been argued that the Secularization of 1803 was responsible for the dramatic increase in illegitimacy.[14] Despite the Concordat of 1817, the Church was slow to recover and the first Benedictine monastery was not reopened until 1830. The reduction in personnel was accompanied by enforced land sales and a reorganization of parish boundaries. As a result traditional moral norms, which had rested on a firm Christian basis, were displaced and the "secularization of sexual life" led directly to the illegitimacy problem. The validity of this explanation rests on an assumed effectiveness of Church control in the late eighteenth century and an accepted over-lapping of Church and peasant value patterns. Behind the impression of conformity furnished by communion attendance figures, however, there is little evidence of effective social control. The Church had ceased to take an active interest in the running of the economy and ecclesiastical foundations were inevitably landlordish in character. Many churches prior to Secularization were incorporated with monastic foundations and the priest was not locally resident.[15]

12   Bayerische Statistisches Landesamt. Survey of 1840. St. A.ObB. G.R. 302/42.

13   Ludwig August von Müller, *Von Riedels Commentar zum Bayerischen Gesetze über Heimat, Verehelichung und Aufenthalt* (Nördlingen, 1887), 151–152.

14   Phayer, *Religion*, III, 255.

15   Cf. Hartwig Peetz, "Der Haushalt des Klosters Polling im 18. Jahrhundert," *Jahrbuch*

Other signs of an ineffective role function in the late eighteenth century can be adduced from the following factors: first, social and linguistic barriers mitigated the significance of face-to-face contact. The majority of theological students came from the better-off sections of society. Latinized ecclesiastical ritual hardly coped with the innate superstitious nature of peasant religious belief. On Good Friday, for example, bread was rubbed on the cross, the crumbs being stored for later use in baking in the belief that doing so would prevent indigestion. The communication barrier was substantial. According to one contemporary (1786) ". . . In the sermons . . . one hears nothing but complaining . . . today over the decadent, irresponsible times, tomorrow over free-thinkers and godless books . . . and all this for an audience, among whom perhaps hardly three have ever held a book in their hands and who do not know what the sermon is about."[16]

Second, evidence is also available for a noticeable decline in peasant support for the Church in the eighteenth century. For the thirteen churches of the Hofmark Massenhausen, voluntary contributions fell from 135 Gulden (1769) to 98fl.33kr.Ih1. (1802).[17] The average decennial frequency of peasant endowments of ecclesiastical foundations also fell from 6 in 1700–1749 to 3 in 1750–1799.

Third, if the reduction in Church authority implicit in the Secularization acted in a causative role in facilitating increased illegitimacy, why did the extensive erosion of the Church's position in the late eighteenth century not produce a similar effect? Restrictions had been placed on the Mendicant orders (1749–1769); the Decimation Bull of 1757 allowed taxation of Church property and the Bull of 1798 had enabled the Kurfürst to appropriate one-

---

für Münchner Geschichte, IV (1890), 318; Rudolf Haderstorfer, *Die Säkularisation der oberbayerischen Klöster Baumberg und Seeon* (Stuttgart, 1967), 14–15. St. A.ObB. Amts Register (A.R.) 2359. Eleven of the 20 parishes in the Pfleggericht Kranzberg were incorporated prior to 1803.

16 Franz Xaver Freninger (ed.), *Das Matrikelbuch der Universität Ingolstadt-Landshut-München. Rectoren, Professoren, Doctoren. 1472–1872. Candidaten 1772–1872* (Munich, 1872), 79. Anita Brittinger, "Die Bayerische Verwaltung und das volksfromme Brauchtum im Zeitalter der Aufklärung," unpub. diss. (Munich, 1937), 8–9. K. Böck, *Das Bauernleben in den Werken bayrischer Barockprediger* (Munich, 1953), 28 ff.

17 On the basis of a list of voluntary contributions for all Massenhausen settlements dating from 1835–36, the average level per head had fallen from 45 kreuzer in 1769 to just over 4 kreuzer.

seventh of all ecclesiastical property. All of these measures struck at the symbolic position of the Church without affecting the "moral" behavior of parishioners or leading to dramatically high illegitimacy rates.

A further explanatory hypothesis regards formalized primary education, with its emphasis on linear logic and a sense of self, as a prime force in the disruption of social values in the nineteenth century. Undoubtedly increased literacy did promote added awareness of optional forms of social behavior. In Austria after the introduction of compulsory attendance in 1774, the increased influx of popular novels from north Germany contributed to the "anti-catholic" feeling of certain social groups. In England loss of faith in the nineteenth century could easily be associated with specific literary works. If this were equally true for Bavaria, increased literacy may have minimized the magical and superstitious elements in religious belief and thereby led to a conflict between individual and socio-religious behavior norms.[18]

There was educational reform in the early nineteenth century. School attendance was made compulsory for children between six and twelve years in 1802 and improvements were made to the curriculum in 1804, 1806, and 1811. The training of teachers was improved by the establishment of nine seminaries between 1803 1817. In 1783 probably over half of the people in Bavaria could neither read nor write.[19]

In the opinion of contemporaries, however, these attempts at educational reform achieved very little. Figures for the Hofmark Massenhausen indicate that in the period 1840–1847 only 58 percent of men and 50 percent of women from small-holdings could sign their names. In Thalhausen 60 percent were illiterate in the period 1820–1839. Given the predominance of small-holders in many rural areas, it would seem that overall levels of literacy had hardly improved from the late eighteenth century. Structural deficiencies in the educational sector still abounded. Secularization did not lead to the utilization of appropriated income for local educational needs, and the rate of foundation of new schools was

18 Shorter, "Illegitimacy," 252. Otto Brunner, "Staat und Gesellschaft im vormärzlichen Oesterreich im Spiegel von J. Beidtels Geschichte der Oesterreichischen Staatsverwaltung, 1740–1848," in W. Conze (ed.), *Staat und Gesellschaft*, 71. Susan Budd, "The Loss of Faith in England, 1850–1950," *Past & Present*, 36 (1967), 109–112.
19 Peter Anton Winkopp, *Bibliothek der Denker und Männer von Geschmack. Der Zustand der Aufklärung in Bayern* (Munich, 1783), I, 471.

slow. Even in 1833 the average teacher-pupil ratio in the Land-gericht Freising stood at 1:103, although in Neufahrn this rose to 1:209. According to Sendtner, Bavaria lagged behind all other German states in the promotion of education.[20] The aims of the educational system were too limited, but despite the narrow terms of reference, the schooling provided was still insufficient and had little overall effect. It seems unlikely, therefore, that the high illegitimacy rates could have been the result of changes in this sphere.

Finally there is the possibility that social isolation and class stratification increased during this period. The gradual erosion of corporate bonds signified the change from a structured society of separated groups (Stände), differentiated even by sumptuary legislation, to a legally uniform civil society, where the internalized corporative constraints no longer held. According to Franz von Baader (1765–1841) traditional German society could only be retained by greater emphasis on corporate professional organizations. It is possible that corporate cohesion deteriorated in the late eighteenth century. In Austria one effect of Joseph II's "Gesinde" legislation abolishing patriarchal authority was to exclude servants from the family by a reduction in cooperative contact within the employer's household. Adolf von Knigge (1798) viewed the sweetest of all relationships between the household father and his dependents (both by kinship and contract) as a thing of the past.[21] It is therefore possible that such phenomena as increased urbanization and the acceptance of new educational theories may have adversely altered the control mechanisms within both the individual Stände and the monogamous patriarchal family.

Once again, however, this general hypothesis proves unsuitable as an explanation of the high illegitimacy rates in Bavaria. The family role hardly altered. It remained, as a unit centered on a specific holding, the immediate source of social welfare, including the provision of marriage dowries, provisions for physically disabled children and for elderly parents. Throughout the period under consideration the legal basis of these obligations did not al-

---

20 St. A.ObB. R.A. 1124/15703. Otto Sendtner, *Ueber Lehre und Zucht in den Schulen* (Munich, 1826), *passim*.

21 W. Fischer, "Social Tensions," 77. Günter Brakelmann, *Die Soziale Frage des 19. Jahrhunderts* (Witten/Ruhr, 1964), 195. Rolf Engelsing, "Dienstbotenlektüre im 18. und 19. Jahrhundert in Deutschland," *International Review of Social History*, XIII (1968), 397.

ter. The retention of this role, connected with the traditional inheritance pattern, was to provide a strong element of continuity in rural society. Equally there is little evidence of an erosion of corporate bonds within the various strata of rural society. In the Gemeinde proceedings an awareness of corporate responsibility is predominant in the early nineteenth century. The Gemeinde was the highest form of organization in most rural areas, and the allocation of increased powers to this body in the course of the early nineteenth century (as in 1825, 1834, 1848, and 1850), together with the maintenance of consensus and participational action would, if anything, have tended to reinforce cohesion within rural society in Bavaria.[22]

None of the traditional explanations of the disruptive factors facilitating high illegitimacy rates appears appropriate to Bavaria. How then is this dramatic phenomenon to be explained? Basically, increased illegitimacy did not imply a dramatic change in behavioral norms. Illegitimacy did not mean exclusion from contemporary society. It did not conflict, in the opinion of the peasantry, either in the late eighteenth or early nineteenth centuries, with traditional moral norms. The increasing number of bastards is to be explained primarily in economic and legal terms and not in connection with Secularization nor a nascent "sexual revolution."

Although tradition in primitive societies often acts as a force for consolidation, social control relies essentially on the application of different pressures to ensure the continued retention of existing norms, including physical and anticipated sanctions and psychological punishment. In Bavaria illegitimacy had been accepted into the framework of rural society in a way which made social controls unnecessary. There was no inherent conflict between illegitimacy and the retention of the family as the basic unit. Illegitimate children received their due share in family settlements. It was commonly regulated that in the event of a bride's death illegitimate children from other relationships were to be accorded the same rights as legitimate issue.[23] In other spheres a similar lack

22 J. Pflaumer-Rosenberger, *Die Anerbensitte in Altbayern* (Munich, 1939), *passim*. Gesetzblatt (GBL) (Munich, 1834), 109; GBL. (Munich, 1848), 98; GBL. (Munich, 1850), 341.
23 St. A.ObB. Hofmark Thalhausen, 10, Marriage Protokoll of 1833. This provides a typical example of the procedure. In the case of the later death of the bride, her three illegitimate children from another relationship were to be granted full inheritance rights.

of ostracism is visible. Cases where illegitimate children inherited a family holding are found in the 1780s as well as in the 1840s, despite the fact that illegitimate children, being institutionally outside the family under Roman Law, would normally be outside it in the legal sense. Medical attention given to children in their first year of life remained pitifully poor (only 7 percent of those dying from weakness, atrophy, or intestinal infection received attention in 1888–1889), but bastards received equal, if not preferential, treatment. There is also no evidence of a policy of slow starvation of newly born illegitimate children, as can be found in certain areas of France in the nineteenth century.[24]

On a further level traditional concepts of social stability were essentially a function of two major variables—(a) the normative and consensual commitment of the individual of the society and (b) the integration of the norms held by these individuals.[25] It would appear in the case of peasant society in Bavaria that consensual commitment did not preclude the wider acceptance of illegitimacy. Church officials frequently complained that the Gemeinde Vorsteher, as elected representatives, were seldom active enough in combating illegitimacy. Reports from the Landgericht Freising stressed that the central courts could not act against infringements of the moral code, especially in relation to illegitimacy, if denunciations were not passed on by local authorities. The absence of sanctions imposed by the peasantry is further emphasized by the frequency of illegitimate conceptions within individual families. In Fürholzen, for example, all listed illegitimate births in the period 1750–1850 came from ten of the twenty-three holdings. Of the daughters from these tenements, 64.9 percent reaching adulthood gave birth to illegitimate children.

It would therefore seem that illegitimacy, at least within certain families, constituted a social norm rather than a threat to the existing family structure. This aspect is also reinforced by the continued practice of naming illegitimate children after their putative

24   Horace H. Robbins and Francis Deak, "The Familial Property Rights of Illegitimate Children: A Comparative Study," *Columbia Law Review*, XXX (1930), 308–329. Jacques Bergeron and Rene Marjolin, "Hygiène des Nouveau-nés," in J. Bertillon (ed.), *Bericht für den internationalen Hygiene Kongress in Paris* (1893), 111.
25   William J. Goode, "A Theory of Role Strain," *American Sociological Review*, XXV (1960), 495.

father, even after the legislation of 1825 had specifically prohibited doing so without a prior examination of the paternity claim.[26] Although the legislation had an immediate effect in urban areas, the situation in rural areas remained unchanged. It can therefore be concluded that individuals responsible for illegitimate children were not themselves subject to criticism from their neighborhood or kinship groups. Their social standing within the peasant community was not endangered by paternity claims and assertions, even if false. Rural society was apparently indifferent as to whether children listed in the parish registers were legitimate or not. It did not follow the Church's lead in the attempted imposition of social controls. One of the key elements influencing role performances—the esteem/disesteem with which peripheral social networks or important reference groups will respond to the performance—was therefore inoperative as a means of controlling rising illegitimacy rates.

There were a number of practical reasons why high illegitimacy rates could be tolerated without disrupting the continued functioning of traditional rural society in Bavaria. In the first instance, infant mortality among illegitimate children remained extremely high throughout the period under discussion.[27] For Oberbayern in the period 1815–1869 infant mortality rates for illegitimate children actually rose from 38.9 to 42.0 per 100 live births. On the Massenhausen estate over 50 percent of all illegitimate births in the decades 1800–1809 and 1840–1849 died in the first year of life. To this extent high rates of illegitimate births did not imply in concrete terms a long-term social or economic problem. Secondly it is also clear that pregnancies resulting from nonmarital unions seldom resulted in a change in work pattern. Routine employment was continued almost to the day of birth, and resumed a few hours afterwards.[28]

If no formal sanctions were imposed within the family, a psychological sanction linked with a monetary fine or corporal punishment had been retained by the state throughout the

26 Josef Klemens Stadler, "Die Familienname der unehelichen Kinder in Altbayern," *Zeitschrift für Bayerische Landesgeschichte*, IX (1936), 434.

27 Georg Mayr, "Die Sterblichkeit der Kinder während der ersten Lebensjahre in Süddeutschland insbesonders in Bayern," *Zeitschrift des kgl. Bayerischen Statistischen Bureaus*, II (1870), 210.

28 H. Küstner, *Leitfaden der Berufskrankheiten der Frau* (Stuttgart, 1919), 90. Gottfried Lammert, *Volksmedizin und medizinische Aberglaube in Bayern* (Würzburg, 1869), 103.

eighteenth century. On the basis of Roman Law draconic penalties were imposed on extramarital relationships, as in the Bavarian legislation of 1649, 1660, and 1727. Although the carrying of the so-called "stone of infamy" is only cited once in late eighteenth century criminal codes, public degradation remained a main prop in the legal system of punishment. In the course of the latter decades of the eighteenth century, however, there was a tendency toward criticism of existing punishments, and an easing in the definition of illegitimacy.[29] By mid-century it was accepted that this easing excluded children born up to one month after marriage and to women who had been promised marriage, but had been deserted later by the prospective husband. The Reichtags-Abschied of 1731 allowed illegitimate children who had been later legitimized entry into urban guilds, and the Prussian Edict of 1765 attempted to remove some of the stigma attached by certain sections of society to illegitimacy.

Although legal reforms in Bavaria had initially been discouraged by the fact that 157,000 Gulden had been collected from fines exacted between 1766–1776 and 1784–1794 under the "Law of Levity," the legislation of 1780 did produce an amelioration by substituting a fine for the first offense in place of public degradation. The edict of 1808, however, abolished all monetary fines for pregnancies arising from extramarital relationships. Illegitimate children were also able to enjoy equal rights at baptism. In stark contrast to the punitive laws of the eighteenth century, the Law Book of 1813 included no form of legal punishment for illegitimate births, and by 1827 the traditional degradation pole had disappeared from all cities and markets in Bavaria. The gradual lifting of legal sanctions undoubtedly had a significant impact on peasant attitudes towards illegitimacy. Certainly in Massenhausen and Thalhausen the initial rise in illegitimacy rates in the late eighteenth century is coincidental with the introduction of legal reforms (see Table 5). The priest in Hebertshausen claimed that the failure of the state to designate illegitimate births as infringements of the moral order had led to the acceptance of bastards as part of the way of life. In Wippenhausen one of the main reasons for the decline in morality was that illegitimacy went unpunished

---

29 Georg Carl von Meyr (ed.), *Sammlung der Churbaierischen Generalien und Landesverordnungen* (Munich, 1773), 111, 116. Wolfram Peitzsch, *Kriminalpolitik in Bayern unter der Geltung des Codex Juris Criminalis Bavarici von 1751* (Munich, 1968), 90 ff.

by the lay authorities.[30] The only way to cure the shamelessness which thereby arose was through the repeal of the lax civil laws and the reintroduction of stiffer church penalties. To the extent that public degradation and heavy monetary fines or corporal punishment did act as a constraint on the actual birth of illegitimate children, then it is arguable that the legal reforms of the late eighteenth and early nineteenth century would have removed an important external sanction.

From a financial point of view the propensity of single individuals to conceive children out of wedlock would also have been stimulated by economic developments in the early nineteenth century. The majority of parents of illegitimate children were normally listed as being in service. This applied, for example, to 70.6 percent of the fathers in Massenhausen and 78.7 percent of the mothers. It is important to note, therefore, that the economic standing of agricultural employees (Gesinde) underwent a definite improvement in the early nineteenth century.

Labor shortages began to be felt in the primary sector from the late eighteenth century onwards. The cumulative implementation of labor-intensive agricultural reforms, without a concomitant rise in labor productivity and in the context of population growth rates well below the European average, meant that the supply situation gradually became acute. In 1809, for example, employment regulations could not be enforced in the Landericht Erding because of acute labor shortages and the competitive bidding-up of wage levels for rural Gesinde to ensure adequate supply. By the end of the eighteenth century peasants with large, integral holdings frequently had to decide whether it was financially more profitable to engage the requisite number of servants to cultivate all available land, or to employ only those necessary to produce a marginal return on investment. Money wages for agricultural servants (both men and women) rose considerably (Table 7). In the Landgericht Tölz, for example, where a "Knecht" had been content with 40-60 Gulden in 1808, he was demanding a year later 60-80 Gulden and getting it.[31]

30 O.A.M. Wippenhausen, Visitation of 1821.
31 Alois Schlögl (ed.), *Bayerische Agrargeschichte* (Munich, 1954), 16–25. Johann Wernicke, *Das Verhältnis zwischen Geborenen und Gestorbenen in historischer Entwicklung und für die Gegenwart in Stadt und Land* (Jena, 1896), 67. St. A.ObB. R.A. 1103/15676. Lorenz von

Table 7 Wage Index for Servants in Gulden (1654–1859)

YEAR	OBERKNECHT WAGE	OBERKNECHT INDEX	MITTELKNECHT WAGE	MITTELKNECHT INDEX	OBERDIRN WAGE	OBERDIRN INDEX
1654	15	100	10	100	6	100
1750	24	160	21	210	12	200
1776	26	173	24	240	18	300
1780	30	200	30	300		
1790	18	120	15	150		
1801	54	360				
1830	50	333	35	350	24	400
1859	90	600	60	600	44	722

In real terms, however, the purchasing power of the agricultural servants in the early nineteenth century had risen by an even greater margin. The effect of a series of good harvests in the 1820s on the Bavarian economy was considerable. By 1825 grain prices had fallen fourfold from their 1817 level. Although this had severe effects on grain producers, the serving class benefited from a further increase in relative purchasing power. The long-term extent of this trend was considerable. If the wage of an "Oberknecht" in 1623 had been equivalent to 2 Scheffel of rye, it amounted to 7½ Scheffel in 1792 and 11 Scheffel in 1895. Evidence of their increased financial security was mirrored in contemporary reports. An increased expenditure on clothing was noted in a number of quarters. Official reports from the 1830s continually refer to their indulgence in "luxury." Little attempt was made to save money despite the foundation of regional savings banks and what did remain from consumer expenditure went to support the payment of alimony for illegitimate children. Agricultural servants by the 1820s and the 1830s, as a result of general economic developments, were in a far better position to indulge their own tastes than their predecessors had been, faced, for example, by the economic difficulties of the 1770s.[32] In economic terms the price paid

Westenrieder, *Gedanken über die Bevölkerung und Landeskultur in Baiern* (Munich, 1788), 237. St. A.ObB. R.A. 1103/15677–8.

32 Gustav Heinrich Haumann, *Ueber die zur Zeit in Deutschland herrschende Noth des landwirtschaftlichen Standes* (Ilmenau, 1826). Jürgen Kuczynski, Studien zur Geschichte der zyklischen Ueber-produktionskrisen in Deutschland 1825–1866. *Die Geschichte der Lage der Arbeiter unter dem Kapitalismus* (Berlin, 1961), I/ii. Hanns Platzer, *Geschichte der ländlichen Arbeiterverhältnisse in Bayern* (Munich, 1904), 205. St. A.ObB. R.A. 1123/15704.

for illegitimate children by the 1820s could more easily be afforded.

Once the economic and legal constraints were removed, a further group of supplementary social factors also help to provide a realistic explanation of the high illegitimacy rates in Bavaria.

Although the nuclear family, based on the husband-wife relationship, was predominant, certain elements of matrifocality can be observed in the structural pattern of peasant families. The economic functioning of the family holding often depended on the role of the wife, whose responsibilities included the allocation of available jobs among the family workers. If the work of the man was relatively well-defined and bound by routine, the wife was expected to modify her labor input in step with economic circumstances. Significantly the customary "year of mourning" was seldom observed and a widower was likely to remarry very shortly after the death of the spouse. Although it would be unjustified to take this argument too far, two established patterns of matrifocality—a low rate of legal marriage and high rates of illegitimacy—were phenomena common to Bavaria, and the eighteenth century did indeed witness an increased discussion of female emancipation, signified by the publication in 1780 of von Hippel's book, *On the Civic Improvement of Women*.[33]

A further social factor affecting the propensity towards high illegitimacy rates was that lower-class illegitimacy did not constitute such a problem as similar rates among higher social groups would have done, and therefore was not faced with extensive social disapproval.[34] On Goode's scale, listing fourteen different types of illegitimacy, lower-class illegitimacy has a particularly low ranking. If it is argued that the level of disapproval is positively correlated with the amount of disruption or status discrepancy created, then once tangible constraints had been removed, little would have stood in the way of an increase in illegitimacy in Bavaria.

Finally, it is clear that children, whether legitimate or il-

33 Sidney M. Greenfield, "Industrialization and the Family in Sociological Theory," in Bernard Farber (ed.), *Kinship and Family Organization* (New York, 1966), 414. H. Scharnargl, "Straussdorf, eine sozialökonomische und soziologische Untersuchung einer oberbayerischen Landgemeinde mit starkem Flüchtlingsanteil," unpub. diss. (Erlangen, 1952), appendix, Table 9a. Klaus Epstein, *The Genesis of German Conservatism* (Princeton, 1966), 229.
34 W. J. Goode, *The Family* (New Jersey, 1964), 23.

legitimate, were not regarded as fully integrated members of society. Until the child had developed skills of one form or another his economic usefulness to the family was limited and the level of parental attention, particularly in the early years of life, was minimal. Children were seldom regarded as individuals. In Mittelfels it was stated that farmers would rather lose a child than a calf and parental attitudes noticeably deteriorated after the birth of the fourth or fifth child.[35] This negative pattern of parent-child relationships is also reflected in the stereotyped naming of children and the absence of medical attention in cases of illness. Given this background of general indifference the "principle" of legitimacy would not have been regarded as being of primary importance.

What then remains of the original concept of a "sexual revolution" in the context of Bavarian conditions? If the conception of an illegitimate child was not regarded as an infringement of existing social regulations, other criteria of morality provide no indication of a cataclysmic change equivalent to such a revolution. Cases of adultery in Massenhausen only rose from nine (1750–1799) to thirteen (1800–1849), an increase hardly indicative of a dramatic reorientation in value patterns. Only two cases of rape are listed. Provided that comments on illegitimacy are omitted, a picture of basic moral and sexual conformity emerges and there is little evidence of a substantial decline in traditional standards of behavior.

Even as an isolated phenomenon, however, the dramatic illegitimacy rates of the early nineteenth century may still be taken to indicate that a greater number of young people were engaging in premarital sex than in previous decades. And yet even this aspect of the so-called "sexual revolution" must be placed in doubt. Such an assertion appears strange, given that 60 percent of all existing and past societies examined permitted premarital sexual realtions and that in Western Europe as a whole the general pattern of courtship during the eighteenth century is known to have included premarital sexual intercourse.[36] Significantly the incidence of premarital conceptions is just as high in individual parishes on the Hofmark Massenhausen in the period 1750–1799 as in the first half of the nineteenth century, and it seems unlikely that young people in their twenties, although employed as Gesinde, would have been effectively excluded from participation on their own in-

35 Hazzi, *Statistische Aufschlüsse,* II, 137.
36 W. J. Goode, *The Family,* 21.

itiative. Various possibilities emerge (verification is a different matter), including a greater resort to foetal abortion, infant murder, and contraception. All three forms of family limitation are known to have been practiced with varying frequency in eighteenth century Bavaria.[37] It is therefore possible that the only major difference in sexual behavior between the late eighteenth and early nineteenth centuries lay in the degree to which precautions were taken to avoid unwanted pregnancy. Once the economic and legal constraints on illegitimacy had been removed, there was no reason why illegitimate conceptions should not have been allowed to run their full course.

In all human societies a high value is placed upon fertility. Human beings are socialized from early childhood to marry and beget children. Bavaria was no exception to this rule. However the phenomenon of high illegitimacy rates does pose problems in that the conception of children even in relatively permissive societies is largely limited within existing marital relationships. There can be little doubt that illegitimacy rates did rise in many parts of Europe in the period from 1750 to 1850, and that this development was particularly marked in the Catholic territories of South Germany and Austria. A great deal of groundwork remains to be undertaken before the causative factors behind this phenomenon can be established with any degree of certainty. In Bavaria, if an interconnection is posited as having existed between the economic infrastructure and changes in social and sexual behavior patterns, it is difficult, given the retarded development of a cash economy and secondary sector, to explain the phenomenon in terms of a revolutionary change. Perhaps existing views of normality in relation to preindustrial social codes, emphasizing a state of equilibrium, did not allow for an element of flexibility sufficient to accommodate considerable changes, including high illegitimacy rates, without involving any substantial reorientation in accepted social roles.

The present study does not pretend to formulate a science of moral/social behavior in preindustrial South Germany. At the most it can be said to reveal a form of agrarian society where norms of moral behavior were intrinsically indigenous, restricted

37 William Robert Lee, "Some Economic and Demographic Aspects of Peasant Society in Oberbayern from 1752 to 1855, with special reference to certain Estates in the former Landgericht Kranzberg," unpub. diss. (Oxford, 1972), 72–97.

on the one hand by the general range of experience of the peasantry, and on the other by economic and legal regulators. In relation to the problem of illegitimacy the conflict of official and indigenous role-obligations was resolved in favor of that course of action adopted by the peasants, both in the late eighteenth and early nineteenth centuries. High illegitimacy rates, once the economic and legal sanctions had been lifted, could therefore be fully accommodated on the local level without involving a "sexual revolution."

Michael R. Haines

Fertility, Nuptiality, and Occupation: A Study of Coal Mining Populations and Regions in England and Wales in the Mid-Nineteenth Century

Without question one of the important concomitants of modernization and modern economic growth is the structural change for the economy.[1] Clark's frequently cited model of economic change, for example, uses the share of labor force in the primary, secondary, and tertiary sectors to gauge the economic progress of a society.[2] In this context, the importance of geographical and occupational mobility appears central to the whole phenomenon of modernization:

> This shift in sectoral structure of the labor force, combined with the demographic trends and differentials in rates of natural increase, had vast consequences for conditions of life, institutions, and the prevailing views of the populations of developed countries that proved to be the dominant factor in changing the consumption structure, the social structure, and even the ideology of society.[3]

It is from this viewpoint that the significance of differential demographic behavior emerges. As the transition from high to low fertility and mortality levels accompanies modern economic growth, the pattern and speed of transition may depend partly on the occupational composition of the population.

Michael R. Haines is Assistant Professor of Economics and Program Associate, International Population Program, Cornell University, and author of several articles on economic demography.

    I would like to express my thanks to the referee who made a careful reading of a preliminary draft of this paper. The research for this article was based, in part, on funds furnished by the Cornell University Western Societies Program and by NICHHD Grant No. R01-HD-07599. In the period since this paper was written, Professor Dov Friedlander of the Hebrew University brought to my attention a paper he has published on nineteenth-century English mining populations. It is encouraging to note that many of the conclusions are the same, although the data were largely different.

1 See Simon Kuznets, *Modern Economic Growth: Rate, Structure and Spread* (New Haven, 1966), 86–284; *idem, Economic Growth of Nations: Total Output and Production Structure* (Cambridge, Mass., 1971), 143–198, 249–302. Richard A. Easterlin, "Economic Growth: An Overview," in David L. Sills (ed.), *International Encyclopedia of the Social Sciences* (New York, 1968), VI, 468–474.
2 Colin Clark, *The Conditions of Economic Progress* (London, 1957; 3rd ed.).
3 Kuznets, *Economic Growth,* 258.

This paper will show that occupational fertility and nuptiality differentials existed historically in England and Wales and have remained through the modern era.[4] It will be argued that these differentials can be partly, even largely, explained by economic factors, although the general social and status "norms" (i.e., tastes in the economists' jargon) surrounding each occupation continue to play a role. The principal emphasis will be on one occupational group—coal miners—though other groups must be used for comparison.

There are several reasons for this emphasis on coal mining. First, coal mining in the nineteenth century, as today, was one of the most basic activities of the industrial revolution. Some have even labeled the nineteenth century the "Age of Coal."[5] Second, coal mining populations are often numerous and geographically highly concentrated. When demographic information on separate occupations is lacking, as it frequently is, then small areas containing high concentrations of a particular occupational group can be used in its stead. Third, coal miners have been observed to have relatively high fertility; for example, the United Nations states that "Miners have also been shown to be a highly fertile group in those censuses where information for them was tabulated separately."[6] Explaining this particular differential behavior, which has apparently persisted over time, should furnish clues as to the causes of general occupational fertility differentials.

England and Wales is also an appropriate area for study because of its early experience with industrialization and heavy dependence on coal mining. By 1851 35 percent of its population lived in urban areas of at least 20,000 inhabitants, over 49 percent of its labor force was in manufacturing, and over 3.3 percent of the total male labor force worked in mining.[7] Considerable material

4 United Nations, *The Determinants and Consequences of Population Trends: New Findings On Interaction of Demographic, Economic, and Social Functions*, (New York, 1973), I, 100–101.
5 M. Gillet (trans. by C. H. Kent), "The Coal Age and the Rise of Coalfields in the North and Pas-de-Calais," in F. Crouzet, W. H. Chaloner, and W. M. Stern (eds.), *Essays in European Economic History, 1789–1914* (New York, 1969), 188–194, 201–202; David S. Landes, *The Unbound Prometheus: Technological Change and Industrial Development in Western Europe From 1750 To The Present* (Cambridge, 1969), 95–100; E. A. Wrigley, *Industrial Growth and Population Change: A Regional Study of the Coalfield Areas of North-west Europe In The Later Nineteenth Century* (Cambridge, 1961), 3–11.
6 United Nations, *Determinants and Consequences of Population Trends* (New York, 1953), 88.
7 Peter Mathias, *The First Industrial Nation: An Economic History of Britain, 1870–1914* (New York, 1960), 243, 260; B. R. Mitchell and Phyllis Deane, *Abstract of British Historical Statistics* (Cambridge, 1962), 60.

exists from the censuses of 1911 and later which can shed light on the issues of occupational fertility differentials. For the mid-nineteenth century, sufficient demographic and labor force data are available for small geographic areas (i.e., registration districts) to permit some analysis of fertility and nuptiality within mining areas just prior to the decline in period fertility rates (c. the mid-1870s). Finally, a tradition of interest in occupation and social class in Britain dates from the work of Charles Booth in the nineteenth century.[8] This interest led to a limited literature on occupation and its social and demographic concomitants, including fertility and marriage, and to a heritage of statistical materials related to occupation and social class.

OCCUPATION, FERTILITY, AND MARRIAGE IN ENGLAND AND WALES AS A WHOLE   General occupational fertility differentials have been observed in both nineteenth and twentieth century England and Wales. The United Nations, surveying the literature in 1953, noted certain consistencies in the data for England and Wales as well as for a number of other countries.[9] As a rule, populations in agriculture, forestry, fisheries, mining, and some types of metallurgical work have had relatively large families; at the other extreme, professional and clerical workers have had relatively low fertility. In between, there is a general ranking from manual, blue-collar to nonmanual, white collar occupations. Table 1 presents data from the Census of Marriage and Fertility of 1911, a remarkable historical social document. As may be seen from the first panel, there was a general progression from the low fertility of high level professional and business occupations (Class I) to the high fertility of unskilled manual workers (Class V). Of special note were the relatively small families among textile workers

---

8 For a discussion of the application of historical data for historical and sociological purposes, see W. A. Armstrong, "The Use of Information on Occupation" in E. A. Wrigley (ed.), *Nineteenth Century Society: Essays in the Use of Quantitative Methods in the Study of Social Data* (Cambridge, 1972), 191–310. A major point of this article is that occupation is usable both as an industrial grouping for the study of the economic features of society and as a measure of social class or ranking. J. W. Innes, *Class Fertility Differentials in England and Wales, 1876–1934* (Princeton, N.J., 1938); *idem,* "Class Birth Rates in England and Wales, 1921–1931," *The Milbank Memorial Fund Quarterly,* XIX (1941), 72–96; W. A. B. Hopkin and J. Hajnal, "Analysis of Births in England and Wales, 1939, by Father's Occupation," *Population Studies,* I (1947), 187–203, 275–300; T. H. C. Stevenson, "The Fertility of Various Social Classes in England and Wales from the Middle of the Nineteenth Century to 1911," *Journal of the Royal Statistical Society,* XXXVIII (1920), 401–444.
9 United Nations, *Determinants and Consequences* (1953), 87–88.

Table 1   Fertility & Child Mortality in Relation to Husband's Social Class & Occupation: England & Wales, 1911. (Children Ever-Born & Children Surviving Per 100 Couples)

CATEGORY	WIFE UNDER 45 AT CENSUS				
	CHILDREN BORN PER 100 COUPLES		CHILDREN SURVIVING PER 100 COUPLES		STAN-DARDIZED CHILD MOR-TALITY PER 1000 BORN
	ACTUAL	STANDARD-IZED	ACTUAL	STANDARD-IZED	
Total population	282	282	233	233	174
Total occupied	282	282	233	233	174
Total unoccupied	236	215	194	179	167
Social class I	190	213	168	187	123
II	241	250	206	212	150
(occupied only)					
III	279	278	232	231	167
IV	287	285	237	236	173
V	337	317	268	253	202
VI	238	247	191	197	203
VII	358	348	282	274	212
VIII	327	320	284	278	129
Selected occupations					
Coal miners (total)	360	349	283	274	213
Coal miners at the coal face	368	356	289	280	214
Iron & steel workers	354	336	274	262	222
Puddlers; rollers	357	340	275	262	229
Blast furnace workers	376	354	294	278	214
Builders' laborers	384	333	302	265	205
General laborers	370	330	293	263	203
Ship platers/ riveters	372	340	293	270	206
Glass manufacture	362	328	284	259	210
Agricultural laborers	330	323	285	279	135
Civil service officers & clerks	190	210	171	187	110
Indoor domestic servants	151	189	134	164	131
Farmers	276	283	248	254	104
Merchants	198	201	178	180	101
Cotton textile workers	232	242	182	190	218
Tailors	286	273	244	233	147
General shopkeepers	292	271	235	220	187

NOTE: The Standardization procedure for wives under age 45 involved taking the actual rates (of children ever-born per woman) in each category of wife's age of marriage cross-classified by duration of marriage for a particular occupation of husband and then multiplying each rate by the number of ever-married

WIFE OVER 45 AT CENSUS			ALL AGES OF WIFE			
CHILDREN BORN PER 100 COUPLES		CHILDREN SURVIVING PER 100 COUPLES	CHILDREN BORN PER 100 COUPLES		CHILDREN SURVIVING PER 100 COUPLES	SOCIAL CLASS
ACTUAL	STANDARD-IZED		ACTUAL	STANDARD-IZED		
487	487	368	353	353	280	—
489	487	372	350	353	278	—
465	489	334	445	310	322	—
365	389	294	249	274	210	I
435	451	341	311	319	255	II
504	489	382	350	351	279	III
498	492	379	356	357	283	IV
533	528	388	399	390	306	V
457	444	331	308	315	235	VI
626	585	445	423	430	321	VII
572	556	457	433	402	359	VIII
630	588	446	423	432	321	VII
652	604	462	427	442	325	VII
603	559	426	422	414	316	IV & V
622	571	434	436	420	322	V
625	578	451	442	432	336	V
536	540	384	435	405	329	V
542	548	396	441	406	335	V
614	555	442	432	415	330	III
600	537	429	426	401	323	IV
574	561	455	451	405	369	VIII
351	369	292	236	265	205	I
282	357	225	192	247	162	III
467	503	387	378	359	322	II
362	367	309	265	258	232	I
459	446	326	296	313	223	VI
496	484	379	355	346	288	III
467	469	339	361	340	276	II

women in each age/duration category for the total population of England and Wales. The marriage age categories used were 15–19, 20–24, 25–29, 30–34, and 35–44. The duration categories were 0–2, 2–5, 5–10, 10–15, 15–20, 20–25, and 25–30. The "expected" children ever-born were then summed and di-

Table 1 (Continued) Ratios to Total Population Averages (Total Population = 100)

CATEGORY	WIFE UNDER 45 AT CENSUS				
	CHILDREN BORN PER 100 COUPLES		CHILDREN SURVIVING PER 100 COUPLES		STANDARDIZED CHILD MORTALITY PER 1000 BORN
	ACTUAL	STANDARDIZED	ACTUAL	STANDARDIZED	
Total population	100	100	100	100	100
Total occupied	100	100	100	100	100
Total unoccupied	94	76	83	77	96
Social class I	67	76	72	80	71
II	85	89	88	91	86
(occupied only)					
III	99	99	100	99	96
IV	102	101	102	101	99
V	120	112	115	109	116
VI	84	88	82	85	117
VII	127	123	121	118	122
VIII	116	113	122	119	74
Selected occupations					
Coal miners (total)	128	124	121	118	122
Coal miners at the coal face	130	126	124	120	123
Iron & steel workers	126	119	118	112	128
Puddlers; rollers	127	121	118	112	132
Blast furnace workers	133	126	126	119	123
Builders' laborers	136	118	130	114	118
General laborers	131	117	126	113	117
Ship platers/ riveters	132	121	126	116	118
Glass manufacture	128	116	122	111	121
Agricultural laborers	117	115	122	120	78
Civil service officers & clerks	67	74	73	80	63

vided by the total number of married women for all marriage ages and durations at the census who were below age 45. This procedure was repeated for surviving children to women aged under 45. Standardized child mortality per 1000 born was then calculated as:

$$\frac{\left(\begin{array}{c}\text{Standardized Children Ever Born}\\ \text{per 100 couples}\end{array}\right) - \left(\begin{array}{c}\text{Standardized Children Surviving}\\ \text{per 100 couples}\end{array}\right)}{\left(\begin{array}{c}\text{Standardized Children Ever Born}\\ \text{per 100 couples}\end{array}\right)} \times 1000$$

For wives over age 45 at the census, children ever born per 100 couples was standardized only for age of marriage since duration was much less important for older women. (Standardizations for duration and age of marriage were done for the eight social classes and little difference appeared between those standardizations for age only). Children surviving per 100 couples was not standardized since child mortality for older women was greatly influenced by factors external to the family and therefore had

Table 1 (Continued) Ratios to Total Population Averages (Total Population = 100)

WIFE OVER 45 AT CENSUS			ALL AGES OF WIFE			
CHILDREN BORN PER 100 COUPLES		CHILDREN SURVIVING PER 100 COUPLES	CHILDREN BORN PER 100 COUPLES		CHILDREN SURVIVING PER 100 COUPLES	SOCIAL CLASS
ACTUAL	STANDARDIZED		ACTUAL	STANDARDIZED		
100	100	100	100	100	100	—
100	100	101	99	100	99	—
95	100	91	126	88	115	—
75	80	80	71	78	75	I
89	93	93	88	90	91	II
103	100	104	99	99	100	III
102	101	103	101	101	101	IV
109	108	105	113	110	109	V
94	91	90	87	89	84	VI
129	120	121	120	122	115	VII
117	114	124	123	114	128	VIII
129	121	121	120	122	115	VII
134	124	126	121	125	116	VII
124	115	116	120	117	113	IV & V
128	117	118	124	119	115	V
128	119	123	125	122	120	V
110	111	104	123	115	118	V
111	112	108	125	115	120	V
126	114	120	122	118	118	III
123	110	117	121	114	115	IV
119	115	124	128	115	132	VIII
72	76	79	67	75	73	I

much less significance for fertility. Thus, standardized child mortality per 1000 born could not be computed for women over 45.

The biases involved in choosing the total national population of married females of different marriage ages and durations as the standard population are evident and were noted by the compilers of the census (lxxx–lxxxii).

Social classes may be roughly categorized as follows:

I: high skill level and high income professional and business occupations (e.g., scientists, artists, lawyers, physicians, managers, high level civil servants).

II: lower skill and income professional and business occupations (e.g. small shopkeepers, agricultural employers and less skilled professional, scientific and artistic workers)

III: skilled manual laborers

IV: semi-skilled manual laborers

Table 1 (Continued) Ratios to Total Population Averages (Total Population = 100)

CATEGORY	WIFE UNDER 45 AT CENSUS				
	CHILDREN BORN PER 100 COUPLES		CHILDREN SURVIVING PER 100 COUPLES		STAN-DARDIZED CHILD MOR-TALITY PER 1000 BORN
	ACTUAL	STANDARD-IZED	ACTUAL	STANDARD-IZED	
Indoor domestic servants	54	67	58	70	75
Farmers	98	100	106	109	60
Merchants	70	71	76	77	58
Cotton textile workers	82	86	78	82	125
Tailors	101	97	105	100	84
General shopkeepers	104	96	101	94	107

V: unskilled manual laborers

VI: textile workers

VII: miners

VIII: agricultural laborers

(Class VI) and the large families among coal miners (Class VII) and agricultural laborers (Class VIII). These differentials held true both for women above and below age forty-five and for total children born and children surviving.

Since different socioeconomic groups in the population experienced differing patterns of age at marriage and duration of marriage, the rates in Table 1 were also standardized to the age and duration pattern of the female population as a whole.[10] The fertility differentials nonetheless persisted, although they were narrowed, after compensating for the earlier average age at marriage and longer average marital duration among the working classes. The same was also true for average surviving children.

More detailed breakdowns of completed fertility by date of marriage indicate that those differentials not only persisted over time but widened from a least the 1850s. Table 2 presents some evidence on this. Married females of completed fertility (i.e., over age forty-five by 1911) were tabulated by date of marriage and social class and then the rates were standardized for age of marriage

10 For an explanation procedure of the standardization techniques, see the note to Table 1. For women above age 45 standardization was only for the age of marriage and no standardization was done for surviving children.

Table 1 (Continued) Ratios to Total Population Averages (Total Population = 100)

WIFE OVER 45 AT CENSUS			ALL AGES OF WIFE			
CHILDREN BORN PER 100 COUPLES		CHILDREN SURVIVING PER 100 COUPLES	CHILDREN BORN PER 100 COUPLES		CHILDREN SURVIVING PER 100 COUPLES	SOCIAL CLASS
ACTUAL	STANDAR-DIZED		ACTUAL	STANDARD-IZED		
58	73	61	54	70	58	III
96	103	105	107	102	115	II
74	75	84	75	73	83	I
94	92	89	84	89	80	VI
102	99	103	101	98	103	III
96	96	92	102	96	99	II

SOURCE: England and Wales, Registrar General, *Census of England and Wales: 1911*, XIII, "Fertility of Marriage," Part II (London: H.M.S.O., 1923), Table XLVIII.

within each group. For higher socioeconomic groups (I and II) completed fertility was declining relative to the national average while that of unskilled, manual workers (V) was rising relative to the average, which itself was declining for successive marriage cohorts. Completed fertility among miners' and agricultural laborers' families (Groups VII and VIII) rose sharply relative to the national average. The rates of decline of children ever-born for marriage cohorts after 1851 were greatest among the highest social classes and smallest among the lower groups. Completed fertility declined from the marriage cohort of 1852/61 to that of 1882/86 at an average annual rate of 1.21 percent and 1.08 percent per annum respectively for social classes I and II but only by 0.51 percent per annum for social class V and by 0.32 percent and 0.47 percent per annum respectively for coal miners' and agricultural laborers' wives. The national decline was 0.69 percent. The lower panel of Table 2 shows that a similar divergence was taking place for effective fertility (i.e., surviving children). Thus, during the fertility decline in late nineteenth-century Britain, class differentials widened as the lower socioeconomic groups, and especially coal miners, lagged behind the national average.[11]

11 This feature of the fertility decline was noted by Innes, *Class Fertility Differentials*, 41–52.

Table 2 Completed and Effective Fertility per 100 Wives By Social Class and Marriage Cohort. Wives over Age 45 at Census, 1911. Rates Standardized for Marriage Age. Total Rates Standardized for Class Composition.

DATE OF MARRIAGE	I	II[a]	III	IV	V	VI	VII	VIII	TOTAL	TOTAL OCCUPIED POPULATION
				CHILDREN BORN PER 100 COUPLES						
1851 and earlier	605[c]	728	681	740[c]	698[c]	*	*	746	697	700
1852–61	625	700	707	700	718	654	759	738	690	701
1862–71	593	650	679	673	698	633	760	702	662	673
1872–81	497	567	615	616	652	567	717	667	605	611
1882–86[b]	422	493	556	562	609	513	684	632	551	554
				PERCENT OF NATIONAL AVERAGE						
1851 and earlier	86	104	98	106	100	*	*	107	100	100
1852–61	91	101	102	101	104	95	110	107	100	102
1862–71	90	98	103	102	105	96	115	106	100	102
1872–81	82	94	102	102	108	94	119	110	100	101
1882–86[b]	76	89	101	102	111	93	124	115	100	100
				ANNUAL PERCENTAGE DECREASE						
1852–61 to 1862–71	0.52	0.74	0.40	0.39	0.28	0.33	+0.01	0.50	0.41	0.41
1862–71 to 1872–81	1.77	1.37	0.99	0.92	0.68	1.10	0.58	0.51	0.90	0.97
1872–81 to 1882–86	2.18	1.86	1.34	1.22	0.91	1.33	0.63	0.72	1.25	1.30

Table 2   Completed and Effective Fertility per 100 Wives By Social Class and Marriage Cohort. Wives over Age 45 at Census, 1911. Rates Standardized for Marriage Age. Total Rates Standardized for Class Composition.

DATE OF MARRIAGE	I	II[a]	III	IV	V	VI	VII	VIII	TOTAL	TOTAL OCCUPIED POPULATION
	CHILDREN SURVIVING PER 100 COUPLES									
1851 and earlier	378[c]	452	420	464[c]	405[c]	*	*	490	432	436
1852–61	433	492	471	472	466	436	465	527	464	478
1862–71	440	479	481	482	480	423	505	535	473	482
1872–81	393	438	460	464	470	406	502	534	454	458
1882–86[b]	345	393	430	434	451	379	497	521	425	428
	PERCENT OF NATIONAL AVERAGE									
1851 and earlier	88	105	97	107	94	*	*	113	100	101
1852–61	93	106	102	102	100	94	100	114	100	103
1862–71	93	101	102	102	101	89	107	113	100	102
1872–81	86	96	101	102	104	89	111	118	100	101
1882–86	81	92	101	102	106	89	117	123	100	101

a   Includes only wives of occupied husbands.
b   Includes a few women not quite age 45 in 1911 (i.e., wives married at ages 15–19 in 1881–86).
c   Based on fewer than 100 cases.
★ = Fewer than 10 cases available.
SOURCE: J. W. Innes, *Class Fertility Trends in England and Wales, 1876–1934* (Princeton, 1938), 42–43; England and Wales, Registrar General, *Census of England and Wales, 1911*, XIII, "Fertility of Marriage," II (London, 1923), Table XLIV.

Returning to Table 1, selected detailed occupations also suggest a ranking similar to social class; but certain occupations, especially coal mining, were notable. For wives over forty-five in 1911, children ever-born per 100 couples where husband's occupation was in coal mining was 630 (and 652 for workers at the coal face). This was 129 percent (and 134 percent) of the national average, and ranked miners' wives first among all occupational groups, closely followed by wives of blast furnace workers, iron puddlers and rollers, ship platers and riveters, iron miners (not shown), and glass workers. In contrast, wives of higher-level civil service officers and clerks were only 72 percent of the national average, wives of indoor domestic servants only 58 percent, wives of merchants only 74 percent, and wives of cotton textile workers only 94 percent. Adjusting for infant mortality (i.e., ever-born children surviving), fertility for miners' wives dropped to 446 for women aged forty-five and over (and 462 for wives of workers at the coal face). For this measure of "effective fertility," coal miners dropped slightly behind agricultural laborers (but not farmers), blast furnace workers, puddlers and rollers, ship platers and riveters, shipyard workers, some construction laborers, and some general laborers. When these rates were standardized by the age structure of marriage for the female population of England and Wales aged forty-five and over, the first rank of coal mining populations was regained and the rates became 123 percent (and 125 percent) of the national average. It is notable that many of the industrial occupations with high fertility had locational and economic characteristics similar to coal mining. For women under forty-five at the 1911 Census (and hence with incomplete fertility), whose fertility had been standardized to the age at marriage and the duration of marriage characteristic of all women under forty-five in England and Wales in 1911, the ranking remained roughly the same. Coal miners were second only to blast furnace workers and agricultural laborers. For children surviving and standardized for age of marriage and marital duration (a calculation not performed in the census for women over forty-five), miners' wives were only behind wives of agricultural laborers, blast furnace workers, and iron miners (not shown). Wives of workers at the coal face were still first, however, despite the relatively high child mortality among the mining population. Child mortality, standardized for duration of marriage and age at marriage of woman, was among the highest for coal mining families, 122 percent of the national average, but this was compensated by high total fertility.[12] The same was true for most of the other occupations with extremely high total fertility. The overall effect of differentials in child mortality was to cause some slight convergence toward the national average for "effective" fertility, but the effect was minimal and often altered by standardization procedures.[13]

Descriptive evidence for the nineteenth century conveys the same impression. For example, Redford remarked in his pioneering work on labor migration in England in the first half of the nineteenth century:

> In general, the evidence for any strong influx of labor into coal mining is not plentiful. A large part of the supply of new labour required by the expansion of the industry probably came from the natural increase of a *notoriously prolific section of the population*. To contemporary observers the coal mining population afforded 'an example of the principle of population in full vigour, in the absence of external influence, and (hitherto) of internal checks. Pitmen must be bred to their work from childhood . . . their numbers cannot be recruited from any other class . . . the increase of the pit population solely from internal sources has in consequence been such that . . . one hundred and twenty-five families attached to a single colliery were capable of annually supplying twenty to twenty-five youths fit for hewers.'[14]

It is notable that similar features are observable in the mid-twentieth century. In the Census of England and Wales of 1951, the mean number of children ever-born per woman aged 45 to 49

12   See note to Table 1.

13   It is important to note that the Census of 1911 presents only surviving married women with surviving spouses. If their marital fertility were systematically different from those who did not survive, a bias is introduced. Of course, couples who do not make it through child-bearing without one or both partners dying *will* have lower fertility, in general, because of the interruption of the marriage. The question is what their completed fertility would have been. Also couples having completed child-bearing but not surviving to 1911 might have been different from those who did survive. Innes and T. H. C. Stevenson, the man who conducted the 1911 Census of Marriage and Fertility, both argued that no important bias was introduced by inclusion only of surviving married women with surviving spouses. (See Innes, *Class Fertility Differentials*, 22–24; *Census of England and Wales, 1911*, XIII, xciv.) Counter arguments are advanced by R. R. Kuczynski, *The Measurement of Population Growth* (London, 1935), 95–96.

14   P. L. C. Report, 1834, Appendix A, Part I, No. 5, 130; in Arthur Redford, *Labour Migration in England, 1806–1850*, (Manchester, 1964; 2nd ed.), 56–57. [Emphasis added].

was 2.60 children for women whose husbands were in mining and quarrying. (See Table 3.) Only 14 percent of these couples were childless, compared to a national average for children ever-born to women 45 to 49 of 2.01 and a proportion childless of .208. Thus completed fertility of miners' wives was 130 percent of the national level and still 106 percent when standardized for age at marriage and socioeconomic composition.[15] Miners' wives ranked first among all industrial/occupational classifications for unstandardized mean number of children ever-born and still first when standardized only for age at marriage. The rank dropped to fourth (among thirteen industrial/occupational classifications) when fertility was standardized both for age at marriage and socioeconomic composition. The completed fertility of wives of semi-skilled and especially skilled workers (i.e., mostly workers at the coal face) was high relative to all other socioeconomic groups in the mining and quarrying industry. Since these workers made up the bulk of those in the industry, standardizing to the national socioeconomic composition, with its much lower share of skilled and semi-skilled workers, would tend to lower the relative standardized fertility in mining and quarrying.[16]

Marriage practices were also related to occupation. Mean age at first marriage for both males and females appears to have been among the lowest in miners' families and in mining regions. In a special study conducted in 1884–85 by the Registrar General, miners and their wives had the lowest mean age at first marriage (24.06 and 22.46 respectively) among all nine occupational groups

15   Great Britain, General Register Office, *Census: 1951, England and Wales,* lviii, 178, 208. Standardization for socioeconomic groups involved standardization of rates for the individual socioeconomic groups within an industrial classification to the national socioeconomic group composition. The thirteen socioeconomic groups were farmers; agricultural workers; higher administrative, professional and managerial; other administrative, professional and managerial; shopkeepers (including proprietors and managers of wholesale businesses); clerical workers; shop assistants; personal service; foremen; skilled workers; semi-skilled workers; unskilled workers; armed forces.

16   This fact was noted in the census, "The high fertility of the mining group as a whole was evidently due to the exceptionally large families of those actually employed as miners (i.e., skilled and semi-skilled), while the unskilled workers attached to the industry . . . had slightly smaller families than the average of [unskilled workers]." *Ibid.,* lvix. The share of skilled and semi-skilled workers in this sample of married couples was 84.18% for mining and quarrying as compared with 46.12% for all occupational/industrial categories.

studied. The rankings by occupational groups for age of marriage was similar to the ranking by marital fertility.[17]

Coale's index of proportion married (I_m)[18] was significantly higher in an 1861 sample of sixty-one coal mining registration districts than in a random sample of 125 registration districts. The same was true for 1871. (See Table 5). In 1861, the highest proportion of persons married at ages 15 to 24 was found in Durham, a county heavily populated with coal miners. In 1834, the Poor Law Commissioners stated that "miners assumed the most important office of manhood at the earliest age at which nature and passion prompted."[19] The census of 1911 noted that "[e]arly marriage is known as a matter of common experience to increase in frequency down the social scale."[20] It was noted that only 7 percent of middle-class husbands and one third of their wives were married before age twenty-five while for coal miners, those proportions were 57 percent and 75 percent for their wives.[21] For the occupational/social class groupings in between the gradation was regular. This differential marriage pattern has persisted,

17 The listing is as follows:

OCCUPATIONS	MEAN AGE AT FIRST MARRIAGE	
	MALES	FEMALES
Miners	24.06	22.46
Textile Hands	24.38	23.43
Shoemakers, Tailors	24.92	24.31
Artisans	25.35	23.70
Labourers	25.56	23.66
Commercial Clerks	26.25	24.43
Shopkeepers, Shopmen	26.67	24.22
Farmers and Sons	29.23	26.91
Professional and Independent Class	31.22	26.40

SOURCE: England and Wales, Registrar General, *Forty Ninth Annual Report* (1886), viii.

18 For a definition see Ansley J. Coale, "Factors Associated with the Development of Low Fertility: An Historic Summary," in United Nations, *World Population Conference: 1965* (New York, 1967), II, 205–209.

19 *British Parliamentary Papers* (1834), XXXVII, 125. Quoted in Margaret Hewitt, *Wives and Mothers in Victorian England* (London, 1958), 40–41.

20 Great Britain, "Fertility Tables," *Census: 1951, England and Wales* (London, 1959), xlvii.

21 Great Britain, *Census of England and Wales, 1911*, XIII, xvi.

Table 3 Mean Family Size and Proportions Infertile by Industry Group of Husband: England and Wales, 1951 (Women Aged 45–49 at Census. All Marriage Ages Combined. Once Married Women with Husband Present.)

| INDUSTRY GROUP | (CHILDREN EVER-BORN) MEAN FAMILY SIZE | | | PROPORTION INFERTILE | | |
| | UNSTAN-DARDIZED | STANDARDIZED FOR MARRIAGE | | UNSTAN-DARDIZED | STANDARDIZED FOR MARRIAGE | |
		AGE	AGE AND SOCIO-ECONOMIC GROUP		AGE	AGE AND SOCIO-ECONOMIC GROUP
1. Agriculture, horticulture and forestry	2.25	2.31	2.25	0.19	0.18	0.19
2. Mining & quarrying	2.60	2.37	2.13	0.14	0.17	0.18
3. Metal manufacture	2.33	2.23	2.15	0.17	0.18	0.19
4. Engineering & vehicles	1.97	1.99	1.99	0.21	0.21	0.20
5. Textiles	1.74	1.77	1.75	0.25	0.24	0.24
6. Clothing	1.69	1.73	1.81	0.24	0.23	0.22
7. Food, drink & tobacco	2.01	1.99	1.99	0.19	0.20	0.20
8. Other manufacturing industries & utilities	2.00	1.99	1.95	0.20	0.20	0.21
9. Buildings & construction	2.34	2.29	2.25	0.17	0.18	0.19
10. Transport & fishing	2.13	2.07	2.01	0.18	0.19	0.20
11. Distributive trades	1.72	1.77	1.97	0.23	0.22	0.22
12. Professional services	1.65	1.81	1.91	0.24	0.21	0.21
13. Other services	1.83	1.87	1.93	0.23	0.22	0.22

Table 3 Continued

		RATIOS TO TOTAL POPULATION (PERCENT)			
1. Agriculture, horticulture and forestry	112	115	112	94	88	94
2. Mining & quarrying	130	118	106	68	82	87
3. Metal manufacture	116	111	107	81	89	92
4. Engineering & vehicles	98	99	99	101	101	100
5. Textiles	87	88	87	120	118	116
6. Clothing	84	86	90	116	112	108
7. Food, drink & tobacco	100	99	99	95	97	97
8. Other manufacturing industries & utilities	100	99	97	98	100	101
9. Buildings & construction	117	114	112	85	89	92
10. Transport & fishing	106	103	100	89	95	98
11. Distributive trades	85	88	98	113	110	105
12. Professional services	82	90	95	120	103	101
13. Other services	91	93	96	111	107	105

SOURCE: Great Britain, General Register Office, *Census: 1951, England and Wales*, "Fertility Report" (London: HMSO, 1959), 207–210.

especially among mining populations. Among women aged 45 to 49 at the time of the 1951 census, the highest proportion married by age twenty-five was among wives of men in mining and quarrying (64 percent). The lowest proportion was among wives of professionals (38 percent), with other industries distributed in between.[22]

THE MODEL   The explanatory model proposed here focuses on the major factors in marriage and fertility decisions as they relate to mining populations. It is important to consider both marriage and marital fertility, since total fertility is the result of both and since both are affected by many common factors.[23] Modified, this model can be applied more generally to other occupational groups but in this instance focuses on coal miners because of their observed high fertility and early marriage customs. (What is said here regarding coal miners is also essentially true for other populations in mining and metallurgy.)

It is argued here that the higher marital fertility and earlier and more extensive marriage of coal mining populations is a product of the interaction of life style (as embodied in tastes and costs) and potential income outlook.[24] By its very nature, coal mining is not especially centered (at least initially) in large cities or established urban centers. Urban agglomerations do grow up around mines or mining centers, but not of the genre of great administrative, commercial, cultural, and market centers. In the early stages of development the population of these mining centers is often drawn from a rural environment. The hypothesis, then is that these persons, who were socialized (i.e., whose tastes were formed) in a rural life-style, maintained these tastes for a desired mix of goods and children in their new situation while experiencing the expanded income outlook and opportunities of industrial wage earners in a rapidly growing sector. In many cases the new miners experienced a cost situation intermediate between rural and

22   Great Britain, "Fertility Tables," *Census: 1951*, xvi–xviii.

23   Nothing is said in this section concerning illegitimate fertility since it was not too important in England and Wales at this time. It should be possible, however, to modify the model to discuss wife's occupation only and therefore illegitimate fertility.

24   A similar approach to the economics of fertility is taken by Richard A. Easterlin. See his "Towards a Socio-economic Theory of Fertility," in S. J. Behrman, et. al., *Fertility and Family Planning: A World View* (Ann Arbor, 1969), 127–156. Also *idem*, "The Economics and Sociology of Fertility: A Synthesis" (1973), mimeo.

urban and were able to supplement their money incomes with income-in-kind from produce raised on small garden plots and farms. The quasi-rural setting and the relative lack of opportunities for female employment outside the home (which characterized most mining areas) reinforced this latter phenomenon. Although the view of mining communities as quasi-rural is not as appropriate for nineteenth century Britain as it was earlier (or for other countries), the social isolation of mining communities nevertheless helped perpetuate these norms longer and caused them to follow general social norms much more slowly.

A generally good standard of living is evidence that miners enjoyed relatively high incomes. With respect to nineteenth century English miners "most authorities agree that miners enjoyed a relatively high standard of living" and that "against a background of ill-planned industrial conurbation the houses of many miners seemed well-ordered, healthy and clean."[25] Mining wages were generally high and above the national average. Miners also often received free cottages and free coal.[26] Evidence presented by Bowley shows that the average money wages of miners were among the highest in the nineteenth century.[27] The wages of printers, skilled iron workers, and sometimes building craftsmen were at times higher, but those of sailors, agricultural workers, and woolen and cotton textile workers were lower. Laborers' wages were always lower. Finally, these higher wages often accrued to miners at an early age (relative to farmers and professionals), thus encouraging earlier marriage and longer exposure to the peak child bearing period.

Another relevant aspect of coal mining is the comparative absence of female employment outside the home. In Britain, particularly, female and child labor underground was forbidden after Lord Shaftesbury's Act of 1842. Further, because of their location, mines often created male employment opportunities distant from factories or shops which employed women. For England and Wales in 1871, the mean proportion of females aged twenty and

25 Brian Lewis, *Coal Mining in the Eighteenth and Nineteenth Centuries* (London, 1971), 38, 107. He quotes from Louis L. Simonin, *Underground Life or Mines and Miners* (London, 1868).
26 A. L. Bowley, *Wages in the United Kingdom in the Nineteenth Century* (Cambridge, 1900), 96, 101.
27 Bowley, *Wages,* 96–109, 130–133, esp. Appendix I, Table II, 133.

over employed outside the home (in sixty-three registration districts with a significant proportion of the male labor force in coal mining) was 24.5 percent as opposed to 30.1 percent for a random sample of 125 registration districts. (See Table 5) These means were significantly different at a .001 level of probability. At the same date there was a −0.50 zero order correlation between the percentage of adult male employment in mining and minerals and the percentage of adult females employed outside the home within the mining districts.[28] For England in the early twentieth century the high fertility of mining districts relative to textile districts has been attributed to differential employment opportunities for women. "In mining districts there are practically no avenues of employment open to women outside the home, whereas in textile districts the bulk of the work is carried on by women."[29] Women are not usually employed in mining, and in the absence of employment elsewhere (in textiles, for example), would be available for work on garden plots or small farms or in domestic handicrafts, activities more compatible with child rearing. Or they simply would not work at all. Hence fewer available employment opportunities for women might simultaneously encourage earlier marriage and higher marital fertility.

As for the impact of employment on marital fertility, following the reason of Mincer, it can be argued that the contribution of a wife's income to family income has two aspects: a price effect and an income effect.[30] The decision of a wife to enter the labor force outside the home thus should have both a positive influence on fertility (i.e., the income effect), since her income should allow more children, and a negative influence (i.e., the price effect) since it now becomes more expensive and difficult to have young children with the mother working outside the home. Mincer found that where most work for women is outside the home (as in the

28 This correlation was significantly different from zero at a .001 level of probability, assuming normally distributed parent populations.
29 Enid Charles and Pearl Moshinsky, "Differential Fertility in England and Wales During the Past Two Decades," in Lancelot Hogben (ed.), *Political Arithmetic* (New York, 1938), 143. Cited in Samuel H. Preston, "Female Employment Policy and Fertility," in Robert Parke, Jr. and Charles Westoff (eds.), *Aspects of Population Growth Policy*, (Washington, D.C., 1972), VI, 380. See also Margaret Hewitt, *Wives and Mothers*, 40–41, 57.
30 Jacob Mincer, "Market Prices, Opportunity Costs and Income Effects," in Carl F. Christ (ed.), *Measurement in Economics: Studies in Mathematical Economics and Econometrics in Honor of Yehuda Grunfeld* (Stanford, 1963), 67–82.

population he studied for the United States in the 1950s), the negative price effect should dominate. That is, higher female labor force participation outside the home should lead to lower fertility. But where there is considerable employment opportunity in agriculture or in domestic handicraft industry, the income effect should dominate because the wife, staying home, can both work and rear her children. (In this case, the opportunity cost of the wife's time in employment outside the home, and hence the 'cost' of a child, should be lower). That female labor force participation outside the home has a negative effect on marital fertility has been confirmed by a number of authors.[31] It has also been found that a woman's participation in domestic handicraft industry is compatible with child-rearing and thus favorable to higher fertility.[32]

As far as female work and marriage are concerned, there is some contemporary evidence that greater female employment opportunities tend to lower proportions married at younger ages (i.e. 20 to 24).[33] Hewitt demonstrates that this was also the case in mid-

31 Kingsley Davis, "Population Policy: Will Current Programs Succeed?," *Science*, CLVIII (1967), 738; Preston, "Female Employment Policy and Fertility," 375–393; Glen G. Cain, *Married Women in the Labor Force: An Economic Analysis* (Chicago, 1966); Glen G. Cain and Adriana Weininger, "Economic Determinants of Fertility: Results from Cross-Sectional Data," *Demography*, X (1973), 205–233; James A. Sweet, "Family Composition and Labor Force Activity of American Wives," *Demography*, VII (1970), 195–209; John Kasarda, "Economic Structure and Fertility: A Comparative Analysis," *Demography*, VIII (1971), 307–317.

For England during this period it has been established by Margaret Hewitt. "[T]he diminution of fertility was common to all married women occupied away from the home. . . . [T]he lower fertility of the mother employed away from home was, in part at least, the almost inevitable result of the conflict between motherhood and the claims of her job." Hewitt, *Wives and Mothers*, 93. The evidence is not always favorable to the hypothesis of a negative relation of fertility and female employment, however, once a number of other variables are controlled. See Geraldine B. Terry, "Rival Explanations in the Work-Fertility Relationship," *Population Studies*, XXIX (1975), 191–206. The argument is also generally made for the relation between female employment and fertility for countries which have already experienced fertility decline. There is evidence that those arguments do operate in higher fertility, less developed societies, particularly in urban areas. See Sidney Goldstein, "The Influence of Labour Force Participation and Education on Fertility in Thailand," *Population Studies*, XXVI (1972), 419–436. The findings of Kasarda also include analysis of a large number of less developed countries. The findings for less developed, high fertility countries are not as uniform as those for developed, lower fertility countries. See J. M. Stycos and Robert H. Weller, "Female Working Roles and Fertility," *Demography*, IV (1967), 210–217.

32 A. J. Jaffe and K. Azumi, "The Birth Rate and Cottage Industries in Underdeveloped Countries," *Economic Development and Cultural Change*, IX (1960), 52–63.

33 Samuel H. Preston and Alan J. Richards, "The Influence of Women's Work Opportunities on Marriage Rates," *Demography*, XII (1975), 209–222.

nineteenth-century Britain, particularly in industrial areas.[34] The other side of this situation is that a paucity of female employment opportunities would lead to earlier marriage. The same factors which acted to increase marital fertility for miners' wives also produced earlier marriage and less celibacy among mining populations.

Another aspect of the marriage issue is the sex ratio (number of males per 100 females) in the peak marriage and childbearing ages. Coal mining, being largely a male employment, attracts disproportionate numbers of young adult males when the industry is expanding. This is a reflection of the differentials in male/female employment opportunity and migration. For 1871, for example, the average sex ratio for the age group 20 to 29 was 107 for the sample of mining districts but only 94 for the random sample of districts. The zero-order correlations between this sex ratio and Im were 0.73 and 0.50 for the two samples. The partial correlations were 0.52 and 0.45 respectively. The factor of heavily male employment often coincided with a relative scarcity of extra-household female employment and hence the tendency towards earlier and more extensive female marriage because the effect of imbalanced sex ratios would be augmented by low levels of female employment opportunity. The zero order correlations between the sex ratio (for ages 20 to 29) and percentage of adult females employed outside the home was –0.70 for the mining sample and –0.46 for the random sample. The sex ratio thus interacts with both nuptiality and marital fertility (inasmuch as it reflects lack of female employment opportunity). The strong relation of the sex ratio to female marriage has been noted by Wrigley for the coal mining areas of northwest continental Europe.[35] As will be seen below, the sex ratio is indeed a good predictor of both fertility and nuptiality.

The cost and utility of children must also be considered. Although it has been mentioned that child labor underground was prohibited in 1842, children could still work above ground. Further, education was not compulsory until 1876, and even then only up to age twelve.[36] Further, besides a "consumption" utility

34 Hewitt, *Wives and Mothers*, 35–47.
35 Wrigley, *Industrial Growth and Population Change*, 142–145.
36 G. D. H. Cole and Raymond Postgate, *The British Common People: 1746–1946* (London, 1961), 361–364.

and productive utility attached to a child of any given birth order, it has been argued that there is also a social security motive attached to children.[37] Thus, expecting relatively short working lives at peak efficiency, it should not be surprising that miners "discounted" their futures more heavily by marrying earlier and providing more children to care for them in old age. (This motive would obviously be weaker where an effective social insurance system was operating, but this was not the case in mid-nineteenth-century Britain.)

In sum, it is hypothesized that coal mining (and some similar occupations like iron puddling) involved a particular combination of income/earnings life cycle, related female labor force participation, and child costs which favored higher fertility and earlier and more extensive marriage. In addition, the migration patterns and less urban characteristics of mining areas lead to costs, tastes, and marriage patterns conducive to larger families. Finally, higher morbidity and debility among miners and higher mortality among their children also favored earlier marriage and more births both to insure the target family size and to help provide for old age and infirmity among the parents.

AN ANALYSIS OF THE CENSUSES OF 1851, 1861, AND 1871   Earlier it was stated that data from small, more homogeneous geographical areas are a partial substitute for detailed demographic information tabulated by occupation. The censuses of 1851, 1861, and 1871 were used to construct samples of registration districts, the smallest unit for which reasonable age/sex, occupational, and vital data were available. The census of 1841 lacked occupational data and sufficient accompanying vital statistics. The censuses of 1881 and later lacked occupational data for registration districts. The sample was thus restricted to 1851–71, which, unfortunately, precedes the period of fertility decline. For each census two samples were taken. One consisted of all districts (sixty-one) with more than 10 percent of the male population aged twenty and over in coal mining employment in 1861. A random sample of 125 districts was also taken at each census date. The reason for taking a separate sample of mining districts is that areas with a significant propor-

---

37 Harvey Leibenstein, *Economic Backwardness and Economic Growth* (New York, 1957), 163.

tion in mining constitute a rare or special occurrence. It is thus appropriate to sample completely this group of special districts in order to make some comparisons with the national sample. In particular, it is interesting to see whether the same relations held *within* the whole group of mining districts as for the national sample. Ten or more percent of males aged twenty and over in mining was the criterion for selecting the mining districts. This was hardly a homogeneous mining population in many cases, but it does allow scrutiny of some of the characteristics of mining *areas*. It must be remembered, however, that a test of the hypotheses advanced above can only imperfectly be studied using data for small, albeit more homogeneous, geographical areas.

Table 4 provides information on the variables used. The principal sources were, as indicated, the censuses of 1841 through 1871 and the *Annual Reports of the Registrar General* from 1841 through 1872. Most of the data were accepted without correction except birth statistics. Following the work of Glass and Teitelbaum, births were adjusted for each district on the basis of the correction factor for its county.[38] The exception was births used in computing infant mortality rates, since infant deaths as well as births were probably underreported. Although several adjustments were tried to correct for underreporting of infant deaths,[39] it was felt safest simply to divide uncorrected infant deaths by uncorrected live births to obtain the infant mortality rate.

The dependent variables used were Coale's indices of overall fertility (I_f), marital fertility (I_g), and proportions married (I_m). These indices are really a form of indirect standardization of birth rates using the highest observed fertility schedule, that of married Hutterite women in the United States in the 1920s, as the standard schedule.[40] In addition, the index of illegitimate fertility (I_h) was also calculated. For the computation of Ig, Im, and Ih, population by age, sex, and marital status is required. This was not available

---

38   D. V. Glass, "A Note on the Underregistration of Births in Britain in the Nineteenth Century," *Population Studies*, V, (1951), 70–88; Michael S. Teitelbaum, "Birth Underregistration in the Constituent Counties of England and Wales: 1841–1910," *Population Studies*, XXVIII (1974), 329–343.

39   Several assumptions about the share of unreported births which were also unreported infant deaths were considered. All were arbitrary and some led to strange results. Some correlations between child and infant mortality were tried but were also not encouraging.

40   See note 18.

Table 4 Regression Variables for Selected Districts in England and Wales: 1851, 1861, 1871

I_f	Index of Overall Fertility[a] (1851, 1861, 1871)
I_g	Index of Marital Fertility[a] (1861, 1871)
I_m	Index of Proportions Married[a] (1861, 1871)
I_h	Index of Illegitimate Fertility (1861, 1871)
MFR	General Marital Fertility Ratio (legitimate births per 1000 married women 15–59) (1851)
MM	(a) Percent of Males 20+ in Mining and Metallurgy (1851, 1861)
	(b) Percent of Males 20+ in Minerals Employment (1871)
FOH	Percent of Females 20+ Employed Outside the Home[b] (1851, 1861, 1871)
PE	Percent of Males 20+ in Primary Employment (farming and animal husbandry) (1851, 1861, 1871)
IMR	Infant Mortality Rate (infant deaths per 1000 livebirths per annum) (1848–50, 1858–60, 1868–70).
URB	Percent of Population in Principal Towns (1851, 1861, 1871)
RNM	Rate of Residual Net Migration in the Previous Decade (Per 1000 per annum) (1841–50, 1851–60, 1861–70)
SXR	Sex Ratio (Males 20–29 per 100 Females 20–29) (1851, 1861, 1871)

For the rates I_f, I_g, I_h, and MFR, births are taken as three year averages around the central date. For IMR, births and infant deaths are lagged two years.

SOURCE: Registrar General, *Census of 1841, 1851, 1861, and 1871: England and Wales*, passim. Registrar General, *Annual Reports of the Registrar General, 1841 through 1872*, passim.

Births were adjusted by county level adjustment figures furnished by Michael Teitelbaum. See his, "Birth Under-Registration in the Constituent Countries of England and Wales: 1841–1910," *Population Studies*, XXVIII (1974), 329–343.

a For definitions of I_f, I_g, and I_m see Ansley J. Coale, "Factors Associated With the Development of Low Fertility: An Historic Summary," United Nations, *World Population Conference: 1965*, (New York: 1967), II, 205–209.

b Females employed outside the home for 1851 and 1861 was arrived at by taking the total female population aged 20 and over and subtracting women classified as keeping house, pensioners, agricultural workers, and certain selected occupations (for 1851 and 1861 only) which could be identified as in the home (such as keeping a store or tavern in the home, or being a washerwoman), or for which a woman was identified as the wife of an occupied male (such as a butcher's wife or an innkeeper's wife). There was little basis for discriminating domestic handicraft industry. For 1871, females employed outside the home is total female population 20+ less pensioners, women classed as keeping house, and women in agricultural employment.

in 1851 and so the General Marital Fertility Ratio (MFR) was computed as a substitute for I_g.

Among the independent variables, it should be noted that the average infant mortality rate is lagged three years to account for the fact that fertility is expected to adjust to infant mortality with a lag of two to four years.[41] Some labor force structure variables (percentage of adult males in mining and metallurgy, of adult males in primary employment, and of adult females employed outside the home) are included, as well as some additional demographic variables (percentage of population in principal towns, rate of net migration in the previous decade, and the sex ratio for ages 20 to 29).

Means of the variables from Table 4 for the two samples for the three dates are given in Table 5. In addition, tests were made of the statistical significance of the differences of the means of each variable between the samples.[42] This table confirms a number of notions about mining areas relative to the national sample of districts. First, the mining areas had, at all three dates, significantly higher overall fertility, marital fertility, proportions married, and even illegitimate fertility. Second, the mining areas, although less agricultural than the national sample, still had a substantial proportion of the male labor force in agriculture (PE). Third, extra household female labor force participation (FOH) was significantly lower at all three dates in the mining areas. Fourth, the degree of urbanization (URB) was initially lower than that in the national sample (1851) but moved to being more urban by 1871. Fifth, the mining areas consistently showed much less net out-migration than the national sample, pointing to greater economic opportunity.[43] Finally, the sex ratio, as expected, was much higher in the mining areas, reflecting differential in-migration of males. Thus mining areas could be characterized as having higher marital fertility, higher levels of nuptiality, higher infant mortality, higher sex ratios, more in-migration, and lower levels

41   T. Paul Schultz, "An Economic Model of Family Planning and Fertility," *Journal of Political Economy*, LXXVII (1969), 160–161.

42   The test is strictly a test of differences of means from two independently distributed populations. The assumption of independence is not completely held since several districts appear in both samples. It is only a modest number (14 in 1851 and 1861 and 9 in 1871) and their removal from the random sample actually *increases* the differences and reduces the variances, thus making the differences even more significant.

43   Positive RNM indicates net out-migration.

Table 5 Mean Values of Regression Variables

VARIABLE	1851 MINING SAMPLE	1851 RANDOM SAMPLE	1851 SIGNIFICANCE[a] OF DIFFERENCE	1861 MINING SAMPLE	1861 RANDOM SAMPLE	1861 SIGNIFICANCE[a] OF DIFFERENCE	1871 MINING SAMPLE	1871 RANDOM SAMPLE	1871 SIGNIFICANCE OF DIFFERENCE
I_r	.422	.364	***	.433	.369	***	.452	.378	***
I_g	—	—	***	.716	.683	***	.738	.698	***
MFR (per 1000)	260.8	245.6	***	—	—		—	—	
I_m	—	—		.563	.502	***	.576	.507	***
I_h	—	—		.069	.054	***	.066	.050	***
MM (percent)	20.7	2.2	***	24.5	3.1	***	39.9	12.5	***
PE (percent)	21.1	41.2	***	18.6	39.3	***	13.4	32.6	***
FOH (percent)	21.7	26.5	***	22.3	26.3	***	24.5	30.1	***
IMR (per 1000 live births)	150.6	137.3	***	149.7	137.5	***	154.3	135.6	***
URB (percent)	22.4	28.6	*	27.3	27.0	—	40.0	31.0	**
RNM (per 1000 population)	−0.28	18.7	***	1.17	5.92	***	0.79	5.68	***
SXR (per 100)	105.2	93.6	***	101.4	92.3	***	107.2	94.0	***

a   Based on a test of significance of the difference of two means drawn from independently distributed populations.

***   Significant at a 1 percent level.

**   Significant at a 5 percent level.

*   Significant at a 10 percent level.

—   Not significant at a 10 percent level.

For definitions of variables and sources, see Table 4.

of extra-household female employment relative to the national sample. In addition, there was much more homogeneity among the mining areas with respect to their fertility and nuptiality. The coefficients of variability[44] were consistently smaller for the mining sample, indicating less dispersion around the higher means.

Ordinary least squares (OLS) regressions were applied to both the mining sample and the random sample at all three census dates, although only the results for the random sample are reported. The various fertility and nuptiality variables were taken in turn as independent variables. Two alternative specifications of each equation were tried, one excluding and one including the sex ratio.[45]

The results for the random sample are reported in Table 6. The coefficients in parentheses are those not significant at least at a 10 percent level. Also presented are the adjusted R-squared values and F-ratios. The results confirm some prior expectations about the effects of the designated independent variables on fertility and nuptiality, at least for areas. The proportion of males in mining and metallurgy (MM) was, when significant, positively related to fertility and marriage. In other words, controlling for the effects of the other variables, the marginal effect of a larger proportion of miners in the population was to increase both marital fertility and proportions married in an area.[46] For the percentage of adult males in primary employment (PE), it appears again, when significant, that a higher proportion of persons in farming and animal husbandry would lead to higher fertility, mostly via higher marital fertility.

It was earlier hypothesized that extra-household female employment (FOH) would result in lower fertility and marriage. Those coefficients in Table 6 which were significant were indeed negative but a substantial proportion of all coefficients (in 10 out

44 Sample standard deviation divided by the mean.

45 The reason for this result was the high degree of correlation between the SXR and FOH, which tended to increase the standard errors of both coefficients and reduce significance levels for FOH. It was desirable to see how FOH performed in the absence of SXR.

46 A question may arise as to why the proportion of adult males employed in mining and metallurgy is included at all on the right hand side of the regression equation. The answer is that it is of interest to see what effect varying *proportions* of miners and metal workers in the labor force have on fertility and marriage. It is also important to control for those varying proportions in the labor force when examining the effects of other social, demographic, and economic variables.

Table 6   OLS Regression Equations: Random Sample of 125 Registration Districts: England & Wales, 1851, 1861, 1871. Overall Fertility, Marital Fertility & Nuptiality.

DEPENDENT VARIABLES	CON-STANT	MM	PE	FOH	IMR	URB	RNM	SXR	R^2_{adj}	F-RATIO
A) 1851										
I_f	.2742	.0030	.0006	(−.0004)	.0005	−.0006	−.0009	NI	.413	15.516
I_f	.1364	.0025	.0007	(.0002)	.0004	−.0003	−.0008	.0014	.504	18.972
MFR	241.3	.6962	(.0955)	(.0359)	(−.0419)	−.3003	−.6436	NI	.254	8.020
MFR	211.6	(.5825)	(.1001)	(.1655)	(−.0595)	−.2537	−.6254	.2968	.263	7.330
B) 1861										
I_f	.2958	.0037	.0010	−.0009	.0004	−.0002	−.0005	NI	.451	18.007
I_f	.2272	.0033	.0006	(−.0004)	.0003	−.0002	(.0004)	.0008	.544	22.135
I_g	.6821	.0030	.0011	(−.0003)	−.0002	(−.0002)	(−.0005)	NI	.396	14.577
I_g	.6484	.0028	.0006	(−.0000)	−.0003	(−.0002)	(−.0001)	.0004	.415	13.562
I_m	.4289	.0025	.0003	−.0011	.0007	(−.0002)	(−.0004)	NI	.248	7.821
I_m	.3618	.0021	(−.0001)	−.0007	.0006	(−.0002)	(.0005)	.0008	.319	9.301
C) 1871										
I_f	.3085	.0008	.0007	−.0018	.0007	(.0001)	(−.0006)	NI	.204	6.313
I_f	.1105	.0007	.0011	(−.0006)	.0007	(.0002)	(−.0002)	.0015	.348	10.461
I_g	.6510	.0018	.0014	(.0005)	−.0003	(.0003)	(−.0005)	NI	.197	6.065
I_g	.6160	.0018	.0015	(.0007)	−.0003	.0003	−.0004	(−.0003)	.197	5.338
I_m	.4986	(−.0006)	(−.0007)	−.0031	.0010	(−.0001)	(−.0004)	NI	.250	7.871
I_m	.2524	(−.0009)	(.0002)	−.0015	.0011	(−.0001)	(.0000)	.0018	.392	12.398

Figures in parentheses are coefficients not significant at least at the 10 percent level (using a one tailed test).

NI = not included

n = 125

For a definition of variables, see Table 4.

of 16 equations) were insignificant.[47] It is notable, however, that *both* marriage and marital fertility were negatively associated with this variable. Related to this is the closely (and negatively) inter-correlated variable of the sex ratio (SXR) for young adults (aged 20 to 29). This variable was strongly and positively associated with overall fertility, marital fertility, and marriage. Both female employment and the sex ratio often reflect the simultaneous effect of differential male employment opportunity, and so interact. In those equations in which both variables were present, the sex ratio generally performed much better than female employment, perhaps indicating a stronger association of fertility and marriage with sex imbalances among young adults than with actual employment of females. The mechanisms through which the sex ratio acted were both higher marital fertility and higher proportions married. The effect on marital fertility was, however, weaker—as indicated by the lower coefficients in the Ig and MFR equations which even became insignificant in 1871.

Of the other independent variables considered, the lagged infant mortality rate (IMR) was positively related to overall fertility and proportions married. The latter relationship is rather puzzling. It might have been the case that people married earlier in response to a higher recognized environmental risk of infant death, but it is more likely that a high level of infant mortality was caused by a low age of marriage. Since infant mortality is higher for young women relative to those in their mid-twenties[48] and since a high Im usually implies higher proportions married below age twenty-five, there might be some basis for a positive relation between proportions married and infant mortality. The relation of infant mortality to marital fertility was, when significant, negative, which is very puzzling since this relation would presumably have been most strongly positive. It would seem more logical that marital fertility would adjust, even in a regime of natural fertility, to high infant mortality. But such, apparently, was not the case in mid-nineteenth-century Britain.

The urbanization variable had a negative effect on overall and marital fertility in 1851 and 1861 and on marriage as well in 1871.

47 A nonlinear specification of the OLS equations resulted in much better performance of this variable, with 14 of 16 coefficients significant, suggesting nonlinearity in this variable.
48 United Nations, *The Determinants and Consequences of Population Trends* (New York, 1974; rev. ed.), I, 127.

The relationship appeared to weaken over time and even turned positive for marital fertility in 1871. It is possible that newer norms increased female labor force participation, and rising child costs associated with urbanization initially operated to depress fertility and marriage but that this altered over time. Perhaps by 1871 a greater proportion of urban population in a district reflected a greater economic opportunity.

The rate of net migration (RNM) was mostly insignificant after 1851 with the significant coefficients showing negative signs (i.e., the expected ones). A higher degree of out-migration would thus be associated with lower fertility and marriage because high net out-migration can be a proxy for poor economic opportunities which should tend to depress both fertility and marriage. It was, however, generally a weak variable.

Overall, the above equations provide some support for several of the hypotheses advanced regarding factors specific to mining *areas* which might tend to promote fertility and marriage. A higher proportion of males in mining and metallurgy was associated with higher levels of fertility and marriage in an area. A higher sex ratio, more infant mortality, and a lower level of extra-household female employment were features characteristic of mining areas relative to the national average of districts and all tended to increase fertility and nuptiality. For 1851, in addition, the fact that mining districts were relatively less urban exercized a positive influence on marriage and fertility. By 1871, when the mining districts had become more urban, the effects of urbanization had become insignificant. These results are supported by the regressions run for the mining samples.

In general, the two sets of equations (from the mining and the random samples) were rather similar at the three dates in terms of the direction and often the significance of the coefficients. The levels of the coefficients were usually different and a few coefficients, like the proportion of males in mining and metallurgy and in primary employment, showed noticeable differences. It is of some interest, then, that many of the same overall relationships held both for the national district sample and for the special subset of the mining districts.

The overall equations were modestly successful in explaining overall variation, as measured by the R-squared values adjusted for degrees of freedom. The group of socioeconomic and demographic variables used explained between 20 and 50 percent of overall variation in marriage and fertility for the random sample (and up to 70 percent for the mining sample). The R-squared values and the F-ratios (measuring the joint significance of all the variables) tended to become higher in both samples for overall fertility and proportions married, as opposed to marital fertility. This was most dramatic for the mining sample where the R-squared values rose for overall fertility between 1851 and 1871 and for proportions married between 1861 and 1871 but fell for marital fertility between 1851 and 1871. The equations for marital fertility in the 1871 mining equations actually had insignificant F-statistics, indicating that the independent variables lacked any significant explanatory power. Since $I_f \cong I_g \cdot I_m$, it is clear that for both samples, variation in marriage, rather than marital fertility, became increasingly important in accounting for variation in overall fertility. This is confirmed by the coefficients of variability which were lower for marital fertility than for overall fertility or the index of proportions married and also declined over time for marital fertility but not for the other measures.[49] Although there *were* differences in marital fertility, and although the *level* of marital fertility was significantly higher in the mining areas (see Table 5), control of overall period fertility for areas was still largely through marriage. Viewed from another perspective, it appears that on the very eve of the decline in marital fertility in Britain (dated from the 1870s), marital fertility was becoming increasingly *less* important in explaining variations in overall fertility. The socioeconomic and demographic factors which might be expected to influence fertility control within marriage, instead of becoming more important, were becoming less so. This certainly presents a challenging issue whose resolution depends, in part, on work done for the period after 1870–72.

It should be said that a number of estimation problems surround the application of ordinary least squares with a simple linear

49 The coefficients of variability (standard deviation divided by the mean) were:

	I_f		I_g/MFR		I_m	
	MINING	R.S.	MINING	R.S.	MINING	R.S.
1851	.108	.140	.077	.109	—	—
1861	.116	.142	.061	.077	.099	.114
1871	.109	.142	.050	.064	.101	.132

specification in this case. First, it is not clear that the relationship has been properly specified. To assess the importance of this problem, a nonlinear specification was estimated.[50] The form selected tried to account for expected nonlinearities especially in percentage variables which are upper and lower bounded. The transformed equations gave slightly higher adjusted R-squared values and one variable, female employment outside the home (FOH), became significant (with the correct sign) in almost all cases. Otherwise there were few differences, indicating that a simple linear approximation was quite good, except for female employment. A further type of specification error arises if important independent variables are missing. If these missing variables are in any way correlated with the regressors in the equation, then biased coefficients and erroneous significance tests may result.[51] The problem is serious, but there is no way to correct for it. The only answer is to bear in mind the qualification that not all desired variables could be included. A third problem which arises is multi-collinearity between the independent variables. This is a problem of experimental design and is tolerable as long as the t-values are not lowered a great deal. One instance was the high correlation between the sex ratio (SXR) and extra-household female employment (FOH). The inclusion of SXR usually caused FOH to become insignificant, so equations were specified both with and without SXR to examine the significance of FOH.

Finally, there is a serious problem with simultaneous equation bias for at least two independent variables, female employment and infant mortality.[52] As an example, low fertility may be a cause as well as an effect of high extra-household female employment. That is, women may be in the labor force *because* they have few children as well as the reverse. Similarly, high fertility may be a cause as well as an effect of high infant mortality because higher order births experience higher mortality.[53] The result of such a situation is biased coefficients, which may lead to erroneous

50 The functional form estimated was $\ell n \ I_f = \beta_1 + \beta_2/MM + \beta_3/PE + \beta_4/FOH \ \beta_5/IMR + \beta_6/URB + \beta_7 RNM + \beta_8 SXR + E$ where $\ell n \ I_f$ is the natural logarithm of I_f, β_1 is the constant, β_i for $i = 2 - 8$ are the coefficients and E is the error term. A small positive number (.5%) was added to MM, PR, FOH, and URB to avoid division by zero.

51 J. Johnston, *Econometric Methods* (New York, 1972; 2nd ed.), 168–169.

52 *Ibid.,* 341–352.

53 Joe D. Wray, "Population Pressure on Families: Family Size and Child Spacing," in National Academy of Sciences, *Rapid Population Growth* (Baltimore, 1971), 409–418.

t-statistics. The solution is to specify and estimate a simultaneous equations system. This was done for 1861 and 1871 for both samples using two stage least squares (TSLS). The system was estimated in the following form.[54]

$$I_f = f(MM, PE, FOH, IMR, RNM, SXR)$$
$$FOH = g(I_f, URB, SXR)$$
$$IMR = h(I_f, MED)$$

where MED is medical personnel per 10,000 population.

The results (not presented) generally indicate that the coefficients of female employment and infant mortality estimated by OLS were downwardly biased, thus causing them to be rejected too often as insignificant. The problem with TSLS equations is that t-statistics are usually lowered by using this procedure (i.e., the estimates have higher standard errors) and that t-statistics, F-ratios, and R-squared values do not have the same interpretation as for OLS (except for very large samples). The results of OLS estimates for relatively small samples may be biased but are often efficient (i.e., have small standard errors). Given the fact that TSLS reveals that OLS downwardly biases both female employment and infant mortality, it appears that the OLS estimates are reasonable and that these coefficients may simply be found insignificant too often. This is encouraging from the standpoint of the original model.

CONCLUSIONS   Looking at historical differences in fertility and marriage among different occupational groups in England and Wales and concentrating on coal mining populations, we found that coal miners have had higher fertility and earlier and more extensive marriage than most other occupational groups. These differentials existed in the nineteenth century and persisted into the twentieth. A comparison of a sample of mining areas with a random sample of districts for 1851, 1861, and 1871 revealed higher average overall fertility, marital fertility, and proportions married in the mining areas than in the random sample.

It was hypothesized that a number of factors favorable to fertility acted on mining populations. Those include males reaching

54 It should be noted that urbanization is now specified as affecting fertility through female employment and not as acting directly. Here URB is the instrumental variable necessary to estimate FOH. The same is true for MED.

peak earning capacity at a relatively early age, relatively low child costs in mining areas, frequent lack of employment opportunities for women, higher infant mortality, high adult male debility and morbidity, and a taste and cost structure more rural than urban in the earlier stages of development. These factors combined to create earlier and more extensive marriage for both males and females in mining and in mining areas and also higher marital fertility. Net in-migration selective of males in many mining areas led to sex ratios further favoring earlier and more extensive marriage for females. Analysis of the mining and random samples yielded support for the hypotheses concerning female employment, infant mortality, the sex ratio, and urbanization for mining areas.[55]

The period under consideration preceded the decline in period fertility rates (after the mid-1870s), and there is some evidence for areas at this time that marriage differentials were much more important in explaining fertility differentials. This was particularly true for the mining districts by 1871, which may indicate that marriage longer remained more important in controlling fertility in more distinctly working class areas. There was virtually no change in period fertility measures and proportions married over this period. Further, there was little evidence of structural change with respect to the determinants of fertility and marriage in the mining areas. Joint F- tests for the mining equations of 1851 relative to 1861, and 1861 relative to 1871, were insignificant even at a 5 percent level.[56] The same tests for the random sample did indicate significant differences in the coefficients over time, however. The later fertility decline among mining populations might be connected to this lag in structural change, although work with individual data must be carried out.

This paper demonstrated the existence and long term persistence of differences in fertility between mining populations and other socioeconomic/occupational groups. There were, however, important changes over time. Marriage was a major explanation

55 No support was found for the adult morbidity hypothesis, using a test assuming that adult morbidity debility was correlated with adult mortality; but there were problems with this assumption and with the test which still leaves this hypothesis a viable one.
56 For a description of this test of significance between two different sets of regression coefficients see Gregory Chow, "Tests of Equality Between Sets of Coefficients in Two Linear Regressions," Econometrica, XXVIII (1960), 591–605.

of fertility differences across regions prior to the fertility decline. On the other hand, marital fertility differentials were the important factor during and after the fertility decline for occupational groups, since the differentials remained after standardizing for age at marriage and marital duration. Differences in marriage patterns were detectable in 1911 and 1951, however. The model described above is general enough to apply to both periods.

The model used in this paper could easily be generalized and applied to other occupational groups. It is not unique to mining populations, although some of the factors affecting fertility and marriage might receive different emphasis. The finding that marriage was more important than marital fertility in explaining differences among regions seems in itself to reflect the general phenomena of the "Western European marriage pattern" and control of overall fertility through marriage observable in early nineteenth century Western Europe.[57]

57 John Hajnal, "European Marriage Patterns in Perspective," in D. V. Glass and D. E. C. Eversley (eds.), *Population in History* (London, 1965), 101–143.

David Cressy

The Seasonality of Marriage in Old and New England

When Samuel Pitts and Sarah Bobbitt of Plymouth Colony were married in Taunton, Massachusetts, on March 25, 1680, they may have remarked on the appropriateness of starting their new life together on the traditional first day of the new year. March 25, Old New Year's Day, still known to Stuart Englishmen as "Lady Day" in vestigial recognition of the Annunciation of the Virgin Mary, was recognized throughout the Anglo-American world as the annual turning point of the calendar. Even New England Puritans who despised pagan names referred to March as "the first month" and calculated the year from its twenty-fifth day.[1]

In old England, Lady Day was a time when rents fell due, a day for entering or concluding contracts. It was a day for fresh beginnings, and therefore an auspicious day on which to marry. Whereas couples in New England could freely schedule their weddings for this day, or any other day throughout the year, their contemporaries in old England faced tight restrictions on the timing of marriage. Hardly anyone in the old country married on Lady Day, or on the other days in March, because marriage was traditionally forbidden during Lent, a time reserved for abstinence and penance, or during Easter.[2]

The wedding of Peter Hunt to Rebecca Paine at Rehoboth, Massachusetts, on December 24, 1673 was similarly free from the calendrical constraints that the couple might have encountered in England. Advent, which stretched from the fourth Sunday pre-

David Cressy is Associate Professor of History at California State University, Long Beach.

0022-1953/85/ $02.50

© 1985 by The Massachusetts Institute of Technology and the editors of *The Journal of Interdisciplinary History*.

1 Nathaniel B. Shurtleff (ed.), *Records of the Colony of New Plymouth* (Boston, 1857), VIII, 82. For the Puritan calendar, see J. Franklin Jameson (ed.), *Johnson's Wonder-Working Providence* (New York, 1910), 88.
2 Lent, a movable fast, comprised the forty days preceding Easter and could include parts of February and April as well as March. Prohibited periods for marriage are noted in Edmund Gibson, *Codex Juris Ecclesiastici Anglicani* (London, 1713), 518. For a seventeenth-century English defense of these customs see John Cosin, *A Collection of Private Devotions* (London, 1627), preface.

ceding Christmas until Christmas eve, was another period during which marriage was restricted in England. Altogether the Anglican ecclesiastical calendar, inherited from Roman Catholicism, marked 144 days as unsuitable for marriage ceremonies. Formal inhibitions against marriage affected almost 40 percent of the year. An English almanac of 1678 reminded readers that "marriage comes in on the 13 of January, and by Septuagesima Sunday it is out again; until the octaves of Easter, or day after Low-Sunday, at which time it comes in again, and goes no more out till Rogation Sunday: for *Rogamen vetitat*; from whence it is forbidden again untill Trinity-Sunday, when it goes out and comes not in again until St. Hillary, or 13 of January next year," whereupon the whole cycle began again. English couples who wished to marry at those times either had to wait, commit fornication, or seek (and pay for) a special licence.[3]

New Englanders, by contrast, were free to marry whenever they wished, without attention to the almanac or arguments with the clerk. Following the lead of the Plymouth pilgrims, who took the idea from the Dutch, New Englanders made marriage a civil matter, to be conducted by a magistrate rather than a clergyman. By secularizing the wedding ceremony they further removed marriage from the realm of traditional liturgical associations.[4]

It would be reasonable to expect that New Englanders, freed from old-world calendrical restrictions, would have arranged their weddings to suit their own particular convenience, and that marriages would have been distributed randomly throughout the year. Marriage is, after all, the one demographic event most subject to individual human control. Yet everywhere, even in New England, a distinct seasonal pattern appeared. Some months were crowded with nuptials whereas others saw hardly any marriages at all.

3 Shurtleff, *Records of New Plymouth*, VIII, 77. Three couples were married in Boston by Samuel Willard on Christmas Day, 1699, which would have been unthinkable in England. Boston Record Commissioners, *Boston Births, Baptisms, Marriages, and Deaths, 1630–1699* (Boston, 1883), 9th report, 250–252. *An Episcopal Almanac for . . . 1678* (London, 1678). Reformers challenged these restrictions on marriage dates, to little avail. See Robert C. Johnson et al. (eds.), *Commons Debates 1628* (New Haven, 1977), III, 26–36. For a spirited attack on the ancient calendar, see Henry Burton, *A Tryall of Private Devotion* (London, 1628), sigs. E4–F2.

4 George Elliott Howard, *A History of Matrimonial Institutions* (London, 1904), II, 121–139; Chilton L. Powell, "Marriage in Early New England," *New England Quarterly*, I (1928), 323–342.

The purpose of this article is to chart the seasonality of marriage in seventeenth- and eighteenth-century New England, comparing the pattern in the colonies to the experience in the old world. How pervasive were the traditional religious prohibitions on the timing of marriage, and what impact, if any, did they have in America? What other factors—social, cultural, and economic—influenced marriage seasonality when the force of old ecclesiastical constraints disappeared? The evidence presented includes marriage records from Boston, Braintree, Concord, Dedham, Plymouth, and Watertown, all in Massachusetts, and from a large sample of English parishes, with comparative material from France. In the graphs and table which follow, the marriage figures are indexed in order to provide a standard scale which takes into account the varying lengths of months. An even distribution of marriages would produce monthly indices of 100. A Kolmogorov-Smirnov test has been employed to gauge the statistical significance of the variation. Significance is defined at the .05 level.[5]

Compared to England and America, France was the most custom-bound and was most tied to traditional ecclesiastical restrictions. French historical demographers long ago noticed how closely the timing of weddings followed the medieval church calendar, which had been reaffirmed with minor amendment at the Council of Trent. At Crulai in Normandy, the Ile-de-France, the Tarn, the Loire, Amiens, Lyon, and Paris—indeed, wherever marriage records survive from the Ancien Regime—the marriages in these French communities follow a constant seasonal pattern, strongly associated with the periods of religious taboo. From the sixteenth to the nineteenth century, in urban and rural areas alike, French couples (and their clergy) avoided weddings in the holy periods of Advent and Lent. Even French Protestants conformed to this pattern. The Huguenots of Sancerrois and Basse-Normandie in the seventeenth century were not constrained by their religion to follow the Catholic calendar, but the custom was so

---

5 I have followed the procedure in Michel Fleury and Louis Henry, *Nouveau Manuel de Depouillement et d'Exploitation de l'Etat Civil Ancien* (Paris, 1965), 103–105, which is comparable to the indexing in Darrett B. Rutman, Charles Wetherall, and Anita H. Rutman, "Rhythms of Life: Black and White Seasonality in the Early Chesapeake," *Journal of Interdisciplinary History,* XI (1980), 30–31. The Kolomogorov-Smirnov test is best described in Sidney Siegel, *Nonparametric Statistics for the Behavioral Sciences* (New York, 1956), 47–51.

deeply engrained that they too avoided marrying during Advent and Lent.[6]

The typical seasonality of marriage in France is illustrated by parochial records from the Ile-de-France (Table 1 and Figure 1). In the eighteenth century, the villages of the Ile-de-France saw virtually no marriages in March or December—the months coinciding with Lent and Advent—during which time the indexes were just 7 and 4. Peak periods were February, July, and November, when the indexes reached 178, 211, and 206. This jagged switchback pattern is characteristic of rural French marriage records in general.

Religious taboo, however, explains only part of the French seasonal fluctuation. Marriage seasons varied with the busy and slack seasons of the agricultural year as well as with religious observances. Low points in late summer, and the February, July, and November peaks, were closely associated with the cycles of husbandry and harvest.

The people of northern France had little time for weddings during August and September when the grain harvest was waiting to be brought home and every hand was needed in the fields. By November, however, the crop was secure, profits and wages could be reckoned, the ground lay temporarily fallow, and couples could attend to their nuptials. French wine-making areas observed a similar rhythm, with a low index of marriages in September and October at the time of the grape harvest, followed by a surge of November weddings when the vintage was completed. November weddings may also have been planned to anticipate the closed season of Advent in December, just as the February peak surely included the weddings of a large number of couples avoiding marriage in Lent. The midsummer peak is the most difficult to explain, but it may have been connected with the long, light evenings and the general cheeriness of that season. In some French fishing villages the peak months for weddings were July, August, and September, which were relatively slack times between the mackerel and herring runs. French marriages, then, were gener-

6 François Lebrun, *La Vie Conjugale sous l'Ancien Régime* (Paris, 1975), 28–40; Jean Ganiage, *Trois Villages d'Ile-de-France au XVIIIe Siècle* (Paris, 1963), 51–54; Pierre Valmary, *Famille Paysanne aux XVIIIe Siècle en Bas-Quercy* (Paris, 1965), 87–91; Pierre Deyon, *Amiens, Capitale Provinciale; Etude sur la Societé Urbaine au XVIIe Siècle* (Paris, 1967), 10–11, 496.

Table 1 Monthly Index of Marriages

PLACE	PERIOD	N	JAN	FEB	MAR	APR	MAY	JUN	JUL	AUG	SEP	OCT	NOV	DEC
England	1540–99		124	86	8	61	98	117	109	70	102	184	201	41
	1650–99		89	102	43	129	137	123	87	60	96	131	135	72
	1750–99		96	102	60	105	117	91	84	79	86	142	127	112
Ile-de-France	1740–92	317	151	178	7	46	118	103	211	48	50	78	206	4
Plymouth Colony	1633–87	349	156	74	75	63	68	53	75	34	49	109	214	231
Plymouth church	1760–98	683	83	76	107	155	41	55	48	60	66	143	219	147
Dedham, Mass.	1638–99	241	103	97	103	121	117	25	64	69	81	88	177	156
	1750–99	781	100	106	82	94	145	87	71	65	70	127	116	137
Watertown, Mass.	1642–99	214	143	79	127	91	61	91	44	55	103	110	137	160
	1737–99	381	71	112	83	121	133	108	52	80	80	105	112	142
Braintree, Mass.	1643–99	153	130	84	107	135	99	63	69	61	126	46	126	153
	1763–92	232	61	156	86	126	132	63	54	86	84	111	131	111
Concord, Mass.	1647–99	256	65	81	115	105	125	76	78	41	38	111	162	203
	1750–99	634	106	106	95	92	110	89	58	99	98	91	123	132
Boston, Mass.	1650–99	1004	122	83	68	87	106	89	87	102	103	89	142	121
	1750–99	1614	101	105	98	85	94	96	80	119	94	111	109	110
New England	1633–99	2217	122	82	87	94	99	72	76	73	86	94	158	158
	1737–99	4325	94	103	94	104	103	86	66	92	84	116	133	126

Fig. 1 Marriages in the Ile de France 1740—1792

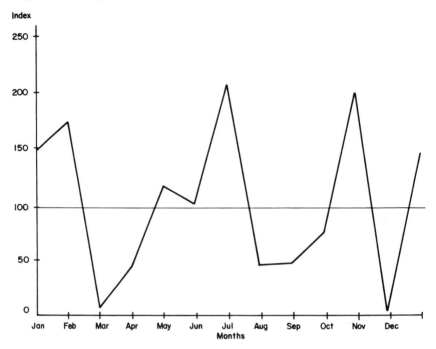

ally coordinated with phases of economic activity, but everywhere, overwhelmingly, they respected the taboo periods of Advent and Lent.[7]

In England, too, the timing of marriage was influenced by the calendrical inhibitions of the church, but their effect was never as powerful as in France. Whereas the French scrupulously avoided marrying during Lent or Advent, a tradition that they maintained throughout the preindustrial era, the English soon abandoned Advent as a taboo time for weddings and gradually relaxed their reluctance to marry during Lent. Table 1 and Figure 2 show the seasonality of marriage in England for the periods 1540 to 1599, 1650 to 1699, and 1750 to 1799. These figures, representing thousands of marriages in a sample of 404 parishes, are drawn from the work of Wrigley, Schofield, and the Cambridge Group for the History of Population and Social Structure.

---

7 See note 6.

Fig. 2 Marriages in England

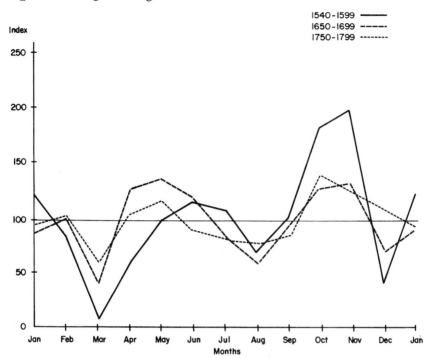

The pattern is coherent and robust, but differs from those of both France and New England.[8]

March was always the least popular month for weddings in England. The index for March was only 8 in the Elizabethan period (comparable to French figures), 43 in the later Stuart period, and still no higher than 60 in the second half of the eighteenth century. Traditional-minded clergy continued to insist on the sanctity of Lent, and couples may have hearkened to the popular saying, "if you marry in Lent you'll live to repent." Even today there are clergy who frown on Lent weddings and seek to reduce their attendant festivities. By the end of the eighteenth century, March weddings had ceased to be unusual, yet the English still retained an attenuated observance of the taboo that had once been almost universal.[9]

8 E. Anthony Wrigley and Roger S. Schofield, *The Population History of England, 1541–1871: A Reconstruction* (Cambridge, Mass., 1981), 298–305, 519–525; Cambridge Group, "marriage seasonality files."
9 George S. Tyack, *Lore and Legend of the English Church* (London, 1899), 183. Cf. "they

December saw a respectably low level of marriages during the Elizabethan period, with an index of 41, but the figure was never so low as in France. December weddings were still below average during the seventeenth century, suggesting some clinging to the custom, but by the eighteenth century the Advent prohibition had been completely forgotten or overruled. Indeed, in some parishes December became the most popular month for weddings. The gradual flattening of the graph, a secular reduction in the amplitude of seasonality, reflects an increasing disregard for calendrical strictures which were, officially, still in force.[10]

Social and economic factors also bore heavily on the seasonality of marriage in England. Few weddings took place during August, the crucial harvesting period. Autumn, by contrast, was generally the most popular time to marry, with peaks in October and November. Autumn in England was a time of relative prosperity, when barns were brimming and larders full. In livestock regions autumn was also the time for killing surplus animals and preserving them for the winter. What better time for marrying than this season of fruitfulness and plenty, at the close of the agricultural year? Only the early summer months rivaled autumn, with a surge of marriages in May and June.

The release of servants from their annual contracts also contributed to the peak periods for weddings. In England almost two thirds of those between the ages of fifteen and twenty-four worked as servants in husbandry. Their annual agreements usually terminated at Michaelmas (September 29), or at the other traditional holidays of Martinmas (November 11), Lady Day (March 25), or May Day (May 1). The weeks that followed often marked their change of status from single dependent servants to partners in marriage.[11]

Closer analysis reveals a regional variation in marriage seasonality which corresponds with the agricultural characteristics of

that wive between sickle and scythe shall never thrive," quoted in Keith Thomas, *Religion and the Decline of Magic* (New York, 1971), 619.

10 Leslie Bradley, "An Enquiry into Seasonality in Baptisms, Marriages, and Burials," *Local Population Studies*, IV (1970), 37; Margaret Massey, "Seasonality, Some Further Thoughts," *Local Population Studies*, VIII (1972), 54; William J. Edwards, "Marriage Seasonality, 1761–1810: An Assessment of Patterns in Seventeen Shropshire Parishes," *Local Population Studies*, XIX (1977), 25.

11 Ann Kussmaul, *Servants in Husbandry in Early Modern England* (Cambridge, 1981), 97–109.

each parish. The autumn marriage peak was most marked in the arable regions of southeast England, whereas pastoral areas like the north and west, preoccupied with spring lambing and calving, were more likely to experience marriage peaks in the early summer.[12]

Urban areas had a more muted seasonality, but they still experienced a peak of marriages in the autumn and a deficit in March. Overall seasonal fluctuations became less pronounced with increased urbanization, industrialization, and economic diversity. In seventeenth-century East Anglia, the region most associated with the settlement of Massachusetts, the low points occurred in March, August, and December, periods clearly related to Lent, the grain harvest, and Advent. By far the most popular time for marriage was October. Social customs, agrarian rhythms, and religious convention worked together to produce a distinctive seasonal pattern.

Did the seventeenth- and eighteenth-century colonists repeat these marriage patterns in America? Before examining the evidence it is useful to consider three hypotheses about the seasonality of marriage in New England.

First, since early migrants to Massachusetts brought with them, as part of their cultural baggage, an engrained observance of English law and custom relating to land-holding and agriculture, it is reasonable to suppose that they also transmitted their calendar for marrying, in the same sub-conscious manner. Demographic studies indicate an underlying continuity between old- and new-world rhythms of fertility and mortality. Lockridge, for example, has argued that "several thousand miles did not alter the pace of the year." The colonists might be expected, then, to have replicated the English seasonality of marriage as they replicated so many other patterns. French Protestants continued to follow the Catholic calendar regarding marriages, despite their new religion. Did the English settlers of New England do likewise?[13]

12 Wrigley and Schofield, *Population History*, 302–304.
13 David Grayson Allen, *In English Ways: the Movement of Societies and the Transferal of English Local Law and Custom to Massachusetts Bay in the Seventeenth Century* (Chapel Hill, 1981). Kenneth A. Lockridge, "The Population of Dedham, Massachusetts, 1636–1736," *Economic History Review*, XIX (1966), 340.

Second, marriage in Massachusetts was entirely free from traditional calendrical constraints, official or vestigial, so that weddings could have been celebrated at random throughout the year. Since the Puritan leaders of New England were so vehemently opposed to the "rubbidge of Romish Reliques," to the point of renaming the months and abolishing Christmas, they may have succeeded in obliterating any hesitation to marry during Lent and Advent. The ancient holidays were pagan, papish, irreligious, erroneous, and profane, according to Increase Mather. "Such vanities . . . are good no where; but in New-England they are a thousand times worse." The religious environment of New England was hostile to ceremony and superstition, but there was continuous backsliding, so that the seasonal pattern of marriages—especially marriages during Lent—may provide an indirect test of the ability of Puritans to overcome deep-rooted traditionalism.[14]

Third, just as economic rhythms clearly affected the seasonality of marriage in the old world, so the agrarian or commercial calendar of the colonies exerted a powerful influence on the timing of marriage in America. An economically-induced pattern could then be expected, shaped primarily by the local routines of labor and leisure, and shortage and plenty.

Lacking the parochial organization of old England, with its established tradition of local record-keeping (begun by Act of Parliament and enforced by episcopal visitation), colonial New England devised alternative methods of vital registration. Massachusetts law required "everie new married man" to deliver a certificate of his marriage, signed by the magistrate or other official who performed it, to the Clerk of the Writs in the town where he lived. The town clerk then had to submit a periodic list of marriages to the county recorder. In 1646 the Court of Plymouth Colony ordered "that the clarke, or some one in every towne, do keepe a register of the day and yeare of every marryage, byrth, and buriall, and to have 3d. a peece for his paynes." Those newly married had to "signify his and her name with the day upon which they were married unto the said clerk or register

---

14 Burton, *A Tryall of Private Devotion*, sig. F2; Increase Mather, *A Testimony Against Several Prophane and Superstitious Customs, Now Practised in New-England* (London, 1687), 35, 40.

keeper within one moneth next after the day of his said marriage," or face a three-shilling fine. Marriages had to be formally registered to discourage fornication, bigamy, and illegitimacy, as well as to establish genealogical and testamentary records.[15]

The system worked well enough, despite occasional expressions of frustration from those charged with its administration. In 1657 the General Court at Boston noted the "general neglect of observing the lawe injoyning a record of all births, deaths and marriages," and set out to rectify the matter with a new schedule of fines. In 1674 Shadrach Wilbore, clerk of Plymouth, submitted his list of marriages, births, and burials, adding, "but many neglect to bring in their names to me." Joshua Fisher, Clerk of the Writs at Dedham, was more confident when he submitted his book in 1675, "and affirmed that in these three pages are conteyned all the marriages that have hitherto bin in ye Towne." Lockridge reassuringly reports that "marriages were nearly all recorded," however tardily. Magistrates submitted lists of marriages that they had performed, and the town clerks prepared periodic returns for the recorder. There may have been some underregistration, but there is no evidence of a seasonal bias in the recording. Since these records usually include the date of the ceremony, they can be used to reconstruct the seasonality of marriage.[16]

Table 1 and Figures 3 to 8, which show monthly indexes, are based on the marriage records of six different communities. Pooled figures from these communities (Table 1 and Figure 9) show the seasonality of marriage in early Massachusetts, somewhat weighted by Boston.[17]

15 *The Book of the General Lawwes and Libertyes Concerning the Inhabitants of the Massachusetts* (Cambridge, Mass., 1648), 46–47; Shurtleff, *Records of New Plymouth*, II, 96; IX, 53.

16 Boston Record Commissioners, *Boston Births, Baptisms, Marriages, and Deaths*, iv; Shurtleff, *Records of New Plymouth*, VIII, 55; Don Gleason Hill (ed.), *The Record of Births, Marriages, and Deaths, and Intentions of Marriage, in the Town of Dedham* (Dedham, Mass., 1886), 127; Lockridge, "Population of Dedham," 319.

17 Shurtleff, *Records of New Plymouth*, I, VIII; "Plymouth Church Records, 1620–1859," *Publications of the Colonial Society of Massachusetts*, XXIII (1923), 492–510; Hill (ed.), *Record in the Town of Dedham; Watertown Records* (Watertown, Mass., 1894–1904); Samuel A. Bates (ed.), *Records of the Town of Braintree, 1640 to 1793* (Braintree, Mass., 1886); *Concord, Massachusetts: Births, Marriages, and Deaths, 1635–1850* (Concord, Mass., 1891); Boston Record Commissioners, *Boston Births, Baptisms, Marriages, and Deaths*; City of Boston,

Fig. 3 Plymouth Marriages

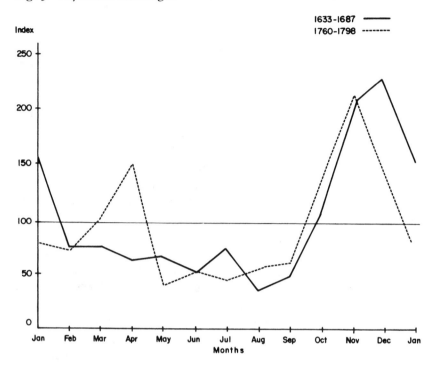

Index

1633-1687 ———
1760-1798 --------

The New England marriage records reveal a striking seasonal pattern, quite unlike anything found in France or England. The colonists easily and swiftly freed themselves from the old-world calendrical rhythms which governed the timing of marriage. Almost at once, however, they instituted a different seasonal pattern, reflecting the new climatic, agricultural, economic, and religious conditions of America.

This seasonal pattern was especially pronounced in the seventeenth century, but the major features persisted beyond the period of the American Revolution. By far the greatest number of weddings took place in the winter, with November and December being the peak months. Weddings were particularly concentrated during these months in Plymouth Colony and to a lesser

Registry Department, *Boston Marriages, 1752–1809* (Boston, 1902). The Boston index for the period 1750–1799 is based on a one-in-five sample of marriages.

Fig. 4 Dedham Marriages

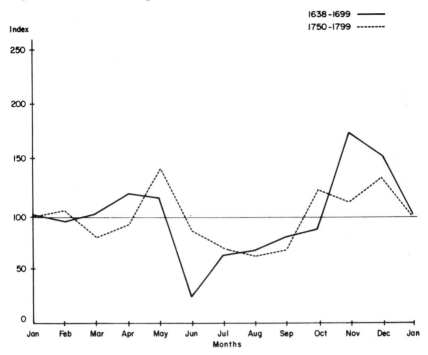

extent in Dedham and Concord. The November and December indexes reached 214 and 231 in Plymouth, 177 and 156 in Dedham, and 162 and 203 in Concord. The mid-winter index for all six communities in the seventeenth century was 158. Braintree, Concord, and Dedham also experienced a secondary peak in the spring, with above-average numbers of marriages in March, April, and May. The summer months, by contrast, saw relatively few weddings, with a trough extending from June to September. The overall mid-summer index was close to 75. June marriages were almost unheard of in seventeenth-century Dedham, where the index dropped to the abstinence level of 25. The August index in Plymouth was only 34.

Boston alone was immune to this volatile pattern. Those who lived in Boston in the seventeenth century showed a mild preference for winter weddings (preferring November to December), and tended to avoid marrying in March. Otherwise their

Fig. 5 Watertown Marriages

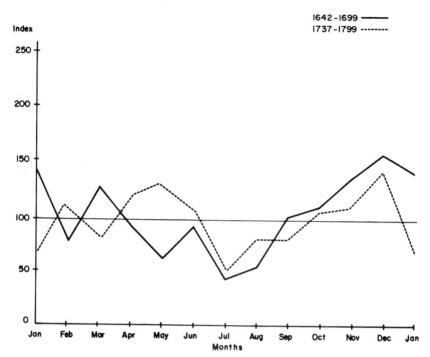

marriages were more evenly distributed throughout the year. A century later the seasonality of marriages in Boston was even more muted. The relative flatness of the graph is only relieved by a dip in July and a compensatory bulge during August.

Early New Englanders paid no attention at all to the old taboo period of Advent and had little, if any, hestitation about marrying during Lent. Only in Boston were there dips in the index for March, as low as 68, which might be associated with some residual regard for Anglican traditions. There are hints, however, of a return to the old ways in the eighteenth century. Everywhere but Plymouth saw the index of March weddings fall below the average. The Watertown index for March was 83, compared to 127 a century earlier. Could this be associated with the eighteenth-century episcopal revival and a limited return to Anglican traditionalism? Earlier American almanacs had omitted

Fig. 6 Braintree Marriages

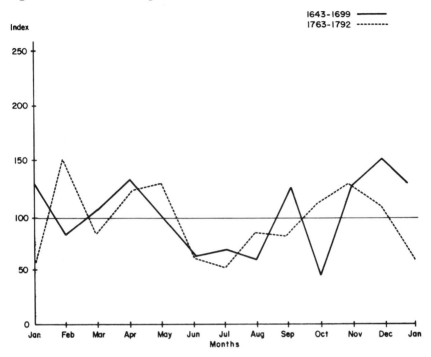

the "times when marriages may not be solemnized," along with the feasts of Epiphany, Easter, and the rest of the traditional liturgical year, but these features reappeared in almanacs of the 1750s and 1760s.[18]

Plymouth, Dedham, Watertown, and Braintree all continued to exhibit a pronounced seasonality in the eighteenth century, with winter peaks, summer lows, and a secondary peak in the spring. The seasonality of **marriage** in Concord, however, had modulated to the degree that it approximated the pattern of seventeenth-century Boston. Marriages became more evenly distributed throughout the year, although Concord, like other rural communities in eastern Massachusetts, still showed a lull in midsummer and a peak in November and December.

18 Contrast Roger Sherman, *An Astronomical Diary, or, an Almanack for . . . 1760 . . . Calculated for the Meridian of Boston in New England* (Boston, 1760) and *Dove Speculum Anni, or an Almanack for the year . . . 1678* (Cambridge, Mass., 1678).

Fig. 7 Concord Marriages

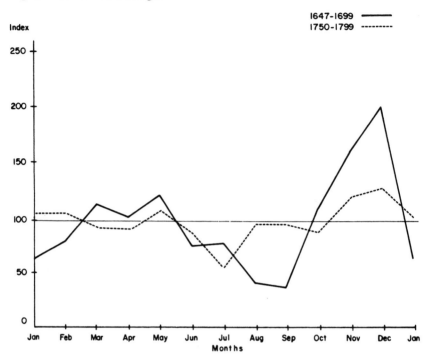

Economic factors provide the primary explanation for these patterns, although the correspondence is not always clear. The evenness of the index for Boston, compared to the switchback seasonality of nearby rural communities, indicates the relative independence of the city from agrarian routines. Like urban centers in Europe, Boston developed an economic diversity with so many contrapuntal rhythms that they virtually cancelled each other out. This independence was especially significant in the eighteenth century as Boston expanded to become an international commercial center. The seasonality of shipping might have influenced the wedding dates of families engaged in overseas trade, but their numbers were insufficient to have much effect. Bostonians, more than anyone in early Massachusetts, were free to arrange their weddings at any time throughout the year.

In the new world, as in the old, the seasonality of marriage in rural areas kept pace with the routines and procedures of the

Fig. 8 Boston Marriages

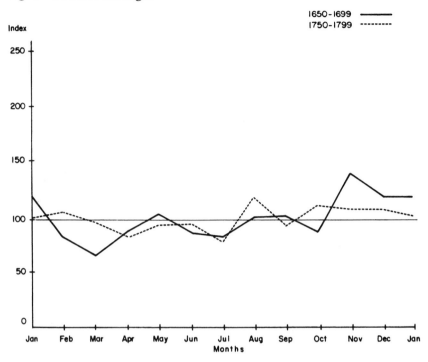

agricultural year. These agrarian rhythms can be reconstructed from diaries, almanacs, and account books.[19]

New England farmers were busiest at the height of summer. The grain harvest demanded an intensive effort in the fields in July and August; August and September were the months for harvesting Indian corn. Few marriages took place in agrarian communities at this time, when activity was focused on the serious business of securing a living. October had been one of the most popular months for marrying in England, but this month

19 Sidney H. Miner and George D. Stanton, Jr. (eds.), *The Diary of Thomas Minor, Stonington, Connecticut, 1653 to 1684* (New London, Ct., 1899). See also Robert R. Walcott, "Husbandry in Colonial New England," *New England Quarterly*, IX (1936), 224–232; D. B. Rutman, *Husbandmen of Plymouth: Farms and Villagers in the Old Colony, 1620–1692* (Boston, 1967), 50–52. Almanacs by Samuel Clough: *The New-England Almanack for . . . MDCC* (Boston, 1700); *ibid.* for MDCCI, MDCCIII; *Kalendarium Nov-Anglicanum* (Boston, 1705); *ibid.* for 1703; *An Almanack for . . . 1708* (Boston, 1708).

Fig. 9 New England Marriages (six communities)

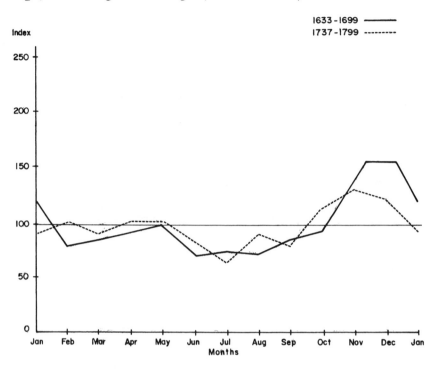

passed in Massachusetts without any noticeable surge of weddings. Indeed, the opposite applied in Braintree where the October index in the seventeenth century was only 46.

Why did New Englanders not follow their contemporaries across the ocean and marry during the month immediately after the harvest? There are several possible explanations. First, because the English custom of service in husbandry, with annual contracts expiring at Michaelmas, was never firmly established in New England, there was no annual flood of nubile ex-servants to inflate the autumn marriage statistics. Servants in New England, as in other American colonies, were indentured for a term of multiple years, and their release occurred on the anniversary of their arrival. (Ships from Europe usually arrived in the summer months, but not all servants were fresh off the boat.) Second, October was still a time of intense agricultural activity in New England because of the sowing of winter wheat. October was also a busy period for those engaged in fishing. Finally, it is possible that New

Englanders simply preferred to wait until November and December, when a combination of environmental and cultural factors produced the most favorable moment for weddings.

The beginning of winter was the peak time for marriage in early New England. The season usually saw an abundant supply of food and a welcome amount of free time in which to enjoy it. Seasonal activities in November included the butchering of livestock and the threshing of grain and corn. It was also a time for planting trees and tending the hearth. Thomas Minor wrote in his diary in November 1655: "the first snow fell . . . we had killed the white sow . . . I did the funil of the chimbly. And Samuel Cheesbrough was married." In November 1662 he wrote, "we killed our swine. The same day Wensday 26 Clemet was married . . . Mr. Stanton's two daghters was married." Stores of grain and corn in the barn and meat in the smokehouse or larder encouraged hospitality, conviviality, and weddings.[20]

Edward Ward, a visitor to New England in 1699, witnessed large gatherings for weddings in November and December and observed the same connection: "Provisions being Plenty, their marriage feasts are very sumptuous." This English visitor also watched the corn-husking parties which followed the harvest season and occurred periodically throughout the winter. They provide, he opined, "as good sport for the Amorous Wag-tailes of New England as Maying amongst us for our forward Youths and Wenches. For 'tis observed, there are more Bastards got in that Season, than in all the Year beside; which Occasions some of the looser Saints to call it Rutting Time."[21]

Indeed, a slightly salacious folklore grew up around the New England winter, associating it with sexual activity which might anticipate marriage. Esther Burr, writing to a friend in 1755, noted the boom in winter weddings and provided a compelling if unorthodox explanation. "Pray what do you think everybody marries in or about winter for: 'tis quite merry, isn't it? I really believe 'tis fear of laying cold, and for want of a bedfellow." Almanac writers marked November, December, and January as a season of short days and long nights, to be spent in the pleasure of meat,

---

20 Miner and Stanton, *Diary of Thomas Minor*, 16, 53.
21 Edward Ward, *A Trip to New-England with a Character of the Country and People* (London, 1699), 10, 11.

drink, warm fires, and close company. "Now is the properest Time for the tearing of sheets, and begetting Bantlings [i.e. babies or bastards]; by reason lazy Lubbers have an Oppertunity to lie long in Bed without the Disturbance either of Daylight or hot Sun-shine." These very months, November through January, saw "a distinct secondary peak" in conceptions (after a peak in the spring), suggesting an accord between folklore and demography.[22]

The evidence from these six communities suggests that although most Massachusetts residents decisively abandoned old-world religious calendar customs, they did not free themselves from other constraints on the timing of marriage. Seasonal activity was still tied to the rhythms of agriculture, which in turn depended on the annual pattern of the weather. Only commercial and manufacturing centers like Boston were buffered against this seasonal rhythm.

It would be interesting to compare the New England experience to that of other colonial societies. How different would the profile be among communities dependent on fishing, forestry, or fur trapping? Did the French Canadians transfer to America the pronounced gallican rhythm, with its avoidance of marriage during Advent and Lent? To what extent did the Dutch in New York modify or maintain the seasonal patterns of the Netherlands? Was there a distinct marriage seasonality associated with the sugar economy, or with the growing and shipping of tobacco or rice? Rutman, Wetherall, and Rutman describe a seasonal pattern in Middlesex County, Virginia, from 1656 to 1746, with a dramatic avoidance of marriage in March and a secondary low in June. The parishioners of All Hallows, Maryland, from 1698 to 1749, also avoided marriage during Lent, had few weddings in the spring and summer, and concentrated their weddings in the winter months. Can we weigh the cultural and religious elements against the economic components of this pattern? What seasonality pre-

22 James Axtell, *The School Upon a Hill. Education and Society in Colonial New England* (New Haven, 1974), 54; Sherman, *An Almanack for the year of our Lord Christ 1750* (New York, 1750), sub. "Winter." Lockridge, "Population of Dedham," 340. In 1628 Burton argued against the unnatural restriction on marriage in Lent, "the most dangerous Season of the Yeere, the Spring time, wherein the blood and spirits are most stirring": *A Tryall of Private Devotion*, sig. F2.

vailed among the English elsewhere in Virginia, or in the Catholic parts of Maryland?[23]

Accounting for seasonal patterns and variations requires a closer study of local social, economic, and cultural history than is possible here. We need to know more about farming routines and the other factors which bore on the timing of marriage in particular communities, as well as the determinants of individual choice. Analysis of the seasonality of marriage in old England demonstrates the influence of different economic regions on demography, and also shows which communities adhered most to religious traditionalism. Further examination of wedding dates may similarly illuminate the social, economic, and cultural history of early America.

23 Rutman, Wetherell, and Rutman, "Rhythms of Life," 36–38. Maryland Hall of Records, Ms.12202 (All Hallows Church). For other examples of marriage seasonality and its links to economic and cultural activity, see Edward Westermarck, *The History of Human Marriage* (New York, 1922; 5th ed.), 79–93; Kussmaul, "Time and Space, Hoofs and Grain: The Seasonality of Marriage in England," *Journal of Interdisciplinary History*, XV (1985), 755–779.

Darrett B. Rutman, Charles Wetherell, and Anita H. Rutman

Rhythms of Life: Black and White Seasonality in the Early Chesapeake

From folk myth to the Bible to modern poetry, Western—and quite possibly all—culture is marked by the image of seasonality. "To every thing there is a season, and a time to every purpose under the heaven: A time to be born, and a time to die. . . ." "In the Spring a young man's fancy lightly turns. . . ."[1] Researchers in medicine, public health, demography, and the life sciences in general have long noted that this seasonal image is reflected in seasonal variations in the vital records of births and deaths. And within the past few years a number of historians, notably of pre-industrial populations, have begun to study seasonal events, hoping to gain not only a glimpse of the fundamental rhythms of a vanished way of life, but also an understanding of what it was in nutrition, in the climate, in clothing and housing, in prophylaxis, in the culture, or, we add, inherently in the biological nature of man, which enforced the seasonal rhythms and to which industrial man seems somewhat, but not entirely, immune.[2]

Darrett B. Rutman is Professor of History at the University of New Hampshire. Charles Wetherell is a doctoral candidate in History at the University of New Hampshire. Anita H. Rutman is a lecturer on paleography and is a bibliographer.

An earlier version of this article was presented at the Organization of American Historians Meeting, 1979. The authors express their gratitude to Maris A. Vinovskis of the University of Michigan who, at an early stage of research, supplied an initial bibliography, and to Franz Halberg, Director of the Chronobiological Laboratories of the University of Minnesota, who facilitated their work in many ways, not the least of which was the providing of extensive bibliographies of the current technical literature.

0022-1953/80/01029-25 $02.50/0

1 Eccles. 3:1–2; Alfred, Lord Tennyson, "Locksley Hall" (1842), in W. J. Rolfe (ed.), *Complete Poetical Works of Tennyson* (Boston, 1898), 90.
2 The literature, particularly on the seasonality of births, is extensive. Ellsworth Huntington, *The Season of Birth* (New York, 1938) summarizes the work to 1935; John C. Bailar, III and Joan Gurian, "The Medical Significance of the Date of Birth," *Eugenics Quarterly*, XIV (1967), 89–102, summarizes the work 1935–1967. Considerable work in biology has centered around the Chronobiological Laboratories at the University of Minnesota and has been reported in *International Journal of Chronobiology* and *Chronobiologia*. See particularly Edward Batschelet et al., "Angular-Linear Correlation Coefficient for Rhythmometry and Circannually Changing Birth Rates at Different Geographic Latitudes," *International Journal of Chronobiology*, I (1973), 183–202, which summarizes modern

This report on seasonality in one Chesapeake county in the late seventeenth and early eighteenth centuries is a by-product of a larger, ongoing study of the total community over the span of four generations. But because the county—Middlesex, Virginia—was biracial during the period, it has particular pertinenence to the growing literature on seasonality. In the county two races lived and worked in a single area but marched, at least in part, to the beat of different drummers. For, as we show, black and white seasonality were clearly and significantly different.[3]

Seasonality refers to the distribution through the year of specific events, in this case the vital events of birth, marriage, and death. The questions asked are simple: Is a particular type of event in the lives of men and women spread evenly through the year, in which case the event would display no seasonality? Or does the event occur more often in one part of the year than another? Historians have been identifying seasonal events by compiling the date of each occurrence over a number of years and subjecting the resultant raw figures of so-many events per month to a procedure designed to take into account the different lengths of the months, leap years with their added February days, and, at the same time, reduce the figures to standard form. Such a procedure allows the comparison of one data set with another even when the total number of events in each set differs. There are several ways of accomplishing this standardization, but the simplest and clearest is by a series of divisions:

NUMBER OF EVENTS RECORDED IN A MONTH
_____

NUMBER OF DAYS IN THAT MONTH, LETTING
FEBRUARY EQUAL 28.25 DAYS
_____

TOTAL NUMBER OF EVENTS RECORDED FOR THE PERIOD
_____

365.25

_____

birth data from 56 areas of the world; Alain Reinberg, "Aspects of Circannual Rhythms in Man," in Eric T. Pengelley (ed.), *Circannual Clocks: Annual Biological Rhythms* (New York, 1974), 423–505. Kenneth A Lockridge first presented the problem of birth seasonality to Early Americanists in "The Conception Cycle as a Tool for Historical Analysis" at a Conference on Social History (SUNY, Stony Brook, 1969). Lockridge drew heavily on the work of French scholars, notably Etienne Gautier and Louis Henry, *La Population*

The resultant product is then multiplied by 100 to obtain the percent of daily average of occurrences for each month. The distribution across the year can be graphically displayed by plotting the monthly percentages of the daily average around a line designating 100 percent of average. A recorded event occurring seasonally would show a significant departure from the 100 line, at some times of the year well above, at others well below. A lack of seasonality would be displayed by a random (therefore insignificant) dispersion about the 100 line.[4]

The result of applying this procedure to 3,216 white births recorded in Middlesex County during the period 1651–1746 is shown in Figure 1. The seasonal nature of the recorded white births in the county is clearly evident, with births occurring above the average from January through a peak in March, dropping steadily from that point to a low in June, then rising gradually into a "random walk" about the 100 line.[5]

The basic configuration of the curve in Figure 1 is not at all unfamiliar to those who have studied the seasonality of pre-industrial births. Data similarly arranged from various Colonial American areas in the periods 1630–1689 and 1720–1777, from Canada in 1700–1760, from Sweden in the eighteenth century, from urban Paris in 1670–1790 and the larger Paris region in

---

de Crulai Paroisse Normande (Paris, 1968), 61; Pierre Goubert, Beauvais et le Beauvaisis de 1600 à 1730: Contribution à l'Histoire Sociale de la France au XVIIIe Siècle (Paris, 1960), 68; Pierre Valmary, Familles Paysannes au XVIIIe Siècle en Bas-Quercy (Paris, 1965), 8.

3 The larger study (hence, indirectly, this study) has been supported by the Central Research Fund of the University of New Hampshire, the American Council of Learned Societies through its Committee for Computer-Oriented Research in the Humanities, and the National Endowment for the Humanities.

4 The procedure described is essentially that suggested by Marcel Fleury and Henry, Nouveau Manuel de Dépouillement et d'Exploitation de l'état Civil Ancien (Paris, 1965). "Significant" and "insignificant" are used throughout in a statistically technical fashion. The alternative to a seasonal distribution is equality across the months; theoretically, deviation from equality will take the form of either random deviation or deviation so extreme as to be improbable as a result of randomness alone—the former insignificant, the later significant. We follow Melvin Zelnik, "Socio-Economic and Seasonal Variations in Births: A Replication," Milbank Memorial Fund Quarterly, XLVII (1969), 161, in considering the Kolmogorov-Smirnov one-sample statistic a more powerful test for this type of data than the more common chi-square test. But note below the cosinor analysis cited in 8n. which uses a variation of the F statistic. We define significance at the .05 level.

5 The prosopography from which the data are drawn is described in Rutman and Rutman, " 'More True and Perfect Lists': The Reconstruction of Censuses for Middlesex County, Virginia, 1668–1704," Virginia Magazine of History and Biography, LXXXVIII (1980), 37–74.

Fig. 1 Recorded White Births, Middlesex Co., Va., 1651–1746, as Percent of Daily Average by Month

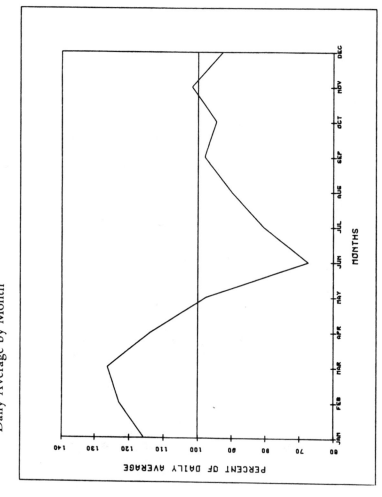

SOURCE: The Middlesex prosopography described in Darrett B. and Anita H. Rutman, "'More True and Perfect Lists': The Reconstruction of Censuses for Middlesex County, Virginia, 1668–1704," *Virginia Magazine of History and Biography*, LXXXVIII (1980), 37–74.

1671–1720, and from the French village of Vexin 1671–1720, all show the same basic outline. In brief, the seasonal pattern of recorded white births found in Middlesex seems very much a part of a general pattern common to at least a large segment of the Western world in the seventeenth and eighteenth centuries.[6]

When recorded black births for the same period in Middlesex are plotted, however, a dramatic and significant departure from the Western norm is immediately evident.[7] In Figure 2, 1,572 recorded black births are plotted with the white births. The black peak occurs in May, not March; and dominating the figure is the near-absolute reversal of the black massif and white valley in the months of May, June, and July. In these three months just over 31 percent of all recorded black births took place, but only 21 percent of recorded white births. The rhythmic nature of the black and white seasonal patterns, and the fact that the patterns are significantly different, is more finitely depicted in Figure 3. Here the data have been disaggregated into twenty-year periods— four such periods for white births and three for black, the latter reflecting a less than adequate number of cases for the period 1667–1686—and the data for each period fitted to a cosine curve.[8]

The seasonality of recorded deaths, too, is clearly evident in

6 From data in Lockridge, "Conception Cycle." In making such comparisons the different calendars (Julian and Gregorian) must be taken into account. The Middlesex births are recorded in Julian form (in common with English recording during the same period) but have been converted to Gregorian to allow comparison with French and modern data. Cowgill's data in "The People of York, 1538–1812," *Scientific American,* CCXXII (1970), 104–112 and "Historical Study of the Season of Birth in the City of York, England," *Nature,* CCIX (1966), 1067–1070, do not seem comparable. She used months of baptism and assumed them to equate with birth months. We suggest that, insofar as English and American data are concerned, this is not always a sound assumption. The Middlesex data include 2,062 cases of known, reliable baptismal months from the years 1651 to 1729; plotting these produces curves quite at variance with curves plotted from recorded births.
7 The Kolmogorov-Smirnov non-parametric test can also be used to define the significance of the difference between two distributions. See Sidney Siegel, *Nonparametric Statistics for the Behavioral Sciences* (New York, 1956), 127–136. Again, we define significance at the .05 level or better.
8 This more finite analysis of rhythmicity is used by Batschelet et al., "Circannual Births and Latitudes." For definitions appropriate to the analysis see Halberg et al., "Chronobiologic Glossary of the International Society for the Study of Biological Rhythms," *International Journal of Chronobiology,* I (1973), 31–63. For the specific analytic procedures see Halberg et al., "Autorhythmometry—Procedures for Physiologic Self-Measurements and their Analysis," *Physiology Teacher,* I (1972), 9–11. For a general discussion of statistical analyses of biological rhythms, see Arne Sollberger, *Biological Rhythm Research* (Amsterdam, 1965), 163–241. The analyses were done using a cosinor program developed by Larry Johnson at the University of Minnesota, supplied to us by Halberg, and converted

Fig. 2 Recorded White and Black Births, Middlesex Co., Va., 1651–1746, as Percent of Daily Average by Month

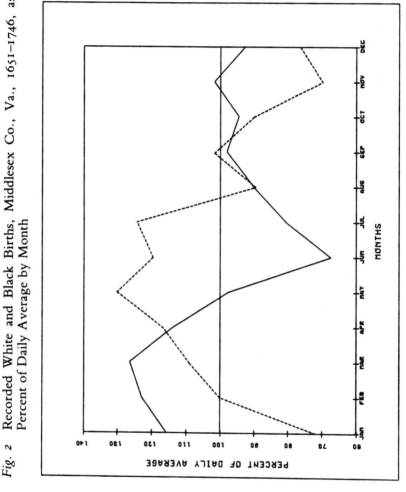

Solid line = white. Broken line = black.
SOURCE: See Figure 1.

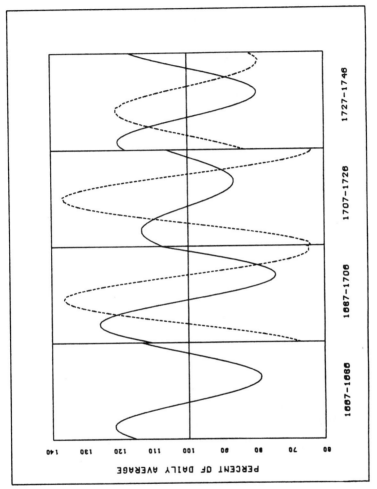

Fig. 3 Recorded White and Black Births, Middlesex Co., Va., 1667–1746, Disaggregated into Twenty-Year Spans and Fitted to Circannual Cosine Functions

Solid line = white. Broken line = black.
SOURCES: Figure 1; Franz Halberg et al., "Autorhythmometry—Procedures for Physiologic Self-Measurement and their Analysis," *Physiology Teacher*, I (1972), 9–11, for the analytic procedure.

Middlesex, as is the marked difference between black and white seasons of death as mirrored in the records, although the difference is not as portentous nor does it plot in as dramatic a fashion as birth seasonality. Figure 4 graphically illustrates the results obtained from 1,842 recorded white deaths and 817 recorded black deaths for the years 1651–1746. The similarities are clear. Both white and black recorded deaths peak early in the year, then fall toward lows in June and July respectively. But at that point the two curves separate, the white rising and falling to form a secondary autumnal peak, the black remaining low and rising only at the end of the year.

Marriage is the third of the vital events of life, and, at least in the case of Middlesex's white population, marriage records exist and are capable of analysis in terms of seasonality. (Black unions in Middlesex were not recorded.) Figure 5 shows a plot of 1,835 recorded white marriages from 1656 to 1746. Again, seasonality of a sort can be seen with highs in February and April bounding an abrupt and deep low in March. But, except for this complex and a secondary low in June—the familiar June bride was not a phenomenon of the early Chesapeake—marriages tend to diffuse insignificantly along the average line.[9]

Recorded births, deaths, and marriages all display seasonal variation in this single Chesapeake county. The first of several questions to be asked of the data is how representative are they. Was there something inherent in Middlesex or in the particular time span (1650–1746) which has imparted a peculiar bias to the data? Counter-indications of bias can, in a general way, be obtained by comparing the results of one data set with results from data drawn from other areas and other times. Differences between sets need not lead to a dismissal of one or the other, for variations might be the results of trends—both temporal and geographical, that is, from one time to another and from one area to another—as well as the result of inherent flaws in the basic data. But similarities can be commanding.

---

to a DECsystem10 environment by the authors. In the interest of comparability we give the estimated rhythm parameters of the cosinor (cosine fitting function) in tabular form in the Appendix. Note that the disaggregated birth data fall below the .05 confidence level in two instances.

9 The insignificant diffusion of marriages through so much of the year lowers the significance of the departure of the entire curve from presumed equality (100 %) below the .05 level.

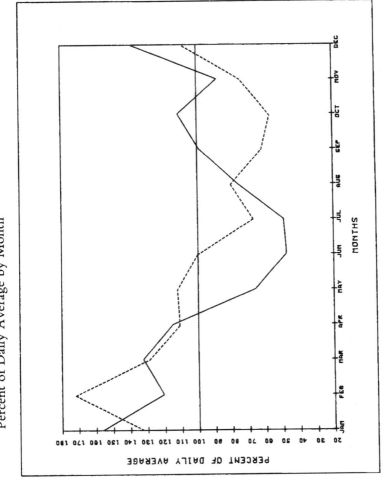

Fig. 4 Recorded White and Black Deaths, Middlesex Co., Va., 1651–1746, as Percent of Daily Average by Month

Solid line = white. Broken line = black.
SOURCE: See Figure 1.

Fig. 4 Recorded White and Black Deaths, Middlesex Co., Va., 1651–1746, as Percent of Daily Average by Month

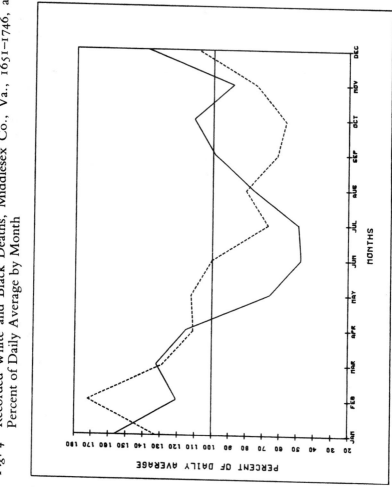

Solid line = white. Broken line = black.
SOURCE: See Figure 1.

The similarities already noted between white births in Middlesex and in other areas of the pre-industrial Western world constitute, in effect, a test for bias from which Middlesex emerges as generally representative. A more immediate test is the comparison with contiguous time periods and geographical areas—comparing, for example, black Middlesex births with black births in nearby Kingston Parish, Mathews County, Virginia, from 1750 to 1770. Such tests, again, indicate the general representativeness of the Middlesex data.[10]

Beyond this first question of representativeness we must ask whether the seasonality of *recorded* events which has been discerned is an accurate reflection of the seasonality of the *actual* events. Are we dealing with the seasonality of births, deaths, and marriages, or only with seasonality in the recording of these events? It is a fundamental issue which forces the historian—even the most statistically minded—to fall back upon logic and internal criticism, upon that unique and traditional questioning of sources which marks the discipline. Who prepared these records? For what purpose? What had one to gain or lose by recording the vital events of his family and slaves? And how might possible gains and losses affect the records and hence what the historian might conclude from them, in this case the seasonality of vital events?[11]

Internal criticism of this sort suggests at least one challenge to our assumption that seasonal curves constructed from the records depict seasonality in life. Heads of families were required to record births and deaths with the minister or, in his absence, the parish clerk. Perhaps some family heads eschewed the discomfort of a long, cold ride in the winter months merely to pass on the fact of a vital event, particularly one pertaining to a black whose birth or death might be construed to be relatively unimportant.

10 Processing the months of 795 black births from Kingston Parish, Mathews County, as transcribed by Sally Nelson Robins, typescript, Virginia Historical Society Library, Richmond, Va., produced only random variation from the Middlesex data.

11 James H. Cassedy, *Demography in Early America: Beginnings of the Statistical Mind, 1600–1800* (Cambridge, Mass., 1969) is suggestive along these lines but weak and sometimes erroneous with regard to southern materials. Compare, for example, where Cassedy notes that "the registration of the vital events of slaves was not required of the parish system" (94) and the citations in 12 n. below to William W. Hening (ed.), *The Statutes at Large: Being a Collection of All the Laws of Virginia . . . [through 1792]* (Richmond, 1809–1823), 13 v.

Or perhaps they eschewed leaving the work of their farms and plantations in the heavier work periods to register an event. The birth or death passed over in this fashion might not be registered at all. Or it might be registered at a later time as a vague, inaccurate recollection, even as the date upon which the head of family finally saw the minister or clerk. In either event, a systematic bias would be introduced into the records, vitiating any discussion of seasonal events in favor of seasonal recording.[12]

The latter possibility, inaccurate registration, seems slim. The nature of white birth records—in which precise dates of birth and baptism are so often included, the interval between the two itself forming a significant pattern—tends to preclude such a misrecording of white births. There also was a positive value, beyond the desire to stay within the law, of entering the precise dates of births and deaths, even of blacks, for tithables (those for whom a poll tax was due from the master of the house) were defined by age. A record of birth insured against premature assessment sometime in the future, whereas a record of death removed the tithable from the rolls, and the head of family from an immediate obligation to pay.[13]

A bias toward the accurate recording of white births and deaths and a sporadic registration of black events can be discounted, for a clear similarity exists between the trends in the black and white ratios of registered births to registered deaths—a situation highly unlikely if such a bias existed. Entry by recollection can be discounted, too, for men recalling the dates of past events will tend to bunch those dates, entering a sequence of similar or patterned dates. Neither sequencing nor patterning is evident. In all likelihood, therefore, those men who consistently

---

12   The law did allow a "grace" period, however—twenty days in that of 1713. Hening (ed.), *Statutes at Large*, IV, 42–45. See also *ibid.*, I, 542; II, 54; III, 153; IV, 550–551. Obviously these biases would not apply to the recording of marriages.

13   An analysis of incidents where both birth and baptism among whites were recorded indicates both a pattern of declining intervals and a tendency in the distribution of intervals within five-year periods toward ever greater statistical normalcy. Philip Alexander Bruce, *Institutional History of Virginia in the Seventeenth Century* (New York, 1910), II, 548–555; Rutman and Rutman, "'More True and Perfect Lists,'" 17 n. One might argue that it would be in the interest of a planter to post-date the record of the birth of a slave or a son so as to make the youth come to taxable age later, saving the taxpayer a year's poll tax. If this had been a common practice slave births just prior to the time the tithable lists were drawn up—roughly the first week in June—would be understated in the records and the existent May peak of black births would be all the more pronounced.

registered vital events did so accurately, entering their information before or after the Sunday services or, if they were delayed, perhaps jotting down the information at home and using their notes to refresh their minds at a later date.[14]

Non-registration according to a pattern remains a possibility, however—in the extreme, men who consistently registered vital events, both black and white, during part of the year (when, for example, the weather was good or the work-load light) and just as consistently omitted registration during other periods (when the weather was bad or the work demanding). A series of tests performed upon the data lowers to an insignificant level the probability of such patterned behavior affecting our results.

To set up such tests we first assumed that within the total society there existed some sub-group more immune than the group as a whole to the patterns of weather and work which, for the sake of the argument, were presumed to have affected the quality of the data. The most prominent families would seem to be such a group. By definition the heads of such families were the political, economic, and social leaders of the society, regular in their attendance at church, and regular in conferring with each other, and with the minister and parish clerk, as members of the parish vestry and county court. If a systematic bias had been injected into the records by weather or work patterns, the results of an examination of the recorded events in the lives of these families should differ significantly from the recorded events of the total sample minus these families. But with reference to white events there was no significant deviation.[15]

To test black vital events an even finer test group was constructed on the basis of blacks who, as part of large estates in probate, fell under the control of executors—men of leading families who had, additionally, legal, financial, and sometimes moral obligations to maintain exact recording. Again, a comparison of

14 This is not to suggest that there was no under-registration (a common phenomenon in all pre-industrial records, particularly with regard to deaths), only that there was impetus toward accurate registration operating upon those who did register an event. For the phenomenon of age-bunching, see David Hackett Fischer, *Growing Old in America* (New York, 1978; expanded ed.), 82–86.

15 Fifteen representative leading families were used: Berkeley, Beverley, Churchill, Daniell, Grimes, Kemp, Perrott, Robinson, Segar, Skipwith, Stanard, Thacker, Vause, Weekes, and Wormeley. In all these tests, no deviation was significant at better than the .20 level.

vital events recorded for such "estate" blacks with the total black record minus estate events showed no significant differences.[16]

It must be stressed that significant deviation in these tests would not be conclusive with reference to the particular question of whether recorded vital events reflect the totality (recorded and unrecorded) of vital events. Social, political, and economic position could conceivably be variables operating independently on recorded and unrecorded alike; one writer, drawing upon twentieth-century data, has even concluded that economic position tends to buffer the modern individual from seasonality. But the lack of significant deviation is commanding. The weight of our testing is on the side of the recorded vital events accurately reflecting the totality of these events in the pre-industrial society of Middlesex.[17]

What do we make of the seasonality that so clearly marked the lives of these men and women, and differently marked black and white? Can we use seasonality to burrow still deeper into their lives? There are some clear answers, and some not so clear at all.

The marriage curve clearly revolves around the Lenten season, consequently telling us something about religious observance in the society. Notably, the Lenten period from Ash Wednesday to Easter Sunday varies from year to year, beginning at the earliest on February 4 and at the latest on March 10. Just under 63 percent of the Lenten days in the period 1651–1746 fell in March, when the number of marriages was minimal. To put the point another way, almost 94 percent of all March days in the period were Lenten days, leaving 6 percent of the March days for the few marriages occurring—*if* we assume that the Virginians of Middlesex adhered to an Anglican proscription of Lenten marriages. But 31 percent of February days and 27 percent of April days fell in Lent. If we do not go beyond our assumption of obedience to a Lenten proscription, Lenten days falling in February and April would suggest that marriages should decline for those months as

---

16 One need only read the executor's record in the MS Wormeley Estate Papers, 1710–1716 (in Christ Church, Lancaster County, Processioners Returns, 1711–1783, Virginia State Library, Richmond, 139–181) to see indications of a felt moral obligation.

17 Zelnik, "Socio-Economic and Seasonal Variations," 159–166. See also, Benjamin Pasamanick, Simon Dinitz, and Hilda Knobloch, "Socio-economic and Seasonal Variations in Birth Rates," *Milbank Memorial Fund Quarterly*, XXXVIII (1960), 248–254.

well. But our curve displays the very opposite—peaks in February and April.[18]

Our reconstruction of the marriage pattern must, consequently, be more complex. We can assume that couples married without regard to season throughout much of the year, when our curve displays a random walk about equality. As Lent approached they tended to hurry marriages in order to avoid the six-week delay (the increased number of marriages during non-Lenten February days more than offsetting the absence of marriages on those February days falling in Lent). As Lent ended they hurried to consecrate marriages which had been put off during the sacred mourning.

The Virginians were not unique in adhering to this pattern. A Lenten proscription of marriage is common in Christianity, and its observance persists in many areas into the twentieth century. Observance of the Lenten proscription shows in Cowgill's data from the city of York, England during the years after 1538. The York data do, however, indicate a sharp November peak (an anticipation of Christmas, she writes) which does not appear in Middlesex. And the whole York pattern tends to disappear gradually as time progresses, becoming all but non-existent by the period 1752–1812. "Evidently," Cowgill writes, "religious festivities no longer set the rhythm of the people's year." In Middlesex the pattern holds strong even when marriages are analyzed in consecutive periods; there are no significant differences between curves drawn on the basis of the data disaggregated into twenty year spans (see Fig. 6).[19]

What of the seasonal variations of death and the differences between black and white seasonality? It is a commonplace to say that the distribution of deaths across the year is determined (certainly in a premodern population) by climate and epidemiological

18 Lenten days computed from Lenten tables in Christopher R. Cheney, *Handbook of Dates for Students of English History* (London, 1961), 83–161.

19 For examples of observance of Lenten proscription see, Huntington, *Season of Birth*, 46, 70; Maria-Luiza Marcilio, *La Ville de São Paulo: Peuplement et Population, 1750–1850* (Rouen, 1968), 181; Joel Halpern, *A Serbian Village* (New York, 1956), 191. But there is no Lenten decline in Virginia Quaker marriages recorded in the MS Chuckatuck Record—Lower Virginia Monthly Minutes and Register of Births, Deaths, Marriages, 1647–1756, Virginia State Library. The Quakers did not observe Lent. Cowgill, "People of York," 107. Cowgill offers her data in rough charts rather than adjusted figures. Hence they are not completely comparable.

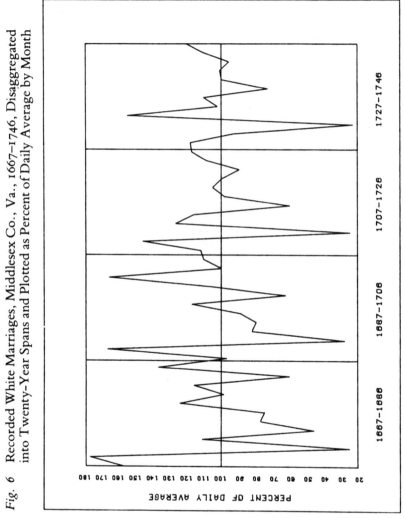

Fig. 6 Recorded White Marriages, Middlesex Co., Va., 1667–1746, Disaggregated into Twenty-Year Spans and Plotted as Percent of Daily Average by Month

SOURCE: See Figure I.

timing. A consideration of the former underlies the greater susceptibility to respiratory infections among blacks noted by Curtin
and others, whereas the latter is the basis of a recent effort to use
the monthly variation in death as a tool in *ex post facto* diagnosis.[20]

Both climatological and diagnostic approaches are applicable
to the Middlesex data. On the one hand, the winter and early
spring months, relatively cold and damp, were, indeed, the killer
months in the Chesapeake for both black and white, a phenomenon apparent in Figures 4 and 7—the second a disaggregation of

Fig. 7   Recorded White and Black Deaths, Middlesex Co., Va., 1667–
1746, Disaggregated into Twenty-Year Spans and Plotted as
Percent of Daily Average by Month

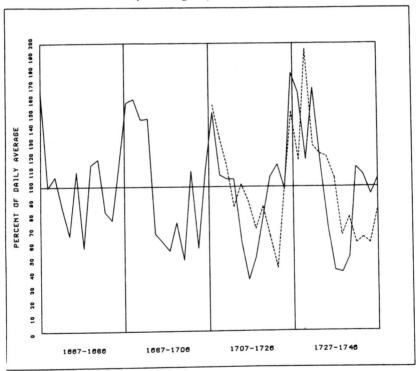

Solid line = white. Broken line = black.
SOURCE: See Figure 1.

20   Philip D. Curtin, "Epidemiology and the Slave Trade," *Political Science Quarterly,*
LXXXIII (1968), 210; Peter H. Wood, *Black Majority: Negroes in Colonial South Carolina
from 1670 through the Stono Rebellion* (New York, 1974), 76–79; Arthur E. Imhof, "The
Analysis of Eighteenth-Century Causes of Death: Some Methodological Considerations,"
Historical Methods, 11 (1978), 3–35.

deaths into twenty-year periods—and confirmed by strong and significant correlations between deaths and weather data.[21] It is not at all clear, however, that blacks were more susceptible to the rigors of the Chesapeake winter than whites; the data neither support nor weaken prevailing views regarding the matter. On the other hand, the secondary peak of white deaths in September and October strengthens a diagnosis of endemic malaria made elsewhere, the "autumnal fevers" so devastating to the whites and from which the blacks were genetically protected.[22]

But there is another aspect to such data which must be considered, if only to pave the way for a consideration of the seasonal variation of births. The study of intrinsic biological rhythms to which the human species is subject is only in its infancy, yet already the rhythmic behavior of scores of physiological functions have been described, including yearly, or circannual, rhythms of such diverse functions as blood serum and testicular activity. The season of death itself, although subject to external phenomena (climate and epidemiological timing), is suspected of having a biological base that is rhythmic. Is it not odd, the chronobiologists ask, that deaths among laboratory mice exposed in a constant

21 Black data are plotted only for the last two periods; they are too sparse in the earlier periods to bear analysis. (Black migration into the county began in earnest only toward the end of the seventeenth century.) The irregularities in the white curve for the first period are in part a function of small sample size and in part a function of heavy servant immigration—servants frequently dying en masse within a short period following the arrival of ships carrying them to the Chesapeake.

  Two eighteenth-century weather diaries are available: one summarized in Thomas Jefferson (ed. William Peden), *Notes on the State of Virginia* (Chapel Hill, 1955), 74, applicable to Williamsburg for the years 1772–1777; the other kept by Francis Fauquier from January 1760 through December 1762, again in Williamsburg, and reported in Rufus Rockwell Wilson (ed.), *Burnaby's Travels through North America* (New York, 1904), 23, 216–251. Neither diary differs materially from the yearly weather pattern presented in more elaborate form by modern weather observers, although Fauquier was reporting a series of years colder than the modern norm. See U.S. Department of Commerce, Weather Bureau, *Decennial Census of the United States Climate: Monthly Averages for State Climatic Divisions, 1931–1960, Virginia* (Washington, 1963), 1; *idem, Summary of Hourly Observations . . . Richmond, Virginia, Byrd Field, 1951–1960* (Washington, 1963). The correlation of modern weather data—taking advantage of their greater detail—with early Chesapeake demographic data does not seem unduly hazardous.

22 Rutman and Rutman, "Of Agues and Fevers: Malaria in the Early Chesapeake," *William and Mary Quarterly*, XXXIII (1967), 31–60. Black resistance to the effects of malarial infection is discussed at length in Kenneth F. and Virginia H. Kiple, *The American Dimension to the Black Diaspora: Diet, Disease, Racism*, forthcoming. We are grateful to them for allowing us to read pertinent chapters in typescript.

environment to a constant X-ray display a circannual rhythm; that circannual peaks occur at roughly the same time for human populations enjoying radically different climates; or that pneumonia deaths in New England and Louisiana peak together, as do cardiovascular deaths in France and Minnesota?[23]

> If, for instance, in the northern hemisphere mortality for certain diseases reaches its peak in January and February, this fact need not necessarily and exclusively be related to perceptive poetical remarks aimed literally and literarily to nurture, such as 'winter months are killers of poor people'; the intrinsic susceptibility (or resistance) of the human organism also varies rhythmically with a period of about 1 year.[24]

We have not entered into the arguments among medical practitioners and biologists that such statements provoke, choosing instead to make two simple points. First, the suspicion that man may be subject to biological periodicities should put us on guard against reading too much "history" into the yearly distributions of death that we find in the past. Rather than being entirely time-and-place-specific, the phenomenon might well be in part timeless. Second, to whatever extent the phenomenon is timeless—that is, a reflection of an intrinsic rhythmicity of the human organism's susceptibility or resistance to disease—the parameters of that rhythm seem to apply equally to black and white. The formal analysis reported in the appendix shows only minimal variation between the two. Such is not the case with regard to births.

Of the three phenomena that we are investigating, the seasonality of birth is the most impenetrable. Historians, viewing birth as a function of fertility, more often than not have lagged their curves by nine months—the roughly 280-day gestation period—and thereby have transformed their investigations into the study of conception. As employed, their approach raises consid-

---

23 Reinberg, "Circannual Rhythms in Man," 424, 476–485. For a general introduction to biological rhythms and their study, see Gay Gaer Luce, *Biological Rhythms in Human and Animal Physiology* (New York, 1976); Sollberger, *Biological Rhythm Research; idem,* "General Properties of Biological Rhythms," *Annals of the New York Academy of Sciences,* XCVIII (1962), 757–774; John D. Palmer, *An Introduction to Biological Rhythms* (New York, 1976); Halberg, "Chronobiology," *Annual Review of Physiology,* XXXI (1969), 675–725.
24 Reinberg, "Circannual Rhythms in Man," 484.

erations ranging from the age structure of the population and the general level of geographical mobility to fecundity and marriage patterns—in short to a consideration of a demographic profile of the population.[25]

Biologists, however, point out that birth is the climax of a long process and that the operative factor or factors enforcing seasonality may lie anywhere—in seasonal variations of fertility, of sexual activity (although some modern work suggests that this is unrelated), and even of the length of the gestation period itself—or they may lie everywhere. Too many physiological unknowns exist for the biologists simply to equate seasonality of birth with seasonality of conception. Between them, historians and biologists have suggestively linked the seasonality of birth to inherent physiological rhythmicities, to periods of religious celibacy (the Islamic Ramadan, for example), to nutritional levels at different times of the year, to work patterns, to customs governing marriage, childrearing, and weaning, and even to the presence of air conditioners in the home. Everything seems to affect the curve, but nothing seems determinative.[26]

There are two exceptions, although not of our discovery and

25 A brief but technical introduction to the concerns of historical demographers, particularly those respecting fertility, can be found in Henry (trans. Etienne van de Walle and Elise F. Jones) *Population: Analysis and Models* (New York, 1976), esp. 47–121, 229–259. See also Charles Tilly (ed.), *Historical Studies of Changing Fertility* (Princeton, 1978), 73–74.
26 The physiological concerns of biologists are implicit throughout the chronobiological literature and to some extent are inspired by clear evidence of circadian rhythms in man, including circadian rhythms in spontaneous births and testosterone (the principal male sex hormone), circannual reproductive rhythms in animals, and evidence of a relationship between circadian and circannual rhythms. See, e.g., Irwin H. Kaiser and Halberg, "Circadian Periodic Aspects of Birth," *Annals of the New York Academy of Sciences*, XCVIII (1962), 1056–1068; Reinberg et al., "Circannual and Circadian Rhythms in Plasma Testosterone in Five Healthy Young Parisian Males," *Acta Endocrinologica*, LXXX (1975), 742–743; Michael Menaker, "Rhythms, Reproduction, and Photoreception," *Biology of Reproduction*, IV (1971), 295–308; *idem*, "Circannual Rhythms in Circadian Perspective," in Pengelley (ed.), *Circannual Clocks*, 507–520; Pengelley and Sally J. Asmundson, "Annual Biological Clocks," *Scientific American*, CCIV (1971), 72–79; E. Haus and Halberg, "Circannual Rhythm in Level and Timing of Serum Corticosterone in Standardized Inbred Mature C-Mice," *Environmental Research*, III (1970), 81–106. On the human gestation period varying in length, see Harry M. Rosenberg, *Seasonal Variation of Births: United States, 1933–1966* (Washington, D.C., 1966), 10; Alan S. Parkes, *Patterns of Sexuality and Reproduction* (New York, 1976), 31–35. Cf. Henry, *Population*, 238–242. J. Richard Udry and Naomi Morris, "Seasonality of Coitus and Seasonality of Birth," *Demography*, IV (1967), 673–697, argue that there is no statistical relationship between seasonal variations in births and seasonal variations in sexual activity. See also Parkes, *Patterns of Sexuality and Reproduction*, 114–119.

drawn from macro-research in chronobiology rather than micro-research in history. Batschelet and his colleagues, in examining data from various parts of the world, have been able to suggest a relatively strong correlation between latitude and the rhythmic timing of the peaks of the birth curves. They imply that whatever biological process is reflected in them is environmentally cued. At the same time, however, the same data suggest a rough, informal correlation between the peaks of the curves and the degree of modernity of the societies involved, which implies that the phenomenon has a cultural basis. Given this morass, chronobiologists, not unnaturally, weigh their words carefully. Batschelet: "Any relationship between the timing of a circannual rhythm in human births and geographic latitude is likely to reflect factors stemming broadly from 'nurture' as well as from 'nature.' However, the synchronized about-yearly population rhythm itself in all likelihood originates at least partly from the operation of intrinsic factors."[27]

What does the introduction of our historical data contribute? Let us start with the simplest of all observations. The society of the early Chesapeake (although historians might strive mightily to find some glimmerings of modernization) must be described as premodern, more in line with the underdeveloped societies of today, with what Batschelet describes as the "agrarian and gaming" societies, than with his "urban and industrial" West. The timing of the peak of Middlesex's white birth curve is clearly more in line with Batschelet's underdeveloped countries and almost exactly the opposite of the modern American peak. "Nurture" in the form of underdeveloped (or premodern) versus modern societies is, consequently, supported. We are, however, dealing with *two* underdeveloped societies: one white with its roots in Europe; one black with its roots in Africa. "Nurture," in Batschelet's usage, would suggest that data from our black and white societies ought to give roughly the same results. They do not.

---

27 Batschelet et al., "Circannual Births and Latitude." For earlier statements of the geographical relationship, see Cowgill, "The Season of Birth in Man," *Man*, I (1966), 232–240; *idem*, "The Season of Birth and its Biological Implications," *Journal of Reproductive Fertility*, VI (1969), Supplement, 89–103; Pasamanick, Dinitz, and Knobloch, "Geographic and Seasonal Variations in Births," *Public Health Reports*, LXXIV (1959), 285–288. Batschelet et al., "Circannual Births and Latitude," 200.

Let us take another approach. We are dealing with people in transit—whites entering the Chesapeake from England, blacks from Africa. For both groups latitudinal shifts were involved, in the case of blacks a considerable shift of 32 degrees if we presume that for the most part they came from the south-facing lands on the African bulge. Unfortunately, pertinent black African data are the most difficult to come by. Batschelet, for example, does not report any in his world-wide survey. Hence we are without even a presumptive starting point. We can suggest, however, that if "nature" in the form of environmental cues linked to latitude is determinative, the white and black curves ought to move toward coincidence.[28] During the period under study there is no indication of this conjunction; indeed, modern American data indicate that there is still a variation—although not nearly as dramatic—between black and white.[29]

In brief, neither nature nor nurture, as Batschelet uses these terms, encompasses (or is supported by) the historical data from the early Chesapeake.

There is, however, far more to nature than simply the habitat implied by latitude, and far more to nurture than is suggested by the simple dichotomy of premodern and modern. On the one hand, nature includes the demonstrable genetic differences between individuals and between groups. Hence, the fact that our data break so dramatically between black and white raises the possibility that race—a word used as Wilson uses it, "to imply nothing more than the observation that certain traits, such as average height or skin color, vary genetically from one locality

---

28 We stress that this is a test of the relatively immediate interaction of environment as implied by latitude and whatever biological clock is operating; it is very much akin to a laboratory situation in which environmental cues—the light/dark cycle or photoperiod, for example—are varied. Such a test is warranted by the rapidity with which human birth rhythms (as currently measured) can change. Cowgill measured a shift of 166 days in the peak of the Puerto Rican birth cycle between 1941-45 and 1956-60. See her "Recent Variations in the Season of Birth in Puerto Rico," *Proceedings of the American Academy of Science,* LII (1964), 1149–1151.

29 See Zelnik, "Socio-Economic and Seasonal Variations," 159–166. The Middlesex black curve is more in line with Zelnik's black data than with the Middlesex white curve. Batschelet uses only white South African birth data. Cowgill does use black South African data ("Season of Birth in Man") and Parkes (*Patterns of Sexuality and Reproduction*) follows Cowgill; but, as Rosenberg (*Seasonal Variation of Birth,* 6) notes, these data are essentially urban since the majority of blacks lived in rural areas where birth registration was not mandatory.

to another"—is an independent variable operating upon the phenomenon. On the other hand, culture—nurture—is an immensely
complex phenomenon. Any interrelationship between culture and
the biology of reproduction (in all its phases) which would affect
what the chronobiologists see as an intrinsic rhythmicity of
births—and specifically, which would account for the difference
between our black and white curves—would be inevitably complex and probably subtle. Still, there are hints of such a linkage
in the Middlesex materials.[30]

In the course of the general study of Middlesex County we
have, over the years, constructed a series of indices—some, of
necessity, quite crude—which describe the year in terms of such
variables as climate, work (and its antonym, leisure), and levels
of nutrition, all of which, as one might expect, vary seasonally.
For the most part the comparison of these indices with the black
and white birth curves has led to negative results, that is to say,
to no apparent connection.[31]

In a few instances, however, the comparisons suggest particular scenarios. Among blacks (but not whites), births rose as
work on the tobacco crop became more intense. Were black
women so foresighted as to plan ahead so that the last stages of
pregnancy kept them from the fields? Probably not. Did labor in
the fields induce early terminations which, when joined with
normal terminations, forced a rise in the number of black births?
Perhaps. Again, among blacks (but not whites) births, lagged
nine months to approximate conceptions, rose and fell with nutritional levels. Was the black diet at times so deficient in nutrition

30 Edward O. Wilson, *On Human Nature* (Cambridge, Mass., 1978), 48. A comparison
of Middlesex black births with the birth months of 781 African girls (born 1935–1947)
reported from South Africa is startlingly suggestive. The data, as reported by A. G. Oettle
and J. Higginson, "The Age at Menarche in South African Bantu (Negro) Girls," *Human
Biology*, XXXIII (1961), 181–190, are not, in and of themselves, significant in a cosinor
analysis. The computed acrophase, however, is −344.0 (referenced to 00 hour, June 22nd),
which translates to *c.* June 2; the Middlesex black acrophase translates to May 30 (see
Appendix). The cosinor analysis of African data yields the following additional parameters:
PR = 37.9; P = .117; AMP = 12.0 ± 3.6.
31 In the same way the relationships between the demographic variables themselves
(births, births lagged to approximate conceptions, marriages, and deaths) were tested
against each other with only negative results. A test of association between white marriages
and births, lagged to approximate conceptions in the months immediately following
marriages (i.e., lagging births by eleven months), failed as well. All tests were also
performed on the white data disaggregated by socioeconomic level of the parents with
similar results: there were no significant differences between levels.

as to mute sexuality or dampen the probability of conception in sexual congress? This is, because of the statistical strength of the association, the most promising thought. Yet we must add that at this point none of our attempts to isolate relationships can truly be said to have succeeded. Our indices are essentially too weak, and the intercorrelations among them too strong.

"To every thing there is a season" the Biblical scribe wrote. And so there was in the early Chesapeake, a time for birth, marriage, and death. Marriage reflects an aspect of the culture of the particular time and place. Death reflects in some measure the fit of man to this particular climate and disease environment. The seasonality of birth reflects a difference of unknown cause between the two peoples who came to live along the Bay. The historian can be comfortable with the first, can easily accept the second, but, we suspect, will be decidedly uncomfortable with the third. We are not.

Our simple statement with regard to the black and white birth data is that they point to a real phenomenon which we ought to try to understand. We offer no firm explanation for the data, but merely point out that explanation could lie in nature—being of one race as opposed to another—or explanation could lie in the culture—being slave at this time and place as against being free. Neither do we postulate the effect that the phenomenon had upon this past society, or even if it had any effect at all. A discipline which is classically devoted to the construction of over-arching truths and causal chains expects more from its practition-ers than such a weak conclusion. We suggest, however, that, as historians become increasingly interdisciplinary, they will increas-ingly find themselves (as we find ourselves) uncovering phenom-ena which they do not understand and for which they can find no immediate use. Rather than dismissing such phenomena, or forc-ing findings beyond their worth by arguing significance in some sort of particularistic scheme, we have presented the data in the hope that others—either in or out of history—will build upon them.

Appendix

Middlesex County, Virginia: Births and Deaths, 1651-1746 Estimated Rhythm Parameters by Least-Squares Fitting of a 365.25 Day Cosine Function to the Percent of Daily Average

	N	PR	P	AMP	±S.E.	ACR	(95% CON. ARC)	DATE
Births:								
White								
All	3,216	62.2	.012	18.5	±3.3	-46.6	(-358 to -96)	Feb 7
1667-1686	349	28.4	.222	21.6	±8.0	-45.0		Feb 5
1687-1706	605	69.8	.005	25.8	±4.0	-66.7	(-27 to -107)	Feb 27
1707-1726	1,154	37.5	.120	13.6	±4.2	-57.2		Feb 18
1727-1746	1,077	71.1	.004	20.4	±3.1	-28.2	(-350 to -66)	Jan 19
Births:								
Black								
All	1,572	84.5	.001	25.9	±2.6	-157.2	(-133 to -182)	May 30
1687-1706	99	48.7	.050	35.9	±8.7	-158.6	(-71 to -246)	May 31
1707-1726	490	73.5	.003	36.6	±5.2	-174.7	(-139 to -210)	Jun 16
1727-1746	972	71.6	.003	20.8	±3.1	-142.0	(-104 to -180)	May 14
Deaths:								
White								
All	1,842	77.6	.001	42.1	±5.3	-21.2	(-350 to -53)	Jan 12
1667-1686	143	18.1	.406	16.8	±8.4	-7.9		Dec 29
1687-1706	297	71.0	.004	50.3	±7.6	-52.9	(-15 to -92)	Feb 13
1707-1726	683	76.4	.002	47.6	±6.2	-2.9	(-330 to -36)	Dec 24
1727-1746	642	65.8	.008	46.9	±8.0	-31.5	(-347 to -76)	Feb 3
Deaths:								
Black								
All	817	80.6	.001	41.8	±4.8	-71.7	(-43 to -100)	Mar 4
1707-1726	300	61.2	.014	36.7	±6.9	-44.1	(-353 to -95)	Feb 5
1727-1746	507	72.2	.003	46.0	±6.7	-83.2	(-46 to -120)	Mar 16

Notes: N = number of cases; PR = percent of variability accounted for by the cosine function; P = probability of the hypothesis (significance); AMP = amplitude of the curve; ACR = acrophase referenced to oo hour, December 22. (95% confidence arcs are reported where P ≦ .05.) In every case the mesor approximates 100. The amplitude is a measure of the distance between the mean of the cosine curve (mesor) and its peak. The acrophase is a measure in degrees from the peak of the curve to 0 degrees, the reference point, in this case the first moment of December 22, hence the acrophase can be construed as an estimated calendar- and clock-moment for the peak of curve. See Halberg et al., "Chronobiologic Glossary," 31-63. Rhythm parameters for marriages are omitted as meaningless; although the Lenten dip is interpretively significant, the cosinor analysis is not.

Edward Byers

Fertility Transition in a New England Commercial Center: Nantucket, Massachusetts,

1680–1840 The attention of American historical demographers has recently been focused on the relatively early fertility decline in northern rural communities. One of the most widely accepted explanations for the fertility behavior of rural families in the late eighteenth and early nineteenth centuries was first put forward by Yasuba and later elaborated by Easterlin. In brief, the argument states that an increasing scarcity of readily available farmland in the older rural areas and a long-standing parental desire to preserve wealth and transmit it to the next generation interacted to produce a change in fertility behavior.[1]

Threatened with the fragmentation of family farms and the increased cost of providing their children with sufficient resources to establish their own households, American rural families adopted strategies of later marriage and family limitation to balance population growth with available land. This economic/ecological explanation implies that in either a rural or urban setting parental concerns about the ability to maintain or expand wealth in the face of decreasing availability of critical resources results in the conscious limitation of family size.

Edward Byers is a graduate student in the department of History at Brandeis University.

This article is based on research begun in cooperation with Carol Shuchman. An earlier version of it was read at the Social Science History Association meeting (1980). Constructive comments from David H. Fischer, Judith C. Taylor, and Alan C. Swedlund were very helpful in revising the original drafts and are most gratefully acknowledged.

0022-1953/82/01017-24 $02.50/0

1 Yasukichi Yasuba, *Birth Rates of the White Population in the United States, 1800–1860: An Economic Study* (Baltimore, 1962); Richard A. Easterlin, "Population Change and Farm Settlement in the Northern United States," *Journal of Economic History*, XXXIV (1976), 45–83; Colin Forster and G. S. L. Tucker, *Economic Opportunity and White American Fertility Ratios: 1800–1860* (New Haven, 1972); Helena Temkin-Greener and Alan C. Swedlund, "Fertility Transition in the Connecticut Valley: 1740–1850," *Population Studies*, XXXII (1978), 27–41; Louise Kantrow, "Philadelphia Gentry: Fertility and Family Limitation Among an American Aristocracy," *Population Studies*, XXXIV (1980), 21–30; Thomas R. Cole, "Family Settlement and Migration in Southeastern Massachusetts, 1650–1805: The Case for Regional Analysis," *New England Historical and Genealogical Register*, XXXII (1978), 171–185.

Some scholars have argued that this explanation by itself cannot account for the fertility decline in America. They contend that fertility behavior was affected by broader social changes. Wells, for example, has argued that not only was the decline in natural resources important but also the development of modern attitudes, including the perception that reduced fertility would aid individuals in either protecting or advancing their economic well-being. In the absence of a prior change in attitudes, families confronted with declining resources would passively accept their fate as they had in the past.[2]

Because the evidence upon which both of these hypotheses rests is drawn almost exclusively from the fertility experience of northern, rural, agrarian communities, neither hypothesis can be conclusively evaluated. Studies of contrasting social settings are required. In particular, a study of a commercial, urban environment, with a microscopic investigation of the dynamics of change in fertility at the family level, would be particularly useful for comparative analysis.

Nantucket, Massachusetts, a medium-sized whaling center, was such a commercial environment. This study examines the marriage and fertility behavior of the white population of Nantucket from the beginning of white settlement in the late seventeenth century through the "golden era" of whaling (1820–1845). Nantucket, an island located thirty miles southeast of Cape Cod, was first settled in the 1660s by whites, most of whom had migrated from the Merrimack Valley. The island's sandy soil forced the first settlers to rely on sheep grazing as their primary economic activity, but by the beginning of the eighteenth century shore whaling had become a major economic pursuit.[3]

---

2 Robert V. Wells, "Family History and Demographic Transition," *Journal of Social History*, IX (1975), 1–19; Nancy Osterud and John Fulton, "Family Limitation and Age of Marriage: Fertility Decline in Sturbridge, Massachusetts, 1730–1850," *Population Studies*, XXX (1976), 481–494; Alan Sweezy, "The Economic Explanation of Fertility Changes in the United States," *Population Studies*, XXV (1971), 255–267; William B. Clifford, Jr., "Modern and Traditional Value Orientations and Fertility Behavior: A Social Demographic Study," *Demography*, VIII (1971), 37–48; Maris A. Vinovskis, "Recent Trends in American Historical Demography: Some Methodological and Conceptual Considerations," *Annual Reviews in Sociology*, IV (1978), 603–627.

3 The general outline of Nantucket's history which follows is based on research still in progress. See also, Alexander Starbuck, *A History of the American Whale Fishery* (New York, 1878); Obed Macy, *The History of Nantucket* (Boston, 1835).

It was, however, the advent of deep-sea whaling that brought commercial prosperity to Nantucket. By the 1720s whaling and its subsidiary activities (outfitting, coopering, boat building, etc.) dominated the island's economy. The present town site around Nantucket harbor, with its large area of protected anchorage and ample space for wharves, warehouses, and homes, was also established by the inhabitants in the 1720s. Total population figures are scarce but it is clear that commercial development was accompanied by population growth: in 1700, the white population was estimated at 300; by the time the Revolution erupted, it had reached 4,525. By the 1840s, nearly 10,000 people lived in Nantucket, and it had become the third largest port in Massachusetts.

Changes in the religious life of the inhabitants accompanied the commercialization of Nantucket in the early decades of the eighteenth century. The original settlers brought a variety of religious preferences to the island, but no formal, community-wide religious observance was held until the first decade of the eighteenth century. Following visits by Quaker missionaries, the Nantucketers formally established their first monthly meeting in 1708. During most of the next century, Quakers dominated the religious and much of the cultural life of the island.

In the decades before the Revolution, Nantucket became the most important whaling center in the world. Its independence from other New England commercial centers was assured in the 1740s when the whaling merchants initiated direct trade with London. Its dominance of American whale fishery was clear by the early 1770s when its fleet accounted for 54 percent of the tonnage and 70 percent of the colonial catch. The Revolution, however, brought economic disaster and political isolation to Nantucket. Tory sympathies among the wealthy merchants, dependence on the London market, the island's isolation and vulnerable position, and Quaker pacifism all pushed the Nantucketers into proclamations of neutrality. These proclamations were ignored as both American and British warships and privateers destroyed about 90 percent of the whaling fleet and reduced the population to near starvation.

A partial recovery in the 1790s was aided by the discovery of new whaling grounds, but it was soon reversed by Thomas Jefferson's embargo and the War of 1812, when once again the Nantucket fleet was largely destroyed. Following the war the fleet was quickly rebuilt, and the 1820s and 1830s were years of unprecedented affluence. But Nantucket entered a period of long-term decline shortly thereafter. The sand bar at the entrance to Nantucket harbor prevented the accommodation of the larger whaling ships of the mid-century and resulted in the movement of industry to better equipped ports such as New Bedford. The social and economic history of Nantucket over this 160-year period was characterized by an expanding, but fluctuating commercial economy; periods of political and military isolation; and a dominant, but variable Quaker religion.

This family reconstitution study is based on data drawn primarily from Nantucket's vital records. Approximately 6,000 marriages were recorded between 1680 and 1840, but out-migrations and underregistration of births and deaths reduced the total number of families that could be reconstituted to 1,873. The large number of families involved dictated the use of a computer.[4]

The 1,873 families were divided into two subsets. The first is a set of 1,013 incomplete families from which marriage data only were taken. The second set is made up of 860 complete families. The criteria for determining a complete family were: (1) the date of birth of the female was known; (2) it was a first marriage for the female; (3) the date of marriage or intention to marry was known; (4) the dates of birth of all children were known and there was no indication that any of the births occurred off the island; and (5) the marriage union remained intact until the wife had reached the age of forty-five (thus, the date of the end of the union had to be known). To be included as an incomplete family, only the date of the wife's birth and date of marriage were required.

All reconstitution studies raise the question of representativeness, and this examination of Nantucket is no exception. The complete families, in particular, are very likely to exclude those who migrated and/or were poor. Of special significance to this study was the extraordinary mobility of at least some of those families engaged in the whaling industry. At different times in its

---

4 FORTRAN was used for the input of data and the date conversions. SPSS was used for the demographic manipulations. This project owes much to the time, energy, and knowledge of Mathew Shuchman. Among many other things, he was responsible for the initial programming.

history, increasing competition and economic downturns drove numerous families from Nantucket. In addition, many Nantucket whalers manned the ships of European fleets, particularly those of England. When the inevitably large number of itinerant seamen are also considered, the problem of migration becomes even more evident. Until probate and tax records are linked to the reconstituted families, their representativeness cannot be known. The primary concern of this study, however, is with the relationship between the community's social and commercial development and the inhabitants' fertility behavior. The fact that these families lived out their reproductive lives on the island is, therefore, relevant.[5]

The trend which is immediately apparent in the fertility behavior of the complete families is the substantial decline in the number of children ever born over the 160-year period. Table 1 reveals a

Table 1   Mean Number of Children Ever Born (Complete Families)

COHORT	CHILDREN EVER BORN	STANDARD DEVIATION	N
1680–1709	6.83	3.37	12
1710–1719	6.75	3.55	12
1720–1729	8.05	3.33	19
1730–1739	7.03	4.29	28
1740–1749	5.82	3.83	34
1750–1759	5.67	3.78	58
1760–1769	5.80	4.26	60
1770–1779	5.77	3.85	61
1780–1789	4.80	3.46	108
1790–1799	4.19	3.30	100
1800–1809	4.20	3.60	90
1810–1819	3.96	3.20	79
1820–1829	3.80	3.26	78
1830–1839	3.45	2.66	121
1680–1739	7.23	3.76	71
1740–1779	5.75	3.95	213
1780–1839	4.07	3.26	576

5   George Rodgers Taylor, "Currents of Migration on Nantucket, 1760–1780," *Historic Nantucket,* XXII (1974), 14–20.

drop from a high of about 8 children for the 1720–1729 marriage cohort to a low of 3.45 for the 1830–1839 cohort—a decrease of just over 4.5 children. This decline was not a steady one. There were two distinct turning points: fluctuating prior to 1740, the number of children per family dropped substantially during the 1740s (26 percent of the total decline); following a period of stability, the decline resumed in the 1780s with the largest proportion (35 percent of the total decline) occurring between 1780 and 1800.

The changing distribution of complete family size indicates a similar pattern. The percentage of complete families having less than five children more than doubled between the periods 1680–1739 and 1780–1839. The proportion of large families with ten or more children declined in a similar manner. This pattern is illustrated in Figure 1. Both the decline and distribution of children ever born point to a very early shift in the fertility behavior of Nantucket's most permanent families.[6]

Fig. 1 Distribution of Children Ever Born (Complete Families)

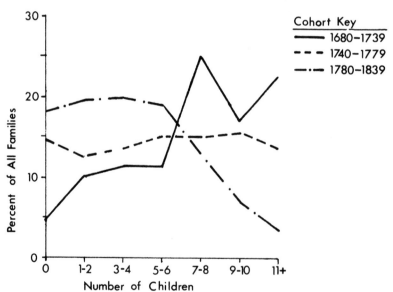

6 Much of the change in both complete family size and its distribution is attributable to the tremendous increase in the number of childless complete families. The increase was so large as to throw into question the reliability of the sources and the findings. As a result, most of the demographic indicators were run without the childless families. Although the values were greater, the same basic patterns were found.

Table 2 Age at First Marriage for Females
(Complete Families)

COHORT	MEAN	MEDIAN	N
1680–1709	19.34	19.50	12
1710–1719	20.24	19.34	12
1720–1729	20.50	19.16	19
1730–1739	19.33	18.20	28
1740–1749	20.84	19.91	34
1750–1759	21.48	20.14	58
1760–1769	22.70	20.77	60
1770–1779	21.52	19.40	61
1780–1789	24.24	22.29	108
1790–1799	24.05	22.25	100
1800–1809	25.34	22.29	90
1810–1819	25.06	22.70	79
1820–1829	23.12	21.66	78
1830–1839	22.71	21.14	121
1680–1739	20.10	19.00	71
1740–1779	21.73	21.10	213
1780–1839	24.02	21.92	576

The first place to look for an explanation of this early decline is the mean age of women at first marriage. It is apparent from Table 2 that the age at marriage for women of complete families did increase over the period of the study. From a low of 19.3 in the 1680–1709 cohort, the mean rose to a high of 25.3 for the 1800–1809 cohort. As expected, the pattern of change parallels that of the decrease in mean number of children ever born. Again, there was some instability as the mean age at marriage fluctuated prior to 1740, increased steadily after 1740, but surprisingly dropped two years between 1820 and 1839. The most substantial increases in female age at first marriage occurred at the same times as the most substantial decreases in mean number of children. When both complete and incomplete families are included, the same pattern, although weaker, appears (Table 3). That the patterns are very similar is apparent from Figure 2.

The mean age at first marriage for males presents a different pattern (Table 3). Prior to 1740, Nantucket men first married at an average age of about 24; between 1740 and 1780 the mean dropped a year; after 1780 it rose steadily until it reached 25.6. The decline during the middle decades of the eighteenth century

Table 3   Age at First Marriage for Males and Females (All Families)

COHORT	MALES			FEMALES		
	MEAN	MEDIAN	N	MEAN	MEDIAN	N
1680–1709	23.84	22.92	10	20.11	19.66	17
1710–1719	23.34	22.95	8	21.57	18.95	18
1720–1729	23.99	22.25	25	20.02	19.16	33
1730–1739	24.56	21.83	24	19.28	18.14	39
1740–1749	22.59	22.08	51	20.04	19.23	67
1750–1759	22.75	22.29	68	20.58	19.54	96
1760–1769	22.99	22.54	82	21.74	20.06	104
1770–1779	23.65	22.89	81	20.50	19.40	114
1780–1789	24.53	23.29	145	23.09	21.77	173
1790–1799	24.84	23.20	162	22.86	21.37	199
1800–1809	24.57	23.20	158	22.80	20.54	206
1810–1819	24.98	23.70	154	23.30	21.11	187
1820–1829	25.34	24.25	133	21.91	20.95	160
1830–1839	25.56	24.72	199	22.30	21.14	236
1680–1739	24.09	22.27	67	20.03	19.08	107
1740–1779	23.05	22.37	282	20.87	19.59	381
1780–1839	24.99	23.79	948	22.62	21.15	1161

may be a reflection of rising prosperity, when opportunities for early careers were plentiful and whaling voyages were short (six to nine months, as compared to two to four years in the nineteenth century), allowing for a faster climb up the occupational ladder. The early career opportunities offered by a commercial whaling center were also partially responsible for the significantly younger age at which Nantucket men first married as compared with their rural counterparts. In Sturbridge, Massachusetts, for example, male mean age at first marriage rose from about twenty-five (1730–1759 marriage cohort) to just under twenty-nine (1840–1859 cohort).[7]

That whaling practices had an impact on family behavior in eighteenth-century Nantucket is also indicated by the data on seasonality of marriage and conceptions presented in Table 4. By the 1770s whaling cruises started in March or April, headed north between May and July, and returned to port by September or October. Thus, the majority of marriages and conceptions before

7 Osterud and Fulton, "Family Limitation," 485.

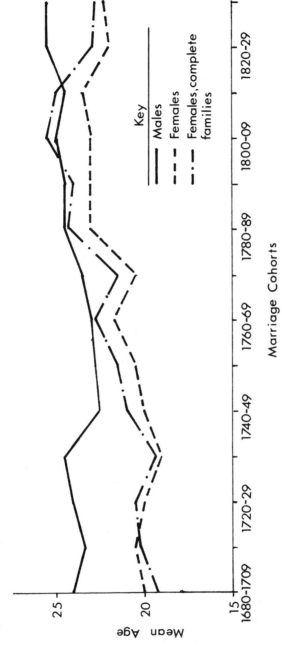

Fig. 2 Mean Age at First Marriage, Males and Females

Table 4 Seasonality of Marriage and Conception (All Families)

MONTH	BEFORE 1780				1780 AND AFTER			
	MARRIAGE		CONCEPTION		MARRIAGE		CONCEPTION	
	INDEX[a]	N	INDEX	N	INDEX	N	INDEX	N
1	173	78	129	212	100	111	101	175
2	129	58	104	170	89	99	90	154
3	78	35	98	161	83	92	101	176
4	40	18	93	152	94	104	94	164
5	42	19	63	104	105	116	88	153
6	40	18	92	151	105	117	102	177
7	56	25	86	141	109	121	94	163
8	69	31	77	127	98	109	124	216
9	84	38	98	160	91	101	129	225
10	176	79	106	174	110	122	94	163
11	147	66	122	200	113	125	96	167
12	164	74	130	214	105	117	91	158

a The indexes were created by dividing the total number of marriages (or conceptions) in each period by 12 (the months) and then dividing that number into the number of marriages per month. Thus, if the marriages (or conceptions) were equally distributed the index would be 100 for each month.

1780 occurred during the winter months of October through February—the off season for whalers. By the 1790s whaling had become a year-round practice, with voyages lasting at least a year. Marriage and conception dates in the late eighteenth and nineteenth centuries reflect these changes by being distributed relatively evenly throughout the year.

For Nantucket, as for other pre-contraceptive populations, change in the mean age of women at first marriage is a powerful factor for explaining changes in mean complete family size. Over the entire 160-year period, the increase in female age at first marriage accounts for just under 40 percent of the decline in mean number of children ever born, assuming a two-year birth interval. However, its impact varied over time. Looking at the shifts between the three major periods will make this clear. Between the periods 1680–1739 and 1740–1779 the rise in female age at first marriage accounted for 55 percent of the decrease in complete family size. The rise in female marriage age between the periods 1740–1779 and 1780–1839 accounted for 68 percent of the decline in mean number of children during the same period. But in the first four decades of the nineteenth century, when mean family size fell by almost a child, female age at first marriage was also falling, thus creating the potential for more children per family.

Clearly, some other factor must have been at work to create this downward shift in mean family size. That this was the case is indicated in Table 5, which lists the age-specific marital fertility rates. Although the decrease in marital fertility was not consistent in all decades and in all age groups, a decline is nonetheless evident after 1740. This decline is especially evident when the rates are collapsed into the three major periods and then indexed by level (Fig. 3). Thus decrease in complete family size that remains unexplained by the increase in female mean age at first marriage is accounted for by this decline in marital fertility.

It is necessary, then, to investigate the possibility that Nantucket families after 1740 were voluntarily practicing some

Table 5 Age-specific Marital Fertility Rates (Complete Families)

COHORT	AGE GROUPS						
	15–19	20–24	25–29	30–34	35–39	40–44	45–49
1680–1709	(0.357)[a]	(0.426)	(0.266)	(0.316)	(0.233)	(0.083)	(0)
1710–1719	(0.220)	(0.358)	(0.371)	(0.363)	(0.309)	(0.145)	(0)
1720–1729	(0.402)	(0.414)	(0.384)	(0.352)	(0.305)	(0.126)	(0.010)
1730–1739	(0.290)	0.375	0.326	0.230	0.272	0.136	0.014
1740–1749	(0.233)	0.382	0.297	0.234	0.177	0.141	0.012
1750–1759	(0.310)	0.335	0.287	0.291	0.173	0.117	0.007
1760–1769	(0.514)	0.376	0.333	0.243	0.242	0.093	0.017
1770–1779	(0.410)	0.352	0.252	0.256	0.211	0.113	0.007
1780–1789	(0.445)	0.368	0.263	0.246	0.196	0.106	0.011
1790–1799	(0.221)	0.276	0.252	0.223	0.191	0.069	0.008
1800–1809	(0.339)	0.326	0.297	0.224	0.206	0.054	0.007
1810–1819	(0.370)	0.264	0.275	0.219	0.211	0.043	0.003
1820–1829	(0.297)	0.209	0.215	0.201	0.169	0.062	0
1830–1839	(0.280)	0.237	0.210	0.204	0.102	0.029	0.002
1680–1739	0.314	0.393	0.337	0.299	0.280	0.126	0.009
1740–1779	0.367	0.358	0.291	0.259	0.203	0.113	0.010
1780–1839	0.320	0.280	0.249	0.220	0.174	0.060	0.005
"Natural fertility"[b]	—	0.435	0.407	0.371	0.298	0.152	0.022

a   All cohort rates based on less than 100 married woman-years have been enclosed in parentheses.
b   The natural fertility rates are taken from Louis Henry, "Some Data on Natural Fertility," *Eugenics Quarterly,* VIII (1961), 81–91.

Fig. 3 Age-specific Marital Fertility Rates Indexed by Level of 20–24 Rate for the 1680–1739 Cohort (Equivalent to 100), for Complete Families

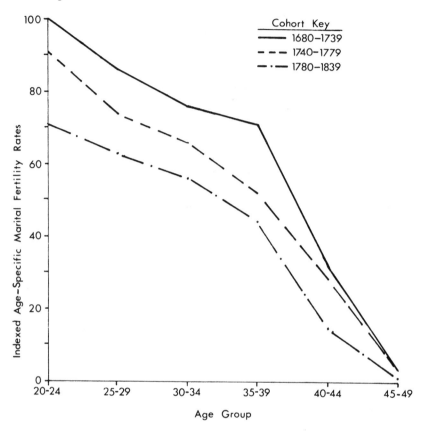

method of birth control. However, birth control is not necessarily family limitation. Knodel has recently reemphasized the distinction between the two terms: "Only parity-dependent fertility control is appropriately considered family limitation, since it alone is directed at stopping childbearing at some given number of children." The assumption underlying this definition of family limitation (or parity-dependent fertility control) is that couples will alter their reproductive behavior by terminating their childbearing once they have reached a target family size.[8]

8 John Knodel, "Family Limitation and the Fertility Transition: Evidence From the Age Patterns of Fertility in Europe and Asia," *Population Studies*, XXXI (1977), 241; see also Knodel's discussion of parity in "From Natural Fertility to Family Limitation: The Onset of Fertility Transition in a Sample of German Villages," *Demography*, XVI (1979), 493–521.

The distinction between parity-dependent and parity-independent fertility control (breast-feeding, abstinence associated with lactation, and spacing) has important implications for the age pattern of childbearing. Most married couples who wish to limit the number of their children concentrate childbearing in the early years of the fertile period. Consequently, marital fertility rates at older ages are particularly low in populations practicing family limitation when compared with populations characterized by natural fertility (fertility in the absence of family limitation). This assumption is so strong that age serves as a proxy for parity in most studies of historical demography.

A number of tests can indicate the age pattern of childbearing. For instance, the average age of mothers at last birth would be expected to decline if family limitation were being practiced. From Table 6 it can be seen that the mean ages of mothers at last birth fell from a high of 38.6 to a low of 32.7 over the entire period of the study—a decline of 5.9 years. Paralleling the decline in complete family size, a shift in the mean age of mothers at last birth occurred with the 1740–1749 cohort. About 36 percent of the decrease took place during that decade. Unlike the changes in

Table 6 Age of Mother at Last Birth (Complete Families)

COHORT	MEAN	MEDIAN	N
1680–1709	35.38	39.16	12
1710–1719	36.68	36.41	12
1720–1729	38.57	39.33	19
1730–1739	37.35	39.00	28
1740–1749	35.59	37.16	34
1750–1759	35.83	37.49	58
1760–1769	35.59	38.58	60
1770–1779	36.29	38.91	61
1780–1789	36.73	38.16	108
1790–1799	36.05	37.74	100
1800–1809	35.98	38.07	90
1810–1819	35.14	37.25	79
1820–1829	34.56	35.75	78
1830–1839	32.70	32.70	121
1680–1739	37.23	39.07	71
1740–1779	35.86	38.66	213
1780–1839	35.13	36.66	576

family size, however, age of mothers at last birth did not significantly decline again until after 1820.[9]

Given the assumption underlying the concept of family limitation, the decline in age of mothers at last birth should be even more evident among women who married young and bore several children well before the end of their fertile period. Table 7 lists the ages at last birth of women who married before and after age thirty. Among these women who married at age thirty or younger the same basic pattern is evident, although the second decline in the mean age at last birth is apparent by 1800 rather than by 1820. For those married after age thirty, the mean increases over time. Figure 4 reveals that the distribution of the age of mothers at last birth gradually shifted downward as the decades passed. Therefore, the data indicate that family limitation began to be practiced on Nantucket by the 1740s—decades earlier than in other New England communities.[10]

Another test of family limitation was provided by Henry, who calculated average age-specific marital fertility rates for pop-

Table 7 Age of Mother at Last Birth, Grouped by Age at Marriage (Complete Families)

COHORT[a]	MARRIED BY AGE 30			MARRIED AFTER AGE 30		
	MEAN	MEDIAN	N	MEAN	MEDIAN	N
1680–1719	36.03	39.04	24	—	—	0
1720–1739	37.92	39.33	44	37.11	37.83	3
1740–1759	35.71	37.49	86	36.25	33.59	6
1760–1779	35.30	38.58	108	41.22	42.27	13
1780–1799	35.67	37.41	185	42.27	43.16	23
1800–1819	34.11	36.08	138	41.94	40.62	31
1820–1839	32.66	33.32	185	42.85	39.90	15

a Cohorts have been collapsed because of the small number of cases.

9 The values for mean age at last birth are low when compared to those found in other communities. This is, in part, because only first marriages were used in calculating the Nantucket values. Women marrying for a second time and likely to give birth later in their lives have been excluded.

10 Because the medians for female age at first marriage were relatively low, the same test was also run using age 25 as the cut-off point. The same patterns were found. Since 30 is the age most commonly used, it was also used here for comparative purposes.

Fig. 4 Distribution of Age of Mother at Last Birth (Complete Families)

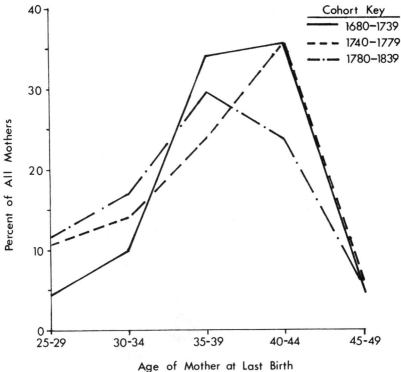

Age of Mother at Last Birth

ulations characterized by natural fertility. Table 8 compares these natural fertility rates with the Nantucket rates. The indexed ratios from the 1680–1739 period reveal that Nantucket's fertility curve is generally the same shape as the natural fertility curve. The indexed ratios for the period 1740–1779 are distinctive in the early age groups, but very similar in the age group 40–44. The last period's (1780–1839) similarity to the natural fertility curve through the age group 35–39 is due to the very low fertility rate for the 20–24 cohort, thus preventing significant decreases in the older groups. The expected divergence still appears, however, in the 40–44 age group.[11]

Another method of comparison is to index the rates so that the shape rather than the level of the fertility curves is emphasized.

11 Louis Henry, "Some Data on Natural Fertility," *Eugenics Quarterly*, VIII (1961), 81–91.

Table 8 Comparison of Nantucket Fertility Rates with Natural Fertility Rates (Complete Families)

	COHORT	AGE GROUP					
		20–24	25–29	30–34	35–39	40–44	45–49
Indexing	1680–1739	100	86	76	71	32	3
by shape[a]	1740–1779	100	81	72	57	32	3
	1780–1839	100	89	79	62	21	2
	Natural fertility	100	94	85	69	34	5
By ratio	1680–1739	100	92	90	104	92	46
and shape[b]	1740–1779	100	87	85	83	90	67
	1780–1839	100	95	92	91	61	36
	Natural fertility	100	100	100	100	100	100

a   20–24 rate for each cohort equivalent to 100.
b   The Nantucket rates were first expressed as a ratio of the natural fertility rates for each age group and these ratios have then been indexed again to the 20–24 ratio, per cohort. Thus, if a curve had exactly the same shape as the natural fertility curve, its indexed ratio would be 100 in all age groups.

Figure 5 demonstrates this graphically. Again, the dissimilarity of the 1740–1779 curve to the natural fertility curve between the ages of twenty-five and thirty-nine, and the similarity in the older ages, is apparent. In other words, the expected disproportionate drop-off in the fertility rates at the older ages did not occur. The 1780–1839 curve is, however, concave rather than convex at the older ages, exactly as it should be when family limitation is being practiced.

Although the data denoting age of mothers at last birth point to deliberate family limitation on Nantucket as early as the 1740s, indications from the shape of the fertility curve are less than clear-cut for the period 1740–1779. Examination of birth intervals sheds light on the fertility behavior of Nantucketers during this time (Table 9). The most striking feature is the marked increase in the interval between the penultimate and last birth. This increase begins, unlike the other indicators, with the 1720–1739 marriage cohort. Although an increase in this interval is expected when a community is beginning to practice family limitation, it should have declined in the later cohorts as families made an effort to contain childbearing within the shortest possible time span. The failure of the Nantucket mean to decrease may be explained by

Fig. 5 Age-specific Marital Fertility Rates, Indexed by Shape, where the 20–24 Rate for Each Cohort is Equivalent to 100 (Complete Families)

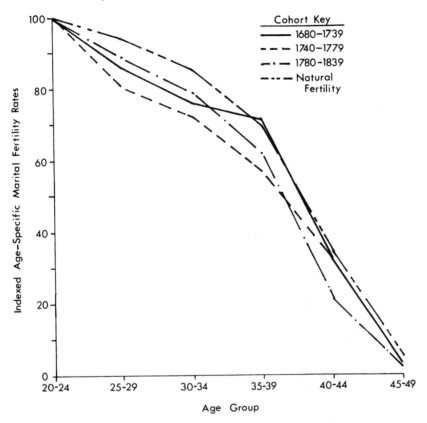

Table 9 Mean Birth Intervals by Month (Complete Families)

COHORT[a]	BIRTH INTERVALS				
	1–2	2–3	3–4	4–5	PENULTIMATE-LAST
1680–1719	21.6	29.4	31.8	23.2	25.0
1720–1739	32.8	35.0	28.7	28.2	35.0
1740–1759	37.2	33.4	33.6	31.2	41.4
1760–1779	31.2	30.6	30.4	32.6	36.1
1780–1799	37.3	39.1	37.4	36.1	40.7
1800–1819	35.9	35.8	31.0	38.5	41.5
1820–1839	44.5	39.8	33.8	32.0	46.6

a Cohorts have been collapsed in order to remove fluctuations.

looking at the other intervals. Given the assumption of family limitation (that childbearing is contained in the early years), it would be expected that early family formation would not be affected by fertility control. It is, then, surprising to find an increase in the average length of these early intervals. The continued increase in the mean of these intervals and the last interval, as well as the shape of the 1740–1779 fertility curve, reflect, in part, the peculiarities of a whaling community, where many of the men spent ever greater amounts of time on longer and longer voyages. It was impossible for many of Nantucket's families to concentrate their childbearing in the earliest years of marriage.

The character of the 1740–1779 period can also be explained by examining the variance and distribution of the mean number of children ever born. Temkin-Greener and Swedlund, in a recent study of the Connecticut Valley, have argued that a "decline in variance of completed family size is probably characteristic of a growing acceptance of some form of family limitation." A reexamination of Table 1 shows that between the 1730s and the 1770s the standard deviation was significantly higher than it had been in previous decades. The increase in the variance of complete family size in these middle decades is an indication that family limitation was at least beginning to be accepted. This observation is strengthened by examining the distribution of complete family size (Fig. 6). The bimodality of the distribution for the 1740–1779 period (and hence the increase in variance) reflects the growing, but not complete acceptance of conscious fertility control. The subsequent decline of variance, beginning with the 1780–1789 cohort, is characteristic of the increasing diffusion of some form of family limitation.[12]

The evidence shows that the decline in fertility after 1740 resulted from the combined impact of rising age at first marriage for women and conscious efforts to limit family size. The transition to family limitation on Nantucket was not, however, an abrupt one. Rather, it was a sequence that involved the gradual diffusion and acceptance of family limitation practices. The first signs of conscious fertility control appear as early as the 1730s and are clearly evident by the 1740s, when an increase in variance and

12 Temkin-Greener and Swedlund, "Fertility Transition," 39.

Fig. 6 Distribution of Mean Complete Family Size

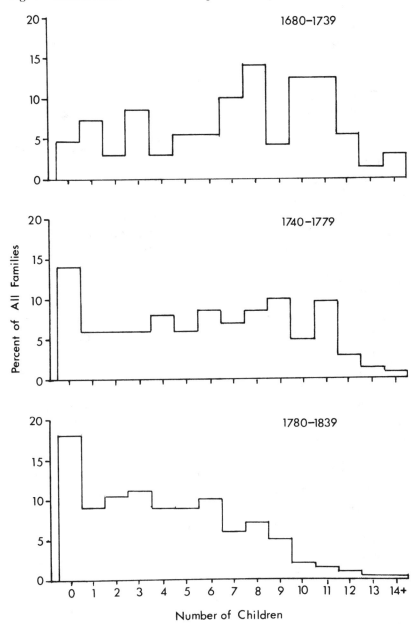

range of family size indicate that some families were attempting to limit the number of their children. Between the 1740s and 1770s there was a growing acceptance of family limitation, as evidenced by the substantial increase in the interval between the penultimate and last birth. In addition, mean complete family size decreased, but the increase in its variance and range of distribution reveals that family limitation had not been fully accepted. The final phase of the transition occurred between the 1770s and 1790s. The marked decline in complete family size and its decreasing variance demonstrate community-wide acceptance of voluntary fertility control.[13]

The greatest dissimilarity between Nantucket's demographic patterns and those of previous studies of early America is in the dating of the fertility decline. The studies of the northern rural mainland generally date the decline in marital fertility somewhere between the last decades of the eighteenth century and the first decades of the nineteenth century. In addition, the absolute values of both marital fertility and the age of mothers at last birth are, in most cases, significantly lower on Nantucket than in these rural areas. Although there was no significant difference in the age at which women first married, there was an atypical decline in age at marriage among Nantucket women in the last decades of the study. Finally, Nantucket men tended to marry at an earlier age than their rural counterparts.

These differences between Nantucket and rural America may represent a general urban-rural fertility differential. Although urban-rural fertility differentials have been observed in most societies, including nineteenth-century America, how long-standing such differentials were remains an open question in the absence of more data. More important, the interpretation and meaning of the differentials have been hotly contested. The contention that urban-rural fertility differentials "are more likely to be determined by the socioeconomic characteristics of an area than by their population size will be elaborated below.[14]

---

13 This chronological model of fertility transition is similar, except in its timing, to the one developed by Temkin-Greener and Swedlund in their study of the Connecticut Valley.
14 Tamara K. Hareven and Vinovskis, "Patterns of Childbearing in Late Nineteenth-Century America: The Determinants of Marital Fertility in Five Massachusetts Towns in 1880," in idem (eds.), *Family and Population in Nineteenth-Century America* (Princeton, 1978), 121. See also Carl Mosk, "Rural-Urban Fertility Differences and the Fertility Transition,"

Some involuntary factors certainly played a role in Nantucket's fertility transition. The mean age of marriage for women increased throughout most of the study, and seasonal migration or work patterns may have affected fertility rates. Such factors as nutrition, weaning practices, and infant mortality, however, did not change significantly in ways that would have led to lower fertility. Since involuntary factors cannot explain the total decline in fertility, some conscious effort at family limitation must have been made by Nantucket families.[15]

The possibility of voluntary fertility control raises the question of what incentives existed for the practice. Although the topic is far too complex to be treated in detail here and research is still in progress, a few tentative observations can be made. First, a number of scholars have pointed out that the shift from premodern to modern levels of fertility involves a fundamental change in the circumstances determining fertility behavior. Premodern fertility is not controlled in the contemporary sense of the word. Rather it is "regulated" by a variety of social and biological circumstances. The shift to modern fertility behavior

---

Population Studies, XXXIV (1980), 77–89; Vinovskis, "Socioeconomic Determinants of Interstate Fertility Differentials in the United States in 1850 and 1860," *Journal of Interdisciplinary History*, VI (1976), 375–396; Easterlin, "Does Human Fertility Adjust to the Environment?" *American Economic Review*, LXI (1971), 399–407.

15 There is some evidence from Europe that seasonal migrations had an effect on fertility by lowering birth rates through changes in the conception rate. Although the effects of whaling's seasonal work patterns could not be isolated at this point in the research, it is possible that they may have had a similar impact on birth rates in Nantucket, especially in the mid-eighteenth century when Nantucket was fulfilling most of its own labor demands. See Francine van de Walle, "Migration and Fertility in Ticino," *Population Studies*, XXIX (1975), 447–462; Jane Menken, "Seasonal Migrations and Seasonal Variation in Fecundability: Effects on Birth Rates and Birth Intervals," *Demography*, XVI (1979), 103–119. There is an additional factor peculiar to Nantucket that may have lowered fertility. Nantucket's isolation and Quaker marriage restrictions seem to have resulted in a high incidence of consanguineous marriages. Although it is difficult to assess the importance of this fact until efforts at record linkage and surname analysis have been completed, it is unlikely that inbreeding accounted for the total decline in family size. First, there were only sixty years between the beginning of inbreeding and the onset of the fertility decline, probably too short a time for any physiological effects to have occurred. Second, it is not certain that inbreeding lowers fertility: see Pierre Philippe, "Amenorrhea, Intra-uterine Mortality and Parental Consanguinity in an Isolated French Canadian Population," *Human Biology*, XLVI (1974), 405–424; idem, "Genetics of Fecundity: A Demographic Approach," *Human Biology*, XLIX (1977), 11–18; Russell M. Reid, "Effects of Consanguineous Marriage and In-breeding on Couple Fertility and Offspring Mortality in Rural Sri Lanka," *Human Biology*, XLVIII (1976), 139–146.

reflects, in part, a fundamental change in the mechanisms determining fertility. Increasingly, childbearing became a matter of free decision by the couple.[16]

What brought about this change in the nature of fertility behavior—a change from a situation where childbearing was taken for granted to a situation where individual households faced problems of choice about limiting family size? On Nantucket, the increasing absorption of families into the commercial economy provided a basis for a new orientation toward family life and economic activity. Problem solving and optimism replaced fatalism, improvisation, and passivity in many areas of life. The family economy and childbearing became matters of conscious awareness and planning. Although such attitudes had, to some degree, existed long before the eighteenth century, the spread of a commercial economy and the accompanying prosperity provided the foundation upon which these attitudes could flourish and eventually prevail. But to say that families consciously planned childbearing does not mean that they always decided in favor of limiting the number of their children. Other factors must have operated on Nantucket to induce a fertility decline. Although the ways in which social and economic factors interacted to produce smaller families are difficult to trace, it is possible to indicate some probable connections.

A scarcity of critical resources—the explanation offered for New England's rural communities—was not a factor in the initial decline of fertility on Nantucket. Population density, however, did increase, particularly in the town itself. In fact, Nantucket was crowded from the beginning. The existence of 1,500 Indians on 45 square miles of island at the time of white settlement created a population density which Massachusetts did not reach until the 1760s. But the rising density and concomitant decrease in the availability of land was not associated with declining economic opportunity. The emergence of Nantucket as a commercial center and the corresponding prosperity in the first half of the eighteenth

16   The discussion of voluntary fertility was influenced by the analytic framework offered by Easterlin, "The Economics and Sociology of Fertility: A Synthesis," in Charles Tilly (ed.), *Historical Studies of Changing Fertility* (Princeton, 1978), 57–133. See also Jean Bourgeois-Pichat, "Social and Biological Determinants of Human Fertility in Non-Industrial Societies," *Proceedings of the American Philosophical Society,* III (1967), 160–163; E. Anthony Wrigley, *Population and History* (New York, 1969).

century provided ample opportunities for parents to bequeath to their children the same opportunities and socioeconomic status that they had themselves enjoyed.[17]

The commercialization and accompanying urbanization of Nantucket created a new set of circumstances that worked to change attitudes so that fewer children were wanted, and also raised the relative cost of rearing those children. Available evidence from recent studies indicates that the relative costs of childbearing are generally greater in urban than in rural areas. On Nantucket, the necessity of importing most of the staples of life would have raised those costs even higher. In addition, the opportunities for paid child labor outside the home were minimal, limiting a child's potential for contributing to family income.[18]

More important were new conditions affecting the role of women. In order to provide for and maintain their families during the absence of their husbands, many eighteenth-century Nantucket women went beyond traditional female activities to manage family and business finances and engage independently in some line of trade. This "petticoat aristocracy," as it was often called, dominated much of the dry-goods trade. Writing in 1826, Eliza Barney, a Nantucket resident, commented:

> fifty years ago all the dry-goods and groceries were kept by women who went to Boston semi-annually to renew their stock. . . . Since that time I can recall nearly 70 women who have successfully engaged in commerce, brought up and educated large families and retired with competence.[19]

Nantucket families may have decided to curtail childbearing because women had other, more financially rewarding activities to occupy their time. Equally important, increased responsibilities and work opportunities created by commercial whaling may have influenced fertility by facilitating the emergence of modern conceptions of the role of women in society and by fostering egalitarian decision making in the family. It is possible that increased opportunities, familial responsibilities, and, most important, the

17 Evarts B. Green, *American Population Before the Federal Census of 1790* (New York, 1932), 17.
18 Easterlin, "Economics and Sociology," 66–67, 113.
19 Quoted in Caroline Dall, *The College, the Market and the Court* (New York, 1972), 197–198.

nature of the work (i.e., work that expanded social contacts, increased financial independence, and removed women from traditional surroundings) changed women's attitudes toward themselves so that they sought greater influence and equality within their families. The island's later history supports this contention. Nantucket was a stronghold of feminism in the nineteenth century and the home of a disproportionately large number of independently prominent women.[20]

Eighteenth-century Quakerism would surely have reinforced these trends. Not only did male Quakers consider women their spiritual equals, but Quaker women played a prominent role in the church by speaking at meetings, writing tracts, and taking up missionary activities. Like other Quakers, Nantucket women established and ran a relatively independent monthly meeting. Finally, Quaker ideology may have strengthened existing desires for fewer children through its assumption of childhood innocence. Quakers believed that neither sin nor grace were conveyed by heredity, but that upon coming of age, a child became susceptible to sin and depravity. This belief in childhood innocence implies a certain amount of malleability—that a child can be taught to remain open to God's grace and to resist the world's evils. The new orientation toward family life that accompanied commercialization may have reinforced this traditional Quaker belief. As a result, parents may have been encouraged to play a more active role in shaping their children's future. To ensure their children's success in both the material and spiritual arenas, parents on Nantucket may have decided that more time for each child was needed and so limited the size of their families.[21]

---

20 J. Hector St. John de Crevecoeur, *Letters From an American Farmer* (New York, 1957), 141–145; Joseph Sansom, *Essays on Nantucket* (Philadelphia, 1811). See also comments by Lucretia Mott on her childhood on Nantucket in the *Proceedings* of Women's Rights Convention (1854). For a similar argument, see Bernard C. Rosen and Alan B. Simmons, "Industrialization, Family and Fertility: A Structural-Psychological Analysis of the Brazilian Case," *Demography*, VIII (1971), 63–87.

21 Crevecoeur, *Letters*, 108–111; J. William Frost, *The Quaker Family in Colonial America* (New York, 1973); Walter J. Homan, *Children and Quakerism* (Berkeley, 1939); Barry Levy, "'Tender Plants': Quaker Farmers and Children in the Delaware Valley, 1681–1735," *Journal of Family History*, III (1978), 116–135; Wells, "Family Size and Fertility Control in Eighteenth-Century America: A Study of Quaker Families," *Population Studies*, XXV (1971), 73–82; Mary Maples Dunn, "Women of Light," in Carol Ruth Berkin and Mary Beth Norton (eds.), *Women of America: A History* (Boston, 1979), 115–136.

Maris A. Vinovskis

Socioeconomic Determinants of
Interstate Fertility Differentials
in the United States in 1850 and 1860

Recent efforts to explain fertility patterns in America in the first half of the nineteenth century have focused on the possible effects of land scarcity and urbanization. The conclusion of most economic historians who have analyzed fertility during that period is that the relative availability of farm land rather than urban or industrial development accounted for fertility differentials and trends.

The major work on fertility in the first half of the nineteenth century is Yasuba's analysis of the fertility ratios of the white population of the United States between 1800 and 1860. He argued that the steadily decreasing supply of farm land is the best explanation of the differentials and trends in the white fertility ratios—particularly in the period before 1830.[1] Recent work has challenged many of Yasuba's points. For example, his work has been criticized for its use of state rather than county or township data; its reliance on rank correlation techniques of analysis rather than the multiple regression procedures which would have permitted him to examine simultaneously the effects of several variables on fertility, and its use of cropland in 1949 as an index of land availability in the nineteenth century.[2] However, most

Maris A. Vinovskis is Assistant Professor of History and Faculty Associate in the Center for Political Studies of the Institute for Social Research at the University of Michigan. This article was written while the author was the Rockefeller Fellow in the History of the Family Project at the American Antiquarian Society and Clark University.

The author would like to thank Allan Bogue, Richard Easterlin, Tamara Haraven, Don Leets, Peter Lindert, R. Marvin McInnis, Morton Rothstein, and James Sweet for their comments on an earlier version of this paper; and the Spencer Foundation and the School of Education at the University of Wisconsin for financial assistance.

1   Yasukichi Yasuba, *Birth Rates of theWhite Population in the United States, 1800–1860: An Economic Study*, (Baltimore, 1962).
2   Susan E. Bloomberg, Mary Frank Fox, Robert M. Warner, and Sam Bass Warner, Jr., "A Census Probe into Nineteenth-Century Family History: Southern Michigan, 1850–1880," *Journal of Social History*, V (1971), 26–45; Richard A. Easterlin, "Does Human Fertility Adjust to the Environment?" *American Economic Association Papers and Proceedings*, LXI (1971), 399–407; John Modell, "Family and Fertility on the Indiana Frontier, 1820," *American Quarterly*, XXIII (1971), 615–634; Francis Notzon, "Fertility and Farmland in Weston, Massachusetts: 1800–1820," unpub. M.S. thesis (University of Wisconsin, 1973); Maris A. Vinovskis, "A Multivariate Regression Analysis of Fertility Differentials Among Massachusetts Towns and Regions in 1860," forthcoming.

of these criticisms have raised questions about certain procedures involved in his analysis rather than challenged the validity of his findings. In fact, the most recent, comprehensive reevaluation by Forster and Tucker of Yasuba's land scarcity thesis strongly supports Yasuba's findings while improving upon many of the shortcomings of the earlier study.[3]

Despite the addition of recent work supporting Yasuba's land scarcity thesis, there is a need to reexamine the entire problem. First, there is the definition of land availability in the nineteenth century. Though Forster and Tucker have improved upon Yasuba's measure by calculating the number of white adults per farm (adult-farm ratio), their measure also lacks conceptual clarity. Secondly, all of the economic historians who have analyzed this issue have ignored such potentially important factors as the educational level of the population. Finally, though the use of multiple regression analysis by Forster and Tucker is a significant improvement on the statistical techniques employed by Yasuba, by restricting themselves to only three independent variables they do not make full use of its potential. In addition, the particular measures of land availability and urbanization that Forster and Tucker have used raise the possibility of multicollinearity in their regression analysis.

In order to reexamine fertility differentials in more detail than has been hitherto attempted, this analysis will be confined to 1850 and 1860, for which we have more detailed census data available than in the early decades of the nineteenth century. The study is based on all states in the New England, Middle Atlantic, North Central, South Atlantic, and South Central census divisions.[4]

DEFINITION OF VARIABLES   The difficulty in analyzing fertility differentials in 1850 and 1860 was to decide how many and which variables to include in this investigation. On the one hand, it seemed necessary

3 Colin Forster and G. S. L. Tucker, *Economic Opportunity and White American Fertility Ratios: 1800–1860* (New Haven, 1972).
4 Regression runs were also made including the territories in 1850 and 1860. However, the territories were omitted in the final regression equations in order to avoid biasing the results by including such unsettled areas as the Dakota territory, which had a white population of only 2,576 in 1860. If the territories had been included, the results would have been very similar in 1850 but not in 1860 because the Dakota territory had a very low white refined fertility ratio (1,157) and an unusually high white sex ratio (1,710). Rather than have the entire analysis distorted by such an extreme case, all the territories in those regions were omitted from the analysis (Minnesota territory in 1850 and the Nebraska and Dakota territories in 1860).

to include as many variables as possible in order to explore the effects of the socioeconomic factors on fertility differentials. On the other hand, it was necessary to limit the number of variables in the final regression equations due to the small number of cases (30 in 1850 and 32 in 1860) and the problem of high correlations among many of the proposed independent variables. As a result, the final regression equations were based on five independent variables though others were included in preliminary runs.

Table 1   Variables used in multiple regression analysis of fertility differentials in the United States in 1850 and 1860

I. INDEX OF FERTILITY
    Y   The number of white children under 10 years old per 1000 white women aged 16–44

II. SEX RATIO OF POPULATION
    X(1) The number of white males aged 15–49 per 1000 white females aged 15–49

III. EXTENT OF FOREIGN–BORN
    X(2) The percentage of the free population that is foreign-born

IV. AGRICULTURAL DEVELOPMENT
    X(3) Value of the average farm

V. DEGREE OF URBANIZATION
    X(4) The percentage of the population living in towns over 2500

VI. EDUCATIONAL LEVEL OF POPULATION
    X(5) The percentage of the white population over 20 which cannot read and write

---

The index of fertility used was the ratio of white children under ten years of age to white women between the ages of sixteen and forty-four. This data had already been calculated by Yasuba from the 1850 and 1860 censuses. By using the white refined fertility ratio rather than a crude one based on the size of the total population, we can minimize some of the differences in fertility due to variations in the age structures among the states. Although it would have been desirable to use a white refined birth rate rather than a white refined fertility ratio, it was impossible due to the lack of accurate information on the number of births during these years. However, the use of white refined fertility ratios probably does not introduce any serious distortions into the analysis as the measures are usually highly correlated.[5]

5   The white refined fertility ratios used in this analysis are based on Yasuba's calculations. These ratios are not standardized for the age-distribution of the women in the

The sex ratio of the population was calculated as the number of white males between fifteen and forty-nine per 1000 white females between fifteen and forty-nine. This variable was included as an indirect measure of the differences in marriage behavior among the states and territories due to the surplus of men over women in the newly settled areas. T'ien has pointed to the significance of this factor in accounting for fertility differentials in 1850 and 1860, though his interpretation has been strongly questioned by Yasuba and others.[6] Ideally, one would have liked to use the median age at first marriage and the proportion ever married, but unfortunately that data was not available in 1850 and 1860. As a result, it was necessary to rely on the crude approximation offered by the sex ratio of the white population.

Debate has often focused on the differentials in fertility between foreign-born and native-born persons in the United States. Therefore, it seemed logical to include a variable on the percentage of the free population that was foreign-born. Although it is possible to differentiate among the national origins of the foreign-born population, this exercise was not carried out in the final regression runs, although a distinction was made between the Irish and German immigrants in the preliminary runs.

Much analysis of nineteenth-century fertility has focused on the relative opportunity to establish farm households. Unfortunately, the connections between the availability of opportunities in farming and changes in fertility at the household level have not yet been fully or carefully delineated. Furthermore, there is little agreement among historians on the proper measure of agricultural development. This is partly because not much data are available on agriculture during most of the first half of the nineteenth century. Only in 1850 and 1860 do the federal censuses begin to provide more detailed agricultural data.

---

child-bearing ages. Yasuba's effort, however, to standardize these ratios for the age-distribution of the women revealed that the effect of the differences among the states in the age-distribution of their women was only minor. Yasuba, *Birth Rates of the White Population*, 61, 128–131.

For an analysis of the reliability of fertility ratio measures, *ibid.*, 23–37; Donald J. Bogue and James A. Palmore, "Some Empirical and Analytical Relations Among Demographic Fertility Measures with Regression Models for Fertility Estimation," *Demography*, I (1964) 313–338; Wilson H. Grabill and Lee Jay Cho, "Methodology for the Measurement of Current Fertility from Population Data on Young Children," *Demography*, II (1965), 50–73; Tamara K. Hareven and Maris A. Vinovskis, "Marital Fertility, Ethnicity and Occupation in Urban Families: An Analysis of South Boston and the South End in 1880," *Journal of Social History* (forthcoming).

6 H. Yuan T'ien, "A Demographic Aspect of Interstate Variation in American Fertility, 1800–1860," *Milbank Memorial Fund Quarterly*, XXXVII (1959), 49–59.

Some scholars such as Modell have used population density as the measure of agricultural opportunity. However, this is an inadequate measure of agricultural opportunity because it does not take into account the quality of the land and the degree of agricultural development of the area. It is a reflection of village and town populations as well as those living on farms.[7]

Yasuba tried to avoid this problem by calculating the number of persons per 1000 arable acres.[8] But his index was based on the cropland in 1949 and properly has been criticized for reflecting the levels of twentieth-century farming technology and practices rather than nineteenth-century agricultural potential.

The most recent effort by Forster and Tucker calculates the number of white adults per farm, using the white adult population in the census year under investigation and the number of farms in 1850, 1860, and 1880.[9] Their index has the advantage of reflecting nineteenth-century farming conditions and practices more accurately than Modell or Yasuba's measures.

However, even Forster and Tucker's index of land availability leaves much to be desired. At the state level, an index of white adults per farm is highly correlated with the percentage of the population engaged in nonagricultural occupations and with the percentage of the population in urban areas.[10] Therefore, we cannot be sure whether the high correlation between the white adult-farm ratio and the white refined fertility ratio is due to the availability of farms, to the percentage of the population in nonagricultural occupations, or to the percentage of the population living in urban areas. Furthermore, because of the high correlations among these variables, if any two of them are included in the same regression equation, the results might be misleading due to multicollinearity.

The number of white adults per farm is not only an ambiguous measure of land availability in terms of being highly correlated with other indices, but it is also conceptually weak in that it does not reflect the relative cost of establishing a farm household. When economists speak of the availability of farms, they are in effect considering the

7   Modell, "Family and Fertility on the Indiana Frontier, 1820."
8   Yasuba, *Birth Rates of the White Population*, 158–169.
9   Forster and Tucker, *Economic Opportunity*, 19–42.
10 For example, in 1850 the correlation between the white adult-farm ratio and the percentage of the population in urban areas was .615, and with the percentage of persons in nonagricultural occupations it was .815. Similarly, the correlation between the white adult-farm ratio and the percentage of the population urban in 1860 was .886.

relative costs of establishing a farm. Forster and Tucker's measure of agricultural opportunity implicitly treats all farms as equally priced, though in reality there were wide differences in the cost of farms in ante-bellum America. Thus, to take an extreme example, the average value of a farm in 1860 in Kansas was $1,179, whereas the average value of a farm in Louisiana was $11,818 in that same year. Surely it was more difficult for a young man to purchase a farm in a state such as Louisiana than in Kansas.[11]

In order to reduce these difficulties, the average value of the farm was used as an index of agricultural opportunity. This index has the advantage of measuring the relative cost of obtaining a farm. Ideally we would like to have data on the cost of establishing a new farm rather than the average value of all farms. However, although these data are unavailable in 1850 and 1860, it probably does not introduce a serious bias as the two measures probably are highly correlated.[12]

Measuring the degree of urbanization is also difficult as few scholars are able to agree upon any single definition of urbanization. Often the term is used as a broad category which includes such factors as industrialization and commercialization of the economy as well as population concentration. However, in order to make the results of this analysis as comparable as possible to the works of earlier scholars,

---

[11] Yasuba also discussed the ability of farmers to assist their children in establishing their own households. He reasoned that to do so was easier when land was readily available and harder when an area became developed. However, there is another aspect of this process that he might have considered. Though farm land becomes more expensive as an area is developed, the value of the farmer's own property also increases. Hence, the farmer is more able to assist his children than previously though the rising cost of farmland in that area might encourage his children to migrate once they receive their inheritance. Again, the relative ability of parents to help their children financially would be better measured by the relative value of the farms than the white adult-farm ratios.

The possible impact of inheritance on fertility has not been resolved. Philip Greven found that the age at marriage for sons was postponed in seventeenth-century Andover, Mass. by the practice of fathers delaying legal transfer of their grants of land to their children. Philip S. Greven, Jr., *Four Generations, Land and Family in Colonial Andover, Massachusetts* (Ithaca, 1970). For a critique of that interpretation, see Vinovskis, "American Historical Demography: A Review Essay," *Historical Methods Newsletter*, IV (1971), 141–148; Vinovskis, "The Field of Early American Family History: A Methodological Critique," *The Family in Historical Perspective*, VII (1974), 2–8.

Notzon's analysis of fertility differentials at the household level in Weston, Mass. from 1800 to 1820 found no statistically significant relationship between the amount of land and the level of fertility. Notzon, "Fertility and Farmland in Weston."

[12] For a discussion of the measurement of the value of the average farm see Thomas J. Pressly and William H. Scofield, *Farm Real Estate Values in the United States by Counties, 1855–1959* (Seattle, 1965), 3–11.

the degree of urbanization will be simply defined as the percentage of the population living in towns over 2,500.

Finally, the educational level of the population might also be measured in a variety of ways. For example, one might calculate the percentage of the white population between five and nineteen attending school during the year. However, this index would reflect the future educational level of the population rather than the current level. Therefore, the level of education was measured by the percentage of the white population over twenty who could not read and write according to the census.[13]

STATISTICAL PROCEDURES EMPLOYED   Multiple regression analysis allows one to study the linear relationship between any of the independent variables, $X(1)$ to $X(5)$, and a dependent variable, Y, while taking into consideration the effect of each of the remaining independent variables on the dependent variable. Multiple regression analysis attempts to produce a linear combination of independent variables which will correlate as highly as possible with the dependent variable. The underlying mathematical procedure is the use of the linear least-squares method which produces the smallest possible residual between the predicted value of the dependent variable from the regression equation and its actual value. In addition, multiple regression analysis minimizes any problems due to ratio correlation.[14]

The relationship between two variables is not always linear. Thus, even though the coefficient of linear correlation between two items may be low, it does not necessarily mean there is little or no association between them, as that relationship might be curvilinear rather than linear. To investigate this possibility, each of the independent variables was plotted against the dependent variable and examined for non-linearity. In addition, each independent variable was transformed into Log_{10} and then correlated with the white refined fertility ratio to see if it provided a better fit. On the basis of this investigation, it was discovered that the independent variables $X(1)$, $X(2)$, $X(3)$, and $X(5)$ should be converted to Log_{10}.

13 For an analysis of the extent and importance of illiteracy in the United States during these years, see Richard M. Bernard and Vinovskis, "Women and Education in Ante-Bellum America," unpub. paper presented at the Berkshire Conference on Women in History, 1974.

14 N. R. Draper and H. Smith, *Applied Regression Analysis* (New York, 1966); William L. Hays, *Statistics* (New York, 1963), 490–577; Edwin Kuh and John R. Meyer, "Correlation and Regression Estimates When the Data are Ratios," *Econometrica*, XXIII (1955), 400–416.

Due to the small number of cases involved, there was always the danger that two or more of the independent variables would be highly correlated with each other. As multiple regression analysis is based on the assumption that no linear dependence exists between the explanatory variables, the existence of multicollinearity among the variables would invalidate our results. Therefore, care was taken not to include any independent variables which were highly correlated with each other.[15]

In an effort to test the relative contribution of each independent variable to the explanation of the white refined fertility ratio, a series of stepwise regressions was run with each of the independent variables individually omitted while the remaining variables were regressed against the white refined fertility ratio. The resultant changes in R^2 due to the omission of each independent variable give us another indication of the relative importance of these variables in accounting for differentials in the white refined fertility ratios among the states.

RESULTS   The mean and standard deviations of each variable are displayed in Table 2.

Table 2 Mean and Standard Deviations of Variables

	1850		1860	
	MEAN	STANDARD DEVIATION	MEAN	STANDARD DEVIATION
White refined fertility ratio under ten	1,406.2	285.8	1,356.4	249.1
Number of white males aged 15–49 per 1000 white females aged 15–49	1,082.9	119.3	1,072.2	114.7
Percentage of the free population that is foreign-born	9.9	8.2	12.4	9.3
Value of the average farm ($)	2,277.2	1,192.9	3,410.0	1,955.7
Percentage of population living in towns over 2500	13.2	13.8	16.9	15.6
Percentage of the white population over 20 which cannot read and write	11.8	7.6	9.5	5.6

15 J. Johnston, *Econometric Methods* (New York, 1972, 2nd ed.), 159–168; Hubert M. Blalock, Jr., "Correlated Independent Variables: The Problem of Multicollinearity," *Social Forces*, LXII (1963), 233–238.

In order to ascertain the relationships between the white refined fertility ratio and the independent variables, simple correlation coefficients were calculated.

Table 3   Correlation Matrices

	Y	X_1	X_2	X_3	X_4	X_5
			1850			
Y	1.000					
X_1	.577	1.000				
X_2	−.409	.273	1.000			
X_3	−.642	−3.05	.444	1.000		
X_4	−.746	−.318	.530	.637	1.000	
X_5	.725	.267	−.550	−.256	−.439	1.000
			1860			
	Y	X_1	X_2	X_3	X_4	X_5
Y	1.000					
X_1	.755	1.000				
X_2	−.285	.153	1.000			
X_3	−.317	−.374	.123	1.000		
X_4	−.733	−.509	.559	.389	1.000	
X_5	.543	.123	−.672	.146	−.419	1.000

The results indicate a positive correlation between the white refined fertility ratio and both the white sex ratio and the percentage of illiterate white adults. The correlation coefficients of the white refined fertility ratio and the percentage foreign-born, the farm value, and the percentage of the population urban are negative. In 1850 the correlations with the farm values, the urban population, and the illiterate white population were particularly strong, though the farm value declines in strength in 1860. Except for the white sex ratio, the correlation coefficients between the white refined fertility ratio and the other variables are weaker in 1860 than in 1850.

Though correlation coefficients are useful in establishing the relationship between two variables, they are handicapped because the relationship may really be caused by a third factor which has not been considered. One way to minimize this danger is to use multiple regression analysis, which allows us to see the relationship between the dependent variable and any independent variable after controlling for the influence of the remaining independent variables on the dependent one. Therefore, regression equations were calculated for 1850 and 1860 in the form:

$$Y = a + b_1 \log_{10} X(1) + b_2 \log_{10} X(2) + b_3 \log_{10} X(3) + b_4 X(4) + b_5 \log_{10} X(5)$$

where Y is the white refined fertility ratio, a is a constant, $X(1)X \cdots (5)$ are the independent variables, and $b_1 \cdots b_5$ are the regression coefficients.

The results of the regression equations for 1850 and 1860 are summarized below in Table 4.

Table 4 Regression Coefficients

	1850	1860
Constant	−1,729.426	−5,981.614
Log$_{10}$ of the number of white males aged 15–49 per 1000 white females aged 15–49	1,330.260	2,430.668
Log$_{10}$ of the percentage of the free population that is foreign-born	69.795	104.157
Log$_{10}$ of the value of the average farm	−385.386	−119.687
Percentage of the population living in towns over 2500	6.882	−6.070
Log$_{10}$ of the percentage of the white population over 20 which cannot read and write	427.131	443.336

Though the regression coefficients indicate the effect of each of the independent variables on the dependent one, it is impossible to evaluate the relative importance of each variable on the basis of regression coefficients since the independent variables are measured in different units. Therefore, it is necessary to calculate standardized regression coefficients (*beta* coefficients) as they indicate the relative importance of the independent variables.

Table 5 Beta Coefficients

	1850	1860
Log$_{10}$ of the number of white males aged 15–49 per 100 white females aged 15–49	.2140	.4391*
Log$_{10}$ of the percentage of the free population that is foreign-born	.1186	.1880
Log$_{10}$ of the value of the average farm	−.2861*	−.0973
Percentage of the population living in towns over 2500	−.3325*	−.3793*
Log$_{10}$ of the percentage of the white population over 20 which cannot read and write	.5143*	.4703*

*=significant at the .01 level

Examining the signs of the correlation coefficients and the *beta* coefficients, we see that there are significant differences. Whereas the relationship between the white refined fertility ratio and the percentage of the free population foreign-born was negative before, it now becomes positive when taking into account the effects of the other independent variables. In other words, the foreign-born population was concentrated in low fertility states so that a simple correlation coefficient revealed the relationship as negative. However, once we controlled for the white sex ratio, the degree of urbanization, the extent of white adult illiteracy, and the value of the average farm, it turns out that the percentage of the free population foreign-born and the white refined fertility ratio are really positively related.

On the basis of the *beta* coefficients, we discover that the value of the average farm and the percentage of the population urban are negatively related to the white refined fertility ratio while the white sex ratio, the percentage of the free population foreign-born, and the illiterate white adult population are positively related.

In terms of the relative ability of the independent variables to account for the fertility differentials, the percentage of the population urban and the percentage of white adults who were illiterate stand out in both 1850 and 1860. The value of the average farm was important in 1850 but became quite insignificant in 1860. The white sex ratio was moderately important in 1850 and became even more important in 1860. The percentage of the free population foreign-born was not very significant in either period.

Besides examining the *beta* coefficients in order to judge the relative significance of the independent variables, we can also examine changes in R^2 when each of the independent variables is removed while the rest of them remain in the regression equation.

In most instances there is a loss in R^2 when any independent variable is removed. However, when the percentage of the free population in 1850 or the value of the average farm in 1860 is omitted there is an increase in R^2 because the loss in R^2 caused by the removal of that variable is more than made up by the gain in an additional degree of freedom in calculating our results. In other words, if we had been interested simply in finding the least number of independent variables needed to predict fertility levels rather than in examining the relative importance of the variables we chose to examine initially, we might have omitted the percentage of the free population foreign-born in 1850 and the value of the average farm in 1860.

The results of this analysis basically confirm our findings from the

Table 6 Change in R^2 due to Removal of each Variable from Regression Equation while the Rest of the Variables are Retained

VARIABLE REMOVED	CHANGE IN R^2	
	1850	1860
Log_{10} of the number of white males aged 15–49 per 1000 white females aged 15–49	−.0154	−.0685
Log_{10} of the percentage of the free population that is foreign-born	.0015	−.0018
Log_{10} of the value of the average farm	−.0401	.0002
Percentage of the population living in towns over 2500	−.0492	−.0437
Log_{10} of the percentage of the white population over 20 which cannot read and write	−.1338	−.0843
R^2 with all variables in equation	.8544	.8117

investigation of the *beta* coefficients. Again the percentage of the population urban and the percentage of white adults who were illiterate were important in both 1850 and 1860. The value of the average farm was important in 1850 but not in 1860, whereas the reverse was true for the white sex ratio. In neither year was the percentage of the free population foreign-born significant.

Though the use of correlation coefficients, *beta* coefficients, and changes in R^2 have given us a good indication of the relative importance of individual variables, we also need to look at the overall effectiveness of the resultant regression equations in explaining the dependent variable. Probably the most useful measure of this is R^2— the ratio between the variance of the dependent variable explained by the independent variables and the total variance of the dependent variable. Thus, if the independent variables perfectly predict the values of the dependent variable, R^2 would be equal to one. On the other hand, if the independent variables have no relationship to the dependent variable and therefore are not helpful in predicting values of the dependent variable, R^2 would be equal to zero.

For the states analyzed in 1850, R^2 is .8544. In other words, approximately 85 percent of the variance in the white refined fertility ratio can be explained by the five independent variables in 1850. The explanatory ability of the same five variables in 1860 is .8117.

DISCUSSION OF RESULTS   The results of this study confirmed the value of including more independent variables in the analysis. Yasuba's and Forster and Tucker's investigations confined themselves mainly to examining the effects of urbanization and land availability, ignoring such potentially important factors as education. In fact, this analysis discovered that the percentage of white adults who were illiterate was the best predictor of fertility differentials in 1850 and 1860.

Another general finding of this study is the need for an awareness of the limitations of analyzing fertility differentials at the state level only. Due to the small number of cases available, we are faced with the problem of high correlations among the independent variables. Although the strictly statistical problem of multicollinearity can be avoided by carefully selecting variables for the regression equations that are not highly correlated amongst themselves, it is still very difficult to interpret the meaning of some of these variables. For example, the percentage of the population living in urban areas was used as an independent variable in order to test whether or not the degree of urbanization of a state affected its level of fertility. Though the results strongly suggest that it does, we cannot be certain that we have really measured the effects of urbanization rather than the effects of the percentage of persons in nonagricultural pursuits, as these two variables are highly correlated with each other. Similar problems exist in interpreting the meaning of Yasuba's and Forster and Tucker's measures of land availability. Furthermore, as there are often significant socioeconomic differences within each of the states, any analysis that in effect treats each state as a demographically homogeneous unit may be quite misleading. Therefore, more research will have to be done at the county, township, and household levels. This is not to suggest that further research at the state level would be unproductive—we clearly need more sophisticated analysis than has been available so far. But it does imply that any general models of fertility that we derive from such analyses will have to be tested and refined using smaller units than states.[16]

We now turn to a discussion of the independent variables in this

16 Forster and Tucker did attempt to analyze New York and Virginia at the county level, but they did not apply the same level of statistical sophistication at the county level as they did at the state level. Forster and Tucker, *Economic Opportunity*, 43–48; Don R. Leet has undertaken an investigation of fertility and agricultural opportunities in Ohio counties from 1810 to 1860 and Vinovskis is analyzing fertility differentials for all counties in the United States in 1850. At the township level, Bash studied fertility differentials in New York, but his analysis was limited by the small number of socioeconomic variables that he used, as well as the statistical procedures he employed. Wendall H. Bash, "Changing Birth Rates in Developing America: New York State, 1840–1875," *Millbank Memorial Fund Quarterly*, XLI (1963), 161–182; Vinovskis is completing an analysis of fertility differentials and trends among Massachusetts townships from 1765 to 1860.

analysis—the white sex ratio, the percentage of the free population foreign-born, the value of the average farm, the degree of urbanization, and the percentage of the white adults who are illiterate.

One area of controversy has been the importance of the sex ratio affecting fertility differentials and trends in the ante-bellum period. T'ien has argued that sex ratio differences were very important as they indirectly affected fertility ratios by altering the likelihood of women marrying. Areas where women were outnumbered by men would probably have a higher proportion of women married than areas where the reverse situation existed.[17]

Yasuba disagreed with T'ien's analysis and minimized the significance of sex ratios. Yasuba argued that the high correlation between the white refined fertility ratio and the white sex ratio was spurious—if T'ien had included other factors, such as urbanization or land availability, the importance of the sex ratio variable would disappear. Furthermore, Yasuba demonstrated that the shifts in the sex ratio from 1800 to 1860 could not account for the drop in fertility over that period.[18]

This analysis suggests that the white sex ratio is an important explanatory variable in accounting for fertility differentials in 1850 and 1860 even after controlling for the other four independent variables. In fact, for 1860 the sex ratio is the second best predictor of fertility differentials, being surpassed only by the percentage of white adults who were illiterate. Furthermore, the analysis of fertility differentials among Massachusetts towns and regions in 1860 confirms the importance of the sex ratio variable.[19] Nevertheless, though Yasuba was too hasty in dismissing the importance of the sex ratio variable in terms of cross-sectional analysis, his critique of its ability to account for the overall decline in fertility from 1800 to 1860 appears to be valid.

Another issue is the role of immigration in determining fertility levels, and in particular whether immigrants had higher fertility rates than the native-born population. This problem is extremely complex and the results so far are not at all clear.

Traditionally, demographers have stressed that the fertility of immigrants was significantly higher than that of the native-born population. However, most of that literature refers to the period in the

17 T'ien, "Demographic Aspect."
18 Yasuba, Birth Rates of the White Population, 125–128.
19 Vinovskis, "Regression Analysis of Fertility."

late nineteenth and early twentieth centuries when immigration was from high fertility cultures in southern and eastern Europe. Forster and Tucker reexamined the entire question in the period before the Civil War and concluded that immigrants to America came from areas in Europe where the fertility rates were actually lower than in the United States at that time.[20]

In order to investigate the possible significance of this factor, the percentage of the free population that was foreign-born was included as an independent variable. The results suggest that the relationship between the white refined fertility ratio and the percentage foreign-born was relatively weak and positive. To gain another perspective on this question, the percentage of the population that was Irish and the percentage that was German were substituted in the 1860 regression for the foreign-born variable. The results of this refinement were that the percentage of Irish was moderately negatively related to fertility while the percentage German was positive and much stronger. Whether these differences actually reflect differences in the fertility of the foreign-born population or merely that more Irish than Germans happened to immigrate to states with lower fertility cannot be determined on the basis of this analysis. It is interesting to note that the relationship between the percentage of Irish and the white refined fertility ratio among Massachusetts towns in 1860 was positive, though not very strongly so—exactly the opposite of our findings at the state level.[21] Again, any definitive statement on this issue must await more detailed analysis, particularly at the household level.

Agricultural opportunity has been the focus of most of the earlier works on nineteenth-century fertility. However, as we have already noted, their measures of agricultural opportunity have not been satisfactory and therefore we have used the value of the average farm instead. Although even this measure has its shortcomings, it does seem better able to measure the relative costs of establishing a farm household than earlier measures.

The results show that in 1850 the value of the farm was strongly negatively related to the white refined fertility ratio, though it was less important than the percentage of the population in urban areas or the percentage of the white adults who were illiterate. In 1860 the value of the farm remains negatively related to fertility, but it becomes quite unimportant in terms of strength. In fact, when the value of the

20 Forster and Tucker, *Economic Opportunity*, 70–86.
21 Vinovskis, "Regression Analysis of Fertility."

farm is removed from the 1860 regression equation, there is an increase in R^2 as the loss of this variable from the equation is offset by the gain in an additional degree of freedom in the computation of the results.

The relative weakness of the value of the farm in 1860 is quite different from the results obtained by Yasuba or Forster and Tucker. Although they acknowledged that the relationship between land availability and the white refined fertility ratio was strongest in the first three decades of the nineteenth century rather than in the period 1850 to 1860, their measures of land availability suggested a much stronger relationship in 1850 and 1860 than found in this analysis. Furthermore, that the degree of illiteracy of the white adult population was much stronger than the value of farms in both 1850 and 1860 suggests that perhaps the particular significance of land availability has been overstated by scholars.

An analysis of Massachusetts townships in 1790 and 1840 using more refined measures of land availability at the state level for those years than were available to Yasuba or Forster and Tucker suggests that land availability was indeed positively related to fertility levels, but that the relationship was much weaker than previously suggested once other factors, such as the level of wealth of an area, were also considered.

Again, there is no intention or illusion of settling the issue of land availability in this paper, especially since this analysis is confined to the period after 1850. However, the results here indicate that future work on this topic should try to develop measures of land availability that take into account relative prices. Furthermore, much more effort must be directed toward clearly delineating the variety of effects that land availability may have on fertility at the household level. One receives the impression that the high correlations between measures of land availability and the white refined fertility ratio found by previous scholars confirm Yasuba's hypothesis, so that little additional work has been done in exploring the actual mechanisms that might be involved.[22] The demographic experiences of farm populations ap-

22 Economists are now developing much more sophisticated models of household fertility. For example, see the proceedings of the Conference on New Economic Approaches to Fertility in the *Journal of Political Economy*, LXXXI (1973) S1–S299. Some very promising efforts currently in progress on the use of the analysis of household fertility for explaining American demographic development historically are by Richard A. Easterlin, Peter H. Lindert, and R. Marvin McInnis. For an attempt to use fertility ratios at the household level to test for rural-urban differences in fertility, see Hareven and Vinovskis, "Rural-Urban Differences in Fertility: An Analysis of Marital

pear to have been much more complex and less dependent upon land availability than suggested by Yasuba and others. Unfortunately, almost no work has been done so far on the determinants of rural fertility at the household level for the first half of the nineteenth cetntury.[23]

The impact of urbanization on fertility has been a major theme of modern demographers. However, the significance of urbanization in explaining fertility differentials or decline in the first half of the nineteenth century has been minimized—largely because the United States was still basically a rural rather than urban society throughout these years. Furthermore, the statistical analysis of the relative importance of the degree of urbanization and land availability by Yasuba or Forster and Tucker have pointed to the importance of the latter factor. However, as we have previously noted, their measures of land availability were highly negatively correlated with the degree of urbanization, so that it is not clear exactly what socioeconomic factors they were measuring by their indices.

The results indicate that the degree of urbanization was strongly negatively related to the white refined fertility ratio in 1850 and in 1860. In both of those years, the degree of urbanization was more strongly correlated with the fertility ratio than was the value of the average farm.

However, again we must remind ourselves of the possible ambiguities in our measure of urbanization. Though the strong inverse relationship between urbanization and earlier measures of land availability was avoided by using the value of the average farm, the extent of urbanization was still highly correlated with other variables such as

---

Fertility, Ethnicity, Occupation, and Literacy in Five Essex County Towns in 1880," paper presented at the American Historical Association meeting in Chicago, 1974.

23 Despite Modell's use of population density as his index of agricultural opportunity, his article is a significant step in the right direction because he attempts to relate fertility differentials at the household level to the characteristics of the family and county. His conclusion is that Yasuba's analysis does not take into account the complexity of factors affecting rural fertility in an area such as Indiana. Modell, "Family and Fertility on the Indiana Frontier, 1820." Bloomberg et al. analyzed fertility changes in southern Michigan between 1850 and 1880 at the household level and also attempted to relate it to the characteristics of the household and the community. However, the results of that study must be cautiously interpreted because of the very small sample size of the 1850 data (used without due consideration of the problems of sampling errors). Bloomberg et al., "A Census Probe."

the percentage of the population in nonagricultural occupations.[24] Therefore, it is difficult to separate these factor at the state level of analysis. Perhaps the degree of urbanization as used in this study is only a proxy for a much more complex phenomenon than suggested by the presence of persons in towns having populations over 2500 persons.

The analysis of Massachusetts townships in 1860 suggested that urbanization, as measured by the number of persons in each of the towns, was not particularly useful in predicting fertility differentials. Instead, the index of commercialization proved to be a much more useful variable in accounting for the fertility differentials.[25] Though it was possible to separate to some degree the effects of commercialization from the effects of the size of towns at the township level, it is virtually impossible to do so at the state level. As a result, though the relationship between urbanization and fertility appears to be quite strong in this investigation, we do not necessarily place much credence on its importance until further work can be done at the county or township levels, where the variety of factors that scholars commonly associate with urbanization can be separated out for more detailed analysis.

Though demographers have frequently pointed to the importance of education in determining the fertility of the population, historical demographers have not seriously analyzed this factor. Although some of the earlier scholars, such as Yasuba, have suggested that education should be investigated as a possible influence on fertility, none of the subsequent research on nineteenth century fertility has attempted to utilize this variable. This failure has been partly because of the general reluctance of economic historians to study until recently the impact of education on American society and partly because the data are unavailable for most states before 1840.[26]

24 For example, the correlation between the percentage of persons in nonagricultural occupations and the percent urban in 1850 was .751.

25 Vinovskis, "Regression Analysis of Fertility."

26 On the recent efforts by economic historians to analyze the role of education in the first half of the nineteenth century, see Albert Fishlow, "The American Common School Revival: Fact or Fancy?" in Henry Rosovsky (ed.), *Industrialization in Two Systems: Essays in Honor of Alexander Gershenkron* (New York, 1966), 40–67; Vinovskis, "Horace Mann on the Economic Productivity of Education," *New England Quarterly*, XLIII (1970), 550–571; Vinovskis, "Trends in Massachusetts Education, 1826–1860," *History of Education Quarterly*, XII (1972), 501–529. For a summary of the type of problems encountered in studying the role of education in economic development from a historical point of view, see Stanley L. Engerman, "Human Capital, Education, and Economic Growth," Robert W. Fogel and Stanley L. Engerman (eds.), *The Reinterpretation of American Economic History*, (New York, 1971), 241–256.

One of the major reasons for undertaking this research was to test for the possible impact of education on the fertility of the population. Therefore, the percentage of whites over twenty who were unable to read and write was included as one of the independent variables. The results were striking—the educational level of the white population was the single best predictor of fertility differentials among the states in 1850 and 1860. Furthermore, when a similar regression equation was calculated for 1840 (though the value of farms was unavailable and therefore excluded), the importance of the educational level of the white population remained strong.

In order to gain another perspective, the percentages of the white population aged five to nineteen attending school in 1840, 1850, and 1860 were also calculated and substituted in the regression equations for the educational variable. Again the importance of an index of education was confirmed.

Finally, in 1850 the percentage of the white population aged five to nineteen attending school and the percentage of white adults who were illiterate were separated by sex and the results were individually run as the educational variable in a series of regression equations. The results were the same—the educational variable continued to be strongly related to the white refined fertility ratio.

In the analysis of Massachusetts townships in 1860, two measures of education were used—the percentage of the population under twenty attending school and the amount of money spent per public school student in each town. The educational factors were consistently negative for the state as a whole as well as for the three subdivisions, and were important factors in terms of their contribution to the explanation of the differences in the white refined fertility ratios among the towns.[27]

The implications of these findings are very important as they suggest that demographic historians should pay more attention to factors such as education in understanding fertility differentials and trends in nineteenth-century America. Considerable time and effort has already been devoted to urbanization and land availability in an attempt to account for fertility differentials and trends, but too little attention has been paid to the role of educational and cultural factors.[28]

27 Vinovskis, "Regression Analysis of Fertility."
28 The use of literacy data in our analysis of fertility differentials in the United States in 1850 and 1860 was adequate because these rates probably do reflect roughly the state variations in the educational level of the population. However, for studies which focus

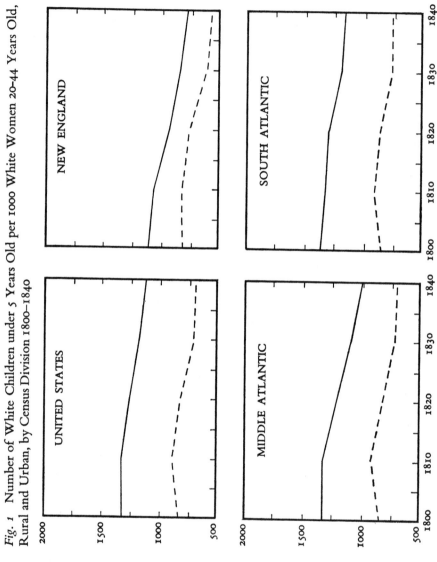

Fig. 1 Number of White Children under 5 Years Old per 1000 White Women 20–44 Years Old, Rural and Urban, by Census Division 1800–1840

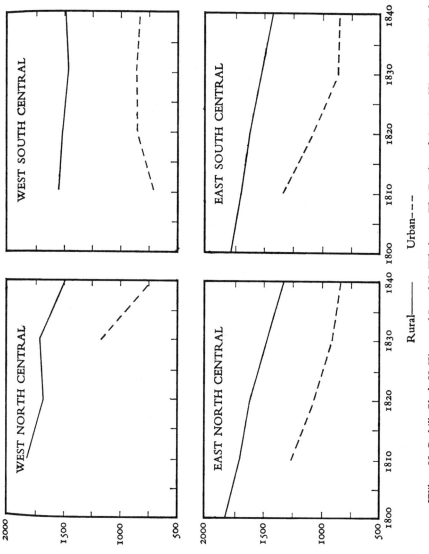

Rural——— Urban----

SOURCE: Wilson H. Grabill, Clyde V. Kiser, and Pascal K. Whelpton, *The Fertility of American Women* (New York, 1958), 17.

One final point should be made. Though this study has focused on fertility differentials rather than trends, many of the same criticisms could be applied to the analysis of changes in nineteenth-century fertility. The debate on the case of the decline in fertility in the first half of the nineteenth century has been focused on rural vs. urban explanations. Yet perhaps the fertility differentials between rural and urban areas persisted because there was a steady decline in fertility in both areas. So much time and effort has been spent on examining the particular causes of declines in rural or urban fertility that demographic historians have not noticed that the declines in both areas may have paralleled each other and both may have been influenced by broad change within American society during those years.

Fortunately, we do have some data on this question for 1800 to 1840 for the United States and for seven of its subregions (see Fig. 1).

It is interesting that the fertility declines in rural and urban areas of the United States and its regions generally parallel each other throughout this period. Similar results were found at the township level in Massachusetts in the period 1765 to 1860.

Perhaps we need to escape from the rural-urban debate long enough to check whether there might not have been some other developments in American society in the first half of the nineteenth century that may partly account for both the rural and urban declines in fertility. That is, though some of the causes of fertility decline in rural areas undoubtedly were different from those for urban areas, we must also entertain the possibility that both rural and urban areas were reacting to the same general changes in American society during the first half of the nineteenth century. Though this paper has not solved this dilemma, preliminary research on this issue suggests that broad attitudinal changes, often preceding rather than being caused by urbanization and industrialization, are probably as significant in accounting for the fertility decline in America as the shifts in economic factors that have dominated the analysis of fertility up to now.[29]

---

on more homogeneous populations, such as an analysis of a particular state or a group of native-born farmers, the variations in adult literacy may be too small to reflect properly the actual differences in their level of educational achievement. Instead, we would like to have the number of years of education each person has obtained. Unfortunately, this type of information is very difficult to find for nineteenth-century America since such data were not often collected.

29 For an analysis of this possibility, see Vinovskis, "Demographic Changes in America From the Revolution to the Civil War: An Analysis of the Socio-Economic Determinants of Fertility Differentials and Trends in Massachusetts from 1765 to 1860," unpub. Ph.D. thesis (Harvard University, 1975).